New Vocal Repertory 2

JANE MANNING

CLARENDON PRESS · OXFORD
1998

Oxford University Press, Great Clarendon Street, Oxford OX2 6DP

Oxford New York

Athens Auckland Bangkok Bogota Bombay
Buenos Aires Calcutta Cape Town Dar es Salaam
Delhi Florence Hong Kong Istanbul Karachi
Kuala Lumpur Madras Madrid Melbourne
Mexico City Nairobi Paris Singapore
Taipei Tokyo Toronto Warsaw
and associated companies in
Berlin Ibadan

Oxford is a trade mark of Oxford University Press

Published in the United States
by Oxford University Press Inc., New York

British Library Cataloguing in Publication Data
Data available

Library of Congress Cataloging in Publication Data
Manning, Jane.
New vocal repertory volume 2 / Jane Manning.
Includes index.
1. Vocal music—Bibliography.   I. Title.
ML128.V7M3   1998   016.78242168—dc20   93-30975
ISBN 0-19-879018-X
ISBN 0-19-879019-8 (pbk.)

1 3 5 7 9 10 8 6 4 2

Typeset by Best-set Typesetter Ltd., Hong Kong
Printed in Great Britain
on acid-free paper by
Biddles Ltd
Guildford & Kings Lynn

Contents

CONTENTS

Preface

Heartened by the fact that *New Vocal Repertory*, in its recent new edition (Clarendon Press: Oxford, 1994), seems to be in regular use in leading music colleges and private practice, I have chosen a second batch of less familiar twentieth-century songs and song cycles suitable for general use. It appears that teachers and singers find it helpful for someone to test the water before they plunge into the bewildering whirlpool of contemporary vocal music, with its vastly diverging styles, idioms, and levels of difficulty. The blanket term 'modern music' is still used too vaguely. The musical difficulties experienced with certain atonal pieces written in the early part of the century by such great composers as Schoenberg and Webern, and the disconcertingly innovative notation of 'experimental' music of the sixties and seventies, have perhaps inhibited further exploration.

'Avant-garde' scores may appear strange at first, but, if given the chance, are often relatively simple to perform. I am inclined to bristle when asked to explain 'extended vocal techniques', since these seem to me to be largely a matter of rationalizing, annotating, and co-ordinating a variety of everyday sounds, which would all be familiar in different contexts. If the tonal inflections of a baby's scream were to be notated exactly, or even the precise rhythmic values of *rubato* in Debussy or Delius, the visual result would be extremely complex.

The choice of texts is also crucial to the artistic experience. As in the much-quoted example of Schubert, not all composers choose great poetry, but many of today's composers are widely cultured and show excellent taste. The choice is not easy, for many reasons. The greatest verse stands on its own, without need of adornment. Succinct or evocatively understated texts are often the most effective for musical setting. Epigrammatic poems such as those by e e cummings, or those with a rich 'sonic music', such as Joyce or Hopkins, have proved justifiably popular with composers. Older texts, such as medieval verses, avoid copyright problems. 'Custom-made texts' by the composers themselves (as in many examples from Messiaen to Alwyn, Casken, and Weir) perhaps provide the ideal solution. The wordless vocalises and phonetic texts found in earlier decades are showing signs of a

1

revival. Awareness of the aural effect of syllables independently of their meaning can affect the interpretation.

Certain individual songs by minor English and American figures do seem to have progressed virtually unchallenged through successive generations of examination and competition syllabuses. Little effort has been made to look for others, even their exact equivalents. Those of us who perform, teach, and listen, should always be receptive to the jolt of the new and unfamiliar, and be ready to break the mould of a repertoire that has remained stagnant, purely because of some random selection made long ago. This is even true of 'standard repertoire'. Many fine Schubert and Brahms songs are rarely heard, while the same few recur constantly. A detailed reappraisal of their comparative degrees of suitability for young voices is overdue. Vocal teachers have sometimes been reluctant to adapt their views. Richard Strauss and Mahler have somehow eluded the 'modern' label, yet early Berg or Schoenberg songs are often undeservedly shunned. There are many historical inconsistencies and anomalies: all Britten's vocal music is deemed acceptable, yet Messiaen's marvellously singable cycles have an unwarranted 'intellectual' image. Surely the specific date of a piece matters little when all have passed on? I am all too aware that the present selection is not comprehensive, and is confined mainly to music of 'Western European classical' origin. It is intended merely to encourage the reader to set out on the path towards further discoveries. No one should rely on the findings of just one person.

The recent popularization of 'classical music', and the somewhat uneasy marriage between art and commerce, means that there is now an even more urgent need for discrimination. The demand for more 'accessible' new music has certainly left its mark, and many of today's composers have adapted to the changing situation. This new volume contains a particularly high proportion of works that would not tax the comparatively untutored listener or performer, yet are of the highest quality. Some could even be categorized as 'light music'. Commercialization of many types of contemporary music has certainly gathered pace over the last few years. The advent of Classic FM, and the corresponding softening of Radio 3's 'image' have enabled the record industry in particular to play a principal role in dictating trends. The lines between 'classical' and 'popular' have become increasingly blurred, and one or two rather odd hybrids have sprung up. The influence of other cultures is even more evident. This diversity is most welcome, but it is often difficult to perceive the difference between the ephemeral 'hit' and the work of lasting value that will not pall on repetition. The prevalence of 'soundbites' has mitigated against an ability to concentrate in longer spans. Nevertheless there is a practical need for short pieces, and splendid initiatives such as Mary Wiegold's Song-Book have made a significant contribution to the repertoire by creating a body of high-quality songs for voice and ensemble, some of them also in alternative versions for voice and piano. Singers should always be ready to ask composers to write for them. It is exciting to spot new talent, and to be able to give support at an early stage. In the last few years, happily, more composers have been writing song cycles, and these include some of the most gifted figures of the younger generation.

There is no substitute for live music-making, with its endless capacity to stir and surprise. Mixed recitals of songs, when presented with polished expertise by such groups as The Songmakers' Almanac and others, have shown the appeal and value of carefully structured 'thematic' programmes. There is a growing tendency for performers to introduce their pieces informally, and the closer rapport with the audience is mutually beneficial. Amongst young artists, standards of musicianship continue to rise, although vocal technique can sometimes be neglected in favour of more superficial aspects of 'presentation'. Potential is as difficult to assess as ever, particularly with the growth in the number of competitions, which encourage snap decision-making at the expense of a more sustained and searching evaluation. The current emphasis on education ought to be advantageous to the emerging talent, but music colleges are now required to place students in the limelight in order to attract funding, thus putting further strain on them to succeed rapidly.

It is possible for an unexceptional artist to enjoy a lucrative career if marketing techniques are applied vigorously, and this can be dispiriting to those with higher aims. No price tag can define levels of artistry. It is often the amateurs, free from commercial pressures, who are left to set an example in commitment and enthusiasm. Organizations such as COMA (Contemporary Music for Amateurs) provide new impetus, and respite from the less attractive aspects of 'professionalism'. Young artists are especially vulnerable now that administrators have gained unprecedented power in the musical hierarchy. Those who actually create and perform the music often seem relegated to the level of hired lackeys; a situation that is mirrored throughout our society.

Opera is now hugely popular, and the 'Pavarotti factor' has made it into something of a spectator sport. It has become more difficult for singers to launch and maintain freelance concert careers. The best voices are often creamed off at college level and placed in opera-houses. This early exposure before technique is secure can take a woeful toll. Only those who are versatile and imaginative and who have a strong instinct for self-preservation are likely to achieve long-term careers. Artists may be diffident about trusting their own instincts, perhaps confused by a mounting parade of less reliable witnesses representing other motives and interests. Damning criticism and fulsome praise should be treated with equal suspicion, and it is advisable to acquire the ability to judge own's own work dispassionately.

Composers deserve the fullest encouragement and co-operation of performers. These collaborations can be highly rewarding despite minor differences of temperament: composers lead a more solitary artistic life, and a very few can be their own worst enemies. Artistic integrity is not always found in the smoothest package—so with performers. Individuality is

3

something to be cherished, and it is surely better to be appreciated by the astute and genuinely knowledgeable, than to be at the mercy of fashion. Those performers who remain bland and anodyne, hoping to please everyone, risk finding themselves interchangeable with many others. The practicalities of earning a living may frequently conflict with artistic ideals, but should never supplant them. Today's artists face an even greater challenge than before. We should all be on our guard against the erosion of our finer instincts, and not be afraid to express our enthusiasms, however unfashionable.

This present volume differs from the first in that works in other languages as well as English are now included. Levels of difficulty are again graded in two separate categories, 'Technical' (vocal skills needed), and 'Musical' (standard of musicianship required), abbreviated to 'T' and 'M' respectively in the text. There is still a lack of recognition of the clear distinction between the two: unfamiliar works are regularly accused of taxing the voice when the real problems concern pitch and rhythm. Works for solo voice are here included for the first time. It is my experience that audiences of all kinds find them exciting and impressive. There are also a few works involving electronics; this seems appropriate in our technological age. The stylistic range is wider than ever, and many works are suitable for comparative beginners. This reflects the demand for works from the 'easier' categories in Volume 1, and the fact that many composers are now writing in a simpler style. The rise in popularity of 'music theatre' has also influenced the choice of several works that allow for a simple theatrical presentation. Featured composers range from the early American pioneers, such as Cage, Seeger, and Antheil, to younger talents such as Turnage and Adès. The geographical spread is also broader: there are works from Norway to Israel, and a number of expatriates: a Briton living in Germany, a New Zealander based in Scotland, and so on. As before there is a substantial contingent from the North American continent, and a very large representation of leading figures in the British musical scene, and some others who seem to have been unduly neglected recently.

I am extremely grateful to a large number of colleagues and friends who have given invaluable advice and support to this project. Publishers, composers, and information centres in various countries have all been most supportive and efficient in providing scores and information. It is particularly pleasing to note the enormous improvement in this area, and I would like to mention specially the splendid work being done by the Contemporary Music Centre in Dublin and the Scottish Music Information Centre in Glasgow. The British, American, and Canadian Music Information Centres have once again proved indispensable, attending to my requests with alacrity and expertise. Most of all, I owe a huge debt of gratitude to the pianist Dominic Saunders, who, with characteristic brilliance, read through a great many of the scores with me, generously giving his time and energy to make my task much easier.

This new selection only scratches the surface of a vast area, and I know that many works of equal stature must have been overlooked. I apologize for disappointing many respected friends and colleagues. The project is potentially endless, but restrictions of time and space eventually meant calling a halt. The Supplementary List provides basic details of an additional fifteen works that do not appear in the main text, but which are warmly recommended. Immediately after I had made my final selection, an important new song cycle by Elliott Carter—*Of Challenge and of Love* (Five Poems of John Hollander for soprano and piano) (Boosey & Hawkes, 1995)—had its première.

Several publishing-houses have recently brought out important anthologies: for instance, *Heritage of Twentieth Century British Song* (4 vols.; Boosey & Hawkes, 1988–91), *A Century of English Song* (4 vols. in separate voice categories; Thames, 1993–6), and *The Young Recitalist* (Stainer & Bell, 1989). The catalogues of these houses, and of Bardic Edition, Lengnick, Maecenas, Ramsey, and Roberton Publications among others, are worthy of close attention. In New Zealand, the enterprising Waiteata Press Music Editions, based at the Victoria University of Wellington, includes songs by many leading New Zealand composers, and a recent initiative by the New Zealand Music Centre (SOUNZ, New Zealand) has produced the splendid volume *Kowhai*. This selection of short vocal works by women with or without piano, is particularly rewarding. Many composers have become their own 'desktop' publishers—another advantage of improvements in technology. A contract with a major publisher may come to have less significance in future. Readers are recommended to consult the current *British Music Yearbook* for up-to-date information on a fluid situation. Addresses of composers, publishers, and information centres are to be found listed alphabetically at the end of the book. As recommended before, those wishing to obtain scores from USA would do well to make contact with a good music store, such as Yesterday Service Inc. 1972 Massachusetts Avenue, Cambridge, Ma. 02140, tel. (001) 617–547 8263, where Esther Breslau and her staff are immensely helpful and knowledgeable.

Finally, I would like to exhort anyone feeling discouraged by the increasing difficulty of balancing everyday realities with artistic aspirations, to fan the embers of commitment and creativity by promoting all that is best in 'living' music. It is infinitely rewarding to work with compositional talent and to initiate new repertoire. Now, as we approach the new millenium, we need to seek out those pieces that will survive the test of time and bring lasting pleasure to coming generations.

October 1996   JANE MANNING

Mon ami
(1974)

Betsy Jolas (born 1926)
Text by the composer (in French)

T I; M I (voice part only)
Female or child pianist/singer
Duration variable, from 1'30" to 4'

An intriguing and wistfully charming one-woman showpiece, from this distinguished French composer, who spent some of her early life in the USA and whose work combines intellectual rigour with musical sensitivity. To sing and play at the same time is not at all easy, as singing teachers and others will know. The composer Michael Head regularly gave one-man recitals of his own songs, and many of today's singers are good pianists well able to accompany themselves informally. However, I recall only one other example of a 'modernist' work to be played and sung by the same person: a piece by the American composer Roger Reynolds, 'Sketch Book', in which, fortunately for myself, the piano part was not too arduous, consisting of gentle chords in between more florid vocal lines. The emphasis was on the voice part; here the roles are reversed. The vocal part remains in a comfortable middle register, avoiding dynamic extremes, and there is a complete absence of the longer phrases that might require a professional's technique. The pianism needed is of a rather higher order, especially in the latter half, which ends with a solo of some virtuosity. The fact that the work is expected to be performed by a child is an indication of the enviable musical grounding that French children receive; in particular their adeptness with the *solfège* system, which gives such security in pitching. All the vocal phrases are based on scales and simple intervals, and the piano consistently cues, echoes, and mirrors pitches, so that the piece is a wonderful training exercise for consolidating musicianship.

The composer has worked out a neat scheme for five possible ways of performing the piece, according to an individual performer's capabilities, selecting the given material to construct a logical whole. The music is divided into four sections, labelled A to D, each progressively longer in proportion to its predecessor. A and B take up half a page, but B carries a repeat version with a slightly different ending. C, twice as long again (whole page), also has a second-time version with a new modulation at the cadence. This leads directly into D, the two-page piano solo, where the performer has a chance to demonstrate real pianistic prowess. The five alternative performing plans are listed in order of difficulty, both of keyboard accomplishment and of the musicianship required to co-ordinate the two parts. The composer has also marked the score clearly to guide the performer through the routes of each numbered version.

The text is a simple, nursery-rhyme-like chant in the form of a riddle. This aptly fits and illustrates the continual interplay between vocal line and piano. One speculates as to whether the music was written first as with Messiaen's own custom-built texts. Roughly translated, the riddle goes thus: 'Do you know who my friend is? . . . it is the mountain's echo'. This 'friend' (or shadow) follows the singer everywhere, repeating all that she says. Musical and verbal relationships are closely woven throughout, and the work is a model of clear-minded organization, and mathematical precision, which yet makes a hauntingly beautiful and spontaneous effect. The vocal tessitura is crucial to the aural concept, and, because of its precise relationship with the keyboard part, it should only be sung by either unbroken boys' or female voices.

Section A is very simple and delicate, and a young boy or girl would sound very touching singing the straightforward, diatonic (in F major) scale fragments. There is a gentle slowing-up at the ends of phrases, and ample time to breathe in between. The piano (but not the voice) is marked legato with 'a little pedalling', and meanders quietly around the vocal range, the hands very close together in the treble clef. Free 'spatial' notation is employed: the most practical method for complete flexibility. The admirably clear printed score is scrupulously aligned—visual accuracy is very important for the dovetailed overlapping entries. There are no actual rhythmic unisons, and a fascinating mosaic effect is achieved. Of course, a child-like naturalness of timbre is not entirely easy for a trained singer to assume, without direct imitation or parody. Sincerity is the keynote, and any artful overprojection or forced naïvety must be avoided. The vocal sounds should flow naturally out of the accompaniment and vice versa, to give the effect of a private reverie. Vibrato has to be kept under control, but not to the extent of rigidity, or the affectation that occasionally mars 'authentic' early music singing. Halfway through, the tempo quickens for a close-knit sequence that depicts the 'following' or 'repeating' of the friend-cum-shadow, before the calmer opening tempo is resumed. The fast section has two different sets of words, but only three out of the five specified combinations feature section A twice, allowing the complete text to be sung.

Section B continues in F major but at a slightly brisker pace, in strict 6/8 metre. The voice part consists largely of 'echo' fragments with plenty of chance to rest in between. The tone can be brighter and more present in keeping with the higher dynamics, especially at the climax at the start of the longest fragment, starting on *forte* high F. This should have a piercing quality. There are also strong accents on 'C'est'. The last two syllables of 'montagne' are used as reverberating echoes to end. These drop low in the voice, especially at the second version of the cadence, where the tuning of the low B flat must be very acute, matching the piano. The keyboard part is sparse and atonal with wide leaps recalling Webern, and a broad range of dynamics within a small space. Resonating harmonics, and almost-plucked staccato effects are subject to scrupulously planned pedallings. Once again, the piano gently follows or anticipates the vocal line, avoiding rhythmic unisons.

The third section, C, goes into C major, and is twice as long. The 6/8 time signature is retained, although the music is punctuated by carefully marked interludes of 'free time', determined in seconds (Example 1). The material of section B is developed and extended, giving the voice more sustained notes, and elongating the 'fanfare-echo' fragments considerably. The angular Webernian atonality of the piano part continues, as does the use of chordal harmonics. Dynamics are much more subtle and varied, including swift changes, and even sharper accents, so that every morsel of sound has tremendous piquancy. At the end, there is a hummed scale reminiscent of the opening, but in C major, for the first time. A portamento is given for the swelling transition across the semitone from E to F, and this must be very expressive and poignant. This is the end of the piece in versions 2 and 3, the piano providing an unexpected, but fleeting, *fortissimo* flourish of staccato intervals to launch this final phrase. Only in the last two versions of the work is the 'second-time bar' heard: this gives a sudden shift up a semitone. The voice intones 'Savez-vous' on 'Do-ré-mi' in C sharp, and the more demanding piano-writing that is to follow is introduced, by a graphically notated rubato of staccato intervals, with a sudden juxtaposition of *fortissimo* and *pianissimo*, within a *rallentando*.

The impressive piano solo that ends the full version of the piece, is based on all the previous vocal and keyboard material, reworking and developing it most thrillingly, gradually bursting into cascades of overlapping scales, and then whirling arpeggios, ever more urgent and electrifying. Fanfare notes and scale fragments resonate throughout the piano's range, and durations of crucial passages are indicated in seconds. The music is written in a by-now-familiar form of free notation, in which 'hairpins' of gradually increasing or diminishing density are used to convey gradual speedings- and slowings-up. This is where a good pianist will have a chance to let off steam: the music goes on to three staves for a while. After a peak of energy, the music calms down to recapture the wistful mood of the beginning, and there is the faintest trace of the work's opening at the very end. In a masterly stroke, the composer creates a mysterious thread-like echo of the first song-phrase, by having the piano's chord, containing the notes of the melody, held silently, while the atonal bass-line picks out the rhythm, so that the aural effect is of a magical wisp of the tune, fading into silence.

An audience will be fascinated by this lovely piece, which proves incontrovertibly that atonal music can be just as much fun as the purely diatonic. Finding one's way through the various permutations is a stimulating game,

Ex.1 Jolas

and it makes the piece very accessible on all levels, focusing concentration and heightening sensitivity to the smallest details. Finding the correct performance context for this rarity will need some thought, but budgetary strictures these days should mean that it provides a welcome chance for a one-person recital. Since the piano will be in use, it would seem a pity not to involve it again, and the singer should be able to find some less demanding items which can be sung seated at the piano. Ideally, some of the early Webern songs (Opp. 4 and 5 for instance) would be a perfect match, for a singer of real pianistic distinction. However, at the other end of the scale, some simple ballads would go very well. Alison Bauld's 'Dear Emily' (see Vol. 1) would be possible for just one performer, and it is to be hoped that other composers will take up this idea of a simple form of music theatre. Betsy Jolas's own assurance and total awareness of the practicalities has resulted in a piece of consummate craftmanship and discipline, not too easily emulated.

It would also be novel, and charming, to intersperse unaccompanied folksongs (especially suitable for the child performer too), with simple piano pieces, such as Grieg's *Lyric Pieces*. With the Jolas in the central position, a memorable and varied sequence can be constructed; a really creative idea for a special Festival event. One could even envisage a family or pupil–teacher evening, with various versions of the piece performed at intervals, almost as a refrain, by members of different age groups and abilities. Repetition will do the work no harm at all.

From 'The Bad Child's Book of Beasts' (1952)

Donald Martino (born 1931)
Text by Hilaire Belloc

T I; M II
High voice and piano
Duration *c*.5′

Donald Martino is a distinguished example from the senior generation of American composers whose work is consistently rewarding and deserves to be heard much more in Europe. His *Three Songs* for bass voice and piano, featured in Volume 1, show him in familiar radical, atonal vein, but his output demonstrates enormous variety. There are large-scale symphonic and choral works including an oratorio on Dante's *Divine Comedy*, and many other intriguing items from his catalogue, of which *Augenmusik: A Mixed Mediocritique for Actress/Danseuse or Uninhibited Female Percussionist and Tape*—invites further investigation. As a former clarinettist, and writer of a considerable amount of wind music, he brings an understanding of breathing technique to his vocal writing.

The composer's adaptability and skill in simplifying his style, is shown admirably in this nicely balanced trio of short songs, set to some of Belloc's *Cautionary Tales*, which have extremely satisfying piano parts too. A light touch and subtle humour are displayed to charming effect, and the vocal lines are unpretentious and naturally shaped. A most welcome straightforward interpretative opportunity is offered to young singers in particular, and there should be no difficulty in learning them. Tessitura is occasionally a little high for sopranos, and a tenor is perhaps the ideal voice for articulating the faster-running passages. The piece is dedicated to Martino's little godson, and the printed (1978) version also bears an inscription to his own small son.

1. The Lion; The Tiger

Marked 'Vigorously', the bold piano solo introduction moves modally in block chords, based in F minor, in irregular patterns. A roaring octave tremolando in the bass depicts the lion, heralding the voice's entry with the same folksong-like theme of the piano's opening. Two fast-moving strophic 'lion' verses are separated by a short piano solo varying the basic motif. The higher-lying second half of each verse may take a little time to feel comfortable and keep words flowing freely and clearly. At the end of the 'lion' section, another piano solo brings a change of key to G major, and a lessening of pace. For the 'tiger', the voice has a simple melody in 4/4, while the rumbling tremolando again features in the bass. At the end of this one verse, the singer suddenly leaps up an octave at the end for the final word 'expense'. High A for the second, sustained syllable of this is potentially awkward, and the singer must avoid pinching the sound and closing on to consonants too soon. The piano's postlude, in the brisker opening tempo, is most ingenious and amusing. It features the 'lion' theme, worked and developed over a wide range, modulating freely, involving some demanding octave passagework before settling back into F minor with a final flourish.

2. The Frog

This most attractive song takes the form of a quasi-Romantic waltz. The composer marks it 'Freely, in Ballad-style', and a one-in-a-bar lilt should prevail through the undulating lyricism of the vocal lines. The words, however, need careful pointing, since there are so many unusual nicknames in the first verse (Example 1). The free flexible approach needed will demonstrate the artists' qualities of natural unforced musicianship. The

11

Ex. 1 Martino

Or   'Gap - a - - grin,'   or   'Toad - gone -

- wrong'.   Or   'Bil - ly   Ban - dy - knees': _____

sudden shifts of harmony and frequent cadences recall Prokofiev, but the language is also redolent of the English Romantics. Despite the almost casual, effortless style required, intervals have to be pitched cleanly, and there are quite a few traps for the unwary. Particular attention must be played to accidentals. However, pitches are quite often doubled in the piano part. There are two complementary verses with a piano solo in between. The second half of each verse travels through different keys and shadings, always flowing continuously. Again some of the lines lie rather high for a soprano, and a tenor will find it easier to make words, such as 'kind and fair' and 'at least', completely clear without restricting the tone.

3. The Microbe

This final song requires extremely good reactions from both performers, and a flexible sense of rhythm. The pianist has to take the main responsibility for piloting the many crucial transitions. At the start, the instruction is 'Gradually finding the tempo', and *staccatissimo* quavers on the piano lead into the singer's rapid successions of parlando writing. Ideally the first vocal paragraph should be taken all in one breath. The only other possibility is to breathe quickly after 'all', if the build to *forte* would be at risk for lack of power. The *fortissimo* pause on the up-beat 'his' (high G) is followed immediately by the softer *molto meno mosso*. The pace then accelerates again ever more relentlessly. The most workable breathing places are after the words 'teeth', 'spots', and 'bands'. Alternatives could throw the rhythm out quite badly, and result in breathlessness. Even at high speed each note has to speak and control is essential. Piano chords coinciding with off-beats could cause ensemble problems during the dizzying acceleration, and the performers cannot afford to get carried away. The two commas placed before large paragraphs are crucial rallying points. The changes of speed, and timings of pauses and restarts have to be managed smoothly and immaculately. The *molto meno, recitante* passage, which brings a sudden *piano* after another *fortissimo* high G, requires a clear cool tone-colour to convey its message, almost confidentially. The singer's diction will be tested fully throughout. The final line must be in one span—like the opening it involves 'gradually finding the tempo' and then letting it subside again in a *ritenuto*—and the pianist should take firm control here. All through the song the vocal manner should be simple and unaffected, with no exaggeration of the humour.

This thoroughly likeable mini-song cycle will suit a young performer perfectly, especially for a family concert. In this context, the songs by Malcolm Williamson, Irving Fine, and Eibhlis Farrell in this book (and the Leonard Bernstein and Richard Rodney Bennett from Volume 1) are obvious companions. Charles Ives's 'The Cage' which describes a lion, would fit very well, and there are plenty of others by him at his most innocent and homespun. This piece could also provide light relief after a more substantial cycle, perhaps by Schumann or Fauré. Groups of more expansive single songs (Brahms, Duparc) could contrast well too. A complete programme of songs with animal references could be assembled, although one should beware of too many jokes in one programme.

Songs from the Good Person of Sichuan (1989)

Dominic Muldowney (born 1952)
Text by Bertolt Brecht
Translated into English by Michael Hofmann

T I; M II
Medium voice and piano
Duration (complete) 22'30"

These songs were written for performance in the context of the play at the National Theatre. Intended for actors, not trained singers, they should prove a great boon to both amateur and professional singer-actors. The composer asks us to bear in mind their original purpose, and one should not forget that these are Chinese characters. The main requirement is to project the drama with persuasive clarity and conviction. A polished vocal technique, with impeccable legato and good breath capacity will not be called upon. It is always refreshing to adapt to different priorities and characteristics, and for trained singers it is challenging to be asked to abandon some of the ingrained habits acquired with care over the years.

Anyone who has spent time working with actors, particularly in a company, will know that they set an enviable example to singers, with regard to memory-capacity, motivation, and ability to assimilate supposedly difficult music. Their sheer zest for hard work often puts the pampered professional singer to shame! Setting words by Brecht inevitably evokes comparison with songs of the Berliner movement, especially those of Eisler and Weill. The Brechtian model still represents a valid goal for those aspiring to the ideal of art for the people. Muldowney is clearly committed to this aesthetic and he is comfortably at home in its special ambience. His is a rare and special talent, and it is important for composers of fine quality to work in the 'straight' theatre. The field of incidental music can attract a type of all-purpose *pasticheur*, not always equal to the task of making a meaningful contribution to the greater stage works.

There are six numbers, and their durations are given separately. These vary from 2'30" to 5'—the fourth is the longest, and the last three the most ambitious in musical terms. Each could be performed separately or different selections made to form a recital group. As a whole they constitute a nicely balanced sequence, well proportioned and satisfyingly varied. The composer is keenly aware of the practicalities of using actors rather than singers. An actor is likely to have limited powers of breath control and sustained pitch. The smaller muscles that make up the singer's apparatus will not be trained for such specific use. A parlando style therefore predominates throughout the songs, with fairly short phrase-lengths, and vocal tessitura is well judged. It is essential for the performer to convey the essence of the text and extract every ounce of drama. Of course, actors are accustomed to exercise, and many keep their bodies in good and disciplined condition, and though their singing may lack finesse, the physical energy is always present.

For young singers, especially beginners, or amateurs, these songs are ideal, and great fun to perform. There is nothing better than something which starts to fall into place right away, and sounds well even when half-spoken. Word clarity is of paramount importance, but trained singers must avoid an 'arty' or knowingly parodistic cabaret style. An unsophisticated direct manner will be much more affecting emotionally. Certainly there is a touching quality about a natural untrained voice, now very much in vogue, but this should not imply any deliberate aim of mediocrity or a lowering of standards, where anyone more vocally sophisticated is liable to be called élitist. Social and artistic attitudes are often difficult to reconcile. Such philosophical points inevitably come to mind when confronted with committed 'political' art.

However, from a cold technical standpoint, to be exposed in the middle of the range can be surprisingly problematic for professional singers, used to exhibiting spectacular extremes. But the trained singer will have some advantage in a wider choice of possibilities of dynamic and vocal colourings. Almost throughout, the manner of vocal delivery is dictated entirely by the way the words fall, as if declaiming or speaking. This natural way of vocalizing may have to be rediscovered, perhaps unravelling layers of self-conscious mannerisms and notions of correct placing. In general, vibrato should be kept to a minimum. Breathing exercises should prove most useful as a preparation, and it is important to stand, and even to move around a little while singing, avoiding set postures. The effect has to be of a spontaneous, personal utterance, the emotions almost visceral.

The piano part takes a good deal of the musical responsibility, and keeps the rhythms moving along. A very safe pair of hands is needed, for though the accompaniments do not require obvious pyrotechnics, they are not all that simple. A player of characterful presence and assurance is needed, someone able to respond to the dramatic content and capture the style instinctively. The printed score is beautifully clear and inviting, and standard notation will cause no problems.

1. Song of the Smoke (2′30″)

The *rubato molto* marking is immediately encouraging, giving great freedom to the vocalist, with the pianist instructed to follow the voice. A generous leeway is given: suggested tempo limits are crotchet = 60–96. The singer is therefore able to pull rhythms around, according to the mood and natural conversational style of the first section of each of three strophic verses. These begin in C major in 2/4 time, with four four-bar phrases divided at the halfway point by a 3/4 bar, adding even more flexibility. The parlando Berliner idiom is beautifully caught from the outset. The voice part proceeds in a matter-of-fact *mezzo-forte* through the straightforward note-for-syllable settings, with their 'casual' cadence points. For the repeated 'chorus' of each verse there is a total change: the key abruptly switches to D flat, in strict tempo (a sinister, slowly swinging 6/8 metre). The voice part is in sardonic, clipped, fragments, quiet and full of suppressed foreboding (Example 1). The usual loud climax is avoided, and the confiding, world-weary ending will be all the more effective in impact.

Ex. 1 Muldowney

15

2. On Suicide (3′30″)

This song is slow-paced and rapt, with a relentless chordal chugging in the piano. The attractive harmonies, with their enharmonic shifts, are strongly reminiscent of those often found in the songs of Hanns Eisler. The voice part is marked 'semplice' but it contains some quite intricate rhythms within the basic pulse. There is much use of of dotted figures, all of which flow naturally according to the articulations of the text, and there is even a triplet cross-rhythm (Example 2). A very wide dynamic range is incorporated, and then, near the end, the music dims to *pianissimo*, and there is a dramatic build from the word 'whispered' (which can indeed be whispered!) to *fortissimo* within a short span. The last note is a low G, and must not be pushed too hard, as it is needs to be soft and very poignant. This is a very strong song, despite its modest dimensions.

Ex. 2 Muldowney

3. Pigs'll Fly (Song of Never Never Day) (3′30″)

This movement is in a sprightly, dancing 12/8, in a modal version of D minor, and there are five verses. These are strophic, almost folksong-like, at first, but the style mutates halfway through to a more bluesy feeling for the ironic, accented exclamation of the refrain 'Pigs'll fly'. The first two verses are quite loud and ebullient, and the piano's repetitive minimalist accompanying figures are replaced by pungent clashing chords at the second verse's refrain. A lilting bridge passage introduces verse 3, which begins softly and gathers force. Here the rhythms are distinctly jazzier over the piano's continuous rocking bass. The piano has a particularly innocent-sounding *pianissimo* introduction to the fourth verse, which gently trips along without emphasis. After this the piano continues the mechanical rhythm but with chromatic modulations, preparing for the final verse, which is very powerful. Marked 'meno mosso', the basic melody undergoes considerable chromatic transformation, including the sharpening of the B flats, and the tessitura dips right down. The last 'Pigs'll fly' should be delivered in a hollow rounded tone, keeping a reasonably full sound on the low As and Gs. The release of the 'l' of 'fly' is crucial for controlling the intonation. The final line is even slower, and must be as silkily smooth as possible, taking special care with the gradual descent.

4. Song of the Inadequacy of the Gods and the Good (5')

This, the longest song, carries a touching plea for sane and reasonable behaviour and for the preservation of the concept of good over evil forces. The voice delivers a quasi-*ad libitum* recitative, with natural 'free' rhythms, marked 'parlando e leggiero' (the latter word in its common misspelling!). The key is E minor, and the vocal style should be casual and confidingly reflective. The music then suddenly moves into a strict march-like tempo. This same pattern is repeated for verse 2, with the freer material alternating with the metric march. After a pause, the last of the three verses is rather different: it is dark and dramatic, and is set much lower in the voice. Beginning in a sombre B flat minor, it proceeds to extreme depths (Example 3), but the passage which includes low E has an upper *ossia* if needed. Some words are highlighted by accents, and chromatic intervals may need extra work to avoid mishaps. Here the start of the verse stays in the march tempo (crotchet = 84) and the second half's 'refrain' is in G melodic minor. It begins gently enough but bursts out into an enraged, accented *fortissimo*. The vocalist has to shout 'Take aim!' twice. It is advisable to keep this very clear and piercing, and not to breathe beforehand: too much force could have a negative effect and even very well induce an irritation or cough. The

Ex. 3 Muldowney

hammered, heavily accented last vocal fragments should be treated with similar care and economy of air. The violent ending has to be controlled, especially if the next song is to follow in sequence.

5. Song of the Waterseller in the Rain (4′)

This is a highly dramatic piece, full of contrasts. It is probably the most demanding song, in view of its continual key-changes, and the use of spoken interpolations to the main melody. Considerable stamina will be needed, and a 'straight' singer will be required to show great acting ability. In this piece in particular, apart from the obvious Brechtian ambience, oriental pentatonic elements are expertly woven into the music to give the appropriate Chinese flavour.

It starts with a call of 'Water!', *ad libitum* in high falsetto. The notes are first cued in the piano, and this avoids any hesitation with pitching: it can be difficult for an untrained singer to switch registers at will. It is definitely for male voice, since the female head register (sometimes labelled 'falsett') will not be so distinctive as a special effect. Once the tempo gets going, the main theme is a Tango in C minor, with staccatos and accents used with great *élan*. This is highly attractive and memorable, and evokes comparison with Kurt Weill. The marked nuances should be inspected closely and observed in every detail. There is a sudden change to five sharps (although it feels more like C sharp than G sharp minor) and the voice has another falsetto call of 'Water!', which involves the same pitches, but is written in sharps, this time in strict 2/2 metre. This also recurs at the start of the last 'chorus'. The construction of the three verses is a rough ABABAB, but there is no falsetto call at the start of the middle 'refrain'. The regular enharmonic shuttlings from the flat to the sharp key, and back, throughout the song, are probably less likely to worry those who do not read music, but instead learn by aural means. Awareness of potential difficulties can be something of a disadvantage, and ignorance may indeed be bliss! Rhythms are not always predictable either, and the spoken fragments (always given as an 'aside') will need detailed work. It is not easy to move naturally from song to speech and vice versa in a short span, and some experience of Sprechstimme would be helpful. All three of these parentheses are notated in exact rhythm, with crosses for note-heads. Only this first one shows the basic pitch contour, and it need not be too high. The others are written on a monotone but this should not be taken too literally—it will sound more natural to drop the voice to a deepish speaking range, remembering always that the intrinsic difference between spoken and sung notes is that, in the former, pitches are not prolonged so that they can be defined. A profusion of explosive syllables in the spoken bits aids a more clipped effect. The sudden 3/8 bar for the second 'aside' may go against the grain at first, but such rhythmic irregularities add a distinctive edge to this number (Example 4). Each spoken phrase is followed by a long pause, including at the very end.

Ex. 4 Muldowney

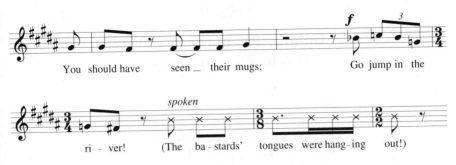

6. Trio of the Vanishing Gods on the Cloud (4′)

After a *rubato molto* piano introduction, the voice enters for a delightful fast waltz in traditional Viennese vein, to be sung with vigour and panache. Here a trained singer will be more at home. The pitches of the preceding Tango movement are found in the almost-improvised-sounding piano interludes that separate the three verses. The first two are in E flat major and the last is subject to a piquant shift up a semitone: a device frequently found in stage musicals. This pithily cheerful and straightforward setting ends quite abruptly with no rallentando, but a snappy accent on the last note.

There are many attractive possibilities for programming some or all of these diverse but appealing songs. Actor–singers may like to place them in a special poetry and music recital. It would be very exciting to revive some of the nineteenth-century melodramas by Liszt and others, so rarely heard these days. The items by Cage and Jolas in this book could also be suitable. Since a good pianist will be available, other cabaret items by such as Weill, Eisler, and Schoenberg would be ideally compatible, especially for more experienced singers. The pieces are also suitable for group performance by a number of different people, perhaps at a student concert. Some of the *Ten Songs* by Martin Wesley-Smith featured in this volume would go exceptionally well. Of course the Chinese theme could also be taken up: several composers have set Chinese verse in translation, and the John Beckwith songs in Volume 1 are not too taxing. It would also be worth looking up some of Cornelius Cardew's *Chinese Songs*. One singer will need to be very versatile to perform the whole set. In this case, it would be helpful to include a brief commentary outlining the play's action. Potential performers should note that the score stipulates very clearly that permission must be obtained from the publisher, before any performance in a dramatic format can take place.

Adlestrop
(1989)

Anthony Payne (born 1936)
Text by Edward Thomas

T I; M III
Soprano or mezzo-soprano and piano
Duration *c*.4′

This enchanting miniature sets a well-loved poem with perfect economy and clarity. The music is ideally sensitive to the especially nostalgic and poignant atmosphere of the poem. The exciting piano part carries the images of the text throughout, depicting the motion of a train at the beginning. It needs effortless virtuosity and the player must take considerable responsibility for shaping the work. By contrast, the singer's spare, uncluttered lines make their point most touchingly. The piece lies comfortably in mid-voice, and is equally suitable for a soprano or mezzo. It could also work for a light baritone, since G is the highest note, but tenors may be less happy with some of the lower-lying phrases. These, however, are always at a gentle dynamic. Audiences invariably respond warmly and attentively to this thoroughly approachable piece, whose harmonic language could be described as polytonal, mingled with strong resonances of the English Romantics such as Delius, Bax, and Moeran. In addition to the 'train' effects, lusciously spaced chords and 'bell-chimes' evoke the hazy summer landscape, and the feeling of being suspended in a time capsule. Histrionics must be avoided: the piece automatically encourages complete concentration and sensitive listening, and poise is a prime requirement.

This composer prefers to use the voice in a simple, unaffected, and non-virtuoso manner, as if speaking. In this way, words can be heard clearly, and the subtle but wide range of colours and dynamics can be achieved without strain. Tonal control and perfect intonation are particularly important, to negotiate intervals cleanly without ambiguities.

One of the most satisfying aspects of the piece from the singer's point of view is that it gives the opportunity to examine and analyse vocal quality while performing it. One becomes acutely aware of the minutiae of gradations of vibrato and higher frequencies, and of the pitch centre of each note. The pianist plays the major role, depicting the text's nature imagery in overtly programmatic terms, and also shaping passagework with flexibility, so that rhythms flow naturally. As with many of this composer's works, choice of tempo is crucial.

The piano's extended solo 'prelude' must begin sufficiently briskly to allow for the train's slowing-down to sound convincing. Cross-rhythms between right and left hand should not sound contrived. Cantabile moments are always to be savoured, dynamics strictly observed, and accents relished.

The voice's unaccompanied entry presents a subtle interpretative challenge. With fullest concentration, stillness, and simplicity of manner, it should seem to arise naturally, as if musing out loud. Tone should be pure and well focused. There is plenty of time to hear the initial pitch, prompted by the piano's lingering cue. The voice's uneven rhythms are actually a form of written-out rubato and must not sound calculated, but the difference between triplets and semiquavers should be apparent. The low tessitura of the first entry falls easily within a speaking range for most voices, and there should be no trouble with text audibility, as vocal phrases build gently and gradually. It is important to observe rests and note-endings exactly, but this does not mean that each fragment needs a separate breath. Indeed, from experience, singers will know that tone is often clearer when air is conserved, removing the temptation to exaggerate explosive consonants. Naturally inflected speech patterns mean that text and music fit together perfectly, as in the best Lieder tradition, for instance in the songs of Wolf. After the fragmented opening, the phrase beginning 'the express train' will seem quite long, and the singer has to control a gentle swell through the sustained low B flat on 'there'. In the next phrase, the word 'June' should be left to resonate naturally, without a crescendo. A subtle increase of speed encapsulates a moment of tension, enhanced by the sibilance of the text in 'the steam hissed'. Once again, large breaths in the gaps are inappropriate. The name of the village of the title, occurring at this point, must provide a moment of sheer magic, placed delicately and securely without emphasis, letting the sparseness of the setting make its poignant effect (Example 1). The Gs on 'name' and on the second syllable of 'willows' can then glow warmly in the longish cantabile phrase which leads to the central section, in which voice and piano are more traditionally in full partnership, instead of alternating as in the first section. The piano takes over from the voice's lingering pitch, reversing the process of the opening. Pitch-matching of this kind is frequently found in Payne's music, and it encourages careful listening, a prerequisite for chamber music.

The piano's figurations can prove difficult to follow here, since they overlap, and both hands alternate quintuplets with four-quaver groups in duple time, but deep left-hand octaves help to plot crucial beats for the singer. The vocal line floats radiantly above increasingly dense texture during a gradual acceleration of speed and rising excitement. Always the sustained syllables at the ends of the climbing phrases lie flatteringly, culminating in the glorious long high G on 'sky' (there is no need to be overconscious of the diphthong, and risk spoiling the end of the note—the 'ah' sound can drift comfortably into space), and the piano continues its repeated figures, giving the voice further support, and enriching the

Ex. 1 Payne

No one left and no one came   on the bare plat-form.   What I saw was

Ad - le - strop   on - ly the name ____   And wil - lows, ____

Wil - low   herb,

and grass,   and mea - dow sweet.   And hay - cocks dry,

resonance with strong bass octaves, rising to a *fortissimo* climax. Again here, it is the pianist's task to shape an important transition. After a pause, a sudden change of mood and pace brings calm, with an echo or 'after-shock', an octave lower, of the piano's preceding material. As at the opening, the voice enters unhurriedly and without stress, and the singing of the blackbird provides another vivid moment of heightened awareness. Intervals at this particular point may need a little extra work, as the voice is left exposed. In this final section, as the piano underpins the vocal line once more, familiar pitch sequences recur, and the singer's C sharps, Es, and Gs should feel bright and effortlessly resonant, within the gentler dynamic. The piano's texture now continues on either side of the singer's last phrases, and, as at the beginning, the touching evocative words can be heard without distraction. The voice drops to a final low B natural, and this will need to be well controlled and poised, taking care not to allow the tone to become too heavy. The pianist's crucially exposed concluding solo continues the deeply contemplative mood, dying away gradually, as figurations peter out, and a perfectly balanced ending brings a whispered echo of the note-pattern that introduced the voice at the outset.

This beautifully balanced little piece works very well at the start of the second half of a recital, but could also form part of a mixed group of English songs, perhaps settings of other War poems. Despite its simplicity of effect, it is not eclipsed by larger scale works, and its brevity is deceptive, since it is packed with detail, and lingers in the memory. It is particularly suited to providing a contrast to a work of extravagant virtuosity.

The Maldive Shark
(1990)

Howard Skempton (born 1947)
Text by Herman Melville

T I; M I
Baritone and piano
Duration 3′

Howard Skempton is a genuine original, with a sharp ear and great imagination, and his music is at last getting the recognition it deserves. He belongs to a group of politically committed composers who have determinedly ploughed their own furrow without regard to current fashion or material success. Always concerned with music's accessibility to all kinds of people, Skempton has consistently supported and encouraged other composers with typical courtesy and generosity. I first encountered him at the Scratch Orchestra's memorable Beethoven concert in the late sixties. An amateur baritone of style and sincerity, his 'Ode to Joy' carried touching conviction.

This tiny gem is a real find for almost any occasion, informal as well as formal. It is dedicated to his friend and colleague, the composer and singer Brian Dennis. A wonderful text muses upon the relationship between the shark and the small fish that encircle it on its ponderous way. The text's imagery is superbly resonant, alliterative ('white triple tiers of glittering gates'), and often lurid ('sawpit of mouth', 'charnel of maw') and can be thoroughly relished by the singer as it rolls off the tongue. The feel of the syllables is irresistible, and the test is to keep crystal clarity while a seamless legato is maintained, *mezzo-piano* throughout. This will be no mean achievement, but the music is so enjoyable that assiduous practice will be no hardship.

The musical idiom is an example of neo-simplicity at its best. The composer himself comments on its 'relentless circularity', happily apposite to the words. Continual crotchet triads in the piano's right hand produce a series of delicious shifting harmonies over slow-moving, deep bass octaves: a pricelessly apt depiction of the text, as the tiny fish dart around the shark on its inexorable journey. The voice weaves a most fetching tune over the top, going round and round, cadencing frequently. This theme is repeated eight times, identically in terms of pitch and harmony, but with an endless variety of phrase-lengths. Anyone who does not concentrate on counting carefully will quickly stumble into a trap. The music continually oscillates between the twin centres of the home key of D major, and its mediant, F sharp minor, with many felicitous transitions and pivot chordings *en route*. Phrases often cut off abruptly, presumably illustrating the snapping of jaws. These punctuate the music in a style that recalls the songs of Eisler or Weill. The main requirement throughout is an even tone, clear and penetrating, perhaps shading individual words spontaneously ('sleek', 'slim', 'liquidly', etc.). Some delicate rubato in response to changes of harmony is also permissible, but nothing must be allowed to disturb the calm, steady glide of the music. It is particularly important to avoid pushing the recurring high Es out of line. The especially arresting detail of word-painting at 'serrated teeth' (Example 1) brings a fleeting moment of potential disruption, and the swung rhythm here has to be negotiated with deceptive ease. It all sounds quite beautiful and lies easily within the voice's natural compass.

This little piece is sure to enchant any audience. Despite its cyclic form, there is no danger of monotony with its constant charm and subtle elliptical shaping. A superb encore, it would also make a lovely start to a programme. Other miniatures about creatures of land and ocean could be added to form

Ex. 1 Skempton

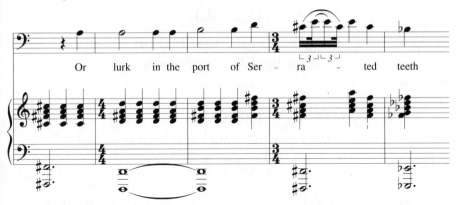

an attractive group. Cage's 'Litany for the Whale' (for two singers) would be a good choice, especially for unsophisticated voices. Poulenc's *Le Bestiaire* and Satie's *Ludions* would also be ideally placed beside it. There is no reason at all why it should not become immensely popular.

Five Songs
(1919–20)

George Antheil (1900–59)
Text by Adelaide Crapsey

T II; M III
Soprano (or tenor) and piano
Duration *c.*7′

This could hardly be called new repertory, in view of its date, but the name of the American composer George Antheil is unlikely to be familiar to many singers. Much cherished as a modernist innovator, he enjoys cult status in specialist circles. His best-selling autobiography *Bad Boy of Music* was published in 1945. Dividing his time between Europe and the USA, he was also active as a pianist, and was championed by the artistic élite of his time, including Joyce, Yeats, Pound, Satie, and Picasso. He eventually moved to Los Angeles, where he orchestrated film scores, wrote a lonely-hearts column, and, in co-operation with the film star Hedy Lamarr, invented a new type of torpedo! He also wrote a mystery novel under a pseudonym.

He was one of the first composers to incorporate jazz elements in a symphonic context, and he was fond of experimenting with odd instrumental combinations and early electronic devices. A distaste for the Romanticism of Strauss and the 'fluid diaphanous lechery' (his own words) of the Impressionists, led him to develop a style featuring the chugging, machine-like rhythms amd violent percussive sounds that now, so many years later, are greatly in vogue. His most famous work remains the *Ballet mécanique* (1926), originally conceived as a film score. Its instrumentation includes eight pianos, a player piano, two electric bells, two propellers, and a siren. His later (1940s on) style contains a wider variety of references, including folk and jazz alongside an almost-classical lyricism.

His small repertoire of songs, often setting major poets, including some of his contemporaries, is well worth seeking out. His *Nine Songs of Experience* (Blake) dating from 1948 is acknowledged to be one of his finest works.

The present brief and delightful example of his work is as quirky and, original as might be imagined, and an unexpected treat for all concerned. Compact cycles of this quality are still rare, and much needed in the repertoire. Although a soprano is specified, there seems no reason why a tenor should not be equally happy singing it. In fact, a few of the higher lines will be easier to articulate in the male register. Some of the piano accompaniments are extremely full-textured, though, so the soprano voice would float more easily above without becoming swamped. The pianist will find the bold, dramatic writing very satisfying. The first three songs are very short, and, interestingly, the vocal tessitura descends as the cycle progresses, whilst the accompaniment becomes more active and dominant. The last two songs have an almost orchestral richness. The poems are aphoristic and understated, and the voice parts correspondingly plain and undecorated, moving either in declamatory speech rhythms, or in long slow spans, often on a monotone, and almost always in close intervals. The descriptive imagery and atmosphere are filled in by the piano's excitingly characterful part.

1. November Night

The brief opening song is written in the key of B major, and the tonic and dominant are sounded throughout, at the bottom of the piano, and also alternating gently in the middle of the texture. Soft high chromatic chords provide the misty effect appropriate to the text, not forgetting the 'frostiness' which is emphasized by tenuto separations of each chord. The singer floats a sustained high line above. Although pitches are constantly repeated, relationships with the piano's chords are not always easy, and a steely precision is needed. The passage would work very well if sung non-vibrato, as words may prove difficult to get across otherwise. The very long 'ghosts' on high G natural should be made to sound unearthly. There will probably be a need for a quick breath after 'crisped' because of the many repeated Gs. A high A sharp forms a nice arching approach to the first of two repeated dropping semitones on 'fall'; each, as well as the A sharp itself, has to swell and fade within a short space, and the A sharp could be allowed to linger a little. Otherwise the only slackening of tempo (a choice of crotchet = 72 or 80—the latter feels the more comfortable) occurs after the long note, giving the singer a chance to recover strength. The piano ends unresolved on an octave D sharp.

2. Triad

The second movement is the simplest and is again extremely brief. In A minor, it almost seems like a folksong fragment, but a rather unusual one. The piano's gently throbbing triads begin softly and sparsely, and gradually gather force and richness. The voice part again stays within a limited range, with close chromatic intervals and repeated notes that make intonation particularly crucial. Phrases are short and not at all taxing. The text is evocative and economical, and one is reminded of some of Ives's exquisite miniature songs. A momentary lyrical interlude, it forms a perfect preparation for what is to come.

3. Suzanna and the Elders

This tiny setting takes the form of a dramatic recitative, and ranges violently in mood and dynamic. Now we see the composer's markings (written in boxes): 'hard', 'more softly', 'tenderly', and 'defiant'. The piano punctuates with chords, its volume fluctuating wildly. After the angry opening outburst, the voice softens to *pianissimo* for 'beautiful', 'delicate', etc. The last bar marks a total change: a defiant cry of 'Therefore', on high G, is left ringing in the air, the piano's strident chords suddenly disappearing to *piano*. A great deal of emotion is packed into a short space.

4. Fate Defied

The last two songs are somewhat longer, and more radical in style, and their accompaniments are more ambitious, exhibiting the pianist's virtuosity. There are some startling changes of mood and idiom, and the music crackles with energy and fresh invention. The singer begins with a simple, intoned, introductory phrase, *pianissimo*. Quite suddenly (the instruction 'defiantly' occurs at this moment though the dynamic remains *pianissimo*) the piano begins a long section of scintillating rapid high arpeggio figures. This continues while the voice spins long lines on repeated pitches, first on G sharp, and then up to (middle) B natural. The written instructions (which contain some odd misspellings, presumably the composer's own) are unexpected but illuminating, especially 'with muted voice'. It is difficult to decide how to achieve this within the legato. Perhaps singing through clenched teeth, or heightening consonants and reducing volume on vowels, might help the effect, but it may well be merely a change of mood, which has somehow to be conveyed vocally by intense concentration. 'Radiently' [*sic*] is easier to obey once the line lifts a little, but there is no guidance as to breathing during the long succession of B naturals. A breath before 'clad' is the most obvious choice, but, so as to maintain a steady line and save something for the crescendo at the end, another may be necessary after it as well, and then again after 'like'. Balance could be disturbed otherwise, since the piano part becomes increasingly loud and manic. At this point the singer is given a higher *ossia*, which would certainly ride the texture better, but could give breathing and placement problems, especially for a soprano. A long E could prove difficult to manœuvre, followed as it is by an awkward transition to E flat with a sudden diminuendo. After a pause, the piano has driving octaves and chords (marked 'harshly') as the voice intones the last phrase on middle B natural.

5. The Warning

The final song begins with a lengthy piano solo, dark and brooding, with arpeggio flourishes before each chord. The voice proceeds in sparse, separated fragments, relatively low in the range. The expressive instructions are increasingly bizarre (and misspelt: 'strindently' for instance!). Fearlessly innovative, the composer asks for 'strangled' tone on the word 'flew'. A sudden exaggerated tightening of the 'w' with the lips should produce a snuffed effect, but it must be done very quickly and then released, so as not to contort neck muscles. Meanwhile the piano has wild pounding triplets and tremolandos and accented chords. For the voice's last line, and its echo, marked 'slower, more deliberate', the same diamond-shaped 'harmonic' note is used for 'cold' (Example 1). This would seem to indicate a further stifling of the sound, perhaps to a whisper. For the second time, without the pause, a swift elision on to 'l' and then a sudden stop on 'd' should work well. The piano's postlude repeats the opening flourishes, and dies away.

Ex. 1 Antheil

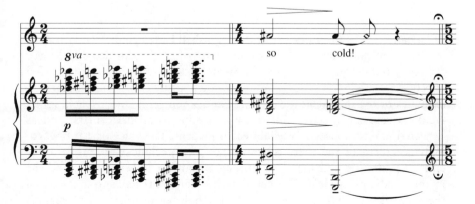

When encountering Antheil's music, it is impossible not to be reminded of other great innovators, in particular Percy Grainger, A Grainger–Antheil recital would be most refreshing. It would also be good to compile a complete programme of 'Pioneers, Experimentalists, and Eccentrics'. Using a major figure such as Charles Ives, whose songs provide the widest possible choice, as the central peg, the programme could include works by Henry Cowell, John Cage, Ruth Crawford Seeger, and Lou Harrison, as well as Antheil, to give an unusual slant on 'Americana'. In contrast, they could also be mixed with the work of Copland, Carter, Barber, Bernstein, and Rorem. The adventurous are also warmly recommended to search out the work of the early Russian experimentalists, especially the extraordinary Nicholas Obouhov, whose songs, written around the same time as this Antheil set, are full of extravagant instructions. A rich field, indeed, for the awakening of curiosity, and one where many treasures may be uncovered.

Beside the Depths of A River
(1969–76)

Tzvi Avni (born 1927)
Text by Mati Katz in Hebrew and English
Translation by Gila Abrahamson

T II; M II
High or medium voice and piano
Duration *c*.10′

I first came across the work of the distinguished Israeli composer Tzvi Avni in the seventies, when I had the opportunity of singing his delightful piece for voice and clarinet 'Leda and the Swan'. It featured many of the special effects associated with post-sixties' experimentalism: chords on the clarinet, extremes of register, aleatoric sections, and so on. This song cycle is somewhat less radical in style, and easily accessible to all performers, and as expected, the composer's excellent ear is evident. The voice part is rewardingly comfortable and there is nothing of great technical or musical difficulty. Tessitura is undemanding, suiting all but the lowest voices, and the layout is admirably clear. The characterful piano part tends to move when the voice is still and vice versa, avoiding balance problems. The piano's notation does involve several standard modern devices, including the slowing-down of repeated notes depicted graphically. There are many inside-piano effects, such as fingered glissandos, and the striking of strings with a metal stick. Tone-clusters are played both outside and inside the piano, and appear on an extra stave. All this is made abundantly clear in the written instructions in the score. The singer's role is a rather more conventional one, straightforwardly lyrical or declamatory by turn. There are many repeated notes, and repetitions of intervals, especially tritones, create a secure tonal basis that allows the voice to focus firmly, so that the singer can monitor each note and match tone-quality to the sound of the piano, without feeling under pressure. The composer provides few dynamics in the vocal line. It is presumed that, as often found in traditional German Lieder, they should match those of the piano, or perhaps stay one notch above.

The exceptionally fine work of the young Israeli poet Mati Katz, killed in military action in 1964, has inspired the composer to produce music of immediacy and memorability, assured yet unpretentious. The attractively presented score includes the original poems printed before each song-setting, with line drawings taken from the poet's anthology *At Sunset*. The text is written in Hebrew script, with a phonetic realization provided underneath. The English translation beneath this is a little difficult to read at first. Ideally the work should be performed in the original language, as some of the English reads a little awkwardly, and the flow of verbal phrases does not always coincide with the music. However, it does seem that a lot of care has been devoted to the singability of the text in either version.

The opening song 'A Star Fell Down' was written in 1969, and the others at later intervals, the complete set of four songs having its première in 1976. They form a beautifully balanced cycle, the third (title-) song the longest, and the last a brief epilogue. Each one has a different character within a cohesive musical style.

1. A Star Fell Down

The music is instantly appealing in its sound quality, exploiting the best resonances of both voice and piano. Tritones figure frequently—always a graceful interval to sing. The piano's expressive introduction has some notes struck inside the instrument, but otherwise the sparse two-part writing gives the impression of a musing dialogue, with flexible rhythmic gestures, ending in a glissando over the strings. The marking is 'contemplative'. The singer begins gently in narrative, recitative style. The composer's fine ear shows in his choice of medium to low tessitura, giving maximum clarity without strain. The piano part contains all the necessary pitch cues. Low repeated notes, a semitone apart are intoned steadily in tempo, and after a piano flourish intensity increases as the line rises, in a *più mosso*. After the slow chanting comes one of the glowing suspended notes which form a feature of the whole work, and contribute greatly to its lyricism. The long F sharp on 'No' in the English version lies very well indeed (the Hebrew syllable is 'yuk'—also a long vowel). Throughout the cycle open vowels tend to coincide in both languages, indicating that the translator is aware of vocal implications. The voice continues in similar vein, each passage of intoning narrative ending in a long-held note, while the piano fills in the pictorial images. For the section beginning 'A life coloured grey' the piano has repeated static chords, marked 'senza espress' and the voice should aim to match this by singing almost non-vibrato on the repeated As until the crescendo on the long E flat. This lifts the voice in readiness for a radiant restart on high G, and two identical descending chromatic scale passages, which sound particularly lovely against the piano's pulsing chords, although the anchoring B flat has to be picked out for accurate intonation. The voice is always given time to place notes perfectly and check exact tuning with the piano. The singer's last statement is simple and unadorned (note the short note for 'laugh', which must not be accentuated), ending in ruminative mood.

2. To Dead Ground

This brief song forms a bold contrast to the opening movement. It is highly dramatic and dynamic, driven along by mechanical rhythms. Repeated notes are again a major feature of the vocal writing. The marking 'rigido e drammatico' neatly encapsulates the mode of performance. The piano's loud clashing chords at the opening are soon replaced by dry staccato attacks in *pianissimo*. The singer's rhythmic incantation begins on repeated middle Gs in sharp stabs, for which tone must be as incisive as possible. However, since the piano's chords are so short, and pedalling is kept to a minimum, there is little danger of being swamped. There is no actual dynamic marking for the singer, but the mood is anguished, and the violent war images in the fast-moving text need to be brought out clearly, and the pulse kept tightly controlled. A suppressed intense *pianissimo* could also be effective in a resonant acoustic. The expressive melisma on 'blood' must be piercingly distinct, especially its final accent. Occasionally the voice is released from the monotone to amplify important images. ('thousands of eyes', 'glaring', etc.) Eventually the line surges up and down (the voice, presumably, matching the piano's *fortissimo*), and the exposed *subito piano* on 'roar', which swells to *forte*, and then back, provides the main technical challenge of the piece (Example 1). The chanting resumes at the end, and the singer should mirror the piano's *pianissimo*, keeping tone absolutely straight and intense, expressing controlled agony.

Ex. 1 Avni

I   crawled on, _____ to the bor-der of the con-stant roar _____

3. Beside the Depths of a River

Marked 'misterioso', the title-song is the most substantial of the cycle. The piano part includes many impressive dramatic flourishes, and its repeated-note figures within a rallentando are notated graphically, as explained in the index. Note-clusters are given an extra stave at the bottom, and the pianist will need to consult the instructions that define them: some involve precise pitches, and some are silent. The voice part has conventional notation throughout, and gestures and tessitura avoid extremes. Again there are many instances of 'intoned' repeated notes, especially at the start of phrases. These need to be sung with great purity, rapt and poised. The lines move along supply and easily, and long shining held notes as found in No. 1 are again prominent. A sustained F sharp on 'High' has a perfect approach (Example 2). The dipping melismatic figure on 'nest' helps to relax the

Ex. 2 Avni

In the moun - tains on high

voice, and unisons with the piano reinforce the line's clarity. Proportions are perfectly judged. The narration continues, plain and unhurried, each note telling with bell-like precision. The end of the next paragraph has a dramatic cadence: a loud held high G descends in ceremonial fashion down a major third, on 'gates' in the English version (the 'rot' of the Hebrew is more comfortable). Breathing decisions have to be made here. A breath after the tied F sharp ('bruised') works best. For the second half of the song, piano interludes, closely related to figures found at the opening, punctuate the smooth sections of vocalizing. They are brief but colourful, and seem almost to speak, in single lines, with reverberating articulations. Each time the voice re-enters calmly in warm mid-register. Again, occasional octave doublings in the piano enrich the sound. The voice part remains simple and unemotional, leaving the piano to convey things unsaid. The singer's last chanted line is accompanied by heavily chromatic chords on the piano, until the last sustained low E, which must be held very steadily. The musical language is sometimes orientally pentatonic, with added tritones, but there are some traces of atonality in this movement, especially in the few chordal passages. After the singer has finished (note the brief moments of 'vocal' melody occurring in the piano during the voice's last two long notes) the music fades gradually, the piano's echoing repeated notes thinning into silence. The mood is introspective throughout this beautifully controlled song.

4. And in Me's Another

A deeply poignant final setting consists of only six phrases. Once again the piano plays a strong role. The right-hand part is highly elaborate and lyrically expressive, as if it were another voice, (the voice of the spirit?) performing a florid solo. The singer's part is not at all showy in the usual sense, but phrases sit perfectly in the voice, and every kernel of resonance can be brought clearly into focus. The recitative-like lines are shapely and flow naturally, pausing on long-held notes at the ends of each phrase, as before. The piano's decorative figures continue through held notes so that the voice is never left exposed, even at the very end. Apart from two passing F naturals, there are no high notes in this last song. The effect of it is all the more moving and absorbing. The dynamic throughout is quiet but always expressive, and singer and pianist end together, on a warm added sixth chord, symbolically united.

It is a real pleasure to find such an immediately attractive and well-proportioned song cycle. It can be recommended without reservation to singers and teachers. Although a mezzo-soprano is stipulated in the score, sopranos and tenors will also be happy in it, and the tessitura should not tax baritones either. Its practicality is one of its most admirable features— everything seems to work perfectly from the outset; a tribute to the composer's experience and acute aural perception. The variety of the songs is impressive, considering that the vocal resources of the singer are hardly stretched. It is a fine example to those who strive to make a big effect by crowding vocal lines with spectacular tricks that can tire the singer and negate the result. Earlier cycles by Avni are also worth attention, and are even more straightforward musically; his 'How Fair Thou Art' (1957) (from the *Song of Songs*), for soprano, could be described as minimalist and should be very popular. It contains some high floating passages, and would be a lovely vehicle for a young beginner.

This cycle would make an excellent start to a programme, since it sets the atmosphere instantly. A lively acoustic, especially that of a church, will further enhance its impact. It would complement standard lieder, especially those of Wolf, Strauss, and (early) Schoenberg, and it contrasts particularly well with strophic songs. Britten's Folksong arrangements, or Holst's 'Rig Veda' hymns are also musically compatible.

Dream Songs
(1986)

Richard Rodney Bennett (born 1936)
Text by Walter de la Mare

T II; M II
Soprano and piano
Duration *c*.10′

This composer's mastery of so many forms and types of music is deservedly admired. The breadth of his experience as a performer in widely varying styles enhances his ability to produce apt and eminently practicable music for all occasions. A large output of works suitable for young performers or amateurs should not, however, lead anyone to imagine that he is a light-weight. His authority is displayed equally in his large-scale symphonic and operatic works as in his music for film, or his jazz-influenced pieces. This is versatility at the very highest level and performers and audiences alike are the beneficiaries. At a time when 'accessible' music is being marketed so aggressively, work of this quality is greatly needed to show that artistic standards do not have to be compromised in order to satisfy a wider public.

This charming cycle was written for and is dedicated to the Scottish soprano Sasha Abrams, always a persuasive and touching artist, possessing exactly the right combination of intelligence and spontaneity to commun-icate directly without seeming arch or coy. The piece is particularly suitable for a youthful timbre, and exploits the soprano range effortlessly in graceful undulating phrases within which the text can be easily articulated. The musical style, mellifluous, clear, and characterful, should cause no difficulty at all. Echoes of the harmonic and melodic features of the English Roman-tics (especially Frank Bridge) are to be perceived, along with the influence of French masters such as Debussy, Ravel, and Poulenc. Conventional key signatures are used. The material is deftly worked into lilting rhythms and flexible phrase-lengths. Piano parts are totally idiomatic and satisfying to play (the composer is a superb and elegantly stylish player). The cycle could also be suitable for unison voices in classroom or choir. The four songs are beautifully balanced, providing contrast in mood and pace, the two slower and more inwardly poignant dramatic pieces alternating with the two 'dance miniatures'.

1. The Song of the Wanderer

Marked 'Allegro giocoso', the rocking rhythms of the piano's introduction elide smoothly into a swaying accompaniment of repeated right-hand triplet figures over a sprightly dancing bass-line, underpinning the voice's supple melody. The voice part is notated in 3/4 against the piano's 9/8, and this two-against-three relationship is a notable feature of the song. It gives an elasticity and natural flow to the music, avoiding any mechanical feeling. The voice part should be sung in four-bar (not two-bar) spans, making full use of the marked crescendos. With careful counting at the initial stages, particularly in the voice's first four bars (where there may be a tendency to move ahead too fast), the tempo and basic pattern will soon be securely established. The second phrase, beginning 'I know where there grows', will require good muscular support, as it will seem quite long in view of the rise in tessitura and dynamic. The phrase that follows also involves a long span through a tied note, this time negotiating a diminuendo on to some neatly turned triplets (Example 1). A gentle glottal attack is appropriate for the

Ex. 1 Bennett

I know where there grows ___ A tree that's called the Tree of Life,

I know where there grows ___ The Ri-ver of All-For - got-ten-ness,

accented 'I's in general. The song is in a basic ABA form with embellishments. Halfway through its middle section the voice joins the piano's compound rhythms, a transition that works perfectly and seemingly without effort, despite the implied and actual syncopation involved. (A misprint in bar 25 gives 4/4 instead of 3/4 for the time signature.) Rhythmic momentum is maintained with increased flexibility of phrasing and accent in the most subtle way. The crescendo to a high accented F on 'Phoenix' may need special care if the vowel is to remain open and yet clear and unforced. A gentler recapitulation of the opening vocal melody with the As flattened to A flats, is followed by a sequence of descending bell-like scales, in subtle chromatic shifts, with tenuto accents. Intonation is very important here. The song ends in the same way as does the opening 'verse', with a longer pause on the final held middle C, and the briefest of piano postludes to finish, *pianissimo*.

2. The Song of Shadows

The piano's opening harp-like arpeggios carry a special instruction from the composer: each top note should be slightly marked, but the arpeggio should precede the beat. Over these the voice intones a sonorous legato melody in the middle range. Nuances of dynamic and accent will make great effect here. The singer can savour all the alliterative and onomatopoeic features of the text, and should give a Scottish articulation to the 'wh' of 'whimpers'. A more metric section follows, with lightly alternating thirds in each hand of the piano forming an ostinato. This later supports the vocal line warmly, the left hand in unison with the voice in pliable phrases, some dotted in contrast to the uniformly flowing quaver movement. After a single 2/4 bar, the voice moves up the octave, and comes to a sustained cadence, with an extended E (marked *mezzo-forte*, the song's loudest dynamic), dropping to a final held A in the middle of the stave, which must remain steady through a long diminuendo. The 'm' on 'more' will help keep the vowel in a forward position, not too 'covered', so that it can float away to nothing. Arpeggios return in the piano's left hand for the close. Although this lovely song will flatter the voice, and an opulent tone could sound particularly well in this range, over-indulgence is to be avoided, as this could spoil the subtly intimate atmosphere.

3. Dream-Song

This is a most fetching waltz song, introduced with four bars on the piano, with 'bell-chimes' on the second beat of the bar, that are sweetly reminiscent of Elgar's orchestral piece *Mina*. The voice takes up the pattern (Example 2). Although rests occur at the beginning of each bar, breaths should not be taken every time. In fact, it is advisable to think in eight-bar phrases, avoiding heavy accents, and taking care to shape the fragments, fading very slightly away from the tenuto second-beat entries. It is important to sustain three full beats on the final low D which rounds off the contrasting cantabile at the end of the paragraph. Words are wittily and aptly set, exploiting their characteristic sonorities, especially with the leaning accents on second beats. The basic waltz tune is repeated, the line decorated and varied, ending in a longer flowing phrase, with a graceful octave descent at the close. The depiction of the roaring lion is particularly delightful, the rolled 'r's used to great effect. After a flourish on the piano, the tempo returns with a third verse of the waltz tune, again subtly varied, with smooth-running phrases moving up and down the scale. Once again the cadence is a gentle one, ending on a long middle note (in this case G). The 'w' on 'a-way' is especially helpful in focusing the tone to a bright resonance which can die away without losing its centre.

4. The Song of the Mad Prince

This final movement is perhaps the most difficult of the cycle to bring off. It features a folksong-like dialogue of mysterious and elliptical questions and answers. Good articulation and expert timing are paramount, and a clear boyish tone is appropriate. The voice part is divided into four-bar segments, but a rigid effect is easily avoided, as a running quaver movement

Ex. 2 Bennett

in the piano part binds it all together. The voice's occasional triplets must be accurately placed. There is also the very special interpretative problem of phrases within quotation marks. Any abrupt stopping and starting would be overfussy in this context, yet the sense must be made clear. Concentration is needed to make this convincing and keep momentum going in mainly parlando vocal lines. Happily, as ever, the tessitura is ideal for attaining a penetrating articulation. Rather unusually, the composer has put in breath marks to indicate the separation of phrases. Rather than taking breath in each of these, creating too hectic an effect (and probably making the voice breathy), it is better to stop and restart the voice without use of air. Changes of dynamic proliferate here, as moods fluctuate rapidly, and much detail has to be packed into the song's short length. The vocal line is clean-cut and crisply rhythmic. The crucial penultimate phrase 'Life's troubled bubble broken' (the alliteration should be enjoyed) will require extra care in tuning the whole tones. The final quasi-casual 'That's what I said' is repeated as an echo, *pianissimo*, at the very end. The vowels need to be kept clear and forward with a thin, thread-like accuracy. The interpreter's challenge is to arrive at a somewhat quirky, piquant mode of delivery, yet not to exaggerate. The piece will only come off when singer amd pianist are so well rehearsed and relaxed that it all seems natural and unforced.

This cycle is a most happy addition to the repertoire, and is adaptable to many different circumstances. It could of course be placed in a programme of settings of established English poets, and would contrast well with Elaine Hugh-Jones's fine 7 *Songs of Walter de la Mare* (see Volume 1—the second poem of the Bennett is common to both cycles). For young voices there are many other choices of material in lighter vein: Malcolm Williamson's 'From *A Child's Garden of Verses*' featured in this volume or Alan Rawsthorne's *Nursery Rhymes* for instance. But for the more advanced singer, this piece will form an ideal opener to a mixed recital, particularly including a major cycle by a French composer. It would go equally well at the end of a programme, perhaps preceded by a solo vocal showpiece of contrasting style. More music by this versatile composer would itself provide an exciting contrast: 'The Little Ghost who Died for Love', an extended *scena* in more ambitious stylistic vein, is an example.

Lacrimosa
(1989)

Glenn Buhr (born 1954)
Text by the composer

T II; M III
Mezzo-soprano and piano plus optional jazz
instrumental part
Duration 15′

A haunting and highly original cantata from one of Canada's most forceful and versatile musicians of the younger generation. His work combines minimalism with strong jazz influences, but is high on individuality and direct communication with an audience. The variety within the four brief movements is considerable, and they fully exploit the mezzo range, often going very low in the voice indeed, especially in the unembellished first verse of the blues at the end of the cycle, which also provides an opportunity for an improvised solo on jazz instrument(s) if available.

Notation is beautifully clear and attractive to look at. The composer's own evocative yet succinct texts fulfil their purpose admirably, with a 'cummings'-like economy of expression, repetition being used most tellingly.

1.

The first movement is straightforwardly minimalist. The piano's continuous ostinato is set in motion, alternating 5/4 and 4/4, in close-knit two-part writing, plus pedal-notes, all in the treble clef. The voice enters with plain, calm statements in middle register, restricted to a narrow range at first, gradually gathering intensity as the lines acquire more rhythmic variety and suppleness towards the centre of the movement (Example 1). The singer should feel extremely comfortable in this range. Natural speech patterns fall easily without strain in this register, demonstrating the composer's excellent ear, essential for vocal writing. In the final paragraphs, the pitch drops low, in a short unaccompanied passage that includes a deep A sharp, and eventually settles on to a long middle C for the resumption of the piano's *perpetuum mobile*. Throughout, intervals must be perfectly tuned (there are enharmonic relationships at times). It helps to be aware of the potential to vocalize 'instrumentally'; to project a clear line through the piano texture, which sometimes rises above the voice's pitch. As ever, a 'simple' vocal part requires careful control of minutiae of tonal inflections and timings, so that it seems effortless to the listener. This movement provides a well-judged warm-up for the voice, setting the atmosphere and focusing concentration, in a gently elegiac mood.

2.

The piano begins with rippling high-ranging arpeggio textures, and these continue throughout the voice's flexible, arhythmic lines. There is no time signature, and the vocal part (the notes written without 'tails') is to be sung freely and naturally, spacing the pitches proportionately as they appear on the stave: a familiar and eminently practical way of achieving a flexible result. Those unused to this type of free notation will find it far easier than they imagine. It has the advantage of allowing for spontaneity and freedom, so that each performance will be subtly different, and the singer can control her own timing, without feeling harried by strict metrical requirements. The tessitura, again, is ideal for clarity and ease: the voice ranges up and down in enjoyably lyrical phrases, whose lengths are also perfectly judged.

3.

This is by far the most substantial movement, and is structured roughly in ABACA form. As with the second song, its appearance is immediately arresting. At the outset the piano part is written in boxes—a familiar and popular device of the avant-garde, and from the performer's point of view, agreeably liberating; even, quite simply, fun! Groups of single notes inside

Ex. 1 Buhr

TECHNICAL II

- fined   and   trans - -

- formed   by

sad

ness.

frames have to be repeated during the allotted time-span (measured approximately in seconds) in random order *ad libitum*. The composer's direction is to play the notes 'sparsely'. Unlike the preceding movement, the two performers' parts are alternated in solo segments: a most effective piece of writing. Passages of silence, measured in seconds, come at the end of each piano box, and occasional *pianissimo* split chords cue in the new voice entry, so there will be few problems with co-ordination. After this opening section of thread-like solo lines, comes a stark contrast; the second (B) section features toccata figures of repeated notes on the piano, alternating 12/8 and 4/4 patterns in which the semiquaver is constant. These become heavily accented in an intense crescendo, the single notes splintering into semitone clusters, as the triple rhythms become gentler in readiness for the voice's re-entry. Here the singer is tested in a series of powerful declamatory outbursts with jagged, wide-ranging intervals, eventually cadencing on a low B flat. The piano's right hand has a faster-moving version of the jagged lines, ending in a trill, leaving the singer's final syllable of 'ug-ly' exposed. After a soft chord, section A, with the piano boxes alternating with the voice's flexible solos, is repeated exactly. The contrasting passage which follows is exciting and challenging, providing a chance for real drama of interpretation. Violent images are portrayed in angular vocal lines which must be searingly projected, taking care to keep words clear. Rolled 'r's will be useful for words like 'screaming', 'extreme', etc. and tone must be incisive without becoming too grating. The composer has a natural sensitivity to the shapes of phrases and his dynamic markings must be carefully followed, as they provide moments of relief from stress (Example 2). The piano part is extremely florid here, with trills, groups of rapid demisemiquavers, and eventually upward-swirling arpeggios at a *meno mosso*. The singer's gradual diminuendo on to repeated, soft F naturals (at the top of the stave) needs skill in placing and controlling the tone perfectly. Once again the voice is left unaccompanied, but at least the words are helpful: the '-nd', 'l', and 'v' of 'and lovers' can be prolonged and placed gently forward, so

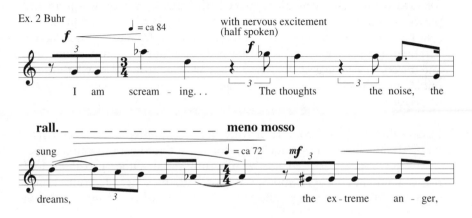

that vibrations of lips and tongue can be felt before the elision into the vowels. It is particularly important for the 'o' vowel not to slip back. For the last, tightly constructed section, section A (piano boxes and voice solos) returns, but is interrupted by a serenely lyrical vocal melody, accompanied by extended piano trills. Then the piano bursts in with a jaggedly chromatic passage reminiscent of those in section C, ending in a huge chord, leaving the voice to cadence, unaccompanied again, descending to a low A. Again, long consonants will help to focus the sound and keep it firmly resonant. The voice's last words, *pianissimo*, are the same as her first 'Stay close', and the piano's last box fades into silence.

4.

This 'Dirge-Blues' exploits the singer's deepest notes, and also provides an opportunity for a jazz instrumentalist to improvise solos in between vocal verses. The second version of the vocal part is highly decorative, but should seem spontaneous in exactly the same way as when ornamenting a baroque aria. This faster-moving part, despite its tricky intervals, will feel easier to sing than the unembellished basic tune (Example 3). The singer may like to

Ex. 3 Buhr

experiment with a smoky tone, but has to remember that any breathiness will make the sound less penetrating, and, more crucially, affect the ability to sustain long phrases. The very low Fs will be clearer if placed directly forward without allowing air to precede the attack. A good warm-up and plenty of muscular support exercises are advisable as preparation! It will also be a great advantage if the pianist has some feeling for jazz idioms. Although the basic material is written out, a certain flexibility is expected, and the composer suggests that 'jazz fills' can be improvised at will throughout. A most memorable end to an attractive and thoroughly enjoyable piece of performers' music.

Placing this work in a concert provides many tempting ideas. Since *Lacrimosa*, despite its generally lugubrious tone, is a fine vocal showpiece, other works surrounding it need not be too substantial. Other jazz-influenced pieces would of course be appropriate; also cabaret songs of various kinds, especially those providing light relief. Britten's *Cabaret Songs* feature a

'Blues' with similar low tessitura, and would make an interesting companion piece, separated by an interval. Baroque arias and *scene* (Handel, Purcell, Monteverdi) would contrast excellently, as would Mozart or Haydn. More North American Music, in particular a varied group by Charles Ives, lyrical and enigmatic as well as rumbustious, could perhaps end the second half, if this work is placed before the interval.

Three Songs
(1993)

Lyell Cresswell (born 1944)
Text by Marco Bucchieri (in Italian)

T II; M III
High/medium voice and piano
Duration *c.5'*

The New Zealand-born composer Lyell Cresswell, now resident in Edinburgh, has become established as an original and vital force in Scottish musical life, yet his music, always bold and individual, retains a strong identification with his heritage. His solo-voice piece 'Prayer for the Cure of a Sprained Back' sets a Maori prayer, and the type of vocalizing required is far from Western traditions. His stature as a composer of power and integrity is now receiving the recognition it deserves, and his development over the years has been most impressive.

Even here, in these brief but arresting settings of Italian verse (an English translation is provided at the front of the score), the vocal gestures tend to be declamatory and percussive rather than traditionally lyrical. The piano parts are particularly striking and characterful, and the vocal lines mostly proceed in short snatches, avoiding flowing cantabile. The piece is not at all taxing vocally, and problems of tonal and breath control over long stretches will not be exposed. The utter succinctness and clarity of utterance is most refreshing, and should make an immediate and dynamic effect on an audience. The poems are pithy in understatement, very similar to Japanese haikai, and eminently suitable for musical treatment. However, the images that the first two evoke are disturbed and restless, despite their modest scale, and it is not until the last song, very much the longest, that stillness and finality bring an icy calm. There are certain minimal elements in the musical language. Many Australasian composers, notably the Australians Peter Sculthorpe and Ross Edwards, have been attracted by these devices, stemming from a South Pacific rather than an American culture base, with the influence of gamelan strongly in evidence. The recurring-note patterns are manipulated with a directness and conviction that evades the trap of monotony. This mini-cycle brims with energy and conviction and packs a wide emotional range within its small proportions. It gives the performers the opportunity to make an electrifying impression with relatively simple means. The Italian language is also an advantage in its syllabic directness, especially in the monophthong vowels, and the lack of composite consonants that can affect timing and placing.

1. Il Nome

This is a fascinating and very exciting song, despite its brevity. Its natural, earthy folkiness encourages a specific way of singing that could be described as primitive rather than pure classical, and will suit the *vizioso* (viciously) marking. The pace is dazzling (quaver = 220) and terrific momentum is instantly generated. The piano repeats a pedal D throughout, while the voice has searing *fortissimo* fragments, spiked with grace-notes, which increase the rawness of the impact. These are mainly in the middle range, and are not intended to sound pretty. The singer should experiment by first declaiming the text, shouting, non-vibrato, making sure to hold diaphragm and stomach muscles firmly in place so that air is not wasted. This can be checked by putting a hand lightly over the mouth: no breath should be felt on the hand. Surprisingly, singing loudly quasi-non-vibrato in a folk manner (as found memorably in Berio's *Folksongs* for example) is considered avant-garde and specialized, when it merely involves natural sounds. To plan and sustain such sounds does of course require solid support and the anchorage of trained muscles. The quavers have to be counted carefully as the time signature fluctuates constantly, and there are many uneven bars. Near the end of the song, the tessitura rises a little (Example 1), but the knife-edge

Ex. 1 Cresswell

quality should be maintained. It is worth taking time to acquire this incisive way of singing, which has much in common with the 'belting' used in stage musicals (although this is often helped by amplification). Greater precision of vocal placing and tuning will result. Once everything is working properly, the voice becomes increasingly sensitive, and any moments of careless production soon begin to feel uncomfortable. The short sharp accents at the ends of some phrases must be snapped off immediately, not allowing the vowel to recede. A minor cavil; dynamics are written below the vocal lines, and are small enough to miss. Oddly, this does not apply to the other two songs.

2. Sfiorarci Le Mani

This tiny, one-page setting consists of even briefer vocal fragments, with moments of silence contributing to the highly strung effect. The singer should retain the biting declamatory style of the opening song. The piano has some loud bravura skirls of oscillating sevenths in between sparse staccato attacks. The sung snippets veer from *fortissimo* to *pianissimo*, and stay within the whole tone from E flat (D sharp) to (high) F natural. Intonation will need to be carefully monitored, especially as this is register-break territory for female voices. However, the resultant tension of quality could well enhance the interpretation, and increase the feeling of suppressed excitement. There is a Webernian economy of texture, and similar concentration of emotion. Each accent and dynamic must be scrupulously followed. As with No. 1, there are some uneven rhythms, and rests will have to be counted out with special care, since the tempo is again quite brisk and unrelenting.

3. Novembre

This final movement is perhaps the most challenging, and is in marked contrast to the others. In keeping with the misty evocations of the poem, the piano, which begins with a lengthy solo, features close-merging, cloudily impressionistic chords, and there is much use of the sustaining pedal. These hypnotic harmonies rotate subtly throughout, and there is no counterpoint. The voice part is considerably smoother than in the preceding songs, and phrases are also somewhat longer. There are in fact only eight, four of them very short, repeating the words 'il respiro'. The singer must produce a fine-spun tone, but not a romantic or sensuous one; the almost instrumental edge of the earlier folk sound should still prevail. The Italian language does of course make it easier to keep a steady legato on the pure vowel sounds. Intonation must be very clean in order to penetrate through the piano's less defined texture, which will not be much help with pitch orientation. The *pianissimo* marking should not mean a tentative or breathy sound or too 'white' a non-vibrato. Plain singing in middle register is not always easy to control, but it is important to grade dynamics accurately. There is a gradual build to *fortissimo* and then back to *pianissimo* again. The tempo is quite fast, so there should be no problem sustaining the longer spans. Swelling dynamics will allow for a more expressive delivery. Dynamic markings are absent from the last two pages, but a chilling continuous *pianissimo* will be most effective. The last phrase requires the firmest control of all.

Cresswell's outstanding skill and imagination has enabled him to create a rich and engrossing miniature song cycle that will be an asset to any recital. It makes a radical contrast to the Romantic song repertoire, and its pungent immediacy should attract many performers. Its concise proportions make it a perfect foil for a longer work. It would also go very well with Berio's *Canti popolari* (which contains, in a voice and piano version, some of the songs included in his celebrated set of instrumental *Folksongs*). The piece by Mark-Anthony Turnage recommended in this book, or, continuing a New Zealand theme with an entirely different style, the cycle by Gillian Whitehead, would both make excellent companion-pieces.

Five Songs for Children (1988)

Eibhlis Farrell (born 1953)
Text by various writers

T II; M III
Mezzo-soprano and piano
Duration *c.*8'

Thanks to the work of the excellent Contemporary Music Centre in Dublin, music from Ireland is now much easier to obtain. This is a delightful discovery from one of the younger generation of Irish composers, a set of miniatures with a direct appeal to performer and audience, immensely practicable yet by no means simplistic. It will make a charming effect in a recital. It is relatively undemanding, yet written with deceptive skill and sensitivity, and lies perfectly in the voice (especially a young one). The composer knows how effective light scoring can be, and the whole impression is economical and finely judged, The flexible vocal lines are enjoyable to perform and there is plenty of variety to sustain interest. The singer will, however, require a good sense of pitch in the atonal passages, and an ability to gauge intervals cleanly. The piano parts are not at all difficult, and would suit a beginner.

The composer's manuscript, it must be said, leaves something to be desired, especially in clarity. There are several discrepancies in accidentals, and texts and beats are not always perfectly aligned. The appearance of the score is not perhaps as inviting as one has come to expect, and it would be a great pity if this were to deter potential performers. There are quite a number of rhythmic traps, too, not helped by the lack of time signatures. It is therefore important for some time to be spent on doctoring the score in advance, but the effort is well worth it.

1. Ridiculous Rose (Shel Silverstein)

This takes the form of a simple *arioso* with free-flowing melismas in the voice, starting unaccompanied. The piano part is spare, providing light cues and commentary, ensuring a transparent texture so that words can be easily heard and the voice may blossom unhindered. The movement is marked 'ad lib. quasi recit', and the singer's rhythmic freedom gives spontaneity to the interpretation. The opening pair of arching vocal phrases on 'Rose' are particularly grateful to sing. As with Bernstein's more famous set of children's songs *I Hate Music!* (cf. Vol. 1) it is not necessary to adopt an affectedly childish manner or voice. A delicately accurate delivery and natural, innocent manner are all that are required. There is no need to overemphasize in the anxiety that the audience may fail to get the point. Poise and conviction invariably win through. The piano punctuates the line with broken, recitative-like chords, as the voice part becomes declamatory, adopting the mother's admonishing voice. The repeated word 'fingers' has an effective downward glissando. Piano and voice exchange material throughout, and all is neatly constructed within the tiny framework. There is another sweeping glissando, this time upwards, near the end, for 'she ate'. This should be pronounced 'ett', with a glottal articulation on the vowel, which will help cue in the pianist, who then has the melisma of the voice's opening solo. The separated staccato notes in the voice will be clearer if no breath is taken in between them. The singer's low, paused notes give her ample scope to control and poise the last, very soft, staccato note of the key word, which must be adapted carefully to the acoustic, and not clipped too short for audibility. It is especially important not to breathe before this.

2. Hiccup! (Shel Silverstein)

In keeping with the subject, rhythms are somewhat unpredictable here. This delightfully apt setting is simple and effective to perform. There are interesting cross-rhythms in the piano, spanning barlines, so it is important for the singer to maintain the quaver pulse, especially in bar 4. Anyone accustomed to singing additive rhythms in the works of Messiaen, for instance, will be familiar with the need to adapt to shifting metric patterns and not be thrown by them. The subtleties should pass by effortlessly, and the singer must breathe in long paragraphs. Word-painting is appropriately and amusingly achieved: for instance, the sudden stop at 'Hold . . . your breath'. For the articulated squawk on 'up' at the top of a glissando, there is an asterisk instead of a note-head, and I would take this to mean *ad libitum* as far as pitch is concerned. Soon after, a cross instead of a note-head on the 'hic-' of 'hiccups' requires a more accurate pitch (perhaps a brief glossary could have been provided to clarify this). The spoken coda is excellently conceived, and should not be forced. The voice must relax down to a normal speaking range. Singers can sometimes sound self-conscious when speaking, and, in some operatic performances one recalls, appear occasionally to have lost the knack of letting go of their trained sound. The last question's rising inflection is indicated by an upward arrow. The loud resumption of the hiccups and the resigned 'oh well!' must be projected strongly. Dynamics written below the text can easily be overlooked.

3. Ratatatat! (Anne King)

Marked 'in march style', this is another sprightly movement. Tempo indications are generally absent, but these songs do virtually sing themselves, and all the performer has to do is to speak the text in the correct mood to arrive at a speed which seems right. This particular song leads me to believe that the composer may have been influenced by Mussorgsky's wonderful cycle *The Nursery*; there could be no better model than the 'Hobby Horse' with its characteristic lilt. The musical idiom certainly has a Russian flavour, and rhythms are catchy yet do not impede vocal flow. The performers must keep on their toes, because there are some tricky irregular patterns. (e.g. the voice and piano relationship on 'rolling'). Upward glissandos on short syllables must be scooped with panache, despite the forward thrust of the rhythm. The vocal range is very broad in comparison with the earlier songs. Words must be given special attention as dynamics alter rapidly, and the effect is exhilarating. At an exciting climax on 'Marches', there is time to place the 'M' carefully on the high A to ensure a full, open sound. A short, echoing coda, parlando, as at the beginning, ends in an unaccompanied whisper, on 'tat'. The 't's should be clipped short and as sibilant as possible, although it is best to retain some element of pitch for the vowel.

4. Lullaby (Anon.)

For this brief movement, the composer again favours asymmetric rhythms, swinging gently between 3/4 and 4/4 at first and then expanding to 5/4 and 6/4, creating a suitably soporific, vaguely swaying, effect. The piano has a glissando across the strings just before the voice enters. Both partners should move almost casually through the shifting patterns, obeying the natural stresses, *molto legato*. Vocal tessitura is deliberately limited to the middle range, with close intervals contributing to the hypnotic atmosphere. Intonation is crucial, and each interval will need careful monitoring, despite the lazily spun lines. The high Fs may not be easy for a mezzo at such a quiet dynamic, and it is important not to force re-entries, but to glide in easily after a gentle, unhurried breath.

5. Squirrel (Anon.)

The cycle ends with another witty miniature, combining elements of the first two songs. There is much parlando writing in keeping with a fast-moving text, but also some melismatic figures that run very easily in the voice. The composer displays a real command of the vocal idiom, and phrase-marks and nuances are all entirely appropriate. The singer is given a chance to show flair and dashing style. Words are delightfully set, with note-groupings acutely judged (Example 1). Staccato and legato alternate with considerable

Ex. 1 Farrell

Whisky, frisky, Hippity Hop   Up ____ he climbs ____   to the tree top

brio, and at the echoed repeat of the opening words, the singer has to gauge a *molto rit.* before a downward plunge on 'scampers to the ground'. Enunciation needs skill in differentiating the rhyming, and not-quite-rhyming, slang syllables. Tempo changes proliferate: hardly a bar stays in regular metre. Glissandos, this time unpitched, and marked by arrows, can be spoken rather than sung, although the unaccompanied pitched cadence has to be well controlled.

Many people have written songs for and about children, including setting famous verses, and this cycle could go extremely well in a special children's concert, including perhaps Malcolm Williamson's *From A Child's Garden of Verses* (in this volume), Alan Rawsthorne's *Nursery Rhymes*, Richard Rodney Bennett's *Garland for Marjory Fleming* (see Volume 1), or the Bernstein already mentioned. The Mussorgsky is of course a more substantial choice, but would make an admirable foil for this modestly conceived yet admirably effective piece. There is a considerable need for genuinely original works in lighter vein, and it could also make an excellent end to a recital of standard Lieder repertoire, or of Russian music in particular. Alternatively, florid Italian arias by such as Rossini or Donizetti would contrast well. Farrell's work is an excellent example of practical and imaginative writing within a small scale—a knack that can sometimes elude even the most well-established composers.

Childhood Fables for Grownups (Set 1) *
(1955–9)

Irving Fine (1914–62)
Text by Gertrude Norman

T II; M III
Medium/low voice and piano
Duration *c*.7′

The early death of Irving Fine robbed American musical life of a rewarding and assured composer, who would by now have come to be revered as a major figure. His work is of the highest quality, rigorously imagined and strong in character. These delightful songs represent the composer in his lighter vein, but there is no sacrifice of compositional intensity. The first set of four are relatively modest in scale, but the later two songs are altogether more ambitious, and demand much of the performers. Each set can be performed separately, but the whole sequence constitutes an exciting and substantial addition to the general repertory. The songs concentrate around the middle range, and will suit those singers who can produce a firm ringing tone, sufficiently strong at the bottom of the register so that key words do not disappear. A counter-tenor would be particularly good in this respect, but mezzos, altos, and bass-baritones should all find the music well within their scope. Ultra-crisp diction and a commanding presence will be called upon throughout. The accessibility of the pieces is deceptive. They will repay close attention and repeated hearings, and preliminary study is recommended before a complete performance is embarked upon. The musical idiom is basically neo-classic, but the last two songs stray into more modernist territory, and there are frequent instances of pastiche and some rapid changes of key and time signature to keep everyone on their toes. Piano parts require a player of great panache and versatility, and this is very much a duo relationship, needing quick responses from each partner.

Each song is dedicated to a colleague, Nos. 3 and 4 to the composers Leonard Bernstein and Lukas Foss respectively. The choices are presumably based on confidential allusions, although the 'Lenny the Leopard' title is a straightforward reference, and 'The Frog' is perhaps allotted to Lukas Foss because of his children's opera on that subject.

Gertrude Norman's succinct poems, though direct and simple in their rhyming schemes, are ripe for sophisticated treatment, and these are definitely not exclusively children's pieces—although young audiences are sure

---

* Set 2 is discussed under Technical III on pp. 143–145.

to enjoy them, without knowing about their musical complexities. Standard notation is used, including key and time signatures.

1. Polaroli

The opening rhyme about the polar bear is set in straightforward ternary form. It starts and ends with a forthright march, with a jaggedly ranging, accented vocal melody in simple time. For the middle section, there is much use of the 'sh' sounds in the poem to contribute to the watery splashing effects. Sinuous triplets have to be fitted into the line, and there are some shorter, separate attacks in contrast. The singer should aim for four-bar, rather than two-bar, phrases. It is important to obey dynamic markings, and distinguish between the triplets and semiquaver–quaver combinations that spring up the octave from low B. The nonsense words will need careful articulation, and this section ends with a sustained series of octave leaps up and down, with a controlled diminuendo (Example 1). The low As and Bs in this must be anchored very safely, especially the louder ones. It is best to keep tone straight and trumpet-like, snapping off note-endings with aplomb.

Ex. 1 Fine

2. Tigeroo

A lively interpreter will have an enjoyable time with this dialogue between the keeper and his defiant tiger. The piano part is particularly vivacious, scampering and slinking by turn, with some elegant neo-classical figures. The basic 2/4 pulse is varied by a syncopated tie across the barline, for the repeated 'Tigeroo' in the first two verses, giving a fleeting flavour of a Latin dance. The music is roughly the same for each of these, but subtle rhythmic variations alter the effect considerably as the story progresses. For the last verse, the Tiger's angry, roaring response (another march) is at the upper octave (although this is still not high—it goes only to a D). Marked 'sempre marcato', the notes have to be punched out aggressively. For the shouted (pitched) 'Pooh!' it is not necessary to take a breath, and the sound should fall away before it becomes too sung. After the last quietly menacing statement ('If he comes in my cage I'll eat him too') the 'too' is shouted in similar fashion, pitched a little lower. It is important not to force the sound at any point. A shout only requires a quick muscular spasm, and the throat should be kept relaxed. A clear tone is all that is needed for this setting, and it is important not to let enthusiasm lead to breathy overprojection—always a danger in this pointed writing.

3. Lenny the Leopard

One hopes that Bernstein enjoyed this small tribute. An endearing little poem is extended by piano solos that frame every section (perhaps a reference to the great conductor's impressive pianism?). A charmingly plaintive, and instantly memorable, theme (perhaps a quotation?) is heard first in the piano, surrounded by wide, spread chords. It moves gracefully in a modal C minor, in triplet figures. There are two verses each consisting of three modal phrases, the third different each time. Changing time signatures contribute to a feeling of barless flexibility. There are short piano interludes at the ends of verses, and these continue the triplet movement. A surprise coda takes the place of a final verse. It is sweetly sentimental (Example 2) and should be sung with utmost simplicity and artlessness. The voice part is marked 'forte espressivo' until the end, when the mood softens suitably, and the music goes into major mode, indicating the soothing effect of the

Ex. 2 Fine

mother's words. The piano has a serene solo to end, and the motto theme is lengthened within the texture, as the music comes to a calm close.

4. The Frog and the Snake

This final song of the first set has a very simple basic tune in D major in 2/4 time, but all is not as easy as it may seem. The music streaks along at a very speedy *Allegro vivace*, never letting up for a moment. In this Poulenc-like *perpetuum mobile* the singer will need swift reactions and slick articulation in order not to be left behind. There is no time for slow breathing: the quick shallow breaths necessary for continuous baroque music such as Bach arias are useful here. As always, accents and dynamics are meticulously thought out. After a very straightforward first verse, introducing the two creatures, the basic material is subject to characterful variation. The middle of the three verses, where the frog 'speaks', is highly chromatic, but notes are doubled in the piano, and the singer must listen to ensure that tuning is exact. Such dialogue is much funnier if pitches are cleanly heard; often with accented notes there is a tendency to splash around and lose the centre of the vowels. The two characters must of course be clearly identified, although this is mostly built into the music, especially with dynamic changes. The final verse is developed and extended still further, and involves some incredibly fast patter. It is this passage that will determine the most practicable tempo: it would be very unwise to risk starting too fast and coming to grief at this point. The long-held Ds, starting suddenly soft and increasing in volume, the latter one lasting a full eleven bars, will need expert control. The earlier one is useful as a 'rehearsal' in gauging the ideal placing, but the impelling consonants are unfortunately not the same. The 'l' of laughing is considerably more helpful in timing the release, whereas the 's' of 'sun' could be more constricting. There is hardly time for a snatched breath before the cadence, although it is possible to take a brief one, imperceptibly, before 'summer' if absolutely necessary. This should not disturb the rhythm but it will impair the crescendo. The last real intake is before 'smiling' and it is then a question of careful awareness in conserving air during syllable changes, and using the alliterative 's's to make sure of diaphragmatic control. The 'u' vowel is not an easy one: it should be kept bright and forward, and not too round, so that the placement is close to that of high-pitched humming, and the final 'n' is positioned easily. The unaccompanied *fortissimo* bar is of course the most exposed moment, and it is important not to have shot one's bolt too soon. The crescendo is a very gradual one, and it is best not to let enthusiasm run away. (See also final paragraph on p. 143).

Anna Blossom Time
(1988)

Christopher Fox (born 1955)
Text by Kurt Schwitters
Translated into English by the composer

T II; M II/III
Medium voice and piano
Duration *c*.15′

For anyone looking for a truly attractive concert piece with immediate appeal, this is a major discovery. Fox is a prime example of a group of middle-generation British composers, many of whom, especially those based outside London, have been unjustly overlooked. Their work is, however, recognized on the continent of Europe, and their musical sympathies are often more in line with European stylistic models than with the earlier generation of British composers. Fox's voice is a clear and cogent one, showing a striking musicality and sureness of touch. Everything is most meticulously thought out and presented. Both verbal and musical material are deftly manipulated, the highest priority appearing to be performability, and directness of communication with the audience: rare and welcome indeed.

Most of this delightful collection was written during the composer's time in Berlin in 1987, Nos. 3, 4, and 6 being completed the following year. Nine epigrammatic and wickedly witty poems by Kurt Schwitters, translated from the original German, find their ideal musical match. The composer obviously feels a deep affinity with the work of this Dadaist artist (who as a refugee, settled in England and died at Ambleside in the forties) and displays his own skill with words as well as music, in a highly personalized and creative approach. So complete is his accord with the spirit of the verses that he admits to having taken considerable licence in Anglicizing the references where appropriate. Riddles, traditional rhymes, and sayings with specifically German references have been most ingeniously adapted, retaining their pungency and aptness. The sharp, often dark humour is conveyed most tellingly. One is reminded of a modern poet such as Wendy Cope in the economy of expression, the ironic word-plays, and so on. For the brief 'adult nursery rhyme' which ends the cycle, the composer has even altered the thematic content to refer to a well-known English jingle. An exceptional punctiliousness ensures that all is in perfect taste and finely judged. It is interesting to note that the poet himself had made a translation of his own work, and had changed 'Anna' into 'Eve', maintaining the palindrome. Fox preferred the original name, using the letters as a four-note motif for musical purposes.

The pieces all sit very well in the soprano voice (the composer's wife is a professional singer), but mezzos, tenors, or baritones are unlikely to be taxed by the generally medium tessitura. Apart from some lightly hummed notes in the sixth song (the most musically 'advanced'), the highest sung note is G flat. None of the movements lasts for more than two pages except for the fifth and eighth songs, which are probably the most demanding for both partners, more especially for the pianist in No. 8. The last (No. 9) is extremely short and simple. Piano parts often feature the motoric repetitions of a fashionable minimalism, but have sufficient panache and variety to remain constantly stimulating.

The composer, ever practical, suggests that the performers can make their own selection, 'picking and mixing' as suits the occasion. The songs do, however, work as a complete cycle in the given order but, with regard to differing levels of musical difficulty, there are a great many other viable possibilities. No. 6 is an affectionate homage to atonality (but quite a gentle example), No. 7 features animal noises, and there are occasional passages of rhythmically notated speech and Sprechstimme, but otherwise the songs are musically straightforward, though not without rhythmic hazards. A thoroughly enjoyable eclectic mix of styles is handled with great authority. It was the composer's intention to make the vocal idiom reflect some of the conventions of the time when the Anna Blume verses were written (1920s and 1930s). Pastiches of Viennese atonality, Berliner cabaret, and American folk and show music are all deftly accomplished, retaining a freshness and vitality despite the magpie-like nature of the collation. Conventional notation, with time and key signatures, is employed throughout, and the score is a model of clarity and neatness.

1. Dumb Animals

The cycle begins with this immediately attractive example of simple Singspiel style, highly reminiscent of Brecht and Weill (specifically invoking the Anna of the *Seven Deadly Sins*) and also of Eisler. The words give an ironic commentary on the cruelly interlocking patterns of life and death associated with fishing, and the punch-line at the end is particularly cutting: a characteristic that is to recur throughout the cycle. The piano's dry staccato chords pulsate in quavers throughout, while the voice utters short, clipped phrases. The motoric rhythm is disturbed momentarily by a quickening and immediate deceleration in the piano's chords at the end of the first paragraph. For the singer, absolute clarity of rhythm and tone is all that is needed. Pitches lie comfortably around the speaking range, often on a monotone, and delivery should be matter-of-fact, making the barbed message all the more effective.

2. Morning

By contrast this movement flows smoothly. The piano moves along in graceful quavers and the idiom recalls the pastoral tradition of the English Romantics, flavoured with elements of Barber or even of Ives at his most artless. The voice part is lyrical and shapely, though phrase-lengths are elliptical, subtle, and well varied, so that beats have to be counted with care. The octave leap up to F on 'void' at the end is a nice touch, and vibrato should not obtrude. There is actually no dynamic marking, but the mood is quiet and intimate. Poetic images and homely phrases alternate with acid observations. Two sustained high Fs should be kept straight and clear. The bitterness of the closing words should not be overplayed: a deceptively calm sweetness should be maintained.

3. 1, 2, 3

The almost childishly insistent patter of this song, and its musical idiom, including the opening pitches, remind me forcibly of little Flora's sudden petulant outburst in Britten's *The Turn of the Screw* when she defiantly asserts that, despite a visitation from the ghost of Miss Jessel, she can see 'nothing, nobody', and unfairly accuses the Governess of stirring up trouble. The manic parlando also evokes Eisler with its underpinning of staccato piano chords. This must be kept strictly in control, rhythmically exact and disconcertingly alien and mechanical. The stuttering effect in the first of the two strophic verses will need special attention, so that it does not sound as if the singer is stumbling involuntarily (Example 1). Dynamics are important: the beginning is very loud, and the statements thereafter alternate between a more thoughtful *mezzo-forte* and a defiant return to *forte*. The piano part is chordal, often syncopated, and fairly static harmonically.

Ex. 1 Fox

♩ = 84

f

I don't know no-thing 'bout love, 1, 2, 3, but no-thing 'bout love, I

don't know no-thing but 1, 2, 3. The de-vil can c-come and c-col-lect me,

1, 2, 3, yeah c-col-lect me, If my love should stray.

4. Cut Up

This begins as a simple ballad, almost a pop song, lilting gently in A flat–F minor with the voice in smooth syncopated phrases. A crooning style will be appropriate, with American-style diction. There is a sudden loud exclamatory interlude, the voice on an E flat monotone, hammered parlando in pidgin English, in rhythmic unison with Eislerian chugging staccato chords on the piano. The gentle rocking ballad then resumes, although there is a further brief snatch of the 'cut-up' fragments, this time chillingly soft and light. As often before, the words are uncomfortably equivocal. The slowed last line and cadence have a real blues flavour, complete with slurred grace-notes and characteristic harmonies (Example 2).

Ex. 2 Fox

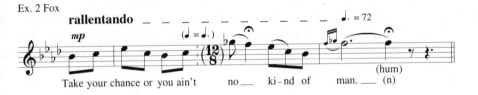

Take your chance or you ain't no ki-nd of man. (hum) (n)

5. Anna Blossom's Book of Chinese Proverbs

This is the second longest movement, and a most agreeable example of minimalism at its most fascinating. The singer delivers a dizzying list of aphorisms, mainly proverbs, or political statements, some well known, some less so, in a rapid staccato stream, starting with 'flies have short legs'. The piano moves in rhythmic unison throughout. Its reiterated pentatonic chords add to the oriental effect, and the style of vocalizing should also reflect this, with little vibrato. An unflurried, impassive manner will be most effective. The piece builds cumulatively, and counting is crucial. Iron control has to be kept, with short breaths taken in strict time. Sudden dynamic changes are important too: everything must be precise, deft, and apparently effortless.

Word-plays, riddles, paradoxes, and cross-references proliferate amid the repetitive patterns, and verbal clarity is therefore paramount. Some fragments are enclosed in brackets ('boxes') and are subject to multiple repetitions. 'Brevity is the soul of wit' is treated thus (a nice in-joke!). Extraordinary insights and perceptions are thrown up by reversing or juxtaposing the fragmented components of the proverbs ('no flies on the bourgeoisie', 'Soul is the brevity of wit', 'expressionism isn't always expressive'). These are worthy of the great wordsmiths such as Lorenz Hart. The opportunity for word games and puzzles provided by 'The beginning is the end of the beginning' and its many variants, is exploited to the full. The music directly illustrates the words here, and even becomes stuck in a repetitive groove at one point. The ending is suitably abrupt, the music stopping dead in its tracks. Ensemble will need to be tidy, in view of the constant unisons with the piano's chording, but the piano part is marked 'colla voce' so the singer should not feel restricted in pointing special details, as long as the basic pulse is maintained.

6. You

This haiku-like miniature is perhaps the only song of the set to give possible pitching problems, but these are not severe. A cue may be needed for the first note, if the songs are not being performed in order (the transition from *The Book of Chinese Proverbs* will not cause trouble). Here we have a delicate parody of Second Viennese School vocal writing, especially of Webern. This does of course mean that there are some flattering wide intervals, in particular a descending seventh. However, proceedings are interrupted by contrasting fragments of Schoenbergian Sprechstimme, the singer chanting naturally on A flat in a fleeting reference to Berliner cabaret style. This lies very easily and should not be exaggerated. Rhythms acquire a jazzy swing for a moment. The text is quirky and charming, with an almost Joycean flavour in its *double entendres*: 'I leafe you', 'I long you', etc. For the high-lying *bocca chiusa* on 'n' near the start, it is important for the throat to remain open and loose. Otherwise the vocal writing is comfortable, inviting rapt floating, with a minimum of vibrato, giving the chance to focus on musical accuracy.

7. Country Life

This begins as a marvellous skit of a folksy American song, in jaunty four-square rhythms above an oompah bass, in the key of D flat. It recalls cowboy ballads, square-dance music, or even traditional favourites such as 'Old MacDonald had a farm'. Words are wonderfully witty ('Wire is the soul of electricity'). An uninhibited performer will relish the opportunity for a cabaret turn in appropriate style, dispensing with the 'high classical' manner. A strong, even slightly rough, delivery will suit the mood, and the accent must be identifiably American. Even light sopranos should fearlessly employ their least polite chest voice! The jogging rhythm of the first verse is followed by a declamatory interlude, before the folk melody resumes. This second verse, abruptly changing into G major, provides the resourceful vocalist with the chance to imitate a hyena and a sheep in rapid succession, without interrupting the line. The breezy mood subtly changes to a more contemplative one, as the piano's chords become lazier and more sustained, and the voice trails off, musing. This transition must be managed thoughtfully, identifying closely with the text.

8. All about A-N-N-A

This is the cycle's most elaborate song. It has a particularly intricate piano part, requiring great dexterity and rhythmic control at high speed. Rapidly repeated figures in contrary motion are basically static in harmony, but the oscillations constantly undergo subtle shifts and twists. Over this texture the voice moves in plain unadorned phrases, centred around the tonic of C major, often rocking back and forth to the third above (E). It is very important to fix the tempo securely (crotchet = 84 is given), and not allow it to get quicker during the simpler passages. The vocal sound should be clean and incisive, cool and detached.

An irresistible reference to 'Tea for Two' occurs in each verse at the words 'me for you and you for me' and here the triplet figures can be swung a little. There are continual contrasts of mood and pace. Syncopated chordal passages alternate with the busy rippling minimalism of the opening, which recurs, each time complete with its 'Tea for Two' motif. The sung lines are interspersed by short passages of natural speech which are rhythmically notated, and marked 'sotto voce'. Now and again phrases suddenly snap off. A loud A major chord heralds a contrasting middle section: 'Question time'. This is a recitative, chanted strongly on a monotone A, accompanied by held chords, and it is full of sardonic comments (Example 3).

Ex. 3 Fox

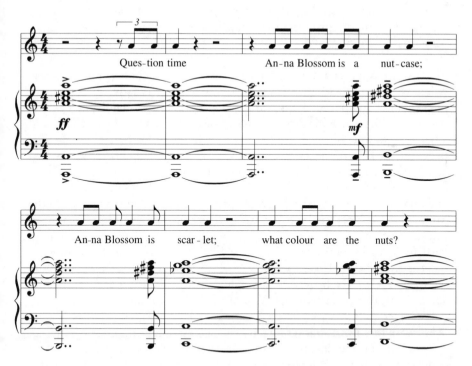

In a sudden change to free notation, there is a hilarious quote, unaccompanied, of the famous American folk melody later used by Berio in his *Folksongs* ('Black is the Colour'), except that here 'black' is changed to 'blue'—the humour is surreal here: 'her green nuts are bright and scarlet fair'. The scintillating figures resume, the voice part sustained as before, with 'Tea for Two' and the 'natural speech' occurring one last time. The florid writing is now extended and developed, and harmonies become (appropriately?) 'bluer'. (It is difficult not to enter into the spirit by trying to discover even more in-jokes!) The spelled-out 'A-N-N-A' is repeated six times (written in a box) with an *accelerando*. After a few last bursts of the *perpetuum mobile* the music suddenly stops. This most substantial movement gives both performers plenty to think about, and would stand very well on its own in concert.

9. Lullaby

The briefest epilogue is provided by this tiny lullaby in C major, all in crotchets. There are just two short verses, the music simple and sweet, the words just the opposite (and not at all suitable for the nursery!). Poise and an immaculately calm and innocent manner are prerequisites. The poet had intended this to be sung to a traditional German tune about a glow-worm, but the composer has decided instead to link it to the familiar 'Twinkle, twinkle, little star'. He admits this to be his most extreme example of 'composer–poet licence', and it works amazingly well, as a particularly outrageous skit on the 'original', which is entirely true to the spirit of Schwitters.

These songs are a gift to the performer. Everyone, including the audience, will have great fun with them, and their practicability is a joy. Since they can be combined in different ways and regrouped, their use is endlessly flexible. Any one of them would of course make the perfect encore after a long and strenuous recital, but they can equally well form the central focus of a programme. The composer recounts an occasion when they were performed as a kind of relay with students choosing their favourites, one even involving an octave transposition! The idea could prove invaluable for universities and conservatoires. The songs' accessibility to the amateur as well as to the professional performer, is also a case for grateful recognition. Writing to genuine demand ought not to be an outmoded concept, and there is a great need for contemporary repertoire that is direct in its appeal and not too dauntingly difficult. This is people's music at its very best. Other composers whose work fits stylistically, and whose musical demands are roughly similar) are Barry Seaman (see Volume 1), Howard Skempton, and Malcolm Singer (in this book). The street-singer able to perform some of Martin Wesley Smith's *Ten Songs* (cf. this book) will also find some choice material.

To avoid too piecemeal a programme it could be as well to have some contrasting material in longer spans, perhaps even for solo voice. A major cycle such as Mussorgsky's *The Nursery* would complement these songs nicely. Obviously, some actual Viennese or German music would be ideal, particularly the *Cabaret Songs* of Schoenberg, and virtually any Eisler songs. American composers, such as Copland, Barber, and Ned Rorem, especially the more substantial cycles, would perhaps be best of all as a contrast. Ives would naturally provide a plentiful source of songs of varying length and atmosphere. The irony of Satie's *Ludions* and other songs would make a piquant contribution to a stimulating occasion, helping to revive enthusiasm in the solo song's vital contribution to art and society.

Five Songs of Innocence and Experience (1980)

Edward Gregson (born 1945)
Texts by various poets

T II; M III
Soprano or tenor and piano
Duration *c*.12′

A most beautiful and moving song cycle from a composer of natural gifts, and great sensitivity. This is a delightful recital item, well proportioned and consistently absorbing. It makes a satisfying whole, despite the fact that the songs were written at different times: the first two in 1965 while the composer was still a student, and the remaining three ready for the first complete performance in 1980. The composer says that he has used William Blake's title because, although the poems are not by him, the sentiments are closly allied. Aptly, the two early songs symbolize Innocence and draw parallels between Love and Nature. The last three dig deeper into areas of strife and inhumanity. The last, inspiring War poem, brings renewed hope through idealism, and victory over death. The fierce integrity and passionate commitment of Gregson's teacher, the late Alan Bush, is obviously an abiding and beneficial influence. The cycle glows with emotional warmth and conviction.

Gregson's ear is alive to the subtlest nuances, and the music is attractive to listen to, voice and piano equally well served in thoroughly idiomatic writing. A young voice–piano partnership will find it rewarding, and audiences will respond to its sincerity and directness. The musical language lies strongly within the English song tradition, with its flowing lyricism and classic interplay between voice and piano. It is tonal, yet with much freedom of modulation and rhythmic impetus. The subtle rubato suitable for English Romantic, and also French, music, is applicable here, and sensitive performers will shape the lines naturally, responding to the innate musicality of the writing. As some words lie a little high, it is perhaps marginally better for a tenor than a soprano, but there should be no real vocal problems.

1. As I pass at dusk (Robert Kent)

Marked 'con tenerezza', this makes a lovely start, and its lyrical sonorities recall the English Romantics. The key signature is F minor but, with D sharpened to a natural, the feeling is decidedly modal. It is a treat to sing and play; words are set comfortably and phrases are beautifully balanced. The 3/8 time gives the music a gentle lilt and the vocal lines expand naturally with the dynamics. In the central section, the voice has accented cross-rhythms against the piano's rippling semiquavers, and these ease into a cadence in 3/4. The gentle 3/8 then returns, this time in the major key. The varying phrase-lengths and constant rhythmic interest are redolent of that master songsmith Peter Warlock, and the whole song is winning in its fresh appeal.

2. To the Thawing Wind (Robert Frost)

This strongly contrasting setting is marked 'Allegro furioso e deciso', and sweeps along with tremendous *élan*. The piano plays a virtuoso role and strong fingers will be needed for the vigorous accents and relentless energy. The key is basically D minor, the time signature an impetuous 12/8, and the form ternary. The vocal line calls for firmness and clarity, with rhythms bitingly emphatic. The text's percussive syllables enhance the turbulent imagery; all are set with awareness of vocal practicalities. The singer should easily find the cutting edge necessary to project through the texture. A sudden recitative brings a momentary lull and a complete change of character. It is marked 'senza vibrato' and 'Lento' and begins quietly. The tenuto accents indicate that it should be sung non-legato, with icy intensity. A steadier beat is then established, and dynamics and tessitura range widely, with a feeling of ritual formality. The singer is given considerable scope for variations of tone-colour in this rewarding passage (Example 1). The furious pounding music returns for the last section, introduced by a lively piano solo, which repeats previous material. The whirling 12/8 is again spiced with duplets so that rhythms are never rigid, and the song hurtles to an explosive end, with the singer on a loud high A on 'door'. Throughout, vocal phrases are judged perfectly: long-held notes and melismas occur at the ends of phrases, so the singer's capacity is used to the full, and physical enjoyment is inbuilt.

3. A Carol (C. Day Lewis)

The fifteen years that have elapsed between this and the previous song are evident, in the more 'advanced' and confidently individual style, yet none of the freshness has been lost. The composer has obviously, in the mean time,

Ex. 1 Gregson

been exposed to a wider variety of contemporary music, including Continental figures such as Messiaen, and transatlantic influences, especially minimalism. C. Day Lewis's disturbingly apt satire of traditional Christmas lullabies alludes to Burns as well as to the easily identifiable 'Away in the Manger'. Any suspicion of cosiness is rudely dispelled by a parade of grim everyday realities and hardships. Two brief stanzas are set in 3/8 time; the first mainly gentle, with the voice floating over semiquaver arpeggios in the piano, and the second a great deal more dramatic and intense, with the accompaniment correspondingly florid and dense-textured. The vocal lines move in five-bar phrases in verse 1. For the hemidemisemiquaver complexities of verse 2's piano part, a regular four-bar pattern is established, but because of the rich and varied harmonies the music never becomes static. It is extremely important to judge the opening tempo accurately, so that there is no slowing-down needed for the second half. At the high point of each verse, the piano's running figures give way to stark chords. The singer should keep dynamics light for the first verse, maintaining an almost unnatural calm, responding only to the exciting descending seventh on 'are dumb', where tension builds for a moment, only to lapse again into resignation. Verse 2, marked 'emphatically', has knife-twisting chromatic shifts, and the vocal part has Scotch snaps to add a cutting impact to the words. The composer has taken care to mark the penultimate phrase 'più legato', so that the searingly accented cadenza climax will be all the more electrifying. Words lie very high here ('Two shillings a week') and a soprano may find it difficult to avoid shrillness, although this is not entirely inappropriate. There should be no breath before the high melisma on 'price', which must be very smooth. The composer has placed a comma after it, and this sudden hiatus makes the dramatic point before the heavily accented cadence. The instruction to 'cut off' abruptly at the end of the bar, is particularly important.

4. Come live with Me (C. Day Lewis)

The second C. Day Lewis parody mirrors the famous Marlowe original (set by Warlock and others) fairly closely, substituting pessimistic contemporary visions for the pastoral delights vaunted by the earlier poet. Our modern-day Shepherd and Shepherdess can only experience such things vicariously, if at all. Marked 'jauntily', it trips along with infectious bounce and delicately pointed irony. A piano introduction exposes the fluctuating time signatures that are a constant feature. They help to keep phrase lengths varied and rhythms intriguingly unpredictable. The writing is wonderfully assured, and cross-rhythmed melismas, accents, and up-beat glissandos are combined in a dazzling display of energy. Musical and dynamic gestures are occasionally reminiscent of Britten (especially the modal scale passages in the vocal part) and the heady shifts of pulse call to mind moments in the works of Messiaen, as well as providing a fleeting reminder of the fast movement of Elizabeth Maconchy's *Sun, Moon and Stars* (see Volume I). The agile vocal line allows for some felicitous decorative touches, for example the delicious reference to 'madrigals', where some florid word-painting occurs (Example 2). There is room for full-blooded lyricism as well as sharp attacks. At a passage marked 'sweeter' there is a particularly lovely long cantabile phrase that flatters the voice. The following section, consisting of short, clipped phrases, is a test of rhythmic control, and well-timed breathing. Tone should be cold and detached here; there is every opportunity to vary the timbre according to the words, which are set impeccably. The voice and artistry of the late Peter Pears would have been ideally suited to this music. The keyboard part too requires an artist of the highest calibre. The final verse is similar in gesture to the opening, but builds relentlessly to a thrilling climax. A succession of ringing high Gs gradually fade, but

Ex. 2 Gregson

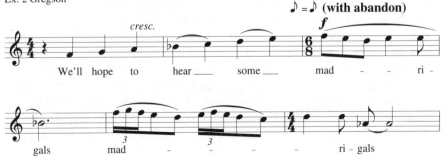

momentum never flags. This is a marvellous song, strong enough even to stand on its own.

5. To My Brother (Siegfried Sassoon)

An affirmative end to the cycle is provided by the setting of this deeply affecting War poem. It starts in dark, brooding fashion, in a 'modal' G minor. The piano's dirge-like opening chords are interspersed with a short bugle motif, of three repeated notes (triplet semiquavers) followed by the major fourth above. This 'muffled fanfare', which is to recur frequently, cannot help but evoke Beethoven's Fifth, and one feels this must be intentional. The harmonies have a preponderance of fourths and fifths, and the atmosphere of sombre ceremony is truly compelling. The vocal line is poignantly simple, and lies very comfortably. The repeated middle Gs on which it begins are marked 'senza vibrato' and this should be no problem. As the song progresses, and the lines move easily up and down by step, the composer writes 'poco vibrato', and again, the lines are so comfortably placed that the singer should be able to monitor the tone exactly. The piano gently punctuates the poem with brief solos, which feature the stark chords and bugle motif of the opening in condensed form. A very bleak *senza espressione* section has chanted repeated notes, and a 'white' tone will work well at this low tessitura. There are no further instructions as to the level of vibrato, but it is to be assumed that for the passionate climax, normal tone will apply. At the word 'fight' the dark mood lifts, and, after the piano's interlude, where the 'bugle call' is reiterated in more ebullient vein, the vocal line gathers strength and soars radiantly to a glorious 'light' on the final held high G, and the last 'fanfares' are hammered out in triumph in the piano's postlude. It is important for the singer to sustain intensity to the very last moment. It will probably help to take a last, short breath before 'the light', since an accent is marked for the up-beat.

This impressive cycle should be a great success with performers and audiences. It would be an excellent idea to compare the fourth song with Warlock's 'The Passionate Shepherd' which sets the original Marlowe. Indeed, a group of Warlock songs would be the ideal complement. The War theme could also be extended, by other settings of War poets such as Wilfrid Owen (Elaine Hugh-Jones's 'Futility', for example) and Edward Thomas (see Anthony Payne's 'Adlestrop' in this volume). Nicola Lefanu's 'But Stars Remaining' (in this volume) also sets a C. Day Lewis poem. The Blake reference of the title could also be taken further. Britten's *Songs and Proverbs* are for a different voice, but his Hardy cycle *Winter Words* would be a happy idea. An all-British recital could also include Holst's Humbert Wolfe cycle. However, Gregson's piece will be particularly easy to programme in a standard song recital. It can hold its own alongside the classic German and French cycles, and its perfect length is a strong advantage. It deserves to become widely known and enjoyed.

Drei Lieder Aus 'Der Struwwelpeter' (1990)

Christopher Hobbs (born 1950)
Text from 'Der Struwwelpeter' (in German)

T II; M III
Baritone or mezzo-soprano and piano
Duration *c*.10′

Christopher Hobbs belongs, with Howard Skempton and others, to a group of British composers associated with the late Cornelius Cardew, who, in the sixties, were especially concerned with preserving and developing the connection between the Arts and International Socialism. Inspiration was found in the examples of Brecht and others, who deliberately eschewed the idea of the artist, including the classical composer and performer, as representative of an élite' or middle-class culture. New music had certainly become polarized in what now seems an unhealthy way, and those whose styles were consciously accessible were often unjustly neglected by the musical establishment. Amidst the political arguments, the musical quality tended to be overlooked. Now that we are nearing the end of the century, a reappraisal seems long overdue, and it is surely high time that a broader range of repertoire is brought into the traditional recital domain.

The directness and honesty of Hobbs' music is most refreshing, and can be warmly recommended in all aspects. Fashion seems less relevant these days, and there is always room for a genuine voice with a clear message, and a well-crafted professionalism. The Continental influence here is obvious, in the choice of three rhymes, sung in the original German, from the renowned, and unflinchingly cruel, set of moral fables, *Struwwelpeter*, which aim to scare children into good habits. Their spirit is captured brilliantly in music of great appeal and memorability. Pitching is not always easy; although the idiom is tonal, there are many chromatic shifts and potential pitfalls in the vocal line. The singer will have a splendid chance to demonstrate accuracy of timing, both in swift, shallow breathing and crisp articulation. Idiomatic German is essential, and it is important to find the appropriately direct manner for storytelling, highlighting colourful images as they occur, but mainly relating the tales and their frightful consequences with a ruthless detachment.

1. Die Geschichte von Bösen Friedrich
The musical style here inevitably invokes comparison with the Brecht settings of Kurt Weill or Hanns Eisler. The verse relates the tale of the boy who

tortures animals and destroys everything in sight until at last the dog gives him a taste of his own medicine. The piano accompaniment drives the rhythm along, the hands alternating with running semiquavers and pulsing crotchet chords, the harmonic base remaining mainly static. Phrase-lengths are fluid, avoiding repetitive rigidity, and the singer will need to count carefully. The composer adds a note suggesting that the right-hand semiquavers in the opening section be transposed up an octave for a female singer, avoiding the possibility of the voice being obscured by the density of notes around the same pitch level. It is comparatively rare, even now, to find such keen aural sensitivity and attention to simple practicality. Overscoring in the middle and lower reaches of the female voice is unfortunately far more frequent than it should be. The voice part has accented octaves to illustrate Frederick whipping the dog, and piano figures change to regular repeated chords at the moment when the dog unexpectedly fights back, after which the running semiquavers are resumed. In total contrast, a piano solo in a steady 3/2 amusingly parodies Bach counterpoint. The singer eventually enters, in a mock chorale, in unison with the piano's left hand, as Frederick's illness is related in minor-key solemnity. This should be intoned with mock reverence, non-vibrato. The opening *perpetuum mobile* returns, at a slightly slower tempo, marked 'tranquillo', for the final verse and its complacent conclusion. It should be sung with sweetest simplicity and little dynamic variation, in contrast to the more piercing emphasis of the earlier violent images. The chorale theme is cleverly used in a more romantic cantabile style for the piano's coda, with triplet movement in the left hand—the effect almost Chopinesque.

2. Die Geschichte von Suppen-Kaspar

Chords announce a dramatic, declamatory start to this dreadful tale of the anorexic child, which seems especially apt in today's world. Strong, syncopated rhythms have to be kept secure, with tone evenly focused. For the refrain, as the boy refuses his soup, the music slows down, and the voice has a nagging, repetitive figure (Example 1). A thin voice, whining and reedy,

Ex. 1 Hobbs

69

will be effective here and, each time it comes, it is very important to observe the variations in dynamics, as the boy's squeaky protest becomes more insistent and then fades. The specific syllables and tessitura aid the characterization considerably. The Kurt Weill influence reappears with the onset of regular, dry staccato chords under the vocal line, as the story progresses. The Berliner cabaret style is caught to perfection and this is all very enjoyable to perform. The regular pulse continues at the original, brisker tempo through the refrain, but after this comes an abrupt change. The music goes into minor mode and note-values elongate. The voice has a particularly exposed interpretative hurdle on 'dünn und schwach'; the glissando down a minor ninth works easily, however, and a deliberate narrowing of the tone will help the effect, with every pitch piercingly clear. After a carefully timed pause on 'schrein', comes the last refrain, with failing strength, its rhythms drawn out still further than before. At a 'slightly faster' tempo a bland matter-of-fact final verse concludes the story, in funereal style, supported only by sustained chords, with deep bass notes. There must be no slackening of speed, and the last word 'tot' has to be placed exactly, *a tempo*, without accent: the percussive syllables will suffice.

3. Die gar traurige Geschichte mit dem Feuerzeug

The third setting again has minimalist repeated figures in the piano: this time gentle rocking chords in 6/8, changing every eight bars. Above this, a pleasant lilting vocal line describes the tragic exploits of little Pauline and her fascination with fire. She ignores the warnings of a pair of watchful family cats, named 'Minz' and 'Maunz'. For the little girl's speech, there is a change to 2/4 in an unaccompanied recitative-like passage. A special naïve childish voice has to be found—one that is quite distinct from the plainer narrative voice. Words are not entirely easy, and German fluency will be well tested. The depiction of the household cats is especially delightful. Their varying 'Miau's (elongated to 'Miaow's as the situation becomes ever more desperate!) give the vocalist an opportunity for uninhibited fun, in as exact an imitation of mewing as possible. There is no need to be too concerned about preserving vocal purity (Example 2). The rocking opening music returns again between dramatic interludes, and the performers must remain watchful during constantly varying phrase-lengths. There are swift changes of mood and pace as excitement and terror build. A solemn verse in lower tessitura brings a steadier crotchet movement for the voice and a chance to show smooth legato singing. Tone can be suitably dark and sonorous. For the cats' most frantic bout of mewing (already too late), the thin 'cat' tone has to be held through a long-drawn-out D on 'Kind', which then crescendos directly into the loudest octave 'miau's. There should be no interruption for breath during the crescendo. The climactic *fortissimo* dies quite suddenly on a low E. The last verse, in 6/4 metre, in E minor, is a varied, expanded version of the opening music, chillingly detached, as the horrific scene is described in detail. At the switch to 4/4 the cats add a slow,

Ex. 2 Hobbs

Miau! Mio! Miau! Mio! lass' stehn! sonst brennst Du lich - ter loh!"

mournful chorus, the wide-intervalled 'miau's plaintively echoing. For the lower and more sustained notes here, the singer will have to compromise between piercing and normal tone, but it is very important to keep a clean edge on the sound, and avoid a heavy chest voice with full vibrato. Dynamics are very light. The final long 'Wo' needs particular control. The poignant picture of the cats' copious weeping is aptly illustrated in the piano's closing solo, with a surprise twist at the cadence.

There will be no trouble at all finding a slot for this in a concert programme, either with lighter fare, such as other nursery rhymes, or with examples of music from, or influenced by the Berliner cabaret movement. (Eisler, Weill, Schoenberg, also David Blake, whose fine instrumental cycle 'From the Mattress Grave' is warmly recommended.) The Christopher Fox work in this book is also an excellent match. Audiences will enjoy it hugely. An artist with interpretative flair should bring it off triumphantly, and the higher the level of technical accomplishment, the better the music will be served. The general effect is easily enough achieved, but detailed work will be amply rewarded. It would of course provide a startling and refreshing contrast to a more traditional art-song group, especially a French or Italian selection.

The Centred Passion
(1986)

Derek Holman (born 1931)
Text by Alfred, Lord Tennyson

T II; M III
Baritone and piano
Duration 19'

Derek Holman was born in England, but has lived in Canada since 1965. He is an accomplished organist, with special experience and expertise in choral and church music. He has also composed much orchestral and chamber music, but the bulk of his output is vocal music, for which he displays a special understanding and affinity. His work shows the influence of the English Romantics, and also, as with so many of his and later generations, Stravinsky, Shostakovich, and Britten have left their mark. This song cycle is a happy discovery: beautifully crafted, with a real sweep to it and a deep identification with the voice as a physical means of expression as well as an instrument. The harmonic language is varied, mostly quasi-tonal, with ninths and thirteenths figuring conspicuously. Conventional notation is used, although there could well be some problems with pitching notes accurately, and the singer must pay careful attention to chromatic intervals and tune exactly to the piano, otherwise a certain muddy vagueness could mar the denser moments. However, the vocal writing is impeccable. Each of the six settings of poems from 'In Memoriam A. H. H.' has a distinctive flavour, with a suitably varied yet always idiomatic keyboard part, and mood and pace throughout are ideally balanced to provide a consistently absorbing experience for performers and listener.

1. Old Yew

The cycle starts in slow, dirge-like tread, marked 'Slow and Melancholy', with deep widely spaced chords in the piano. The effect is sonorous and mournful, exploiting the voice's full resonance in broadly spanned legato phrases. The piano supports, sometimes follows, or is occasionally in unison. Some sonorities remind one of early Britten in their poignant tonality. Grace-note groups in the piano part occur before the beat, and there are clear instructions for this. The composer gives meticulous attention to detail, and his Italian terms of expression and tempo are very helpful. The few vocal melismas naturally enhance the flexibility of the uncluttered vocal lines, allowing the singer to ease his way comfortably through them. There should be no difficulty in floating 'the seasons' in a smooth *pianissimo*, and words should be easily understood. The composer has natural facility and a fine ear for vocal balance. Tessiture and intensity rise considerably at the centre of the song's three sections. The gloomy final paragraph has shorter phrase-lengths which are subtly varied, involving a deeper register. Dynamics rise gently with the range, and rhythms obey slow speech patterns: 'rubato' is stipulated, and a final hushed *pianissimo* phrase brings a gradual slowing-down to an unresolved close, hanging in the air.

2. Tonight the winds begin to rise

This movement is, in complete contrast, bursting with vigour, and goes at a breath-taking speed (crotchet = 152 at the outset). The piano is marked 'non-legato' to emphasize the rhythmic bite and thrust. The vocal phrases must all be taken in one breath; if not they will be difficult to control and will become exhausting. Clear enunciation must be a priority, but it is important to keep short notes also within a basic sweeping legato, which should provide contrast to the piano's detached writing. The swirling images are portrayed in piano triplets against the voice's regular metre. The verse is full of onomatapoeia, and the singer encompasses a wide range, including some tricky melismatic moments. The basic pulse must be felt beneath the surging lines. Slight respite comes with a *più tranquillo*, where the vocal range is judged with particular sensitivity. Large triplets in the voice have to be fitted with the piano without sounding contrived. The music again plunges on at breakneck rate, exploiting the baritone's high range just when he is likely to be well warmed for the task. A profusion of syllables in the text will need preliminary work to get them running unfalteringly. 'Dote and pore on yonder cloud' may prove awkward to articulate at first. Practising the text at a fast, intense, well-supported whisper immediately highlights problem moments, and ensures that energy is used constructively. It is especially important not to bluster, and to maintain discipline within this brisk tempo, avoiding tumbling ahead on subsidiary syllables and short notes, which often need to be held back. Choice of breathing places is crucial, very much as in a typical continuously running Bach aria, where there is time only to snatch a breath and proceed in strict rhythm, without disturbing the pulse. This song hurtles to an exciting and strenuous end. Some almost Handelian figures are a reminder that experience in singing 'Why do the nations' from *The Messiah* could be an appropriate point of reference! (Example 1). The final accented, sustained high E flat on 'Fire' leaves little room for hesitation or insecurity. The triphthong must, of course, be modified to a general 'a' sound until the very end, and it is probably better to end in a short rolled 'r' to avoid a bumpy extra syllable (although a staccato on the end of the note could indicate a deliberately articulated 'y' to add extra force and fury). A good deal of technical prowess is needed to make all the note-groups equally clear, although it is also true to say that less skilled singers can enjoy themselves with this movement.

Ex. 1 Holman

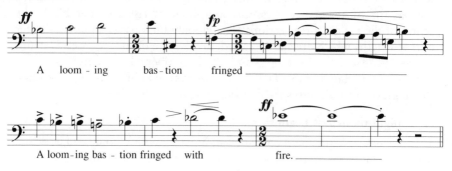

3. The Path by Which We Twain

This *Allegretto* creates yet another contrast in atmosphere. Continuous right-hand semiquaver sextuplets throughout seem to indicate the sounds of nature: at first, a gentle murmuring (bees humming?) giving way later on to more threatening and oppressively insistent images. The *tranquillo* marking at the beginning is a reminder that the effect is intended to be more impressionistic than mechanical. The left hand meanwhile picks out high, syncopated figures, starting with crossed hands, in plain descending octaves. Phrase-lengths again use the singer's full capacity. The basically contemplative mood yet carries momentum, the piano's left hand, which continues in duet with the voice, controlling the rhythm. In the middle of the movement the mood changes dramatically to one of terror and foreboding. The piano part requires considerable technical command and stamina, especially for the relentless right-hand figures. As before, the vocal lines rise and burgeon naturally; idiomatic and satisfying writing for a true baritone with a good high range. Once again there is a rapt, soft final phrase that is somewhat exposed, beginning in a comfortably low register to allow for a careful climb to the poised 'me' on middle C, in which the 'm' is an obvious aid to placing.

4. The Time Draws Near

It is difficult not to be reminded forcibly of the Britten of *The Turn of the Screw* when hearing the piano's opening theme, with its bell-like repetitions that answer and comment throughout. The harmonic sound-world, too, evokes early Britten. This is a particularly lovely song (marked 'Slow and tranquil'). Its poignant spirituality immediately draws the listener in. The singer must spin a perfect legato in this slow tempo (Example 2). Again, phrases seem perfectly balanced, using the whole range, and there is scope to dwell on special words. An *agitato* section interrupts the reflective mood, bringing an urgent, more personal immediacy. The tension rises to an impassioned declaration, but then subsides as quickly to a compressed recapitulation of the opening, with the phrases fragmented in a similar way

Ex. 2 Holman

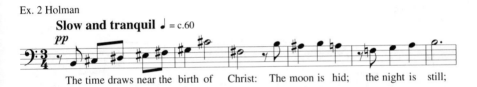

Slow and tranquil ♩ = c.60

The time draws near the birth of Christ: The moon is hid; the night is still;

as in the first movement. The singer ends on a hushed, held B natural on the word 'Yule', for which it will help to prolong and vocalize the 'y', and end with a long 'l'.

For this movement in particular, the singer would do well to aim at a pure, clearly placed, sound, avoiding the over-rich vibrato that mars so many mature baritones—often the result of pressure on a young voice. The timing of progress from note to note must be exact, as if playing an instrument. The coda should be very moving, and there is much opportunity for dramatic imagination with word-painting and mood-changes.

5. Now fades the last long streak of snow

This movement provides another telling contrast in the relationship between voice and piano. Lavish, often dense, harp-like arpeggios accompany and support the voice, as in the traditionally idiomatic writing of earlier masters, notably Fauré. Balance could be a problem here, and it is probably wise for the singer to bring his dynamics up a little, although the composer has set the piano part high enough to avoid clogging the register (a basic mistake of many composers with less good aural sense). The exhilarating flow of the music virtually dictates the singer's interpretation: he merely has to be swept along, being careful to point up special features, such as dotted rhythms, along the way. Some enharmonic changes will require concentration and reliable musicianship. Except for the final section, the voice part remains in the middle compass. The piano part is spectacular but even its fullest textures must not be allowed to overwhelm details of the text. The voice part continues without a break, so breathing must be organized with fore-thought. There is once again a tender, quiet coda with a long, luxuriant melisma on 'blos—soms'. Apart from this, the song maintains a uniform style and textural layout, similar to that of an intermezzo in a Romantic suite, as found in the piano music of Schumann, for instance.

6. Thy voice is on the rolling air

The cycle ends with a return to the solemn tread of the opening, but in dislocated rhythms, mainly in 7/8 patterns. This movement is the most difficult both technically and musically. Dynamics are loud and impas-sioned, and vocal lines are sometimes quite elaborate: for instance the melisma on the second syllable of 'diffusive' (Example 3). Pitch and rhythm are by no means easy here. The mood is intense and sombre, and large

Ex. 3 Holman

intervals arch across the range, some more than an octave. The required volume and cumulative tension make considerable demands on the singer's stamina. The tessitura rises gradually, and at the very end, there is a forceful climax on a high F sharp (an *ossia* is provided) at the beginning of a broad-ranging melisma. The last note of all on 'die' will call on special reserves of energy. Here, the given alternative is for high F, if the singer feels up to it, but D flat is the safer option. In general, it is always better to choose the note on which one can be really sure of projecting firmly and staying in full control, so that risk is kept to a minimum. The end of the work should be tremendously exciting.

With these basically straightforward settings of well-loved Romantic poems, as with the songs of Warlock and others, which are often tackled by performers of mixed abilities, the more polished singers can add an extra dimension, by maintaining a scrupulously clean delivery and attention to the smallest points of musical detail. These can sometimes be overlooked when concentrating on purely verbal nuances that can interrupt the line and sound a trifle prissy. Certain mannerisms in the interpretation of English music have occasionally meant that music of finest quality has not always been given its due status.

Holman's attractive cycle follows the tradition of the English Romantics, and can be compared with Elaine Hugh-Jones's work in displaying the gifts and flair to say something fresh in a well-tried idiom. Emotions are depicted in a conventional yet highly persuasive way, and it all works beautifully. Holman's special understanding of the male voice is to be warmly welcomed. The baritone voice is a particularly flexible and rewarding instrument. This work is a most valuable and substantial vehicle for a musicianly young singer with a firm centre and a ringing top register. There are many fine cycles that would complement it in a recital. Finzi, Vaughan Williams, Britten (especially the Blake songs, but also some of the *Folksong Arrangements* for light relief) and Shostakovich are particularly suitable. However, there will be a need for contrast in immediate juxtaposition. Some Wolf or Schumann, perhaps, or as a complete change, more avant-garde material that uses the voice in an entirely non-traditional way: Cage, or Bedford, for instance. Some lighter pieces from the American repertoire would be appropriate: Virgil Thomson, and some of the shorter Ives songs. A composer who changes domicile in mid-career is sometimes in danger of neglect in both countries. Holman's work deserves to be more widely known. He is a real 'vocal' composer.

A Cornford Cycle
(1972–4)

Elaine Hugh-Jones (born 1927)
Text by Frances Cornford

T II; M II
Baritone or contralto and piano
Duration c.18′

A consummate song-writer, and one of the most rewarding 'discoveries' of Volume 1, Elaine Hugh-Jones has confined herself almost entirely to the medium of voice and piano. Her zest for composing and a natural gift for communicating show in all her work. Many years as a professional accompanist have given her special insight into the practical aspects of the singer's art, and a superb ear and meticulous craftsmanship combine to produce music that is as pleasurable to sing as it is to listen to.

Her imaginative response to these eight evocative texts is as unerring as ever. Her keyboard parts underline and enhance the atmosphere and pictorial content of each poem, in unfailingly idiomatic fashion, with balance and layout admirably planned. A rigorous approach to verbal and musical detail—the composer admits to spending lengthy periods honing and polishing each phrase until it feels exactly right—is concealed within music of great spontaneity and variety. Rhythmic and harmonic interest never flag, and the expressive range of the songs is immense, despite their modest dimensions. The style owes much to an earlier generation of British Romantics, but Hugh-Jones's rare gift is that of saying something entirely fresh and personal within the familiar idiom. The sheer quality of her work should win her a much larger audience, and young singers and teachers will find it invaluable. Even beginners can shine in such grateful material, and accompanists are certain to enjoy themselves hugely.

1. A Back View

The opening song is a mere fragment lasting just one page of manuscript, yet with characteristic histrionic flair, the composer paints a vivid picture of an old man entering Heaven. Flexible speech rhythms dictate the movement of recitative-like vocal lines within a *Maestoso* tread, in D minor. The piano part acquires a third stave for some tolling bell-chords, and clearly marked cross-rhythms in the phrasing of the accompaniment create a subtly woven texture. Precise articulation of syllables is aided by the use of staccato and accents, and tenuto marks in particular help to project the most important words. There is even time for some expressive onomatopoeia on 'lean upon a gate', at a *poco meno mosso*, before the solemn 'march' resumes for a while, followed by a boldly affirmative final declamation, where the tempo is allowed to broaden. Tessitura is undemanding, and the singer will gain in confidence from being given this chance to establish contact with the audience by way of this relatively simple initial task.

2. To a Young Cat in the Orchard

The composer's skill in conjuring up light, scampering figures for the piano is exhibited here to delightful effect. Marked 'Scherzando' and mostly in 6/8 time, this setting trips along irresistibly, the piano taking the major role in characterizing the cat's movements, in delicate staccato figures, bubbling groups of semiquavers, and even a delicious 'mini-waltz' that oscillates between each hand (Example 1). The key is B flat minor, but there are so

Ex. 1 Hugh-Jones

many chromatic notes that tonality is always fluid, and the singer has to be very careful to plot intervals accurately, giving special attention to whole tones and semitones. The voice part is fragmentary, with accents highlighting words such as 'stalking'. In the whirling waltz passage, the voice should spin a smooth legato through the texture, allowing the duplets against the beat their full value. The ending is suitably enigmatic and unresolved. Sliding chromatic semiquavers round off the the last questioning 'or wrong or right', delivered 'Very slowly' and deliberately.

3. The Old Woman at the Flower Show

Another exquisite miniature, this third setting provides a perfect contrast to the preceding song. Rocking chords in 6/8 in the piano support a smoothly floating vocal melody in 3/4. The subtle rhythmic relationship gives the line a distinctive freedom and flexibility, avoiding a mechanical pulse. The composer's helpful 'Leisurely' instruction is just enough to ensure the appropriate mood, and prevent overprojection of the character of the old woman, who is speaking and reminiscing. The feeling of detached nostalgia is captured in hypnotically continuous music. There should be no lapse into overt drama or sentimentality. The sibilant consonants 's' and 'sh' can be heightened a little: 'Sash', 'shade', 'dust', 'ash'—each can summon up a picture in a flash. As always with legato singing, the shorter notes must be sung to their full value as part of the line.

4. Bicker's Cottage

In a masterly piece of writing, the composer depicts a ticking clock in *staccatissimo* attacks, embedded in the piano's warm legato texture of murmuring, sleepy quaver groups, underpinned by their expanded version in crotchets in the bass part. This texture continues through the first half of the poem, setting the peaceful scene in the cottage, and leaving the voice to describe the domestic details in clear, simple phrases, as always, in a comfortable register that allows for subtle colorations. The accompaniment changes abruptly to rising arpeggios as the scene shifts to the more threatening world outside. The turbulence of the approaching storm draws a dramatic outburst from the singer (Example 2). The composer always judges breathing spans to a nicety and there should be no need to divide this phrase with a breath after 'night'; it would be a pity to interrupt the exciting surge upwards and corresponding *accelerando*. The final section is full of

Ex. 2 Hugh-Jones

Out - side the un - plumbed night and gath - er - ing storm. _____

foreboding. Split chords in the piano, ominously deep, underline the voice's fearful message. This much slower passage can be delivered in a haunted, covered manner, making the most of the sinister quality of text and music. The composer has made a varied dramatic *scena* within the smallest framework, and every detail seems absolutely right.

5. The Road to Coursegoules

Yet another pithily brief encapsulation of atmosphere, this is a most fascinating and memorable song, despite its extreme brevity, and apparent folksong-like simplicity. The key is an ambiguously modal A flat major, The plain quavers of the vocal line must be sung very evenly, without stress, but allowing for the most delicate dynamic nuances according to their rise and fall. The transparent piano part, in gentle two-part counterpoint over pedal-notes, is clearly phrased to guide the shaping of the phrases. At the central point the voice becomes declamatory, with the repeated 'a fool' coming to rest on a pause. A slower tempo then brings gently dropping phrases for 'does not fall asleep', and a sudden flicker of urgency (crescendo and *accelerando*) at the placename of the title. The opening tempo returns, leaving the singer to intone the last few words very simply, as the accompaniment becomes fragmented and comes to a halt without slowing up.

6. The Watch

The last three songs show the composer at her most compelling, her sense of drama displayed to superb effect. This sixth song is marked 'Restless' and the piano's continual weaving chromatic patterns are to be played 'legatissimo'. Later a ticking watch makes an appearance, with its faster staccato pulse, in both voice and piano, complementing that of the clock in No. 4. The singer's short phrases are intensely emotional, rising to an outburst of agony and despair, inviting Death to 'come quick'. Repeated words and syllables make the most of rhymes and percussive endings, focusing concentration on their exact timings and varied accents. There are some unexpected stresses against the beat on 'continual discontent' that are clearly indicated. 'Tick', 'sick', 'quick' are all reiterated with cumulative tension bordering on hysteria. This movement is quite difficult to bring off at first, as the close chromatic intervals of the voice part could become ambiguous in pitch and uneven, if accented too vigorously. Control and economy of breath are essential, and despite a 'gasping' quality, the phrases should be thought in longer spans. The music hurtles forward towards the climax in a continuous *accelerando*, and the singer has to sustain *fortissimo* to the very last, fragmented cries of 'come quick'. This may not feel entirely comfortable at first in view of such brief attacks. However, patience will also be needed to polish the interpretation, and arrive at a perfect timing of the whole structure, and repetitions will soon iron out any unnecessary bumps.

7. The Madman and the Child

In this most extraordinary and memorable song, the composer has succeeded admirably in characterizing the two protagonists of the dialogue.
The singer will enjoy the interpretative challenge, assured of a rewarding
result. The child's question at the start of each verse is accompanied by
repeated quizzical curving figures high in the piano's treble line, halting
and gently expressive. The vocal part requires a direct and uninhibited
approach, curious and fearful, but should not sound exaggeratedly naïve.
For the Madman's replies the music takes on a totally different quality: soft,
sinister arpeggios roam around the range, while phrases of longer chromatic
notes provide an ominous hymn-like tread. The chillingly slow vocal line is
marked 'sempre senza espressione', even when the melody rises. It can be
tempting to depict madness by employing a parodistic non-vibrato that
merely sounds weird, but a *molto legato* crooning will be more effective.
The tuning of close intervals and enharmonic shifts in conjunction with the
piano is crucial (Example 3) and long breath-spans will help keep the tone

Ex. 3 Hugh-Jones

clear. For the second verse, the Madman is no longer marked 'senza espress'. The slow tempo is resumed as before, the voice moving in measured
tread for just one phrase, but the piano part suddenly accelerates, propelling
the singer into a reckless and revealing description of hell. At the climax, the
tempo broadens for an wild, impassioned cry, and, during a diminuendo,
the piano's figures descend in sequence. It is extremely important for the
Madman to maintain tension through the quieter final fragments. The
singer's last line has a portamento on 'Nothing' that can be incredibly
menacing, and there is an ideal opportunity to prepare for the last searing

'despair', by placing the 't' of 'but' carefully and deliberately before taking breath. The basic F minor is left unresolved, the piano left hanging on an E natural at the end.

8. Night Song

The last song is a classic example of modern-day Lied, the relationship between voice and piano traditional, in that the singer declaims the text dramatically, while the accompaniment provides a *perpetuum mobile* of galloping figures, arpeggios, and tremolandos. Once again the key is F minor, but an alternative version is available in E minor, in case the highish tessitura causes problems for deeper voices. The pianist will relish the chance to demonstrate panache and virtuosity throughout this scintillating piece. The voice part will need to be practised slowly to make sure of unexpected intervals, including the familiar double flats and enharmonic shifts. Rhythms are full of life, often dotted or accented, but fluctuating time signatures create flexible phrase-lengths within the pounding *Vivo* tempo. The barking of the dogs is amusingly captured in short stabbing notes in the piano's left hand; at first high-pitched, then in louder alternations of high and low. At the entry of the second dog the accompaniment growls appropriately, with fast tremolandos in both hands. His contribution to the barking is even more emphatic, and the voice articulates his loud protest in heavily accented crotchets, within an *allargando*. The original tempo then returns, and with it the racing figures of the opening, and the high-pitched barking of all the dogs recedes into the distance. For the first part of the song, in particular, the words have to be put across very deftly: 'dogs bark shrill' and, especially, 'strawy lair' are not at all easy at such a pace. As often with sharply rhythmicized vocal lines, it is important to keep a continuous thread through them, and make sure that the pitch of even the smallest notes is definable. The piano arpeggios drift upwards and disappear, and a dashing *martellato* flourish rounds off the cycle.

This work should find a place in the regular repertoire of young altos and baritones looking for an ideal English group for a standard recital, to stand alongside groups of Schubert or Brahms songs or the classics of the French or Russian repertoire. The variety of pace and mood of the cycle makes it quite complete in itself. It would also go very well at the end of a recital, since, because it lies so happily in the voice, it is unlikely to tire the singer. The composer's other works include many for soprano or tenor, but it is particularly pleasing to be able to recommend this outstanding and substantial cycle to the many low-voiced singers who complain, quite justifiably, that the modern repertoire seems at present to favour high voices unduly. Hugh-Jones's single song 'Futility', for medium voice to a Wilfrid Owen poem, should also be mentioned—a lovely setting, and suitable for a mixed group of songs, or as an encore to this cycle. This work also exists in a version with clarinet and piano.

Songs from Letters
(Calamity Jane to her daughter Janey, 1880–1902)

Libby Larsen (born 1950)
Text adapted by the composer from Calamity Jane's Letters

T II; M III
Soprano and piano
Duration *c.*13′

The work of the American composer Libby Larsen has recently received considerable attention, and it is a pleasure to recommend this most engaging cycle, which is sure to prove attractive to audiences and performers. Her music demonstrates clarity and assurance, combined with flair and imagination. A forthright, highly accessible style is flexible enough to allow for a sensitive response to words, and a close identification and sympathy with the emotional world of her chosen subjects. Not surprisingly she is particularly strong in portraying the woman's point of view, and is a persuasive advocate of a broader understanding of the conflict between work and family duties. She has found a fruitful stimulus in women's writings, and her vocal output also includes a major cycle for voice and instruments, set to Elizabeth Barrett Browning's *Sonnets from the Portuguese*, which was written specially for the late Arleen Auger.

Her choice of subject here is a very happy one—quite a coup, in fact. It will invoke special affection and nostalgia amongst those who, like myself, have happy recollections of Doris Day's exuberant performance in the title role of the enjoyable Fifties' film musical *Calamity Jane*, Doubtless 'Jane' was caricatured and sentimentalized in such examples of popular culture, and the historical facts were distorted. The one-dimensional tomboy-pioneer image is very far from the true picture. However, wide public awareness of this particular heroine of the Wild West cannot be viewed as a disadvantage, and concert promoters will welcome this piece as something refreshingly different.

The composer's programme note informs us that 'Martha Jane Canary Hickock' (her real name) wrote these letters to her daughter Janey (by the equally famed Wild Bill Hickock), during the time when she sent the child to live with a friend in a 'normal' environment. She raised the money to support Janey by taking on all kinds of work, some of it dangerous or humiliating, in the brutal and uncompromising West. Her defiant independence will strike many a chord today, and the letters reveal a multifaceted human being, with whom the interpreter can feel great sympathy. The ambivalent mother–daughter relationship is a potent source of mixed emotions, and these provide the focus for the work. The music is full of vitality, alternating between dramatic declamation and intimate contemplation. The effect is often operatic and volatile, but the singer will find it practical and relatively straightforward in technical requirements. The idiom is freely chromatic and wide-ranging, and intervals will need to be keenly tuned. American diction will aid a natural legato delivery. There are occasional resonances of Samuel Barber, even of Menotti, and some enjoyable moments of pastiche, recalling vividly the popular music and spirit of the Wild West. Heavy vibrato should be avoided, since the lines are amply expressive in their own way, with dynamics aptly plotted. The occasional high notes (including a high C) are set very skilfully for maximum effect, and a light operatic mezzo could also sing the work comfortably.

1. So Like Your Father's (1880)

The brief introductory setting is tender and reflective, beginning with a simple unaccompanied recitative. A sparse piano part in 4/4 reiterates a short rhythmic motif (marked 'warm, bell-like' in the left hand). The singer has a series of short graceful phrases, all to be sung very sweetly and naturally. The composer's expressive markings ('wistfully, 'warmly') provide all the interpretative guidance needed, and the finely judged pitches should glow beautifully.

2. He Never Misses (1880)

This is a lively and memorable action narrative, enjoyable to perform. Marked 'with abandon', it tells of the intrepid exploits of Wild Bill Hickock, Janey's father, in a dramatic *arietta*. A galloping piano part is notated in 6/8 plus 2/8 against the voice's 4/4, creating a feeling of nervous energy. The tempo is very fast indeed, and the voice is set in middle range, heavily accented at the outset, in forceful declamation. Economy of air flow is essential to avoid gustiness. The singer alternates loud outbursts with a crucial sinewy legato phrase 'I crawled through the brush to warn him', which is set against the piano's jagged rhythms. This is repeated twice over each time, in a rising sequence, marked 'with growing intensity'. The triumphantly emphatic 'Bill killed them all' also comes twice, and the voice is left alone to carry the impact. There is no need to breathe during the line commencing at bar 24 (Example 1). It would be a pity to interrupt the brief crescendo on 'face', and the accents at the end will be punchier with less air. At this point, the singer is instructed to make a 'gun-toting' gesture! This must be done with great panache, while the piano underlines the action with considerable gusto, fiercely reiterating the Scotch snap rhythm featured earlier. After 'Calamity's final recitative passage, marked 'proudly', the pianist is left to depict the 'final shoot-out'.

Ex. 1 Larsen

3. A Man Can Love Two Women (1880)

The piano's opening solo introduces the two types of contrasting music to be found in this song: lyrical musings and passionate diatribes, marked respectively 'calmly' and 'fiercely, freely'. The first two bars expose the motto that is to recur at intervals. The exhortation: 'Don't let jealousy get you, Janey' is first sung warmly, and after the forceful 'it kills love' the lines become smooth again, with a diminuendo at the end of a long phrase. It is important to keep this in one breath-span, despite the slow tempo. The opening advice is then repeated with vehemence, and the singer will need considerable power for a series of relentlessly loud phrases. A huge build-up on the climbing reiterations of 'I lost everything I loved' leads to a melismatic climax, incorporating a high B flat, and the arching phrase melts gradually back into a warmer cantabile at the end. This will make a fine effect. If lack of breath should inhibit the expressive range, a breath can be snatched before 'except' if necessary (Example 2).

Ex. 2 Larsen

The music continues in calmer vein, confiding and tender, to the end. The style is identifiably American, recalling Copland in his homespun mode, touching and direct. The penultimate phrase, marked 'freely' but then moving into tempo, is quite long, and will be even more affecting if kept in one breath, as if speaking.

4. A Working Woman (1882–1893)

A richly varied and substantial movement, this forms the focal point of the cycle, and is really a full-blooded operatic aria. Calamity Jane graphically describes her life in the West, and the gruelling and often shameful work which she undertakes with a mixture of resentment and relish. She starts almost pensively, and then launches into a catalogue of adventures. Opportunities for musical pastiche are firmly grasped. The atmosphere of the saloon and its music, complete with honky-tonk piano, is most expertly captured, as is the repeated depiction of Jane's stagecoach driving. The singer should have a field day with all this. The lines are placed well in the centre of the voice to allow for the greatest range of colour and dynamic without strain. The composer's instructions are, as always, a great help ('with growing anger', 'bitterly', etc.). Jane continually rails against the 'virtuous women' and their hypocrisy. The opening refrain 'Your mother works for a living' punctuates the action, and is varied in mood and pace. A sudden, free recitative brings an exhilarating episode describing Bill Cody's 'Wild West Show'. The piano's jagged rhythms recall No. 2, and the marking 'as if shooting a Colt 45' gives another chance to enliven the performance with some physical action. The music surges forward irrepressibly in burlesque fashion, and the singer's emphatic triplets and hammered semiquaver groups ensure a firm attack. The throwing of her stetson into the air is illustrated by a couple of marvellous descending octave portamentos on first G sharp and then high C. These are approached by way of climbing intervals that lie extremely well in the voice. After this show interlude the singer is left unaccompanied for a while as she muses, but momentum soon whips up again. This time, her anger at the 'forces of virtue' is even stormier. Tension rises, and the words are 'spat out', culminating in violent, accented cursing at the climax. Quite suddenly, all her vehemence subsides, and the last line's 'Epilogue' is a slowed-down, world-weary version of the refrain, while the last strains of bar-room music die away in the piano. This ambitious movement runs the whole gamut of emotions, and will certainly demonstrate the singer's acting skills. However, it should not prove unduly taxing, thanks to the composer's awareness of the practicalities of good vocal writing.

5. All I have (1902)

A moving final song returns to a loose recitative style, and again has an authentic Western flavour in its harmonies. The motto used in the third movement occurs here in a different guise, poignant and bitter. Jane tells of her impending blindness and cries out against her ill-luck. Once again, the composer's markings are illuminating. The emotions are visceral, and there is no need for exaggeration: the poignant images will speak for themselves, especially if the singer lives the text intensely, allowing for subtle shadings of tone-quality. The tempo fluctuates with the sporadic bursts of energy, and corresponding lapses into weary reverie. Nostalgia becomes increasingly painful, and the motto is reiterated agonizingly in the build-up to the passionate melisma on 'Ah!, which gives the singer a splendid moment of vocal display (Example 3). The closing section gradually brings a calmer mood, with gathering tenderness and warmth, also reflected in the harmonies. Emphatic, accented final exhortations follow the distant echo of 'I am going blind', which can be sung non vibrato. The repetitions of 'Goodnight, little girl' are used with touching effect, one 'sadly, wistfully', almost questioning, before the piano's chords resolve the doubts. The singer's last gentle phrase has a lovely cantabile sweep. The piano is left to echo the left hand rhythmic figures of the cycle's opening; the marking is, as before, 'warmly, bell-like'.

Ex. 3 Larsen

This work will make a rewarding centrepiece to a recital, and could even be partly staged, with lighting. It would make a particularly interesting contrast with Alison Bauld's letter-writing *scena* 'Dear Emily' (see Volume 1) which is intended to be performed at a writing-desk. Famous operatic letter scenes include Tchaikovsky's Tatiana (*Eugene Onegin*) or Britten's Governess (*The Turn of the Screw*). An intriguing quasi-theatrical programme could be based around the central prop of a desk. Nicholas Maw's cycle *The Voice of Love* (Volume 1) features an exchange of love letters. However, the 'Wild West' theme can also be developed. 'Charley Rutlage' by Charles Ives would be an obvious choice. Outside the classical art-song field there would be rich pickings from musicals, such as *Annie Get your Gun* (that other famous Wild West heroine), *Oklahoma!*, *Paint your Wagon*, or *Seven Brides for Seven Brothers*. Traditional American songs of the period, such as Stephen Foster's 'Beautiful Dreamer' would be appropriate too.

Six Songs, op. 14
(1954–7)

Per Nørgård (born 1932)
Texts by various writers (English and Danish words)

T II; M III
Voice (any) and pianoforte
Duration *c*.13″

These brief but charming songs by the leading Danish composer of today are examples of modern Lieder stemming from the German tradition, yet with echoes of Grieg. The delicacy and precise detail recall Wolf's vocal writing in particular and the accompaniments are especially well integrated. Trickier than they might at first appear, they are well suited to a young singer with a light flexible voice and tone neatly placed. The idiom is fresh and clear and the voice flows naturally in gently articulated rhythmic fragments: staccato is used frequently in the first three songs and so there is every chance for the singer to perfect the art of placing each note precisely and lifting it without taking unnecessary breaths. The last two songs are strophic with several verses each. Moods are generally understated with considerable subtlety and there is an undeniably Nordic flavour to the music which is basically tonal but with many chromatic inflections. Word-setting is very well judged. The first song contains a few floating high notes that may prove awkward for heavier voices.

1. Winter Night (Jens August Schade)

A time signature fluctuating between 4/4 and 6/8 gives an immediate feeling of seamlessness to this opening song, marked 'Allegretto, leggero' with no detectable strong beats to disturb the still snowscape depicted in the poem. The opening line is marked 'sonore', so the singer should not be afraid to start with a firm tone making full use of tenuto marks: this will make the sudden *pianissimo* staccato which follows even more telling (do not breathe after the crescendo). A *secco* phrase is more effective if enunciated clearly, without huskiness, then the tone can glow on the word 'snow' (the only smooth word in the phrase). Sibilants and percussive consonants help greatly in pointing the many delicate staccatos: the word-setting is exemplary and every effect works beautifully, even at such a soft dynamic. A more cantabile passage is supported by a busier piano part (the accompanist has hitherto kept a steady quaver movement, clear and transparent). The thicker texture adds weight and warmth to the voice part which nevertheless stays soft. Keeping a line through a progression of short attacks requires special concentration—tenuto marks can be used fully, and the composer's marked nuances are important, giving a subtle range of muted colours. The last line of the song is problematic at first: the singer should place the 'l' of 'listen' well forward with the tip of the tongue almost appearing between the teeth, and the accent should be exaggerated. It is difficult to divide the syllables in a way that can be clearly understood. 'Li—s(t)en' is the most practicable distribution, then the second note too has a good starting springboard—likewise 'cra—ckles'. The two syllables of 'starlight' should leave a bright glow, even within such a short duration (Example 1). All the words and syllables are to be enjoyed: the direct contact with lips and teeth can be clearly felt throughout and should help to control and poise the phrases.

Ex. 1 Nørgård

2. On the Himmelberg (Jens August Schade)

This very short song, marked 'Moderato—un poco burlesco', sweeps along in phrases full of quick-fire syllables that require adroit enunciation and much practice. There is no need at all to breathe in intermediate rests: the song must be thought of in whole paragraphs and strongly characterized. The dynamic range is very wide and the text must be made clear to put across the frequent amusing twists and throw-away jokes. This is a whirl-wind scherzo, infectious and crackling with vitality, and many repetitions will be needed to bring it off naturally and effortlessly.

3. Landscape (Thøger Larsen)

In vocal style this brief song, marked 'Tranquillo', bears close resemblance to the first, though the line is less rangy and flows gently along mainly in the middle of the voice, punctuated by staccatos and tenutos to emphasize and clarify the text. Absolute evenness of tone should be attained and dynamics carefully regulated. The sudden *pianissimo* in the final paragraph must come as a complete surprise—the 'and' should be treated as an up-beat (non-staccato). The warmth of 'summer' is enhanced by the tenuto. As before, word components give impetus and rhythmic life to the phrases and are used skilfully.

4. My Soul is like a lonely brook (Johannes Jørgensen)

Marked 'Andantino e semplice', this is a beautiful and expressive song with strophic elements. The opening phrase is subtly transposed at each repetition and delicate chromatic twists mean that special care will be needed for perfect intonation: nothing is worse than notes slightly off-centre with uncontrolled vibrato. The pitch range is warm and comfortable and ideal for the wide spectrum of dynamics and vocal colourings required.

There are plenty of satisfying long legato phrases, good for demonstrating smoothness of tone (Example 2). A more fragmentary recitative-like passage

Ex. 2 Nørgård

interrupts the general flow in the centre of the piece and some long triplets have to be plotted securely within the more flexible movement of the music. The very last note offers the only real hazard—a diminuendo to *pianissimo* on E natural on 'waking'—female voices will find this hard at first. Do not explode the 'k' too vigorously as this will hamper continuity and jar the sound. Try to keep a steady 'ee' or 'i' and do not allow the soft palate to drop too early for the final 'ng'. Even as this 'ng' trails away into silence there should be a feeling of space behind nostrils and eye-sockets and the jaw should remain relaxed and open—avoid clamping any muscles unnecessarily, and support the tone well. It is probably best to take a breath before the tenuto on 'life's' since the 'k' of 'daybreak' will make a brief interruption in any case. The 'al' of 'eternal' and 'w' of 'waking' can be lingered upon and elided to great vocal benefit, keeping a good forward placing for that last hurdle.

5. The Thunderstorm (Thøger Larsen)

A slow, entirely strophic song in five verses. The rubato marking suggests an opportunity to linger over individual words and syllables where appropriate in the different verses and to let the natural rhythms take over. For all that, dynamics and nuances are precisely notated. As throughout the cycle, words and their syllabic components are physically and sensually pleasing in the act of enunciation: an important factor in enjoyment for performer and audience, and one often overlooked by composers. Nørgård shows the true Lied composer's awareness of detail in verbal and musical inflections woven together. This is an especially striking poem full of resonant images and all have, to be projected within relatively quiet dynamics. There is no indication that volume levels should alter radically from verse to verse. Presumably, from verse 3 onwards, when thunderstorm elements become violent, a feeling of suppressed excitement, or hushed wonder, is appropriate.

Tremendous intensity must be generated and this may prove strenuous since so much control has to be exercised to avoid bursting out into too loud a dynamic. This is a most original and understated way of depicting a storm scene, but should be highly effective, and a challenge to the interpreter.

6. The Jutland Wind (Johannes V. Jensen)

This final song is also strictly strophic with five verses and the somewhat unusual marking of 'austera e pesante'. A stark clarity of delivery is needed here (Example 3). Tessitura is low and sopranos may have to work hard to

Ex. 3 Nørgård

firm up the low B which occurs frequently: keep it straight and cutting rather than warm and full. In contrast to the previous song, here dynamics are widely ranging and rise to a passionate *fortissimo* at the climax of each verse (the penultimate phrase). The last line is quiet and bland after this outburst, leaving an enigmatic feeling in the air. At the end of the last verse the piano accompaniment repeats the soft monody, in unison, two octaves apart with tiny grace-notes, as at the beginning of the piece. A most evocative completion to the cycle.

It would be intriguing to balance these songs with a cycle by either Wolf or Grieg, the two composers who seem to have the most in common with this style. The piece would fit easily into any classical programme, but would probably form too stark a contrast to French music. English (especially Delius, with his Scandinavian influences) and Austro-German Lieder would be the best of companions.

Three Japanese Lyrics
(1990)

Martin O'Leary (born 1963)
Text from *The Penguin Book of Japanese Verse*, translations
by Geoffrey Bownas and Anthony Thwaite

T II; M II
Soprano and piano
Duration 6'

Ireland has produced so many of the world's great literary figures that other
aspects of her rich cultural life have perhaps tended to be overlooked.
Thanks to the excellent work of the Contemporary Music Centre in Dublin,
information and material on Irish composers is now readily available. It is
all immaculately presented and co-ordinated, performing a most valuable
service to all concerned, especially to performers seeking fresh repertoire.
Formerly, just a few leading figures had attained international recognition,
but this sterling project reveals a wide variety of gifted composers. As would
be expected, a sensitivity to language, atmosphere, and imagery is a common feature, and singers and teachers are exhorted to investigate further.

The young composer Martin O'Leary, also an accomplished pianist, has
produced a winningly practical and appealing group of miniatures. He has
chosen to set traditional Japanese verses in their English translations. Their
spirit and atmosphere are most beautifully encapsulated, in economical
writing which displays natural musicality and fine judgement: a model of
taste and simplicity, that a young soprano will find ideal. With such economy of means, each pitch tells and a pure, pearly tone is essential.

Each of the three brief songs has a distinct character of its own, and the
relationship between voice and piano is also subtly different. All are linked
Attacca, and the final song, the most substantial, is the only one that may
require some preliminary technical work on the part of the singer.

1. (Priest Saigyo)

Marked 'Steadily Moving', this provides a practical way for the soprano to
ease herself gradually into the work and feel the acoustic. There is an
extended piano introduction in plain flowing arpeggio quavers, shared
between the hands, interrupted by pauses. The voice part is very simple and
sparse, and the piano has the dominant role throughout, moving the music
onward with long solo passages between each of the slow, delicate sung
fragments. The effect is most poignant, ebbing and flowing, and throwing
the smallest detail into relief. There is an attractive melisma on the word

'changes' needing clarity and pinpoint accuracy. Two-thirds of the way through the song comes a change of style: the piano's arpeggios are suddenly rapid, and the voice has a cantabile phrase, surrounded by gleaming widely spaced chords (depicting the shining of the moon). After this the piano's postlude continues in rhetorical vein, ending quietly on a pause which leads directly into the next movement.

2. (Hitomaro Kashu)

This is the briefest of fragments but, with its rapt, wide-ranging vocal line, and quiet, subtly graded dynamics, it evokes Webern at his most crystalline. The marking is 'Very Slow—Meditative', and a hushed atmosphere should prevail. The piano touches in soft legato chords, broadly spaced, and these often contain pointers for pitching the vocal line. The singer is very much in the foreground despite the restrained volume. Supple dipping intervals encourage tonal beauty.

3. (Anon. from 'Manyoshu')

This final movement is 'quite fast', and is the most vocally demanding of the cycle. The piano begins with varied arpeggio figures over which the singer's phrases include some very long notes. A change to 12/8 from simple time is managed smoothly, the beat remaining constant. Just before the voice enters each time, the piano's last note provides a clear pitch cue. For the second half the time signature changes to 4/4, and the singer must adjust immediately to the new pattern, keeping a steady pulse. The piano now has close-interval chords, and the pitch security achieved earlier will need to be maintained with determination through combinations of semitones that could prove disorienting. The soprano has to hold a clearly defined C sharp through all this. Towards the end comes the main vocal hurdle: a rapturous soaring up to a paused high C (Example 1). Thankfully, both the approach, from a tenth below, and the arching descent afterwards, give a chance to relax, and the singer can dictate the timing of the pause according to comfort. As before, crucial pitches are mirrored in the accompaniment to ensure a safe launch and landing. A slower coda follows, with another long-held note for the singer, and, at the very end there are two hummed fragments to be floated *pianissimo*. The first goes to high G sharp, so the throat must be kept well open. Muscular support will pay off here, and it should make a lovely effect.

Ex. 1 O'Leary

A young duo would be particularly well suited to this modest but attractive cycle. Its brevity means that it is useful for a short lunchtime or late-night recital. A good number of composers have been inspired by oriental verse. There are works by, for instance, Thomas Wilson, Alexander Goehr, and the Canadian John Beckwith (*Five Lyrics of the T'ang Dynasty*, featured in Volume 1) that would go well with this in an 'East–West' programme. Early music, especially lute songs, will have the requisite delicacy to provide a complement, and folksongs, too, could prove a rich source of appropriate material, even sung unaccompanied. Best of all, one of Webern's exquisite short sets of songs—(Opp. 4, 5, 12, and 25) would make a fascinating point of comparison. If sharing a programme with something in richer romantic or dramatic vein, it will show the singer's control admirably.

Five Songs
(1929)
Ruth Crawford Seeger (1901–53)
Text by Carl Sandburg

T II; M IV
Contralto and piano
Duration *c.*10′

The importance and exceptional quality of the work of the American pioneer composer Ruth Crawford Seeger is at last beginning to be recognized after years of neglect. These fine settings of poems by Sandburg, who was a personal friend of hers, have recently become available in a new printed edition prepared from material in the Library of Congress. The songs were not originally conceived as a cycle, but were performed in this order at their première. There is a shortage of true contralto repertoire, and these songs are especially welcome. They exploit the deep range particularly well. The words are set simply and naturally, and the idiomatic piano parts are evocative and appropriate to the poems' imagery. There is a subtle and distinctive flavour about this music, which may appear straightforward on the page. However, its Schoenbergian atonality means that pitching needs some care. Crawford Seeger makes every sounding harmony tell, and the mainly fragmentary, understated vocal part is contrasted by a considerably more elaborate and flowing piano accompaniment. The vocal lines on their own will give very few technical problems, except that of maintaining a clear line. Singers already accustomed to a serial idiom will know that one's ears soon become attuned to the logical progressions, and sevenths and diminished fifths rapidly feel as natural as thirds, sixths, and perfect intervals. Singers who are, or aim to be, good musicians, will find this kind of music makes one acutely conscious of the need to focus the voice more accurately. As we know, there is a great deal of woolly between-the-note singing to be heard in tonal music: often the listener is merely imagining that he hears the correct pitches because the melody is already familiar. The composer, who often played her own accompaniments, shows a real mastery of the art of songwriting and the relationship between partners is carefully balanced. A confident and characterful player will enjoy this work. Conventional notation, including time (but not key) signatures, is employed throughout.

1. Home Thoughts

Marked 'leggiero' (a misspelling so common that it is even now rarely found in its correct form without the 'i'), the song begins quietly and intimately, and the voice's musing opening fragments are unaccompanied. The piano then builds to a more passionate and expressive mood, in surging, wide-ranging phrases. Pitching is undoubtedly tricky at first, but words are set comfortably, so that they are always audible at the given dynamics. The composer's ear is unerring in this respect. Throughout, the compact vocal phrases convey a wealth of meaning with extreme economy. It is the piano which acts as pilot for the changing emotions, guiding, responding, and impelling the music forward, and providing gentle support, and never covering the voice, which is often left alone for the most significant phrases. Everything seems perfectly balanced and textures are always clear. The vocal delivery should feel as natural as in speaking, and the rare moments of heightened tension are thus thrown into relief. A particularly effective piece of writing occurs on 'The iron drag of the long day' when tenuto notes in the middle of the voice will be especially plangent, and there is ample time to place each one. The song ends, as it began, with a parlando recitative passage, but at a slower tempo, with a sudden, loud, imploring 'Speak', until the voice fades on to a long-held G, underpinned by low throbbing F pedal-notes in the piano's bass-line.

2. White Moon

The style and layout of this movement is entirely different to that of the first setting. Here, repeated triplet figures, high in the piano, help to create a silvery texture for the moonlit landscape, as the voice enters, floating in a smooth flexible middle register, below the piano. The lilting triplet rhythm on 'flimmering' works beautifully (Example 1). Some wider intervals then occur, leaping down major and minor sevenths, and the piano's changing figurations dictate and control the pulse. A flowing 6/8 is established, the

Ex. 1 Seeger

voice in dotted rhythms against it. 'Metric modulation' (where an irregular division of the beat becomes the regular beat in a following section, and vice versa), more familiar in the works of Elliott Carter and others, occurs here. It may take a little time to acquire adaptability to the changing pulse relationships, but it is an immensely helpful lesson in musicianship. At the return to 4/4 the voice is unaccompanied for alternate phrases ('flimmering' recurs during the one phrase supported by the piano). The voice rises to a held E flat, in what feels like a closing statement. After this a short coda balances the opening bars, with similar piano figures, in inverted form, and the voice murmurs the last few words, on repeated low Fs. The final long note, low E on 'Moon', should be easy to float with a pure quality.

3. Joy

This song is in sharpest contrast to the preceding one. In a miniature prelude the piano has a brilliant and extrovert solo, full of bright staccatos and flourishes. This serves to announce the voice's rhetorical opening unaccompanied fragment. The sudden surge of energy is immediately interrupted by a more flowing, *meno mosso* section, in triplets, which in turn gives way to another abrupt outburst. Here the voice must punch out some percussive syllables: 'As the Apache dancer clutches his woman'. The tessitura drops very low and it is important not to force and risk losing the centre of the tone. The triplet motion resumes in a passage marked 'grazioso'. The rocking rhythms build to a cadence, leaving the voice alone for another declamatory gesture (Example 2). (The tenuto marks on 'ter-ri-ble' may take some time to attain evenness of each vowel.) The final section extends the sharp disjointed material of the opening, the voice alternating with the piano's flourishes. The last (*meno mosso*) vocal phrase again dips low on to a series of tenuto notes: 'lit-tle deaths'. Since the voice is again left solo, there is no need to overproject, and the second of the 'l' sounds should help the transition into the last note, before the piano rounds off the movement in characterful style.

Ex.2 Seeger

Tempo primo

Sent on sing - ing, sing - ing, Smashed to the heart ___ Un - der the

ribs With a ter - ri - ble love.

4. Loam

A sombre mood pervades the fourth song, again a far cry from the previous movement. The piano provides organ-like soft chords low in the bass, with a slow, sustained melody above—all this necessitates an extra stave at the beginning, but the texture gradually becomes more translucent as the song progresses. The voice too, starts very low, intoning a long sequence of low As. Balance is absolutely crucial here, and the piano part is marked 'sotto voce' so that the sustained melody is subdued and does not obtrude. The music flows with measured tread, and as the vocal tessitura rises, a *legatissimo* marking must be carefully observed, incorporating the notes of shorter value within the line; for example, the 'And the' during the *accelerando* which follows. The piano has an expressive cantabile solo passage preparing for a warmly flowing vocal entry, totally different in character from the opening. This is, however, short-lived, and there is a return to fragmentary vocal utterances rather similar to those of the opening song. A *Maestoso* strikes an affirmative mood, and the characterful flourishes of the preceding song reappear in the piano. Another unaccompanied vocal phrase must maintain the exuberant rhythmic impetus. The singer holds a long F at the end, and it should be noted that no diminuendo or *rallentando* is marked.

5. Sunsets

As in the second setting, the piano performs a pictorial role here, and three staves are necessary for the opening *Lento* section, marked 'tranquillo'. Each carries different material: high chiming chord couplets at the top, a lilting melody in the middle, and sustained repeated chords in the bass. This will prove a challenge to the pianist, but the effect is wonderfully poetic, even slightly reminiscent of Debussy. This impression is enhanced by the parlando rhythms of the voice part. As so often in this work, the voice is left alone for whole phrases, especially those containing successions of words which might have been difficult to make clear otherwise. At the end of the first paragraph, 'e' vowels on repeated low B flats ('sleep is easy') will need to be kept open to allow the sound to resonate. A short piano solo then encapsulates, in just two bars, most of the opening material. As before, it is the piano which shapes the progress of the poem's colourful images. The voice part becomes ever sparser towards the end of the cycle, and the composer controls the close of the work with masterly judgement, and a precise aural imagination. Particularly telling is the voice's final unaccompanied passage ('Ribbons at the ear', etc.). A ringing high F sharp on 'Dancing' is rewarding to sing. For the resumption of the opening *Lento* tempo the pianist again has an extra stave, and the dancing rhythm is now also woven cleverly into the texture. The voice part gradually peters out, with a last held 'dreams'.

This is certainly not a showpiece for the vocal soloist, but its musical integrity and unity of material are impressive and memorable. It makes its effect by the aptness and assurance of the settings: an extension of the traditional voice–piano idiom translated into a more 'advanced' musical language, yet retaining spontaneity within its rigorous compositional processes. This is very far from being academic music. The test of a composer's natural musicality is always in the performing of a work: even at a first readthrough, this lies perfectly in both instruments, and is far less difficult than might be feared.

Because of stylistic similarities it would be tempting to put this work in a programme with some mid-period Schoenberg—most particularly his magnificent cycle *Das Buch der Hängenden Gärten*, Op. 15, which exhibits the same extreme sensitivy to words and their natural vocal inflections. A natural companion would be Charles Ives, that greatest of pioneer American composers, whose songs are of astonishing variety.

French music, especially Debussy's *Chansons de Bilitis*, would provide an interesting and stimulating comparison, but it is important to include something else in the programme which features the voice in a more spectacular solo role—perhaps even a work for solo voice, or a florid aria from an earlier period. It is very much to be hoped that Ruth Crawford Seeger will now take her rightful place in music history. A relatively short life and a smallish output should be no deterrent. Duparc wrote only thirteen songs, but these have become standard repertoire.

Six Blake Songs
(1949–50)

Russell Smith (born 1927)
Text by William Blake

T II; M III
Medium voice and piano
Duration *c*.14′

A distinguished American composer of the senior generation, who has lived in Germany for some years, Russell Smith has been unjustly neglected. He has written some beautiful songs displaying tremendous variety within a basically traditional idiom. There seems no reason why they should not be widely admired, and, if more readily available in print, they would surely attract those singers who are always on the lookout for repertoire which will please an audience, yet be stimulating to sing and interpret. There is still not enough quality material in English-language settings outside the obvious and more prolific song composers, such as Britten and Barber, and Smith perhaps occupies similar ground to that of Elaine Hugh-Jones. This cycle sets six of Blake's best-loved poems from *Songs of Innocence* in an assured and thoroughly responsive way. Keyboard-writing is also rewardingly idiomatic and textures luminous. These songs are a happy addition to the repertoire, and will suit any singer with a flexible voice and warm tone. They are not at all difficult musically, but there is enough variety to maintain interest, and they are immediately effective. Even less advanced singers can fully enjoy them, and develop their abilities by studying their exemplary vocal writing. Conventional notation, including time signatures, is used throughout.

1. Introduction
A sparkling start to the cycle is provided by the piano's tripping 6/8 rhythms, often moving in thirds in the right hand. The voice swoops delicately up and down the range with a bright energy, in smoothly flowing phrases. The image of the piper is beautifully captured. Each of the two verses ends with long shimmering held notes: hushed and silvery the first time; warm and exultant for the end. Momentum is never lost as the music is propelled along, and words, too, will not be covered by the piano's transparent textures, which mix staccato and legato in fluid patterns.

2. Spring
This brief, poignant setting is extremely economical in its construction; a recurring motif of two sequential descending minor sixths followed by a

whole tone sets an elliptical rhythmic pattern in motion, 2/4 time signatures alternating with 5/8 to create a barless effect. The harmonic implications are almost Elgarian. The voice part consists mainly of short fragments, which expand to a more mellifluous series of repeated 'merrily's at the end. The slowish tempo is perhaps surprising for a universally cheerful subject, and warmth and radiance of tone should be exploited so that it does not become melancholy.

3. The Lamb

This song is more ambitious in scale, and contains several bars of composite beats within the quaver movement (4 + 5, 3 + 2 + 3, etc.). The dynamics are extremely important. The idiom is modal, quasi-pastoral, as in the English style. Vocally, the dynamic and expressive range is quite extensive; a rapt concentration is needed to make every poetic point in the series of rhetorical statements, each of cumulative weight and import. Tenuto marks are used for emphasis, and the words are set plainly, syllable by syllable. The piano part flows warmly and sonorously in contrast to the shorter vocal phrases. *Accelerandi* and *ritenuti* are dictated by the significance of key words and arise naturally from the declamatory style of the text. The final section rises ecstatically upward to end on a rather loud and hearty blessing. Again, this is an original response to familiar words that have been set by others where a more reverent hush might have been the obvious choice for the benediction!

4. The Little Boy Lost

The nervous cries of the child in the poem are depicted in short, halting vocal phrases. It would be appropriate to try for a boyish timbre, without vibrato for this opening. Piano harmonies are more dissonant than hitherto: the G minor tonality is disturbed by repeated C sharps in the bass-line and the musical idiom seems to have something in common with early Britten. Lengths of phrases contribute to the disjointed, insecure effect. A piano arpeggio signals the change to reported speech for the second half of the song, which is suddenly much louder, and dramatic and threatening in its dark sonorities (the piano part is marked 'legato' through a sombre unison with the vocal line). At a climax, the voice is left alone to shape a gradual diminuendo, with tenuto accents leading to the final held note, which is accompanied by a repeat of the piano arpeggios. It could be difficult to keep the tone firm and maintain the crescendo through basically low-lying phrases, but volume must not slacken until the word 'away' is reached (Example 1). The final breath should be taken before 'and away' to make sure of a clean attack on each accent and a smooth, non-breathy last note.

5. Little Boy Found

This movement continues and complements the preceding song. It starts bleakly, with thin piano textures illustrating the barren landscape. Icy

Ex. 1 Smith

staccato notes in the left hand, in uneven rhythms, cross over the right, and increase the feeling of numb disorientation. Tessitura is in a comfortable middle range, allowing scope for varying vocal colour. A sudden warmth and tenderness suffuses the line, as God appears, bringing comfort. This very quick change of atmosphere needs special thought and concentration to make it convincing. The staccato notes under the word 'white' seem far less threatening in this context. The last sentence begins glowingly, but then harks back to the mother's lonely search, and so ends very quietly, the voice left unaccompanied in a poignant *pianissimo* on 'little boy'. A comma at this point indicates a short break, to give special emphasis and colour to the following word 'weeping'. The composer has provided suggested breathing places in the last section (commas in brackets), as the phrasing is not obvious, and individual words need to be pointed up for clarity. It may be helpful (although not entirely necessary) to take a breath before 'weeping' so that the paused ending can have plenty of space, and the singer should make sure of a real *pianissimo* during the final *ritenuto* up-beat (Example 2). The last movement follows *attacca*, breaking the spell.

6. Sweet joy befall thee

Somewhat surprisingly, this short, aphoristic verse, which might be expected to inspire a haiku-like setting, draws the cycle's most extended number. It makes a radiant, rhapsodic finale, ending with an optional vocal cadenza. Avoiding the coy prettiness suggested by the baby girl's speech, the

Ex. 2 Smith

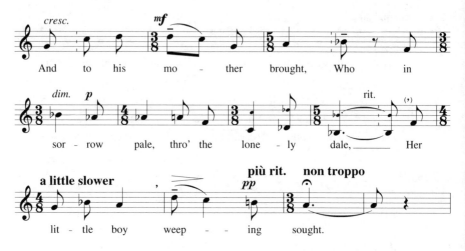

vocal line begins strongly, at first alone (the pitch is continued from the top of the piano's chord in the preceding song), in a confident announcement with emphatic cadence. After a break, and a lighter, free-flowing question, a cheerful quick tempo features a delightfully exuberant passage of 2/4 alternating with 5/8, the piano in sprightly staccato quavers. The short vocal phrases are like the pealing of bells. The piano part becomes livelier still, with tripping rhythms and sharp accents, in a style that bears a resemblance to some of Peter Warlock's more popular songs. Indeed, throughout, Russell Smith seems to display a closer affinity to English rather than American influences, perhaps because of the Continental habits of crisper enunciation of consonants dictating rhythmic patterns. Vocal lines are now much more expansive, with longer-held notes and a wider range of dynamics. A lengthier piano introduction, continuing the tripping, accented material, leads to a delicate 3/8 section, where the left hand now carries the running semiquavers high in the treble clef, and voice and piano right hand continue in lilting patterns. The singer's joyful peals rise to *fortissimo*, and one feels that this could put lighter voices under some strain as the lowish tessitura and brisk tempo make it difficult to produced a firmly centred sound, without pushing too hard. It will help to be economical with breathing. However, as soon as this risky moment is past, the singer can luxuriate on longer, mellifluous phrases, especially if she takes advantage of the suggested cadenza, which gives a good opportunity to exercise the voice in long, arching lines. The piano's final coda repeats more of the tripping music in loud, extrovert style, suddenly ending softly.

This extremely appealing and meticulously written cycle will fit very happily into any standard recital programme, and as it avoids extremes of register, all voices should find it comfortable. Other Blake settings could be chosen to go with it: Britten's *Songs and Proverbs of William Blake* or Virgil Thomson's *Five Songs of William Blake* (featured in Volume 1) for instance. A fine contrast could be provided by French music, especially Ravel or Debussy. Because of its ideal length and the fact that it is not taxing vocally, it could open a recital very well. It would be particularly suitable for a first recital by a young singer.

The Palatine Coast, Op. 21
(1953)

Bernard Stevens (1916–83)
Text by Montague Slater

T II; M II
High voice and pianoforte
Duration 8′

The late Bernard Stevens is an example of a composer of great distinction and integrity whose work has been badly neglected. He was also a most valuable influence as a teacher of composition, and his music is an authoritative and memorable contribution to the British heritage. These songs, written for Sophie Wyss, would suit soprano or tenor equally well. The musical idiom is fairly conventional, containing unmistakable stylistic features of early twentieth-century English Romanticism, yet with its own pungent flavour and an unusually strong sense of pulse. Vitality is abundant throughout and these brief 'folkish' songs (the composer's own choice of word) display this quality vividly, employing fairly simple traditional elements in a most individual way.

1. Mother Shipton's Wooing

This sprightly opening song consists of two bipartite strophic verses, with flowing piano figurations sustaining a continuous driving impulse right through to the end. Subtle changes of tempo and dynamic colour the lines, and words are set so that they can be projected without any strain. Phrasing is unusual and irregular, giving added piquancy to the vocal lines, and ensuring against rigidity. Breathing has, therefore, to be thought out very carefully. The golden rule to remember with music which seems to be continuous, is to obey the musical flow, even when it is at variance with verbal considerations. Musical shapeliness must be maintained. Too much isolation of words for exact observance of minutiae of punctuation can result in the sort of preciousness, sometimes found in hymn-singing (Psalm 23 provides several examples). When lines are elided at the expense of comfort, a very obvious gap has then to be made for a breath *in extremis* in mid-phrase, destroying rhythmic balance. In the first half of the first verse, here, breaths can be taken after either 'woo' or 'saying'. The latter will highlight the quotation that follows but this should not be exaggerated. Musically, the other alternative is better, since there is more time, and a skilled interpreter ought to be able to convey clearly the transition from narrative to actual speech by the subtlest accents, and use of a glottal attack on vowels. The next obvious breathing place is after 'pleasure', and then comes the problem. Ideally, the singer should phrase through to 'walk'. Such an expansive phrase will make muscles work hard and the last part of the verse will then come through firmly. However, there is something to be said for the snatching of a quick, unhurried breath after 'mother', taking advantage of the aspirate, Scottish-style 'wh' of 'when', which would have to be separated in any case. Then, a breath will be needed after 'catches her breath' and this can be used for deliberate effect to illustrate the words and heighten excitement appropriately, but it has to be well timed (Example 1).

In all strophic songs, it makes an enormous difference if the singer takes the trouble to analyse verbal and musical phrasing possibilities, and tries to vary them from verse to verse, creating new shapes and tensions. The second half of the verse (in a new key) again has quotation marks and offers a good possibility for attempting a sweetly innocent timbre for the young girl's speech, but this should not be allowed to lapse into coyness. Words must come out clearly and brightly without exaggeration. Tunes are basically modal in implication, the piano swings back into D major again as in the

Ex. 1 Stevens

opening, and verse 2 is an exact repeat except for slight rhythmic differences according to verbal needs. This time it could be a good idea to make a feature of breathing before the quotation 'O', if this was not done before. Extra impetus will thus be gained, with a fitting emphasis for this last time. There must be a breath after 'corner' in order to manage the rather subtle elision on 'burn a log'; 'a' comes on a long note but must not be too loud— a small crescendo towards 'log' will help preserve the sense. The 'little maid' again speaks up for the last half of the verse, and this time she soars into a bright and resonant area of the voice. For the last phrase it is best to breathe after 'kitchen', strictly *a tempo*, and make the most of the *poco accelerando* which follows on through the higher notes and then a sustained D, lifting again on 'turn'. This is helped greatly by the 'v' sound on 'love' and the voice ends deftly on 'spit', coinciding with the piano's *più mosso* postlude.

2. Lunar Attraction

A flowing medium tempo has to be found for this song and it must not be allowed to flag. The voice part is marked 'misterioso ma semplice' and requires a beautifully steady coolness of tone, with the singer shaping the unusual phrase-lengths with effortless grace (the song is in 5/4). Ideally, the whole of the first phrase should be sung without a break. It is most important to grip the audience with a feeling of rapt commitment from the very beginning. After this, dynamics warm up a little and gaps occur in the line but breaths should not be audible.

The four strophic verses of this song are most cleverly varied so that interest is always kept alive, and word-painting is an important aspect. It is a good idea to straighten the tone to an ethereal thread for the second verse describing the moon as 'a pallid ghost', for instance. The bitter irony of verse 3 must be brought out strongly. It is best to wait for a breath until after 'prevail', so that the following glottal stroke for 'only' is clearly separated. Despite the comma after 'swims' I feel it is better not to breathe here as this may throw the syncopated rhythm off-balance. The best opportunity for a breath is after 'cork' and this will help the singer to be ready for the low melisma on 'spring', which is followed by a long-held low D.

For the last verse the sibilant end of 'Hush' can be used to poetic effect, and dynamics are particularly important, especially the magical *pianissimo* on 'Mirrored' which has to be sustained continuously. It is difficult to find a good breathing place in the last line: a quick one could be taken, if timed perfectly, after 'lullaby', if absolutely necessary. It is as well not to risk any discomfort on the last very long note, as it would be noticeable.

3. May Day Carol

The infectious jollity of this song evokes many other lilting folksong settings on similar themes. The piano part has an ingenious counterpoint with the voice, right hand only for the first verse and then both at once, the left hand providing an inverted version in canon. The 12/8 quaver movement is continuous, and the singer will have to time breathing well so as not to lose momentum. The six strophic verses alternate between soft and loud dynamics, and the long up-beat anacruses to each line are a crucial stylistic feature, giving a special lift and bounce.

For the last verse there is a change to a slightly steadier tempo and the piano's two hands now play two octaves apart in unison. The singer's tone must be clear and precise, swinging easily between quasi-staccato and legato, letting this depend on the syllabic opportunities of the text. Liquid consonants, for instance, help to make a smooth liaison between notes and form inner shapes within the basic four-in-a-bar framework. Conversely, more percussive, silent consonants can punctuate the line and help promote rhythmic vitality. Text analysis is especially desirable for a relatively straightforward setting such as this. As an example, the second phrase (each four-bar phrase should be sung in one span) can be made more lively by singing through all the 'l' sounds ('we'*ll*' and 'te*ll*') and then treating the double 's' of 'blossom' exactly as in Italian, with a very slight stop–start effect making a fleeting lilt. The word 'buds' can be deliberately shortened, and it is very important to sing the word 'tree' through to the next note (Example 2). All other phrases can be given detailed preparatory thought in

Ex. 2 Stevens

this way and the effort will be well rewarded with extra crispness and attack. Alliterative and illustrative properties of individual words can also be brought out clearly (e.g. 'fresh', 'nimbler toes', 'springs'). The singer must make sure to save some strength for the *fortissimo* ending when the last phrase expands into longer note-lengths in a gloriously exuberant outburst.

This short cycle will prove a delightful addition to the repertoire and will not be too difficult for an inexperienced singer, even a complete beginner. It will fit very happily with other British music of all periods and would make an excellent start to a recital, its complete lack of affectation giving it an immediate attractiveness to the listener. It could also go well at the end of a programme of mixed standard repertoire, perhaps including works based on folk music of other countries: Spanish music would make a good contrast, or Bartók's *Hungarian Folksongs*.

Ten Songs
(1965–88)

Martin Wesley-Smith (born 1945)
Text by various writers

T II; M II (except for No. 5: M IV)
Soprano and piano (some also suitable for mezzo
or male voice)
Durations variable, between 1′–4′ per item

The Australian composer Martin Wesley-Smith has the rare attribute of being able to write music that is immediately accessible, witty, and often hilarious. A self-confessed eclectic, he also has a great gift for words, and an original mind, combining a perpetually youthful outlook with a burning commitment to political and environmental issues. One of his major preoccupations is with the work and ideas of Lewis Carroll and this has led to some delightful instrumental pieces, such as 'Snark-Hunting', as well as vocal settings. He is also closely involved with electronic and computer music, and has pioneered many multi-media events, along with fellow creative artists, including his brother Peter, with whom he has often collaborated on lyrics for his songs. His is a rare and refreshing spirit and his musical output reflects an astonishing variety of influences and tastes. Always considerate of the performer, and aware of practicalities, he presents his material with admirable clarity and attractiveness. His lively approach shows even in minor details such as his instructions for obtaining copies of his works (amid eloquent pleas against illegal photocopying!). Wesley-Smith would seem to be the natural successor to Percy Grainger in terms of his versatility, deep interest in ethnic music, and flexibility of attitude to performance, preferring immediate impact to undue academicism. Like Grainger, he allows for several versions of pieces, involving different keys and combinations, so that the songs can be adapted for any occasion.

This collection of songs covers a large portion of his working life, and includes items from his two choral cantatas *Boojum!* (a music theatre work in its original form) and *Songs of Australia* as well as much earlier pieces. They do not have to be sung as a cycle, and should provide a most invaluable source of short pieces for use in informal settings, including parties, as well as cabarets and concerts with a light-hearted flavour. This is just the kind of repertoire that singers really need to develop their interpretative skills and ability to adapt to different styles. Even total beginners, and the vocally unsophisticated, will greatly enjoy the songs, which are also eminently suitable for non-classical singers such as folk artists and street-singers. I cherish the memory of one such (bass) singer from Finland who brought the house down at one of my classes with the first song of this set.

1. I'm a Caterpillar of society (Martin and Peter Wesley-Smith) (from *Boojum!*) (Duration 3′)

This piece is an out-and-out hit. The words are brilliantly witty, and especially appropriate for a party involving food. The easygoing syncopation of the basic tune gives scope for rubato and the improvisatory elements found in popular song. Phrasing is vitally important as is a sense of style. The piano part appears simple, but some experience in popular idioms will be an advantage. The accompanist has to lead the 'metric modulations' and help pilot the singer through pulse transitions that must, of course, seem entirely natural. The vocal line features exuberant shouts of exclamation, which tend to occur near the ends of the three verses, before the repeat of the laid-back refrain. Word- (and even rhythm-) painting is deftly incorporated at suitable moments (Example 1). The music undergoes an exciting transformation at verse 3 as the gentle swinging syncopations, and well-spaced chords are suddenly replaced by relentless driving rock-'n'-roll

Ex. 1 Wesley-Smith

rhythms, with repeated chords in the piano's high register, above bass octaves, with the vocal tessitura also rising accordingly. Vibrato should be kept well under control so that words can be clear: it would be a great pity to lose any of them. The singer's lines break into a series of shouted exhortations ('Try this for thighs', etc.—puns come thick and fast!), during which appropriate actions will add more fun to the proceedings. After a pause, the refrain comes back in an augmented version, rounded off with a delightful coda in swing mode: 'Banish the blues with a bowl of greens'. The light touch, musical and verbal wit, and infectious vitality of this song will endear it to all audiences. A marvellous vehicle for a natural performer (each vocalist can adapt it to suit their particular attributes, or even limitations), it is perfect as a surprise encore piece.

2. Tommy Tanna (Anon.) (from *Songs of Australia*) (Duration 3′)

This is a straightforward traditional folksong, in three strophic verses, the last somewhat extended, in a basic modal G minor. It can be sung by any voice, although the words are those of a lady extolling the charms of a black planter. Folksong convention certainly does not require specific gender identification, and countless art songs, such as Debussy's *Ariettes oubliées*, which constitute professions of love from the male viewpoint, are frequently sung by female artists.

A one-in-a-bar waltz rhythm is sustained throughout this song, with natural rubato to round off musical paragraphs. The simple accompaniment figures change subtly as the song progresses, and help to characterize descriptive elements in the (anonymous) poems. The impact will be more effective if the text is not overdramatized, but projected clearly and unaffectedly. The range stays comfortably within an octave span in medium register. After two relatively conventional verse-settings, each followed by eight bars of piano waltz figures, the slow (dotted minim = 48) tempo is suddenly replaced by a speedier one (bar = 60), at the start of verse 3. Halfway through the verse the music slows to dotted minim = 32, and the voice part is further elongated by pauses at the ends of phrase fragments. These should be floated softly and raptly, the piano reduced to plain chords in support, leaving plenty of room for freedom of expression. After this the slow waltz is resumed in tempo, with a slight ritenuto at the end.

3. Climb the Rainbow (Ann North) (Duration 1′30″)

This charming one-off song has the nostalgic, magical feeling of the traditional dream-song found at a central point in a popular musical: 'Over the Rainbow' being a classic example of the genre. Its catchy, two-in-a-bar 6/8 theme, starting with a gentle swaying, and then tumbling ahead in a burst of cumulative speed for the second half, is repeated complete three times. The piano part becomes spectacular and virtuosic in the middle verse, in contrast to the calmer chords of the outer stanzas. The accompanist has to negotiate some very swift chord progressions during *accelerandi*, and quick reactions will be necessary to co-ordinate the flexible pulse (the whole piece is marked 'con rubato'). The vocal line is by no means as easy as it appears. A glissando (this should be exaggerated to paint the word 'slide') leads into each surge ahead. Here the lowish tessitura and fast-moving syllables may mitigate against the desired legato and cause breathing problems. A strong voice is needed to cut through the dense piano texture. The choice of where to take breath during the last half of the verse is crucial, and no easy solution presents itself, as there is little time until the 'molto rit e dim' which ends the two outer verses. After 'chance' is perhaps the best place, though it is often good to vary phrasing in strophic verses, to make different shapes. (After 'side' is an alternative; after 'top' is less satisfactory, leaving too short a fragment after it, with a potentially awkward restart on 'and', interrupting the lilting rhythm.) For the floridly accompanied middle verse it would be unfortunate to have to interrupt the piano's running semiquavers, and, ideally, no breath at all should be taken between 'before' and 'dance'. The slowing-down here does not occur until after the voice has finished, so the tempo, marked 'faster', should not relent. In the last verse the music slows and softens towards the end, giving space to float the final, wistful lines, ending on a held low D. It is always worth taking the trouble to observe the subtle variations of pace and stress in what may appear a simple piece.

4. Andy's Gone with Cattle (Henry Lawson) (Duration 1′30″)

Although not part of the set *Songs of Australia*, this setting of a poem by Australia's best-known pioneer writer Henry Lawson clearly belongs stylistically alongside No. 2 of this collection. The syncopated G major tune has a slight Scottish flavour, and this is enhanced by the piano's dotted rhythms in verse 2, appropriately at the reference to Andy's 'whistle'. Typically, Wesley-Smith manages to maintain a keen and lively musical interest throughout three seemingly straightforward repetitions of the folk-tune, and once again, 'con rubato' is a prime feature, the pulse fluctuating naturally according to the verbal phrases. Tessitura will not tax even the most inexperienced singer, the span covering a ninth up from low D. As before, there is plenty of scope for colouring individual words: ('dejection', 'snarling', 'torrents', etc.) and the piano part undergoes subtle transformations in layout in response to the mood of the text. Block chords predominate, but some are arpeggiated to evoke a strummed accompaniment (perhaps a guitar), and others gently rock in rhythmic unison with the voice, becoming denser in texture and developing even more punch and swing for the last verse. Slow descending chromatic scales in octaves in the left hand are also in evidence in the latter half of the piece. There are constant surprises in chromatic harmonies and unexpected shifts, especially at the return to tempo for the last line of each stanza, which is a repeat of the first. For the final verse, the third line's rise to E has a diminuendo as well as a *ritardando* to prepare for a characteristically delicate slow ending. This time the line flips up the octave to pause on the high E for a moment before subsiding into a gentle cadence (Example 2).

There is also a version of this piece for voice, clarinet, and piano.

Ex. 2 Wesley-Smith

a tempo - slow

And when the sum-mer comes a - gain   God grant it brings us An-dy___

5. Jubjubby (Peter Wesley-Smith) (from *Boojum!*) (Duration 2′30″)

This parody of the already parodistic and much-loved Jabberwocky rhyme of Lewis Carroll, is by far the most musically 'advanced' of this collection. Although bearing a key signature of G minor, the music is basically atonal, and also quite complex rhythmically. It therefore needs considerable time spent in preparation, quite apart from the verbal co-ordination required to project the special nonsense language with its unexpected puns and syllabic niceties. It works beautifully in performance, and the many time-signature changes enhance the spontaneous and effortlessly flexible effect. A pianist of flair and versatility is essential to capture the mercurial switches of mood and emphasis and respond to the minutiae of the vocal articulations.

The form is ternary, the outer verses virtually identical, framed by a piano solo introduction and coda, in an exuberant (crotchet = 140) tempo, which are mirror images of each other. The voice enters at a greatly reduced speed, and there is a Latin-American feel to the rhythms at the outset. A bolero pattern in the piano punctuates the voice's hesitant opening fragments. A glissando up a ninth works very well vocally. Pauses at the end of phrases have to be led clearly by the singer. The long central section describes the mystic creature's battle and capture, in surreal and highly dramatic fashion. The Jub-Jub's entrance, to a brisk march (heralded by piano 'fanfares') hints at old American tunes, in particular 'Marchin' thro' Georgia'. This is surrounded by a succession of volatile recitatives, diverging wildly in character and pace, with much use of onomatapoeia as usual ('groagley toes', 'shuddered', 'squeak', for example). For the section beginning 'The forest shuddered' (another helpful glissando here) it is as well to be cautious with the horrified gasping effect of the splintered line, saving breath to aid clarity. A breathy sound is invariably an unfocused one. Careful counting of irregular beats is essential: it will be all too easy to come unstuck as the drama unfolds. The text should appear to flow naturally without a feeling of strict divisions. At the height of the battle the word 'Attack!' has to be shouted; it will work perfectly as long as no breath is taken before it. 'Forlorn it flew' must be tuned carefully. This mock-poignant moment features some crucial

Ex. 3 Wesley-Smith

For - lorn it flew in - to the air _____ a

tan - trum and a ne - t.

intervals, the downward plunging minor ninth in particular (Example 3). The bar of unaccompanied singing that follows has to be very poised and well timed, leading in the piano's slow march in 4/4. This is a lovely passage, allowing the singer to croon cantabile (more plunging minor ninths—a slight portamento will be appropriate) in quite a romantic style. The resumption of the opening verse leaves the listener hanging in the air with an unresolved cadence, as the voice dies away, and, after a brief pause, the piano rushes headlong into the coda at the dizzying opening tempo, finishing in dashing burlesque fashion with a loud emphatic cadence. This is an excellent party-piece, guaranteed to entertain the widest audience, but it does require technical skill and musicianship to master its intricacies.

6. My Knight in Shining Armour (Peter Wesley-Smith) (from *Boojum!*) (Duration 4′)

Another number from *Boojum!*, far away in character from the previous one, this features a lovely melody set in gentle foxtrot rhythm in F major, the supple vocal lines undulating easily through long-spun notes and dreamy triplets. It is subtitled 'A Love Song to the Rev'rend Charles Lutwidge Dodgson', and the style and idiom of the traditional romantic musical is most beautifully caught. Of the five verses, four repeat the basic melody, but each is slightly varied and gradually extended at its close. Verse 4, in sharpest contrast, is a quasi-military march in B flat major, in strict tempo. As all are sung by Alice herself, it would be inappropriate to exaggerate the romanticism, but to aim instead for a sweetly unaffected delivery, letting the contours of the music and the rhythmic subtleties convey the expression. The added bars at the ends of verses 2, 3, and 5 are the most crucial to the interpretation, as they seem to represent Alice talking to herself and hinting at equivocal emotions that she finds difficult to express adequately. 'I want to know him', coming after a piano interlude at the end of verse 2, seems especially poignant. At the end of verse 3 there is a rapt pause on a high A flat, a delicately sensuous glissando on 'tender love', and then the musing 'A gentle man' and 'I cherish him' with their long-held final notes enhancing the deeply contemplative feeling. The sudden transition to the cheerful march is quite a shock. The voice's fanfare figures must be well focused and words are extremely fast-moving and may be difficult to make clear (Example 4). One suspects a hint of irony in the bluesy minor third at the climax of the verse. The cadence, and the join into the resumption of the main theme, have to be timed with care. At the end of the last verse, the coda is marked 'slow, almost out of tempo', leaving the singer free to deliver the final slow 'I honour you', 'I cherish you', 'I love you' with touching simplicity. A young person could sing this very well, although a trained singer will fare better on the longer phrases, and clean intonation is very important.

Ex. 4 Wesley-Smith

7. Ode to Technology (Peter Wesley-Smith) (Duration 1′)

This tiny song features the composer in his familiar role of sharp satirist and observer of the absurdities of everyday life. It consists of just one verse in a slow 6/8 metre in F major played first on the piano alone, and then repeated by the singer, and tells the sad tale of the demise of a parking meter. The dotted rhythms can be used to convey a quasi-ironical maudlin quality, but the piece should be performed absolutely deadpan with perfect control. It is better not to breathe after the tied high F, so that the octave-leap down can have a slight portamento. The piano's unexpectedly extravagant chromatic arpeggios at the close should raise a laugh.

113

8. I wish I wasn't me (Martin and Peter Wesley-Smith) (Duration 2'15")

The brothers Wesley-Smith have collaborated on this very funny and topical lyric. Basically a music-hall number, it is enormous fun to perform, but as with others of this nature, the fast-pattering text will need time to fall into place naturally and make its full effect without any stumbling. There is no respite for the singer here: the lines follow one another without a break.

The tune is in E flat major in a jaunty 6/8, with heavy use of dotted rhythms, including the Scotch-snap versions. The first two verses cite two public favourites, Paul McCartney and Princess Diana (there is nothing in the lyric that would make the current situation inappropriate!), as objects of envy, for their imagined freedom and glamorous lifestyles. Then follows a particularly amusing interlude, while the singer muses in more realistic fashion, chanting on a monotone in free triplets (marked 'slow, out of tempo') and eventually decides that being famous has drawbacks. The final verse then declares the joys of being oneself after all, savouring the things that money can't buy. A gradual crescendo throughout it builds to a triumphant, repeated 'Oh I'm glad that I am me (little me)'. Words are quite hilarious and will have the audience in stitches. It is important to maintain aplomb and not let rhythms rush ahead. The tessitura is somewhat high for so many quick syllables, and the piece might suit a tenor better than a soprano for this reason. Vibrato will certainly have to be well controlled if the text is to make its full impact. As so often with apparently easy music, a good breathing technique is needed. Discomfort often results from too hectic a delivery of words without heed to phrasing. The subtle variations in rhythm, small rests, and so on, must not be ignored, but there is room for a very free approach to the chanting section, obeying natural speech patterns and almost talking. The pianist has some fairly fast-moving block chords to negotiate, especially at the end, so will need considerable dexterity. This is bound to be a riot with audiences, and there is probably scope for added verses as time goes on.

9. For more than sixty years (Peter and Martin Wesley-Smith) (from *Boojum!*) (Duration 4')

This song has a footnote describing it as 'A reflection on the life of the Rev'rend Charles Lutwidge Dodgson [Lewis Carroll]' and is marked 'gentle, relaxed'. Three strophic verses in F major in 12/8 repeat the same material exactly. They are surrounded by a solo introduction and coda on the piano, which throughout the setting has a cantabile tune low in the bass-line, with regular chords in the right hand controlling the pulse. This runs in counterpoint to the voice's melody, and there is much syncopation in both lines. The music swings gently along in a blues mode. There are quite a few sustained high notes which must be kept very straight in tone, almost crooned: the slow 'y' of 'years' will help this. The contemplative mood is emphasized by an absence of dynamic markings. This means that the performer has to sustain the atmosphere by extreme concentration and poise. At the end, a slow glissando down a third must be carefully planned, using the 'l' of 'love' to ensure continuity of sound.

10. Lost Snail (Martin Wesley-Smith) (Duration 40″)

The last song in this varied collection is one of the composer's occasional 'fun' pieces. This priceless miniature lasts only about 30″, but has to be delivered with consummate precision and artistry. Elliptical references in the text to twin brothers may indicate some family in-joke here, but the somewhat surreal quality of the lyric increases its charm and freshness. As the tessitura rises, there could be a stressful moment or two for the singer: 'mine' is not the easiest of words for a long high note, and the second part of the diphthong is best left to fend for itself ('mahn' is the safest option). It should be remembered that many Australians pronounce the vowel of 'Lance' in the American way, and that too goes for the rhyming 'Aunt's'. The punch-line is unexpected, and needs a deadpan approach, and then perhaps a little bow on 'Thank-you'.

Performers should cherish composers who provide them with such richly varied and entertaining material. Wesley-Smith's unfailing musicality carries him effortlessly through territory where the less skilled and witty have come to grief. Lightness of touch is a special gift, and performers too have much to learn by working on this repertoire. Singers can make their own selection from this exceptionally rewarding store of gems. A whole evening's entertainment can be built around some of these songs, and the nostalgic–romantic pieces are ideal for late night cabaret. A mixed group of the songs would round off a traditional recital to great effect. Other 'Australiana', such as songs by Grainger, could be included. It might be a mistake to juxtapose other examples of wit and humour in music, although the *Newspaper Announcements* of Eisler could go rather well in the opposite half, and even some Kurt Weill. American songs, by Ives, Cowell, Barber, Ned Rorem, and others would be suitable, as Wesley-Smith's music often bears traces of the influence of American popular music and jazz. An extended solo voice piece, including several recommended in this volume (Rainier, Knussen, Aston) would clear the air ready for the rumbustious fun of the satirical pieces.

From a Child's Garden
(1968)

Malcolm Williamson (born 1931)
Text by Robert Louis Stevenson

T II; M II
High voice and piano
Duration *c.*25′

Malcolm Williamson, the present Master of the Queen's Music, has always written superbly for the voice. His operas display to the full his lyrical gifts. They are packed with the expansive, wide-ranging lines that singers revel in. As a performer-composer (he is a brilliant pianist) he is alive to the practicalities of performance, and his music has a tangible physicality and spontaneity. These settings of Stevenson's endearingly familiar poems are expertly crafted and winningly direct in appeal. The cycle is ideally varied and moves effortlessly from impishness to nostalgia, highlighting and illustrating the words with refinement and insight. Such a collection ought to be very widely known. It is a heaven-sent gift for the repertoire; equally suitable for young people as for fully trained adult professionals; a perfect item for a young singer's recital. Individual selections can be made to form balanced groups according to the occasion, such is the richness and variety of the choice available. However, strong thematic links within the cycle make it into a satisfying whole. It is no easy thing to produce music of sterling quality in lighter vein: the pitfalls are obvious. Many examples of mere clever pastiche assail us at every turn, but fresh original music in a traditional idiom is less frequently found. Williamson deftly hones and adapts his own individual style to the smaller canvas, maintaining musical integrity with elegance and *élan*. His lightness of touch and aural acuteness never fail him, and his mastery of his forces seems effortless.

These songs will sound equally well in the tenor or soprano voice, and young children of either sex could also manage some of the simpler numbers very effectively, especially nos. 2–5, or 10–12. Although the musical idiom is straightforward and basically tonal, there are a number of rhythmic and chromatic complexities, and, in the eighth song in particular, there are sustained lines needing considerable breath control. As might be expected, piano parts are completely idiomatic and rewarding for an accomplished player. It is essential to avoid a sentimental interpretation. The performance should be natural and unaffected without any simpering.

116

1. Time to Rise

A delicious opening number with a light, pearly staccato accompaniment. The voice part consists of two-note 'pecking' figures, gracefully shaped, and breaths should not be taken in the gaps between them. The long–short (trochee) patterns make a delightfully appropriate effect. The flip up the octave on 'cocked' is particularly apt. Syncopations need watching; it would be useful to mark out the beats when preparing the song, as it will save time in the end. Phrases gradually expand in both length and range. The F flat on 'said' may be a little more awkward for a soprano than a tenor, and chromatic intervals will need careful tuning. A sudden burst of repetitive coloratura 'birdsong' for the final phrase will benefit from a good professional technique. At the end of the semiquaver figures, the lift to E flat (only to drop down again an octave—a characteristic and favourite interval of this composer), should be floated and not forced.

2. Marching Song

The sturdy, dotted rhythms of the piano's accompaniment are marked 'non legato', and the forthright vocal line is double-dotted for extra clarity and emphasis. The singer has to produce an incisive sound, punching out each note at a steady beat without hurrying. After a straightforward start in D major, which ends suspended on the leading note, there is a succession of characteristic chromatic shifts, often enharmonic, each of which subtly alters the colour of the music. The introduction of 'Mary Jane' brings a slight reduction in volume, but the dogged double dots continue. The piano is at a light dynamic, with the composer showing awareness of potential balance problems. Ideally, the regular two-bar phrases can occasionally be joined together in longer spans if breath allows. A suitably swaggering effect can be achieved by slightly eliding 'hearty' to 'Each', with tenuto marks on 'Feet in time' well separated (Example 1). Any possible monotony is avoided by subtle rhythmic details: a triplet swings against the march beat at the return to D minor, which ends in a held C sharp, with the accompaniment providing a jolly bugle-and-drum effect. There is a sudden hiatus, when the piano stops on a loud E flat major chord, and the voice has a strong declamation, still in double-dotted march style, but with an interesting cross-rhythmed cadence across the barline: a similar device to the hemiola of early music. As the children gradually become tired, dynamics slacken, and breaths become shorter, turning to exhausted gasps, while the march

Ex. 1 Williamson

Feet in time, a - lert and hear-ty, Each a Gre - na - dier!

dies away to *pianissimo*. This setting is amusingly apposite, and provides the singer with an interpretative task that is immediately workable.

3. Where go the boats?

This is the first of several charmingly lyrical movements, where the composer's gift for melody is fully shown. He seems to have an inexhaustible fund of simple yet highly memorable melodies which modulate and develop within their natural flow. Characteristic key shifts, wide vocal intervals, and frequent cadences occasionally remind one of Prokofiev. Phrase-marks are provided for both the strophic A major verses. Their pattern is interesting: four-bar phrases predominate, yet mechanical repetition is avoided. Verse 1 has bars of 4 + 4 + 4 + 2 + 2, and verse 2 consists of 4 + 4 + 2 + 2 + 5, with the last cadence subtly extended by prolonging the C sharp on 'boats'. This gives a momentary ripple to the basic lilting waltz rhythm. The piano flows easily and gently around the voice in quavers throughout.

4. Looking Forward

A brief, one-page fragment that requires great panache and crisp rhythm. The basic 6/8 motion is set in two-bar patterns, but it is better not to breathe until after four bars. There is little time for this, so another short breath could be taken after 'boys' to prepare for the crucial final phrase with its tricky high-placed syncopation on 'meddle' (this may sound better with a tenor voice). The surging crescendo on the last note will need some muscular strength behind it so that the throat is not put under strain. Tone should be kept light and precise, and not too loud.

5. Whole Duty of Children

This is one of the most testing songs for the interpreters, but it is also a delight to perform, full of wit and irony. As with the first song, the piano plays in a light staccato throughout, and the rhythm has an infectious sparkle. The voice part features some exhilarating glissandos up the octave. These are always flattering vocally, and make a spectacular effect with very little trouble. Here they are particularly apt to the satire. Notes in pairs, smoother than those in No. 1 (and with a reverse rhythm of short–long) precede the upward slides, setting them in relief perfectly. For the second half, the voice part is also staccato, and phrasing is again planned with care. Slurred and unslurred notes must be clearly defined. The shortened attacks give an appropriately mincing effect, in a parody of self-consciously correct table manners. Relaxation brings a final line of unabashed cheerfulness, adding a mischievous edge to the proceedings. The final melisma of 'able' is particularly pleasing to sing, and the close intervals at the end need scrupulous intonation, so that the piano's echo of the last two notes chimes exactly.

6. The Flowers

This is one of the undoubted hits of the cycle: a setting of endearing simplicity, yet with an abundance of melting chromatic cadential shifts in characteristic style. There should be no vocal problems at all, as the voice coasts smoothly through each lovely phrase (Example 2). The dropping intervals lie very comfortably, as phrases seem ideally balanced within an AABA format. The B section may need a little care in tuning intervals, especially in the last phrase. The key slides evoke a fleeting reminder of Fauré's masterly Verlaine setting 'Mandoline'. The main (A) melody must

Ex. 2 Williamsom

Andante allegretto

All the names I know from nurse: Gard-ener's gart-ters, Shep-herd's purse, Bach-'lor's but-tons, La-dy's smock, And the La-dy Hol-ly-hock.

never be allowed to become coy or sentimental: it is very touching, and needs only a natural unaffected performance. It could help to imagine a child singing it (and it is indeed within a schoolchild's range), but a falsely imposed naïve timbre could spoil its unadorned delicacy.

7. Rain

After the undemanding charm of 'The Flowers', it is time for something a little more complex musically. The modest dimensions of this setting contain much to engage the performers' concentration: a fascinating patter accompaniment supports a graceful legato vocal line in 6/8, which is complicated by an unexpected distribution of syllables which gives rise to some catchy cross-rhythms. There are just four lilting two-bar phrases, with the last note lengthened, as the piano's 'droplets' peter out, still in the strict (*Andante*) tempo.

8. My bed is a boat

This recipe for peaceful sleep is beautifully captured in the hypnotic, gently rippling 6/4 of the accompaniment, and serene vocal lines, which will demonstrate the singer's control. The piano's oscillating thirds shimmer above a bass pedal, which at first remains static on the tonic of G flat, except for a typical harmonic shift at the end of paragraphs (Example 3). There are four strophic verses. The first three are identical for the singer, but the fourth and last is markedly different. The rhythmic structure remains

Ex. 3 Williamson

basically the same, and the melody is a closely related variant of the main verse. However, the 3/4 bar that contributes an intriguingly irregular pattern halfway through each verse, is absent in this last. There is a sudden switch to F sharp minor, *mezzo-forte*, and then, characteristically, back to G flat, *subito piano*, for the last half. The absence of earlier dynamic markings is significant. Singer and pianist have to maintain a mesmeric *Andante tranquillo*, avoiding expressiveness. The finely spun vocal line should have a trance-like steadiness, and the composer's phrase-marks must be noted with care. There should be no subdivisions despite the longish spans, and the singer has every chance to display a perfect legato. For verse 3, the piano texture intensifies, with the left hand taking over the quaver movement in the form of wide-ranging arpeggios, and the right hand rocking in octaves. The last verse ends with the voice suspended on the dominant, after some crucial chromatic intervals. The singer should aim for a rapt, hushed quality that floats easily and safely, as the piano slows and recedes.

9. From a Railway Carriage

This is the most ambitious and testing of the movements, and is likely to take longer to prepare than any of the others. It will certainly require a high standard of musicianship, particularly with regard to rhythm and pitching. Intervals have to be negotiated cleanly at some speed, and fast-moving syllables will need the slickest articulation. The composer portrays the train's clattering motion quite wonderfully. Fortunately, the piano's staccato chordal figures mostly carry cue notes within the texture, but reactions will need to be very quick to pick them up. The singer will have to listen while singing, and, since the piano's dynamic is a bold *mezzo-forte*, there should at least be no danger of the voice's own resonance obscuring the detail. It is necessary to anchor firmly to the piano's low opening notes, which contain the B flat needed for the first syllable, and not to be put off by the subsequent chromaticism just before the voice's entry. The interval of a minor third is of crucial importance throughout. Tone should be bright and clear, with very little vibrato. The recurring 7/8 pattern (3 + 2 + 2) will come naturally with sufficient repetition, and this is a useful exercise in additive rhythms that will serve the singer well in the works of Messiaen and others. Once the knack is acquired, there is an agreeable freedom and swing to the music. Breaths will have to be accomplished swiftly and neatly, but there is no need for a breath after each fragment. Ideally, rests should be thought through and breath left until the end of the two opening 'paragraphs'—the first consisting of four fragments, and the second of two longer phrases. As ever, the less air used, the clearer and more controlled the sound. The singer can enjoy the percussive consonants and the poem's sheer vitality in this expert setting. Wisely, the composer has not cluttered the score with dynamics, aware that the words provide endless interest and a variety of captivating images within their natural shapes and sounds. The section beginning 'All of the sights' can perhaps be a little smoother, but this will happen naturally on the slurred 'thick' and 'driving'. The sibilance of 'stations', and especially 'whistles', can be exaggerated for effect. A change of key, and a rising tessitura for 'Here is a child', brings a change of colour and a brighter resonance, and rolling the 'r's will enhance clarity (Example 4). The frequent word-painting opportunities must not, however, be

Ex. 4 Williamson

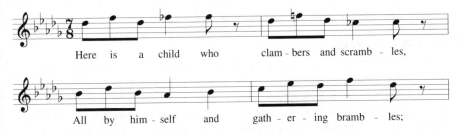

allowed to obscure musical contours. The phrase 'Here is a tramp', taken in one span, makes an especially lovely shape. The last verse, which brings a gentler dynamic after the more hectic *mezzo-forte*, is the most challenging musically. The range is high for a soprano to articulate at speed, and intervals are tricky. The swoop across 'along with man' should provide momentary respite from any tiredness. The tempo must be kept under control, especially for the up-beat into the last 'paragraph' (four fragments again, as at the beginning, but with the last two joined). Here a diminuendo has to be manœuvred skilfully, ending with utmost precision on the final dropped *pianissimo*, without any slackening of pace.

10. The Lamplighter

Strict repetitive rhythms, at a speaking pace, form a minimalist pattern that continues throughout this appealing song. Legato phrase-marks above the vocal part remind the singer to ensure that shorter notes remain part of the line, and are not neglected. This again means that diction must be crisp and unhesitating. A mechanical 6/8 is set up in the piano, and the singer joins after two bars. Breaths between phrases must be quick and shallow, and, despite an *Allegretto*, the words must not seem rushed. Every note should have a clear centre, released on to a vowel, however brief, leaving enough time to highlight individual words and images such as 'driver', 'banker', 'rich', and so on. The boyish enthusiasm can be projected without over-doing it. The exclaimed 'O's should be articulated on the glottis to make them fully expressive. For the last of three identical verses, the final phrase is extended by a lengthening of note-values, introducing a tripping dotted figure to end.

11. A Good Boy

Perhaps this song and 'The Flowers' are the two most obviously destined for great popularity. Again the main melody is worthy to become a golden oldie alongside the classics of the genre. Its supple lyricism lies perfectly in the voice, in a smoothly modulating F major, and its proportions seem ideal, enabling all the phrases to fall naturally without problems of breathing. Once again, the composer succeeds in avoiding the trap of sentimentality, and creates a touching cameo that is memorable in its sincerity, and bears no suspicion of worldly cynicism. The slight slowing-up before the last of the three verses gives singer and audience a heightened awareness of the poignancy of the simple trust expressed in the poem.

12. Happy Thought

This minute epilogue is set in typically brilliant fashion. The piano's exhil-arating introduction repeats the material of 'Looking Forward' and the bouncing 6/8 rhythm even bears echoes of the motion of the train in No. 9. The singer has just two phrases, to be sung with spontaneity and directness, in an exuberant *Presto*. Extreme clarity of rhythms must be preserved right up to the final punch-line 'happy as kings'. The piano's cheeky staccato figures in the postlude again recall Songs 1 and 5.

A cycle of this stature and accessibility by such a gifted and experienced figure is a godsend for performers and audiences worldwide. It is odd that certain items in lighter vein, with considerably less charm and wit, should have been promoted over the years, and established in the repertoire, while a work of this quality has been heard far less. Its sterling worth will win hordes of new admirers, and it will prove a delightful choice to end a recital. Performed complete it will make a fine complement to a major cycle by a French or Russian composer. Single songs can of course be used to enhance special occasions aimed at young people, or informal or late-night pro-grammes.

   Postscript: Just as I had completed this article, my attention was drawn to a most detailed and perceptive study on the cycle by Ian Bartlett in *Music Teacher* (Oct. 1970). A rigorous musicological analysis, yet full of insight, it is to be highly recommended.

Her days shall pass
(1981)

Avril·Anderson (born 1953)
Text by Charlotte Brontë

T III; M II
Soprano and piano
Duration 4'

Avril Anderson and her husband David Sutton Anderson have made a lively and enterprising contribution to British musical life in recent years. Their consistency and integrity have won them much admiration amongst the new music *cognoscenti*. Not only have they created a stimulating body of individual work, but they have also devoted considerable energy to promoting other composers of like mind. Avril Anderson's output contains quite a number of vocal works, including an opera *Edward II* (1976) as yet unperformed, and, more recently, she has become involved with the re-creation of traditional Sephardic music for voice and guitar. Wide-ranging sympathies and a fresh and direct musical utterance make her work immediately arresting, and ideal for a singer looking for something unusual to spice up a standard recital.

This short but very poignant and intense work is a typical example of her vocal writing. A brief, movingly elegiac verse by Charlotte Brontë is set with a seeming simplicity and spareness of texture that is perhaps somewhat deceptive in appearance. It is by no means easy to achieve a perfect evenness in the frequently exposed vocal lines, and dynamics are often unexpected, including some violent changes. Rhythmic discipline will be needed: there are strong elements of minimalism in the repeated patterns or mobiles, and the whole piece is very tightly constructed. Pitches and motifs recur throughout, and there should be no trouble with intonation, as cues for the singer's notes are almost invariably present at some point in the accompaniment.

There are many phrases, including the opening, that have to be sung wordlessly on 'Ah', and these help to sustain the feeling of desolation and deep misery. This is emphasized by repeated notes, often bearing tenuto accents, which create a sobbing effect. It is unusual to find passages of wordless vocalization that contain so many separated notes without consonants to help impel them. It almost seems as if a text is implied, rather than written, and that the music is expressing emotions that are beyond words. The phrases would seem to fit some silent declamatory recitative, and thinking of this should help clarify the interpretation. It may be necessary to modify the vowel-sound a little according to context, particularly when dynamics become stronger. It is important not to let the 'Ah' go back, and become too throaty or artificially covered. Holding a vowel-sound, and articulating notes too enthusiastically, can result in bad habits, such as gripping the jaw or neck muscles. This can be very uncomfortable, and dangerous for future vocal health. As singers will already know, consonants can be extremely helpful in launching and planting notes accurately, and their absence can expose problems of attack. A vocalise is more usually a display of mellifluous legato on a constantly shifting line, but this composer shows a refreshingly different approach.

Neither vocal nor piano writing is idiomatic in the usual sense, but both singer and pianist complement one another in spare, uncluttered lines. The piano is in two 'voices' almost continually, apart from some chordal progressions nearer the close. The thin texture of the accompaniment is warmed by use of the sustaining pedal. Long-held resonances are built into the music, giving it a distinctive, haunting quality. All pedallings are meticulously annotated, with half-pedalling a significant feature. The voice itself is often used as an instrument, and tone should be clean-edged, with vibrato well controlled. However, the tessitura is sometimes quite high, and a dramatic voice will sound well in the louder passages, and in the two expansively lyrical lines that form twin high points of the work. There are also many phrases that centre around the potentially vulnerable register-break area, and these will tax stamina. The composer's manuscript, though clear and bold, has the dynamics below the stave and text above; the opposite of the usual procedure, and this may cause confusion at first, since expressive markings are often found where words might be expected. There should be no ambiguities with accidentals, which are used conventionally and apply throughout bars until cancelled. Despite 'normal' barrings, there are no time signatures, and it would be wise to go through with a pencil and mark beats, so as to avoid any delaying stumblings during early readings.

A powerful piece, yet tautly economical in scale and proportion. The performers will need a deep, intense concentration and absence of mannerism, as if participating in some private, agonizing ritual.

The opening tempo is a very brisk one, but there are no notes of small value. The piano starts *fortissimo* with a declamatory fanfare figure, and the voice enters gently and wordlessly on high E flat—not an easy way to begin. This first sung phrase will test smoothness of placing. It is repeated exactly, and then once more at the lower octave. Interestingly, vocal dynamics increase as the tessitura drops. The piano then introduces a series of rocking contrary-motion figures, which are grouped in two-note patterns, three pairs to a bar, in alternating sequences, with oscillating minor sixths in the right hand and diminished fifths in the left. This creates a soft (*pianissimo*) texture, and the voice eventually joins in at a high register, *mezzo-forte*. A shorter piano announcement is followed by a very brief vocal fragment, still without words. No accents are marked here, despite the repeated notes, and it may be difficult to achieve a secure legato, especially in mid-register at a *forte*. The mobile effect returns in the piano, *pianissimo*, and this time each bar is an exact repeat, high in the treble clef. The soprano's first line of text is set memorably, with a wide-ranging and eventually extremely high tessitura. From another aspect, too, it represents a challenge: rhythmic unison is abandoned, and voice and piano beats are placed so as to be interspersed, and rendered deliberately out of kilter (Example 1). However, a strict tempo

Ex. 1 Anderson

must be kept by the pianist, whose patterns continually repeat. It is the singer's more difficult task to maintain an identical tempo but not to coincide. The voice can be allowed a little flexibility, and the long pause on F sharp (rather uncomfortable, after such a high line) is a rallying-point, as is the close of the sentence. A good deal of support will be needed to sustain this strenuous vocal part, especially the pause on '-ly', not the easiest of syllables. The singer should try to keep the tongue relaxed, and the throat as open as possible so that the sound does not deteriorate, and the ending is clean. The partners must be sure to catch each other at the beginning of the following, metric minimalist section, which is again wordless, and the voice cannot rest till after this. The last note of each 4/4 pattern changes alternately, and phrasing and breathing will need keen attention, especially since the note-groups end with an upward curve, and afford little time for breaths. In order not to tire, the singer may need to take very shallow breaths at the end of each bar. When the voice is used in *perpetuum mobile* in this way, it is wise to play safe and not risk disturbing the pulse. Ideally, a singer with a strong and reliable technique might prefer to take the whole passage in one breath-span, with each group clearly articulated. The dynamic here is an unvaried *piano*. For the repeated Cs, in expanding rhythms at the cadence, the tenuto accents should be made with the diaphragm and not the throat.

A *meno mosso* brings a change of texture for the piano: successions of sustained chromatic chords, each half-pedalled in turn. As the voice enters, *molto legato* with a strong, swooping lyrical phrase (Example 2), the piano stops playing, but the pedal controls the overhanging resonance through the vocal melody. The singer should find this phrase very rewarding. Again, there is a snatch of 'wordless recitative', with reiterated notes, rising to a hefty *fortissimo*, which is not particulary easy in this range. The phrase is repeated, slower and quieter, this time with words, dying away to nothing.

Ex. 2 Anderson

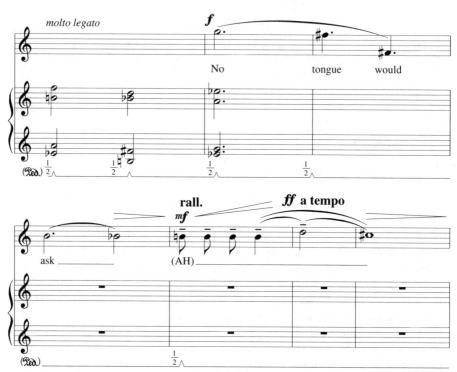

The composer consistently avoids the obvious: one would have expected the louder version to have the text, and the second one to be a wordless echo. Again the singer is left exposed for a further passage of highly-charged vocalizing, made more flexible by smooth triplets that are to be a feature of the last section of the piece. The piano's resonances are again the only accompaniment. Slow piano octaves have acciaccaturas preceding the notes in alternate hands, giving a fascinating bell-like effect. The voice has to place four more accented notes at a carefully plotted juncture, indicated by a dotted line. Quaver subdivisions will have to be counted out silently, so that it all works out perfectly. The voice actually enters at the fourth quaver of the 4/4 (or 2/2) bar: a rare moment of rhythmic complexity to keep the singer on her toes. Suddenly a violent change from triple *piano* to triple *forte* in the piano, begins a 'funeral dirge' in heavy treading chords at a new tempo of crotchet = 96. One presumes this to be even slower than the preceding *meno mosso*, preparing for the voice's final lament. The piano's right hand traces a poignant melody, which is then taken up by the singer, for the last line of text, beautifully set in the middle of the voice, for a most plangent tone-quality. The relentless tread of the piano's left-hand chords continue and fade (aided by the soft pedal) with a last fragment of right-hand melody at the very end.

This thoroughly engrossing piece should make a memorable impression, if placed carefully in a recital, preferably at the start of the second half. It could conceivably be performed with the singer accompanying herself at the keyboard, and, with that in mind, could combine very well with the Betsy Jolas piece in this book. Its controlled, internalized passion would make it suitable for a special ambience, such as a theatrical venue, or late-night event. It would make an excellent contrast to the Romantic song repertoire, and would go well before a major Austro-German cycle, or after something florid and fast-moving from earlier periods. A more cheerful and light-hearted piece will also be needed to follow it. American works would be suitable for this, including many in this volume. The composer herself studied in America with David del Tredici.

Epigrams
(1985)

Violet Archer (born 1913)
Text by David McCord

T III; M II
Baritone or tenor and piano
Duration *c*.8'

One of Canada's most distinguished and prolific senior figures, Violet Archer has written a good quantity of solo songs. Her music is not as widely known as it should be, and this short and extremely witty cycle is a gift for a performer: a most delightful addition to the male voice repertoire of light-hearted fare so often needed for recitals. A great deal of musical skill and variety is contained within its brief length, and the stylistic idiom is imme-diately attractive. Texts are taken from *The Pocket Book of Humorous Verse* by David McCord. The composer displays a fondness for bitonality and 'wrong-note' harmony, always used skilfully and to the point, never sounding ugly. Her natural aural refinement never deserts her. (One can think of other supposedly hilarious party-pieces where cheap tricks substi-tute for genuine wit and style, and performers leer and wink to distract attention from the music.) Quotations are also used to appropriate effect, and the vocal tessitura is finely judged for verbal clarity. Piano parts are extremely undemanding and would suit a beginner. They demonstrate how to gain the maximum effect with an economy of means. *Ossie* are given at the upper octave to suit the tenor range, so the piece is equally viable for both voices specified, and performers will relish the opportunities for some gently sardonic, highly civilized fun.

1. If the Man who Turnips Cries

This song features a sparse but telling piano part, with two distinctive types of material. Series of parallel bitonal thirds in each hand are featured before, after, and in between the vocal phrases, and, in contrast, the singer's lines are introduced and accompanied by staccato chugging rhythmic figures, all in the bass clef. The tempo marking is *Larghetto*, and the singer is given room to expand unfettered at high points. As always it is important to maintain a legato flow through a fast-moving text, and therefore essential not to take unnecessary breaths. For instance, the opening vocal phrase, at first within the motoric rhythm set by the piano, immediately broadens to the reiterated cry of 'Turnips', with a crescendo on the second of these. The shouted passage that follows, with pauses on each note, will actually be clearer without a large breath beforehand. The notes are written as in traditional Sprechstimme with crosses through their stems (Example 1). The

Ex.1 Archer

If a man who turn-ips cries Turn - ips turn - ips   turn - ips   cries.
(Cups hands around mouth and shouts)

singer is instructed to cup hands over his mouth in a theatrical gesture that will be very effective. Pitches are of course specified, and the most practical and usual way to ensure that there can be no confusion with normal singing, is to touch the notes lightly and glide off them immediately (trying not to slide past the next note in the series). A non-vibrato quality is the safest, with a direct and natural production. Many trained singers create difficulties by being reluctant to incorporate natural everyday sounds into their vocal apparatus. A useful trick is to imagine that, when uttering a cry, you are drawing the sound in, rather than pushing outwards. The feeling is as if making an involuntary reaction to a sudden dig in the ribs.

The whole of the last phrase should be sung in one span, resulting in firm resonance and control of the *fortissimo* 'father'. The voice part is enclosed by short piano solos, and there are just three morsels of text in which to project plenty of personality.

2. My Bishop's Eyes

Here the voice part is mainly unaccompanied (marked 'to be sung freely, like a chant'). The obvious ecclesiastical connection is emphasized by the use of the famous 'Old Hundredth' (All People that on Earth do Dwell) in the piano part throughout. This undergoes a hilarious series of modifications and reharmonizations: first in long spans, and then with false starts and unexpected modulations towards the end, veering finally into E flat (having started on the traditional base of G major) with a crazily sliding cadence, left unresolved by the sly introduction of a low E natural at the very last moment! The singer's incantations involve quasi-modal lines with close intervals that require careful tuning and even tone-quality: the words are amusingly apt for the tongue-in-cheek religiosity of the music. Melismas on key words need to be shaped expressively. A diminuendo at the end of a phrase on 'his' can move into falsetto very effectively. Dynamics must be sharply differentiated, especially at the end, where the singer rounds off the hymn tune, firmly intoning each pitch. He must take care to separate the last two words, as it is crucial to control the diminuendo on 'mine'.

3. Lord Clive

The piano part adopts a mock-classical motif here, with semiquaver turns followed by brief trills, accompanied by an oompah ostinato bass. The effect can loosely be described as 'wrong-note Mozart' in his military or Turkish mode. This brief movement requires precision of vocal delivery and careful timing of the shorter note-values, ensuring that they are part of the line. To sing such passages as these tidily, in natural parlando rhythms, is by no means easy. It is important not to rush the smaller syllables and to keep the pulse steady. The more declamatory closing paragraph, with its increasing emphasis on descending fourths, leads to the sudden blurting-out, in snarling *fortissimo*, of the words 'for being dead', marked 'senza rit.'. Deciding where to breathe is the problem: probably the best choice is just before the time signature changes to 6/4. It is especially important not to breathe before the final shout. Note-heads written as crosses here suggest a vehement non-legato, abandoning normal 'sung' tone. The 'd' consonants can encourage tightness of jaw and neck. Once engaged, these muscles must be released instantly. Moving directly from singing to speech is not as difficult as often supposed. A break for breath in between will create unnecessary problems and arrest momentum.

4. This House where once a Lawyer Dwelt

Here is yet another song consisting of just three well-contrasted vocal phrases. A mock dirge is set up in the piano part, with rhythmic chords over a very deep bass-line. Marked 'Largo Maestoso', the singer begins with a smooth and expressively descriptive phrase. When the singer reiterates 'Alas!', the upper octave is suggested as a tenor alternative. Mock solemnity is called for, and a mercurial shift of mood and pace follows immediately, for the ironic final comment, again with an upper *ossia*, at a swifter tempo. Considerable aplomb is needed to bring this off, and verbal clarity is imperative.

5. I Like to Quote

This is a charming waltz movement, the piano remaining in simple two-part counterpoint throughout, the left hand with a continual ostinato that shifts pitch at regular intervals. The movement is gentle and dreamy in character, marked 'sognando'. Such indications from the composer are enormously helpful to interpreters, often confirming their own intuitions. The voice floats lyrical phrases in praise of Romantic poets: the first, Keats; the second, Shelley (Example 2). Here the tenor version reaches a very high tessitura. Dynamics rise and fall naturally with the undulating lines. The punch-line is that the poet actually prefers the pithier elements of his own verse. For either voice, this involves a slow fade on the last note—the tenor's a high F. A smooth legato must be maintained, and the subtle chromatic inflections should seem effortlessly deft.

Ex.2 Archer

And oft - en I am caught by Shel - ley's tone,_____

6. The Bee Hive Inn

Bitonality is again a significant feature in this exuberant final song of the cycle, in which the singer takes the role of a drunken bee! Characteristics of baroque music are immediately apparent, with verbal and musical repetitions strongly featured. Pitching could be a little problematic, were it not for some helpful doublings in the piano accompaniment.

Fast-moving close blocks of chords in either hand, joined in off-beat couplets, convey a busy, buzzing effect in the piano's opening phrases. The marking is 'Allegretto gioioso', and the singer begins in high spirits, his second line rising up (again with higher alternatives for tenor—both doubled by the piano's left-hand octaves), until, at the climax, it splinters into merry laughter, which is notated rhythmically, but without pitches. Fanfare figures on the piano herald the next voice entry, which proceeds upwards in mock-Handelian fashion, accompanied, as previously, by conventional baroque figurations. Tonal ambiguities mean that the singer will be glad of the anchorage provided by strong bass octaves in the piano when the final peak is reached. Here the tenor has an exciting high B flat, and the last burst of laughter can be extended *ad libitum* according to histrionic abilities, not forgetting to leave enough energy for the last one. This must be indicated very clearly, as at the end of a cadenza, so that the pianist can catch it and place the final chord to best effect. 'Laughing' passages can fall wherever they will feel spontaneous, but basic contours should be observed as written. A manic effect is entirely appropriate, and pacing must not seem at all laboured. Pitches need not be calculated too precisely, but a few 'dummy runs' will help consolidate a basic approach and get breathing organized. 'H's should not be articulated consciously, but should happen naturally.

Such an enjoyable yet concise work should be extremely easy to programme in many different settings. It could provide an ideal contrast to a major cycle by Schumann or Schubert, or songs by Brahms or Beethoven, preferably mainly of a rapt and slow-paced nature. It would also go excellently with earlier music, especially something from the baroque period: Handel, Purcell, or Monteverdi perhaps. One of Poulenc's cycles, particularly *Le Bestiaire*, or some Ravel would be stylistically apt. However, it should not be juxtaposed directly with a work of extreme length, as this could create an imbalance. It would go best next to a mixed group of songs or arias, or a modestly scaled cycle of fairly simple lyricism. It makes a good end to a full recital as it is not at all taxing.

Five Songs of Crazy Jane
(1960)

Peter Aston (born 1938)
Text by W. B. Yeats

T III; M III
Unaccompanied soprano
Duration *c.*10′

An invigorating and thoroughly enjoyable showpiece, with strong elements of folksong, in elaborated and extended form, this dramatic *scena* deserves to be much better known. Audiences always respond most warmly to its strong-flavoured immediacy. Peter Aston has special experience in working with singers, especially in the field of choral music, and his understanding of the voice is already clearly evident in this, his first acknowledged work. Singing unaccompanied always brings special problems, particularly that of maintaining clean intonation. However, this music is basically tonal, and should not prove too daunting to the inexperienced. It should be noted that double barlines divide each song into sections, and this should be apparent in performance, helping to shape the interpretation.

'Crazy Jane', now an old hag, recalls the lusty passions of her youth, and reflects bitterly upon the cruel realities of passing time and spent beauty. The performer is given enormous scope for vocal acting and heavy characterization, although there should be no lapse into caricature for an exaggerated crone-like quality. An Irish accent, however, softening final consonants, will make a great difference to the authentic effect of the interpretation and it is certainly worth taking the trouble to get this right. The singer should read the poems aloud as a preparatory exercise. Contrary to belief, this piece was not actually written with the present writer in mind, although some later settings of poems from the same collection, for voice and ensemble, by Richard Rodney Bennett were indeed written to take advantage of the happy coincidence!

Although a skilled and versatile singer will make the most of the constantly varying moods and colours, a totally different kind of vocalist—such as a folk or jazz specialist—could also find this a good vehicle. A raw, unpolished sound is greatly preferable to an undernourished overpolite rendering. As familiarity with the notes develops, subtle rubato can be allowed to free the lines from undue rigidity, yet, as always with solo singing, an underlying pulse must still be felt, so that the music does not become shapeless. The ideal result is of a quasi-improvisatory freedom, the thoughts and emotions spontaneously expressed. The tessitura is rarely taxing, although there are just a few places where vowels may need some modification to avoid discomfort when singing high, and, in general, words are set skilfully.

1. I am of Ireland

A 'straight' folksong melody in G minor begins the cycle in relaxed and reflective mode. The composer's instruction is apt: 'With easy movement'. Some nice details of staccato and accent contribute to a natural delivery. This refrain is repeated after two very disparate verses, the last time as a hushed echo at the end. The verse material is more direct and warmly passionate, rhythms falling very flexibly. The repetitions of 'man' can be stressed very slightly, adding bounce to the line, whose springy quality is a joy to sing. The middle of the voice is a rewarding area for colouring the voice and encompassing a large range of dynamics. The composer judges his nuances expertly, and breath-spans, too, are well thought out. A good lung capacity will be a great advantage. Singing alone tends to expose the slightest wavering of tone or flagging of energy. Phrase-lengths are well varied, time signatures continually changing to produce a barless effect. The long central paragraph will need an organized phrasing scheme. The best places to breathe are after 'there' and 'head'. The crescendo through 'off' should not be interrupted. When there is a straight choice between musical and verbal priorities, the musical one usually turns out best. Unusual punctuation of words can even enhance their impact, as long as the music flows well and the singer is able to project the meaning convincingly. The refrain's second appearance is somewhat louder, and the second verse, a jigging dance, is faster and very different in character from the first. It features some delightful portrayals of instruments, deftly and accurately caught (Example 1). The snapped-off, accented 'cock'd a malicious eye' works perfectly too. Lingering use of the liquid consonants in the repeated

Ex. 1 Aston

'time runs on' will contribute to the drowsiness of the gradual winding-down which leads to the almost-whispered last refrain. It is good to aim for the most daringly thread-like *pianissimo* when singing alone, as it draws the audience into intimate contact with the performance.

2. Crazy Jane Grown old Looks at the Dancers

From now on, there are no key signatures, but modal versions of minor keys prevail, often unresolved at the end. Here, for instance, a restless, angry outburst in uneven quaver groupings is centred around E minor, with much use of the intervals of the melodic scale. The C naturals and C sharps need to be tuned especially well, and later on there is still more chromaticism, during which the singer must take care not to lose track of the pitch. The B natural forms a central point on which to focus, and this must always be kept bright and high. A repeated wide-ranging motif on 'love is like the lion's tooth' frames each brief verse of this short movement, which otherwise hurtles along impulsively, almost breathlessly. The text can almost be spat out: a comma given by the composer provides for a gasped intake at a particularly hectic moment. A somewhat stressed sound could even add to the dramatic effect but control has to be reasserted soon after, to make sure of landing safely on the held notes at the ends of phrases, which are very important in allowing some resonance to hang in the air. Successions of short syllables can easily become haphazard and arhythmic without a restraining pause or two. The swung accented duplets on 'coal-black' and 'strike him' should not be rushed. There is an opportunity to word-paint (and retune if necessary) on 'gleam' making good use of the 'l'. This puts the brakes on just in time for the 'Love' motif with its swirling melisma. Each piece of narrative has different music, yet they are all closely related in style. For the last verse the melody is extended still further, introducing some tripping dance figures in response to the text. Pulses and shapes undergo rapid changes in a heedless and almost intoxicating way. All through the last section, high Gs ring out like bells, and enough room must be found to float them into the head register, even in the little time allowed.

3. Those dancing days are gone

After the heady excitement of No. 2, Crazy Jane is found in a more confident mood for this strophic song in three verses, each followed by a rapt, shining refrain in 'E minor' with an enharmonic twist (Example 2). The pitches in this movement may give some problems as there are places where they shift quite far from the tonal centre before switching back again. The pivotal tied note before the refrain is absolutely crucial: it changes from C sharp to C natural for the last verse.

Marked 'Moderately, with a gentle, lilting rhythm', the music flows along with elastic phrasing, incorporating some rather pungent details along the way, although Jane remains in ebullient form throughout, wickedly relishing her discomfiting perceptions born of long experience. The radiantly high

Ex. 2 Aston

I car - ry the sun in a gol - den cup, The
moon _____ in a sil - ver bag. _____

tessitura in the second verse may make it difficult for the text to be audible, and enough time must be allowed for 'the children that he gave'. This is quite a tiring passage, and intonation and tone-quality could suffer if the singer attacks the words too strenuously, gripping so hard that the taut muscles prevent the sound from being placed high enough. This requires a real effort to keep the support low and the tone free. The refrain should be floated as ravishingly as possible in contrast to the more assertive vein of the verses, the last of which soars to A flat on 'sing' (not entirely comfortable at first) before an extremely tricky chromatic transition back to E minor. Throughout, dynamics are varied and all marked details make a great difference to the performance, as does an acute awareness of the sibilance of the refrain, especially on 'sun' and 'silver'.

4. Crazy Jane Talks with the Bishop

The briefest movement encapsulates a bizarre dialogue, in which Crazy Jane emerges defiant and self-justifying. The composer asks for it to be sung 'simply, like a folk tune', despite its somewhat unsavoury subject-matter. The characters should therefore not be acted too obviously. The Bishop could have a more detached air, with a minimum of vibrato. Shocking images can quite often have a stronger impact if sung clearly and unemotionally. Dynamics are gentle at first, and only as Jane warms to her theme is there an increase of volume, reaching an exultant *fortissimo* climax at the very end. A breathing pattern is not immediately apparent, and in view of the loudness of the last paragraph, there may be need to snatch air after 'stiff' and 'mansion'. It would be a pity to disturb the crescendo through the last syllable of 'excrement'; the final accented cadence will maintain power if breath is taken after the tenuto on 'whole', where there is plenty of time.

5. Three Things

A more surreal text, in which the dead bones of Crazy Jane recall memories of their former life, brings a return to the formal scheme of No. 3. Three different, but closely related, verses are divided by short refrain motifs, in this case two separate ones: the first after the opening line of each verse, and the second in the usual place of chorus. Both are reflective in character, and are in fact the only pieces of reported speech. The 'singing bones' are unexpectedly expressive: the movement is marked 'Passionately, with restless movement', and the singer will need to use all her imagination and sensitivity to arrive at a style of delivery which feels and sounds appropriate. 'White' tone would be suitable for the refrains, especially at the end, which fades away to nothing on B natural (the unresolved dominant of yet another 'E minor'). As before, the long notes that form a bridge between verse and refrain have to be tuned with extra care. Dotted rhythms contribute to the disturbed, desperately yearning effect, and there must be no loss of momentum. The refrains can be noticeably more relaxed with a gentle lilt. The composer's setting of the ecstatic and highly erotic penultimate line seems ideal, especially the *meno mosso* at 'stretch and yawn'. The final diminuendo 'a niente' will be made easier by closing early on to the 'n' of 'wind', and continuing this with half-closed lips, holding till the end of the breath

Consistency of the main tonal centres and rhythmic patterns give the cycle a cohesive quality, yet the music moves so effortlessly through a wealth of subtle modulations, that it all seems satisfyingly varied. It gives the interpreter a real chance to shine, demonstrating musicianship and flair. It will be particularly effective between contrasting works for voice and piano. A solo piece always comes as a refreshing change and shift of emphasis, and one as accessible as this is a real find. Other Yeats settings by earlier English composers such as Frank Bridge, would make a nice basis for a special programme, perhaps with some of the many works that have texts by James Joyce.

Banquo's Buried
(1982)
Cry Cock-a-Doodle-Doo!
(1989)
(The Witches' Song*)
(1990)

Alison Bauld (born 1944)
Text by Shakespeare

T III; M III
(Mezzo-)Soprano and piano
Duration 8' (No. 1), 5' (No. 2)

This composer's dramatic gifts are always evident in her work. Early professional experience as an actress in her native Australia, and an appetite for a wide range of cultural influences, especially the literary and visual art forms, equip her ideally to express herself with eloquence and flair. Although her music may appear relatively simple in its appearance on the page, it is highly disciplined and conceived with a very clear idea as to its interpretation, although she is keen to help a performance develop through the rehearsal period, and is not afraid to discard, adapt, and fine-tune details right up to the first performance. Her ear is extremely acute, but sometimes her notation gives ambiguities, which can easily be settled by live demonstration or tape. Hers is very much performers' music and full of immediacy and vitality.

This trilogy of vocal works sets Shakespeare, one of the composer's most potent influences. Her sense of the timing of declamatory verse is outstanding, as is her response to the myriad possibilities of verbal nuance and pitch inflection. She uses conventional notation in the main, but occasionally dispenses with time signatures for rapidly running passages of speaking or whispering.

'The Witches' Song' (from *Macbeth*) is for solo voice, and the other two pieces have highly dramatic and distinctive piano parts. 'Banquo's buried' sets Lady Macbeth's famous soliloqy, and 'Cry Cock-a-Doodle-Doo!' Ariel's song from *The Tempest*. They can each be performed separately, but, sung as a group, they complement each other admirably. 'The Witches' Song' requires the most virtuosity, written on three staves, conveying three

---

* In their most recent edition, these songs are published separately: *Banquo's Buried*, and *Cry Cock-a-Doodle-Doo!* and *The Witches' Song* together as *Two Shakespeare Songs*, all from Novello. *The Witches' Song* is discussed more fully under Technical IV, pp. 231–235.

different 'voices' and swift changes of timbre. 'Cry Cock-a-Doodle-Doo!' also has some role-playing and the singer has to sing into the piano in one section. 'Banquo's Buried' is a highly successful dramatic *scena* which invites staging, but also makes an exciting effect as a concert piece. It has already attained considerable popularity with young singers, who find it rewarding and enjoyable. It makes a splendid audition piece.

All three pieces employ different shadings of vocal utterance: speech effects, whispering, Sprechstimme, and even more subtle variations of groans, shrieks, and rasps where appropriate to the text. These are used sparingly, but to great effect in 'Banquo', slightly more in 'Cry Cock-a-Doodle-Doo!', and, for 'The Witches' Song', are exploited most tellingly. As always, these special effects are much easier to negotiate than others may imagine, and the main challenge in all three pieces is that of sustaining and controlling a smooth line in the middle of the vocal range. Bauld's music does not always sit easily in the higher reaches, or range around in a relaxed way, and often requires a rigorous approach to breath control and evenness, frequently focusing on close intervals in mid-stave. The music is therefore by no means as simple to perform as it may first appear. It amply repays the hard work needed to iron out any areas of vulnerability, and gain the freedom to react quickly in making the transitions between singing and speech. Printed scores are now available of all three pieces: *Banquo's Buried* is published separately, and *Cry Cock-a-Doodle-Doo!* and *The Witches' Song* are together in one volume, as *Two Shakespeare Songs* (Novello).

1. Banquo's Buried

The piece starts impressively, in strongly ritualistic style, with a 'processional' piano prelude, full of strong trills and series of fourths and fifths. A march-like chordal theme is stated, and this is to play a significant part throughout. Lady Macbeth makes a dramatic entry, with repeated B flats in carefully shaded dynamics. It should be noted that this composer often favours a breathy quality, especially in Sprechstimme, which makes an especially intense effect, but will affect dynamics, as the sound will be less penetrating than clear tones, so volume should be adjusted up accordingly. Rhythms are notated exactly, obeying the natural impulses of the dramatic outbursts, and glottal attacks on 'Out' are marked *sforzando*. Phrasing is crucial: despite the fragmented line, the performer should think and breathe in long spans, continuing the sense through. The music has great clarity and spaciousness in the metric 'processional' or 'bell-chiming' sequences, which are interrupted by asides in a free-running parlando. 'Why then, 'tis time to do it' is hissed in an intense whisper. The piano's bass octaves on A will help the singer with pitching the next sung phrase. Moving between speaking and singing can be problematic in this respect. For the contemptuous 'Fie, my Lord' sequence speech is entirely free and unnotated, but there is a particularly close transition into *fortissimo* singing, so the performer must plan breathing carefully. A breath before 'When' is the best choice, going directly into the sung note on E flat, but even this will require stamina, because of the percussive sounds in the text.

Another quick change of delivery brings reiterated low B flats: this should not be rushed, but a quasi-legato should be maintained, threatening and sonorous. The singer suddenly goes into a strange refrain; fey, distracted, and Ophelia-like (Example 1). This gives considerable licence to act with the

Ex. 1 Bauld

The Thane of Fife _ had a wife Where is she now

voice and produce a suitably mad sound, pallid and non-vibrato, landing breathlessly on the paused 'Now': the composer prefers a husky quality here—the weirder the better! The rhythm of this passage needs care, as it is is quite complex. Lady Macbeth suddenly comes back to reality in a scooped 'What?', Sprechstimme leading to normal singing. Hand gestures will be appropriate here in a staged version, but could also enhance a concert performance if not too greatly exaggerated. The composer's own instructions here are 'liberamente—free to spread, pause, stretch'. During the next 'free' passage, a hoarse quality will help the 'low rapid whisper' to be audible, since a loud piano trill is also competing for attention. Throughout the piece, grace-notes indicate phrases that are to be articulated as fast as possible. Timing is all-important in effecting the mercurial changes of mood and pace, and of modes of vocalizing. The verbal images become more horrific and bloodthirsty.

The singer must convey the sensuality of 'all the perfumes of Arabia': the 'm' and 'n' sounds will help with this, as will a crooning quality for the repeated 'Ohs' that grow naturally out of the phrase. As before, a breathing plan has to be worked out, as phrasing does not automatically suggest itself. Ideally there should be no breath before 'will not sweeten' but this requires considerable support, and a crescendo during the last note on 'hand' may make it difficult to sustain tone to the end. A snarling, loud whisper of 'Wash your hands' is potentially dangerous if forced, but sibilance in the text can be used to penetrating effect. A typical crescendo–diminuendo on 'pale' again requires vocal skill.

The refrain 'Banquo's Buried' is the work's most significant theme (and is to recur later). A ringing cantabile is called for. In a novel effect, the piano's notes fit in between the voice's, following close after each fanfare-like attack. Lady Macbeth's muttered 'To bed, to bed' needs care in differentiating singing from Sprechstimme. As always in the piece, note-values must be scrupulous: dotted notes make a subtle but crucial effect. Once again there is a stage whisper (a favourite gesture of this composer).

The music changes character considerably for the final section of the piece. This is almost entirely tonal and musically straightforward. The word 'Come' is reiterated in a seductive chant, with some beautiful lingering glissandos on the 'm's. Register problems may be encountered here, as they focus around E natural and F. A graceful, flowing melody unfolds, mainly in the middle range, and this will need to be controlled extremely well (Example 2). The piano provides a rapt, rocking accompaniment, breaking

Ex. 2 Bauld

off suddenly for a solo repeat of the striking, loud, ritualistic chords of the opening section. The flowing lullaby melody resumes, and the process is repeated. After the third repeat of the lullaby, in which the voice stops significantly before the word 'undone', the 'Banquo's buried' theme reappears in full. This must be performed in even more menacing style than before, ending with the contemptuously thrown away 'To bed', which now drops lower in the voice.

2. Cry Cock-A-Doodle-Doo!

Ariel's famed song from *The Tempest*: 'Come unto these yellow sands' is already familiar in settings by other contemporary composers including Tippett. Bauld's version bears close similarities to 'Banquo's Buried' in harmonies and pitch relationships, and is highly characteristic of her personal style. As with 'Banquo' tempos, moods, and articulations vary constantly. Ariel's singing is interrupted in between verses by a speech from Fernando, which provides great contrast. The singer must adopt a distinctive character and tone-quality for this passage. As usual, the composer employs a huge variety of vocal inflections covering the gradations between speech and song, and this time the inside of the piano is also used to great effect. Fast-running passages obey natural speech patterns, and it is helpful to practise by declaiming the Shakespeare first and then see how easily it fits the notation.

The piece starts with a soft refrain on vowel sounds and gentle humming, in long phrases, floating around the middle octave from middle C sharp upwards, ending with a whistle on low C sharp. This makes a lovely effect. The piano part is less soloistic than in 'Banquo'. Soft, high, dissonant chords introduce Ariel's aria which begins in a breathy Sprechstimme. Rhythms are clearly indicated, and glissandos, accents, and other expressive marks are used liberally. The composer responds acutely to the specific sounds of consonant groups. 'Foot it Featly' is marked staccato. Pitches here do not have to be as high as marked, but they should obey the contours indicated. The first actual sung note is 'Hark!' on C sharp, a recurring resonance—the composer's sense of pitch is also extremely acute. Perhaps surprisingly the dog's 'Bow-wow' is given a very low whispered tone, *subito piano*, and then repeated on sung C sharp grace-notes, marked 'breathy and very fast'. Rhythmic control is important here. Reactions must be quick, as the first sung phrase, consisting of the leaps of octave and ninth often favoured by the composer, accelerates into yet another characteristic piece of onomatopoeia for the cockerel. It is interesting to note the closeness to Tippett's version. The chromatic sliding line should be crowed non-vibrato, observing the written accents clearly.

A short motif in the bass-line of the piano heralds the arrival of Ferdinand. The singer should adopt a more forthright masculine tone, conjuring a commanding presence, clearly identifiable from Ariel's ethereal brightness. At Ferdinand's question, the piano repeats gently oscillating sequences of fourths and fifths and then stops. The sung phrase 'And sure it waits' is perhaps a little difficult to pitch, but the sonority of the held, pedalled chord in the piano should be a help. The following phrase fits exactly with the piano and must be counted out carefully. Similarly, the flowing *Allegro*, where the piano has arpeggios and the voice unpitched speech, has to be strictly rhythmic. There is a quick transition into sung tone on the word 'air' and this needs clarity. The voice then has a chance to shine in a rhapsodic 'aria', which just as suddenly peters out. Ferdinand listens intently, and the mysterious strains begin again. Once more the singer has to change roles for Ariel's wordless chant (Example 3). This is to be sung into the piano, across

141

the strings, while the pianist keeps the pedal down. It is therefore necessary to plan positioning carefully, so that the audience does not have an ungainly back view of the singer. The passage at least (and others which follow) should be memorized, and the angle of the piano should be such that the singer has to lean sideways, retaining contact with the audience, and avoiding long hair flopping over the face. The higher strings of the piano will yield the brightest resonance and clear vocal quality always draws out the best sound. The effect is most exciting, and well worth the effort to make posture adjustments work smoothly. The singer reverts to normal concert position for the start of the familiar ballad (marked by the composer as 'a melancholy sea shanty') 'Full Fathom Five', but at the 'sea change', appropriately, sings over the strings again. The song is in a basic A minor tonality, and must be sung very sweetly and winningly, with bell-like precision, always remembering the spirit-world to which Ariel belongs. Phrasing is a little difficult, as crescendos at the ends of lines prevent a relaxation at these natural points, so quick breaths have to be taken without losing momentum. Another 'normal' phrase is sung before the final series of bell-sounds. The last group of these go into Sprechstimme again and have to be projected into the piano. This means that they should be declaimed strongly, exploiting the prolonged 'ng's and accenting the 'D's to draw as much sound as possible from the piano. The piano's rocking chords gradually die on to a pause.

This short work is packed with detail and makes a perfect foil for the more overtly melodramatic world of 'Banquo's buried'. The characterization calls for a special subtlety and sensitivity from the singer, and the interpretation needs much prior thought and imagination. It would be a good idea to begin by speaking the lines unpitched. (See also final paragraph on p. 235.)

Childhood Fables for Grownups (Set 2)*
(1955–9)

Irving Fine (1914–62)
Text by Gertrude Norman

T III; M IV
Medium/low voice and piano
Duration *c*.7′

1. Two Worms

This song and its companion have considerable musical weight and sophis-
tication, despite the light-hearted subjects, and the accompaniments are
even more demanding technically than Set 1. Simpler melodic elements, as
found in the first set, are developed in a more advanced musical idiom, and
voice parts are a little more showy. However, generally speaking, the pianist
bears the brunt of the responsibility for the interpretation.

A key signature of A flat is given, but there is a modal E flat feeling to the
opening music. Appropriately there is considerable legato writing. The
piano's introduction, moving slinkily in mainly 6/8 time, sounds quite
atonal, dark, and mysterious. Elaborate shivering trill figures are to be an
important feature of the setting. These continue through the first verse, with
its sad picture of the lonely worm. The voice has poignant cantabile lines
over the piano's bass staccato arpeggios, creating a fascinating texture.
There are quite a few rhythmic traps for the singer, and it would be as well
to mark in beats, as the appearance can be deceptive.

The character of the music changes suddenly and the texture lightens at
the move into C major in 5/8 time. The piano has staccato chords, but the
voice must remain smooth and plaintive. This is not so easy with such
percussive consonants and uneven metre, but it is to be noted that there are
no accents. 'Rat' and 'cat' should be held for their full length. The 6/8 is
resumed, and the voice's lament ends in a throbbing melisma on 'loves'. The
squirming trill figures reappear momentarily in the piano's bass-line, as the
second worm is introduced. Singer and pianist will need to keep their wits
about them in a passage of irregular rhythms. A short piano solo recalls the
opening music, leading to a charming, happy *Allegretto*, in which lilting
6/8 rhythms are interrupted by 5/8s and 7/8s. Anyone who is accustomed to
the irregular beats found in more 'advanced' music, will know how useful
it can be to subdivide fives and sevens into combinations of three and two,
according to the natural sway of the music, and then mark the score this

* Set 1 is discussed under Technical II on pp. 52–55.

way. Conductors do of course work like this, but even here, it is much simpler to think in patterns of short and long beats than to count out every single quaver, especially in fast music. The usual way of indicating three subdivisions is with a triangle, and a plain beat (or 'two') has either a downward stroke or a mark similar to an inverted violin down-bow sign. One quickly gets used to letting the rhythms swing naturally, and the music will flow much more easily. In this final section, the elongated trills are contracted into bubbling triplet mordents. Breathing must be judged well: the best place to take air is after the second 'squirm', and it should not be necessary to breathe after 'wife'. Every opportunity should be taken to keep the music dancing along. A very jolly coda, compressing the material, builds to an exuberant finish, with the short squirling trills continuing on every beat.

2. The Duck and the Yak

A thoroughly captivating final song, packed with incident, and carrying a dizzying momentum that never lets up, but hurtles headlong to a confident close. It starts with a most substantial, extrovert piano solo that contains some pastiche baroque contrapuntal features, and ends with strongly accented chords, that even involve a third stave at the cadence. Immediately afterwards mechanical staccato triads introduce the voice's narrative. This is a classic patter number but very far from being strophic or straightforward in any way. Words, rhythms, and pitches abound with potential pitfalls, and slow practice of separate sections is essential. A first sight-reading is guaranteed to collapse in seconds!

The first (duck) stanza may seem simple enough, but then everything begins to go off at a tangent. It would be folly to become reliant on a basic 'rum-ti-tum-ti-tum' pattern, for, as soon as the complementary second (yak) verse starts, pulse and tonality shift abruptly to an elliptical E flat minor in which down-beats are never where one would expect (the 'quack, quack, quack' is a rallying-point, and very easy to interpret!). The piano's darting staccato arpeggios change to accompanying triads again for a declamatory cadence, where the last line of the verse is expanded by lengthening the notes and bringing in a 5/4 bar. A two-bar flourish including a 3/2 bar announces the next verse. These transitions between sections are crucial in impelling the music forward into a new metre. Now we have an extended verse in *alla breve*, which modulates skilfully from E flat, through chromatic accompanying chord progressions, and almost back to the home key of A minor, avoiding a full cadence. The voice is marked 'legato, espressivo' and has a welcome chance for some more 'romantic' singing, as well as a Handelian run at one point (Example 1). There is an exciting build from long low notes up to a climactic 'duck' on a penetrating high F. The dynamics are important: this note starts *forte*, fades quickly and then crescendos more slowly to a loud cut-off. Baroque fragments are heard in the piano under this. The music does not stop there but rushes on to a

Ex. 1 Fine

Don't you cry, don't you cry

a - las, a - lack!

rhetorical summing-up in crotchet triplets, which needs strong emphasis and a straight, cutting tone. A gentle, confidentially musing section gives the voice very simple statements, punctuated by successions of dry staccato chords. The singer's pitches consist of broken triads, like a muffled fanfare. The repeated 'Not at all's' strongly recall Britten's conversational word-setting. The low B flat has to be sustained firmly. Slow chords prepare for the final section, which takes off at a terrific gallop. (*Allegro vivace*, minim = 144.) Here the singer's diction will be thoroughly tested: distinguishing between 'auk' and 'hawk' at speed is no easy matter. Britten's vocal gestures are again called to mind in the continually accented separate attacks which constitute the voice's closing material. Much stamina will be needed, as every note must have searing intensity like a high trumpet. The 'alas, alack' very near the end does not carry accents, and so there is a last chance for a momentary contrast in mournful legato, before the final, piercing 'yak' on D sharp that ends the piece, again with the chords unresolved, lurking around A minor.

The whole cycle if performed complete is quite a *tour de force*, building to a grand climax with the final setting. There are stylistic features in common with both Stravinsky and Britten, but the vocal writing is more idiomatic than that of the former. Both these composers would provide a rich field from which to gather companion-pieces (Britten's *Winter Words* and Stravinsky's *Russian Songs* or 'The Owl and the Pussycat' leap to mind.) There are also other American pieces, such as the songs of Barber, Ives, or Copland that would accord well. The present volume contains several other 'children's' or 'animal' songs, but a complete contrast such as groups of Brahms or Liszt could also work. Russian song cycles (Shostakovich, Prokofiev, Mussorgsky) are especially suitable. Groups of young or student singers could even perform the work in relay, selecting individual songs for their needs. Each set makes a viable recital item, and the second pair in particular will make quite an impact in a standard recital.

Despondent Nonsenses
(1979)

Julian Grant (born 1960)
Text by Mervyn Peake

T III; M III
Medium/high voice and piano
Duration 8'

A perfectly proportioned miniature cycle of six songs, this should be very popular indeed with performers and audiences. It is not quite as simple to sing as may at first appear, because of the many subtleties of nuance and phrasing. Julian Grant's work is always a pleasure to encounter, and his special knowledge and experience in dramatic forms is a great asset to the impact of his vocal works. He already has several operatic successes to his credit, including some outstandingly imaginative works for young people. His musicality and sense of timing are never in doubt, and he captures the fantastical imagery of Mervyn Peake's mercurial poems ideally, responding alertly to all their many-layered allusions, alliterations, puns, and surreal 'word-music'. The musical idiom is attractive to both eye and ear, often neo-classic, with considerable rhythmic verve. Conventional notation is employed, and presentation is admirable.

Although young performers will undoubtedly relish this piece, the technical assurance and versatility of an experienced singer will also be shown to good advantage. Reliable intonation is certainly needed, especially in the close intervals, and the female voice's vulnerable register-change area is repeatedly exploited. It would be all too easy to use it as a superficial entertainment vehicle, with an approximate rendering, neglecting finer points of detail and emphasis, but a more rigorous approach will do it full justice.

The fourth and sixth songs are a little more substantial in scope, and in their vocal and musical demands, but the three tiny vignettes featuring fly, spider, and crocodile, are exquisitely apt, and should lie very naturally. It is a good idea to practise them slowly at first to make sure every minute detail is incorporated. The composer's own markings provide a helpful guide throughout. Piano parts are non-virtuoso, complementing the vocal lines with lively and clear-textured passagework. The constant witty interplay between performers means that enough rehearsal time must be allowed to produce a deceptively effortless result.

1. O here it is! And there it is!

The opening song immediately draws us into a magical world of mysticism and ironic humour. The 'fairy creature' is encapsulated most delightfully in dancing figures in 9/8 time; the voice part deliciously light and airy, with lines floating over a broad range, and loud and soft dynamics alternating. The piano part trips and swings its way infectiously through a continual *Allegro vivo*. There should be no vocal problems here. It is important to establish a deft, flicked staccato that is light and clear, holding the rhythms in perfect control. This will be needed at junctures all through the work, and, in the frequent elliptical phrase-lengths, the voice should seem as if it is speaking naturally. Too rich a vibrato should be avoided: everything should be fine-edged and precise, with extra volume attained by laser-like accuracy of placing rather than by increase of breath pressure.

The composer has set the words with the most acute sensitivity. The strong exclamation at the start will be the firmer if only a very shallow breath is taken before it. The soft legato phrase that follows should be extremely finely spun, with the text's more sibilant sounds contributing to the eerie effect. Later, the contrast between the staccato 'A thug it is' and the smoother 'and smug it is' must be brought out, with the help of the consonants. (The 'm' of 'smug' can be lengthened a little.) The nimble phrase on 'and like a floating pug' must not become too loud. Ideally the whole span should be taken in one breath, up to 'trees', as long as the speed is right. This will help intensify the *pianissimo* duplets that are the launching pad for the appropriately set 'soaring' with its surge to *forte*. The vowel on the rising sixth must be kept well forward, so that the singer is still well poised for the final phrase of 'with chilblains', sung in quasi-pathetic mood, and doubled by the piano's lower octave to droll effect.

2. O Little Fly

The symmetry of the verse here, in regular, alternating rhyming couplets, dictates the shape of this little song. A catchy tango rhythm spices it up, with syncopations, and lazily swung triplets neatly avoiding monotony. Meanwhile the piano has continuous whirring semiquavers, going back and forth over chromatic scales, moving from one part to another. Just one 3/8 bar interrupts the regular pulse for a moment, and this must be scrupulously observed; there is often a danger of inserting an involuntary extra beat. There are, as expected, some winning vocal touches, such as the glissando (marked 'caressando'—caressingly—the correct Italian spelling is actually *carezzando*) at the beginning. The only loud note is on 'fist' and occurs quite suddenly. After that the voice can remain fairly strong until the *subito pianissimo* at the end. Words can be slightly clipped where appropriate, making use of any sibilant or percussive sounds to tidy up note-endings. Glottal opening vowels are useful too. In contrast, slurred pairs of semiquavers may slide along more lazily. The rests in the line beginning 'for surely here' give the phrase a special piquancy. The tempo is quite steady

(*Andantino*) and the effect is all the better for not bring rushed. The last line is most enjoyable, affording a fleeting moment of 'cabaret' at the sudden *pianissimo* on 'mood'. The 'm' can be prolonged as smoulderingly as possible, but the tempo must not sag.

3. Little Spider

This insect portrait is even briefer than the previous one. It is much faster, and in a graceful lilting 12/8 metre. Contrasting with the piano's staccato introduction, the singer has four smooth one-bar phrases in a gentle swaying motion. The surreal text, with the made-up language evoking the world of the Jabberwocky, must be projected with utmost clarity, savouring the rhymes, puns, and alliterations. The heavy 'grieves' on low C sharp must be supported well, so that air does not seep out and cloud the tone. The voice should fall naturally down to a chest sound without extra throat pressure, but the 'e' vowel will need to have space: the rolled 'r' should help. The final throw-away line should be poised and delicate—the soft glissando up the octave to a staccato '-bly' ought to be very comfortable.

4. O Love! O Death! O Ecstasy!

This is a miniature aria, with long cantabile phrases followed by shorter parentheses. It needs fine technical control since it covers a considerable range of dramatic moods and colours. The parody element is particularly broad here, with the composer satirizing Second Viennese School gestures, such as leaping intervals and extremes of dynamic. The opening *ad libitum* line is almost Webern-like (Example 1). The *a piacere* gives the singer ample time to plot the rather difficult intervals, and gauge the upward glissando carefully. It is better not to articulate the 'E' of 'Ecstasy' in this instance, but to keep the line absolutely smooth and uninterrupted. Once the dirge-like *Adagio* begins (with heavy treading bass) the singer can produce a fuller tone (marked 'con intensità') in a manner suggesting suppressed agony. All the 'b's in 'rhubarb burning' should be defined clearly. In stark contrast to the preceding songs, there is room for expressive singing, but vibrato must be monitored to make pitches clear. The mournful sliding melisma on the second 'pity' may need extra care. For the second part, there is a change to sobbing, halting figures in the voice part. Despite a 'misterioso' marking, the tone should not be too breathy, as this may impair the focus of the following cantabile phrase. It is best to think through the successions of rests without breathing. The onomatapoeic setting of 'coughing' should work very well, (note the double rest). For the transition into legato the 'H' on 'Has' should

Ex. 1 Grant

be gentle (using the trick of making the German '-ch' sound instead of expelling air vigorously). The higher-placed 'i' vowels are a little awkward for female voices. The second *ad libitum* phrase is set with great flair: pauses must be fully exploited. The unpitched grace-note preceding 'noisily' invites a special effect, such as a low glottal 'rumble' on the 'n'. At the resumption of the tempo, close intervals must be very clean. The 'parlando a piacere' on 'her irritating wasp-like waist' should come out of the preceding legato without a break, with 'her' joined smoothly to the first syllable of 'irritating' as a neat springboard device. A swift breath should have been taken after 'passed'. The final cadence will need some attention. The glowing 'loves' on high G is no problem, but it requires skill to convert this *forte* into a sudden *pianissimo*, before closing on to a voiced '-ves' and then sustain 'it so' on the exposed E sharp and F sharp. Sopranos and especially mezzos will have to engage strong muscular support to keep transitions even and tone unwavering. This is by far the most difficult moment in the work. It will help to retain the light quality of the 'wasp-like waist' phrase, keeping the tone pliant and placed well forward. A non-vibrato for the last two notes may be the safest option for reliable tuning.

5. Crocodiles

Another fragment of great charm and wit, this has exceptionally long bars (18/4 and 16/4 respectively), for its two main bursts of narrative. Beats may need to be pencilled in while learning it, as, in the second of these, syllables are not always perfectly aligned under notes, even with the advantage of Grant's beautifully neat handwriting. These passages are marked 'meccanico', and this can be conveyed by a deliberately colourless tone-quality as well as by rhythmic rigidity. A quasi-non-vibrato delivery is appropriate for the characterization, keeping notes as long as possible, with consonant transitions very swift. The *forte* opening will need low muscular support to keep it steady. For the second phrase, the obvious breathing places are after 'hints' or 'thick', but a more interesting alternative is to take just one short breath before 'hide's', giving a special emphasis to the word. This leaves a better phrase-length to end, with a clear glottal separation on 'it', and enough time to make 'de trop' sufficiently telling. For the expressive fragments in between, there is scope for rapt and beautiful singing. Tenuto markings during 'or roses in a . . .' must be emphasized, and the timing of the *rallentando* is crucial. The mechanical quality returns immediately on the word 'bush'. At the end it is especially important to make the final change of tone absolutely clear. After the rhapsodic 'tender', there should be an abrupt return to 'crocodile voice' on 'bride's', which should have a cutting resonance to match the piano's sudden *fortissimo*.

6. An Old and Crumbling Parapet

The final song is the most ambitious of the cycle. A flea sits on a parapet, and is involved in an enigmatic moonlight dialogue with the poet. Three verses in 3/8 are well varied and full of sparkle. As in the earlier songs, staccato markings respond delicately to the text's syllabic structure, enabling the singer to snip off words with panache, or glide easily through smoother passages without any vocal difficulties. *Ad libitum* phrases begin and end the first verse, and natural parlando rhythms are used for parenthesis. Otherwise the rocking one-in-a-bar motion gives a delightful swing, and phrases flow easily over the voice's full compass. Rhythms are not always predictable though, and every sound has to be timed scrupulously (e.g. the subtle syncopation on 'And on its top'). There is a particularly rewarding swooping phrase, complete with downward glissando on 'and the moon uprose' (Example 2). For the second *ad libitum* passage, a delayed release of

Ex. 2 Grant

the 'l' of 'flea' is helpful, both for the tenuto accent, and for opening the vowel sound. The tongue should be kept close to the teeth, and it is better not to breathe in the pause. The second verse lurches forward into a *più mosso* for a section of dialogue in which diction must be foolproof. It is always worth making a special effort to convey question marks vocally: largely a matter of intense concentration and inner conviction. A reflective and nostalgic final verse features tiny nuances on 'ogres' and 'flopped' that must be perceived by the audience: this often means exaggeration. It is surprising how many small touches can go unnoticed. The verse should otherwise be very poised and still, with the most innocent and plain delivery of the final *pianissimo* 'paints', letting the piano's rippling accompaniment control the fading end. A most delectable climax to a rewarding piece.

The sheer enjoyability of this music is destined to win an audience's heart, and it could be placed in virtually any programme, as light (but not trivial) relief from more substantial recital fare. It would go very well alongside French or Italian music, and even more modernist British works. Excellent choices could be Poulenc's *Le Bestiaire*, Ravel's *Histoires naturelles*, or Chabrier's 'Animal songs', and other items involving birds and beasts in this book. Numbers from stage musicals could make up a lovely late-night cabaret-style programme. It would also be ideal for a 'poetry and music' evening. Its modest scale and immediacy makes it suitable to begin or end a recital-half, and not be buried in the middle.

A chamber instrumental version of these songs is also available.

Fatal Harmony
(1993)

Piers Hellawell (born 1956)
Text by Andrew Marvell

T III; M V
Solo voice (high)
Duration *c*.3'

This is a brief but delightfully lyrical setting of a much-loved poem. It makes a lovely showpiece for a singer of strong musical gifts, and a fine sense of relative pitch. The vocal writing is in long spans and moves in decorative figures for much of the time. The music is divided into three sections, and the composer envisages two different ways of presenting the piece: either in its entirety, or with each section interspersed with other works. Each 'verse' consists of fifteen bars, based on similar material, and the piece is really an elaborate form of 'strophic' song. It begins and ends on E (in the case of the middle verse only, it cadences on the lower octave) and has a strong tonal focus, despite many chromatic and enharmonic diversions.

Though written for soprano, it seems equally well suited to a mezzo (the highest note is G sharp) or light tenor voice, and the latter will have the advantage in maintaining clear diction through the higher passagework.

The composer's note provides two contrasting aspects of interpretation for a soprano version: first, that the singer is celebrating her own attributes, and alternatively (suggested by the singer for whom it was written, Victoria McLaughlin) that she is musing on her own vocal art, referring to her voice ('she') as a sort of *alter ego*. Male singers will of course have less problems feeling a direct identification with the text in the more traditional way, as a hymn to the beloved. However, specific sexual identity can often seem irrelevant in the world of poetry and art song, as opposed to the more obviously defined role-playing found in opera.

It will be a tremendous advantage for the singer to be able to develop some kind of aural orientation, by dint of assiduous practice. It helps to memorize the vocal feel of a handful of the pitches which recur most often. The 'tonic' of E is the most important of course, and it anchors the whole piece. There are whole-tone scale passages, and a clear impression of an underlying melodic minor scale, with the sharpened leading-note of D sharp given special emphasis. In particular, the flattened dominant of B flat, and its crucial tritone interval with the tonic E, is a constant feature. If this can be focused securely, the pitch framework will stay in place through the chromatic weavings.

The basic tempo is crotchet = 54, but with rubato, and the singer should keep the pulse swinging along, despite the natural freedom and flexibility that will come from physical enjoyment of the shapely lines.

Notation is bold and clear, and the music is barred conventionally, mostly in 3/4 or 4/4, with occasional 7/8 bars. In fact the barring scheme is absolutely identical in all three sections. Dynamics are placed below the text, which means that it is easy to miss them as the eye travels up, incorporating first the syllable and then the pitch. For practical purposes it is better to have them above the vocal line, where they can be read and assimilated along with everything else. Phrasing is all-important, and wrong decisions about breathing places could have unfortunate consequences, throwing whole paragraphs out of line. It is always best to aim for broad spans, making use of technique and training, and allowing support muscles to work properly.

The ideal place to take a breath in the opening sentence is before 'love'. The next choice is a little less obvious, but an unhurried intake just after 'enemy' works well, as long as the restart on 'in' is gentle and unaccented. The lines arch and undulate naturally, and dynamics fluctuate accordingly, intensifying as the tessitura rises. A luxuriant and seamless legato should prevail, except for a few contrasting moments of dancing staccato, which are particularly good to sing. These immediately provide different breathing opportunities, which may go against the text, but preserve the rhythmic impetus. An extra buoyancy is given to the line if there is no real break after 'agree'. It makes a witty musical and verbal point too, if there is a join to the first 'joining', breathing at the rest. After the radiant soaring to 'fatal harmony', it would be a pity to disturb the graceful swoop down an octave. Breath can be snatched neatly after the staccato 'that'. This also has the advantage of clarifying the 'wh' of 'while' at the beginning of the light repetitive staccato figure (Example 1). Ideally the singer should take the remainder of the sentence in one span, as far as 'bind', but this is quite a tall order. There is perhaps just enough time to take a shallow breath before 'my', but the louder dynamic at the end is crucial, and it is better to take a breath in the gap between the two percussive consonants, after 'heart', rather than risk a loss of power on the melisma on 'bind'. Again this has the effect of intensifying the consonant of 'does'. In the echoing, bird-like repetitions of 'she with her voice' each note, however short, must have a

Ex. 1 Hellawell

clear pitch centre and be part of the legato. The final chance for a breath in section 1 is an easier one: a *ritenuto* as the word 'captivate' is repeated, confirms that to separate the two will emphasize the coming cadence very effectively and allow for considerable slowing up according to the composer's expressed wish. The 'n' of 'mind' can be elongated, and this will help to keep the final E in tune.

The second section is even more varied rhythmically. It features some delicate triplet semiquavers, and two upward-running scales, one staccato, the other a septuplet gliding up to a *pianissimo* high G. For this melisma on the word 'hair' it is best to treat it as a single vowel ('eh') rather than attempt to articulate the triphthong. Ideally the first two lines should divide into three phrases of three bars each, but if the staccato run needs more volume, a quick extra breath could be taken after 'itself'. There is of course a short break after the first 'breaking' (another in-joke), but a deep breath on either side of just one word is to be avoided. The composer's comma after 'hair' signifies a noticeable gap. More light staccato–parlando follows in the second half of this section. Here the ideal breathing places are after 'slave' and the first 'fetters'. Baroque rhythmic gestures and Scotch snaps give the music added panache, and grace-notes further enliven the rhythm. The lovely smooth cadence contrasts with its light staccato approach. The only problematic corner could be the somewhat high-lying 'invisibly', which leaves little room for opening the fast 'i' vowels.

Many of the rhythmic features of the first two segments occur again in the 'finale', which begins legato, exactly as section 2, but at a quieter level. The fanfare-like staccato figures on 'fighting' and 'victory' are aptly imagined, as is the descending staccato run on 'hang' (another piece of word-painting). The first breath should be taken after 'plain', and this also helps the articulation of the following 'where'. In this section the music is less continuous, and rests determine other phrases. Interestingly, the composer has made small vertical marks: the first to indicate a glottal start on 'is' in mid-phrase rather than a breath although a short one could be snatched in an emergency, especially in an unfavourably dry acoustic. The restart must be poised, however. Throughout the piece, quintuplets add a suppleness to the lines, and they should not be at all metronomic. In the *sotto voce* phrase, the syllabic distribution of the words 'who has the advantage' is not entirely clear. It seems that '-van' should have the first two semiquavers of the group of four, and then '-tage' should continue until 'both' (which is clearly written). 'Th'ad-' has a single note. This is a fairly long phrase, and it may be difficult to manipulate all its details without running out of steam for the important crescendo. However, it is worth making a special effort to keep it all in one breath, since the music curves and flows so naturally. If absolutely necessary, a breath can be taken after 'eyes'. Dynamics are very important for the final two lines. They are basically quiet, but there is a sudden *mezzo-forte* for 'and all my forces' (another 'fanfare'). At the end of the penultimate phrase comes another of the small vertical marks. This seems to be more of a comma, and the singer should pause just long enough to make it obvious that the work is about to enter its last phrase. The final cadence is most beautiful, and there is plenty of time to place the *ritenuto* (the composer likes this to be drawn out luxuriantly), fading gradually on to a luminous E, and closing to 'n' on 'sun' to prolong the diminuendo.

The sectional version of this attractive piece will work particularly well if the intervening items are instrumental rather than vocal, either chamber ensemble or solo instruments, especially winds. Choral pieces could also be interspersed, either, ideally, English madrigals or Tudor church music, or work of the English Romantics. As a single piece, the possibilities for companion pieces are almost endless. It could form part of a 'Music in Miniature' sequence, including songs for voice and one other instrument: Vaughan Williams's 'Along the Field' for voice and violin, for instance, or Holst's *Four Songs* for voice and violin. Other songs which refer to the art of the singer would be appropriate, such as Warlock's 'To the Memory of a Great Singer'. There are of course a great many songs that celebrate the art of music, from Purcell and Schubert to modern composers. In a programme for solo voice only, contrasting works by Cage or Berio (*Sequenza*), or the Rainier and Lefanu pieces recommended in this volume could surround it, and, if tape facilities are available, the Simon Emmerson work would be a happy choice.

154

Altra Risposta
(1989)

Bjørn Kruse (born 1946)
Text by Quasimodo (in Italian)

T III; M III
Mezzo-soprano and piano
Duration *c.*7'

A vibrant and haunting one-movement dramatic *scena* which exploits the natural glowing colours of the female voice, this is an especially happy discovery, and thoroughly deserves to be taken up by young performers. Bjørn Kruse, one of the middle generation of Norwegian composers (he was actually born in England), is extraordinarily versatile, with first-hand experience of jazz and popular music, and the widest possible range of musical sympathies. His awareness of practicalities and of the desirability of performer-satisfaction is always evident, and there is meticulous attention to detail, informed by innate musicianship, in an attractively presented score. Ritual chanting or declamatory parlando vocal sections alternate with more wide-ranging cantabile lines. Repeated note-groups and patterns are strongly featured in the piano part in particular. Toccata-like passage-work gives an impression of springy energy and drive, with accents being used to excellent effect. The mainly conventional notation gives way at times to *ad libitum* passages which allow greater freedom of expression, often leaving the voice alone in a free recitative. However, a *perpetuum mobile* feeling binds the whole together, and changes of mood, pace, and metre seem to happen naturally with the text. So many repetitions help greatly to promote confidence in pitching, and tonal centres are for the most part clearly identifiable, anchored by the piano's bass line.

This is a piece where some advance work on the score will pay dividends. Careful marking-out of beats through the complex divisions of note-groups will save a lot of rehearsal time, as will some detailed attention to the elision of vowels. This is always of crucial importance when singing in Italian, where maintaining a legato is made relatively easy, but prepositions and clusters of short vowels need to run smoothly and sound natural, avoiding any artificially imposed rhythmic organization. The singer is given plenty of space to place sounds perfectly in tune and to savour individual resonances with a special sensitivity.

The violent images of despair and yearning in the text are matched by music of great vitality and impetus. The singer is given ample scope to project and portray a proliferation of changing moods. After a powerful, virtuosic piano solo, the music suddenly quietens for the voice's entry on repeated mid-stave Gs. The tone must immediately register firmness in a gradual crescendo, penetrating the piano's texture of intricate triple-time counterpoint. The voice declaims a series of rhetorical phrases, mainly in middle voice, in which D flats recur as central points of resonance and tuning, and the lines gradually expand into wide intervals, with octaves leaping upward that are especially good to sing (Example 1). After the quiet parlando 'Ma non

Ex. 1 Kruse

accade nulla' ('but nothing happens') the piano has some more toccata-like bursts of action, punctuated only by a quietly intoned vocal phrase on a monotone, in free rhythm, hushed and reflective. The piano propels the music along until the singer's next loud outburst, describing a vision of repulsive spiders hanging from golden webs. Repeated high Gs here could result in a somewhat steely quality, but this could be well in keeping with the image of the text. The piano ends this section with another dynamic solo, suddenly dying down at the end. Now the singer has a complete change of mood, in a gentle recitative, written in space-time notation: that is, without note-stems, values, or rests, but spaced according to rough proportions, so that the pitches can be placed flexibly according to interpretative intuition. This passage should not be hurried, and it is punctuated with commas to emphasize this. In the following section, the voice ceases its restless reiterations, and has a looser, less insistent paragraph of recitative-like fragments through which a flowing legato should be maintained. Gradually, the lines become more melismatic (and satisfying to sing) while the piano has patterns of repeated notes, used to gently pointillistic effect (Example 2). It is interesting to reflect upon the fact that a harpsichord could also be highly effective in this piece, and of course, gestures from earlier keyboard styles are readily apparent throughout the piece. Use of the piano as a sustaining instrument is not so frequent. The piano's texture is further enlivened by grace-note groups before beats, and the voice part now

156

Ex. 2 Kruse

Nell'- a - - ri - a ___ on - da di suo - ni e a - mo - re

descends into a lower tessitura. The low As should not be too quiet in this
context, since the piano part, in the same register, could cover them, but a
darker tone-quality will be appropriate. As ever, quiet dynamics should
provide an opportunity to intensify consonants and ensure audibility. The
piano part calms into arpeggio figures. The singer may experience some
difficulty with the leap down a minor seventh on the second syllable of
'affondo': this covers a potentially vulnerable area of register adjustment,
and will need skill in achieving a perfect join.

The music becomes freer, with light piano arpeggios repeated *ad libitum*
beneath the singer's statements, which again fall into chant-like successions
of repeated notes, eventually descending to a long-held cadence, left unaccompanied. After this the piano has a gentle arpeggiated transition into
the final section, which resumes the opening tempo (crotchet = 72–76),
and also features the accented toccata figures heard earlier. This time they
are almost immediately broken off for an extended vocal solo, in free
notation, and punctuated by commas, as before, but developed over a much
wider range, and, once again, accompanied only by a sustained chord. This
gives the soloist a tremendous opportunity to make a poignant effect,
carefully monitoring the quality of each pitch, giving scrupulous attention
to intonation and evenness, and leaning on important syllables, guided by
the tenuto marks provided. Rhythm should be entirely free of regular metre,
so that the thoughts flow spontaneously. The mood is one of anguish, and
intensity must not flag despite the lack of formal pulse. Thereafter the voice–
piano relationship resumes in a similar manner as at the beginning, the
singer playing a strictly rhythmic declamatory role, supported by motoric
figures in the piano's left hand. This lasts for only a short while, as the
piano floats upwards, a triplet figuration with cross-rhythmed accents now
used impressionistically as a pedalled texture, *pianissimo*, through which
the singer has a second freely notated passage of extraordinary beauty, a
mirror image of the first in tessitura and dynamics. This rises to a glowing
repeated high G, and then gently descends to a more inward mood as the
piano stops.

The work ends with two poised, eloquent phrases where the utmost
concentration and control will be needed. The drama is concluded in an
atmosphere of awed mystery and contemplation, still equivocal and unresolved. Both voice and piano end with plain, unadorned lines (including a
brief, hushed parenthesis in free time for the singer), and a question mark
hovers in the air, as the singer ends *mezzo-piano* on middle F, while the
piano fades and winds down into silence.

This impressive and colourful piece is certain to be widely admired for its attractive sonorities, lively piano part, and idiomatic use of the female voice. Baroque features in the keyboard-writing tempt one to set it in a programme of earlier music. Monteverdi would be the obviously appropriate companion, but other early Italian composers would complement it well—a selection of *arie antiche* could be ideal. As for other modern pieces, Dallapiccola, Henze, and Britten spring to mind. Indeed, any cantata built on classical lines, old or new, would be a good choice for the opposite half of a programme.

As a complete contrast, some light-hearted miniatures could find their perfect foil in this wonderfully spontaneous and cohesive work, which is a gift to any singer with a natural sense of drama and a sensitivity to language.

Requiem Sequence (1971)

John McCabe (born 1939)
Text from the Requiem Mass (in Latin)

T III; M IV
Soprano and piano
Duration *c*.12′

This work, by one of our most versatile and gifted composers, also a superb pianist, was written in memory of Sir John Barbirolli and Alan Rawsthorne. It is simple in structure and highly practical to perform. As would be expected, the keyboard effects are particularly striking, and an ideal balance is achieved between a suitably liturgical atmosphere and the immediacy of impact in concert performance. An Italianized pronunciation of the Latin text, as most commonly used for concert purposes, is appropriate here. The cycle's basic tessitura, concentrating on the upper middle range, could expose any vulnerability in keeping a steady line and pitch, but will also prove useful in training to acquire these, especially with regard to preserving an even legato between registers. For a high-lying voice, such as a coloratura soprano, the piece should be immediately comfortable, but the darker tones of the lyric voice, with a firm lower range, will be heard to advantage in the faster-moving sections. Rhythms are frequently exhilarating, but will need careful work. There is a great deal of contrast in mood and accent, even including a brief passage of declamatory Sprechstimme. The repeated use of a plainchant idiom gives rhythmic flexibility, while the distinctive harmonic implications require the singer to exercise control of intonation, at the same time maintaining some lengthy, raptly flowing lines in slow tempos. She then has to switch quite suddenly to a series of exuberant *scherzando* fragments of irregular rhythms that come thick and fast, requiring extremely quick reactions—a sustained exercise in projection and agility.

The cycle is most rewarding to perform, full of energy and rather more variety than is often found in settings of these words. The composer has always envisaged an eventual orchestral version of the work, and many of the warmer sonorities readily invite this. There should be no problems of balnce between voice and piano. The keyboard-writing is admirably translucent and registers are arranged judiciously to provide clear textures throughout. The work has a radiant, spell-binding quality to which an audience instantly responds.

The plainsong opening needs scrupulous tuning, with vibrato well under control, yet not eliminated completely. A clear but brightly glowing tone is preferable to a disembodied boyish sound. Smoothness and simplicity are essential. The opening phrase patterns are to recur throughout the work, and they need to be anchored well in the voice. It is worth spending time to acquire the appropriate tone-colour, preserving a sinewy flexibility that can adapt to the most meticulously observed dynamics. The basic melody undulates gently, alternating duplets and triplets, the line rising and falling quite naturally (Example 1). Rhythms here can be interpreted in a relaxed fashion. The composer uses the now-accepted convention of marking 'free' passages with a cross instead of a time signature, giving a greater interpretative freedom to the performers. The sudden arrival of a strict tempo is thus all the more effective, at the *Movendo* of 'Te decet hymnus'. This should be sung forthrightly, with a direct expressiveness, in contrast to the contemplative poise of the opening section. The calm plainchant then returns, interspersed with rhythmic flourishes, where singer and piano must co-ordinate carefully. A nervous energy is generated in the 'Hostias' (*Andantino*), and the piano part becomes notably busier. The singer must be assiduous in counting beats and their subdivisions precisely. An element of physical tension could even be appropriate at this point, accentuated by the

Ex 1. McCabe

con moto ♩ = 80

mp   *liberamente*

Re - qui-em, ___   re - qui-em ___ ae-ter - nam   do-na e-is Do - mi-ne:

frequently high tessitura, which may contribute to an almost manic, but never uncontrolled, effect. In this, the Italianate syllables should also be a help in projecting a dramatic and fearful quality.

The 'Kyrie' needs a beautifully even legato, the piano chords gently pulsating in syncopation. Even the subtlest dynamics should be followed with care. Some experience with the additive rhythms found in Messiaen's song cycles would prove a positive advantage here. The final, whispered 'Kyrie' can be half-voiced, pitched low, and inflected the way it would naturally fall.

The fiery 'Sanctus' forms the work's central focus. The soprano is propelled headlong through a series of tricky rhythms, timing each attack perfectly, so that accents, rhythmic groupings, and syllables are all clearly defined and the music swings along spontaneously and without hesitation. Panache and rhythmic discipline will be far easier to achieve if breaths are kept to a minimum. It will be helpful to place 'triangles' over the triple beats. The word 'Sabaoth', suddenly spoken 'normally' in the midst of all this, is highly effective. The 'Pleni sunt coeli' section now provides a further test of vocal steadiness, this time in a lower range, perhaps requiring some special work to keep each note firmly centred. Some loud 'Hosannas' break out thrillingly—also in a somewhat awkward register; the singer should be careful not to force the accents. The 'Benedictus' has an unexpectedly sprightly tempo, and dramatic tension continues to build, until some high-lying semitones are hammered out almost like brass fanfares. A bravura flourish in the piano gives a momentary respite from the singer's task of negotiating jagged rhythms in exact co-ordination with the accompaniment. It is crucial not to lose volume or impetus in the 'Libera animas'. The *forte* must be maintained to the end of the passage, on 'lacu'. Some even spikier rhythms are reiterated at the start of the work's most challenging section. The piano begins a build-up of suppressed tension, proceeding with the voice, in nervous fits and starts, almost spluttering in effect (Example 2). It is helpful for the singer to listen to the piano's left hand. These are exciting passages to perform and listen to, and their vitality is palpable, with notes almost seeming to tumble over themselves. Relief comes as the singer reaches a spectacular high cadenza for the final 'Ne cadant in obscurum', and the music gradually unwinds itself after this bout of violent activity.

The eerie effect of the sudden change to pitched Sprechstimme on 'Sed signifer sanctus Michael' is most telling. Ideally, this should flow directly into the normally sung notes which follow, with no perceptible break. A highish, rhythmic coda, almost identical to the end of the 'Hostias', leads to a welcome rest for the singer, as the piano prepares the way for the 'Agnus Dei'. This final section returns to the calmer atmosphere of the opening and of the 'Kyrie'. Again, a velvety smoothness of tone is called for, keeping a firm grip on ensemble with the piano, especially the left hand. There may be some initial trouble with counting rhythms here, especially at the 'Qui tollis' entry. The soprano rises to a radiant high G on the last syllable of

Ex. 2 McCabe

'Requiem', which may not be easy to poise at first. Some melismatic decorations are flattering to the voice—at the second of these, the soprano has to
catch the top note of the piano's split chord, entering cleanly and effortlessly. Here the vocal lines involve some even wider leaps than before and
these are grateful to sing (Example 3). As the opening words of the 'Requiem' are repeated, a gentle, free-flowing line is maintained, with alternating
triplets and duplets as before. This time, strict notation is used, and voice
and piano must take care in co-ordinating. The very last notes on '-is' of 'eis'
will probably need some work before they sit easily in the voice, and the

Ex. 3 McCabe

* soprano comes in precisely with the top note of the arpeggio.

singer can let go of the throat, neck, and tongue muscles and let the sound float spaciously. The choice of register, and the slow diminuendo contribute to the task. It is particularly important not to overprepare the 's' at the end, and to be aware of the need to avoid constriction at this point. A lovely feeling of serenity is reached at the end of this outstandingly attractive work.

Requiem Sequence makes a particularly fine opening to a concert, immediately focusing the audience's attention, and inducing a quiet concentration. It goes well in a mixed recital, especially next to some Haydn or Schubert. A Debussy cycle in the opposite half of the programme would make a perfect foil. It is also, of course, eminently suitable for a recital of sacred music in a church setting. This is an invaluable piece for any soprano's repertoire: its difficulties are easily solved with care and practice, and it is always received with exceptional warmth by many different kinds of audience.

Prelude 8
(1981)

Edward McGuire (born 1948)
Text by the composer

T III; M III
Tenor and tape delay
Duration *c*.10′

The Scottish composer Edward McGuire has long been a personal favourite. An innate musicality and thoroughly original approach make his work consistently fascinating, full of surprises. Endearingly idealistic and politically committed, he always seems able to produce something fresh and memorable, drawing on an extraordinarily diverse range of influences from many cultures. A clarity of utterance is his special gift, and this is often spiced with a droll and distinctive sense of humour. Yet his work remains inherently Scottish in flavour. His experience and knowledge of folk music (he plays in the band 'The Whistlebinkies') is integrated perfectly with his straight classical style, and his vocal works over the years provide a rich choice of material for the enterprising singer. His natural flair is

complemented by meticulous attention to detail and exemplary consideration for the performer. Practicalities are always taken care of, and his scores
are a pleasure to look at. His handwriting, in both music and words, is
ideally bold and neat, and he often adds attractive drawings and decorative
motifs. His unassuming artistry and easy command deserve to be valued
much more widely.

It is a special pleasure to find a relatively simple piece involving electronics,
in this case a straightforward 'tape loop', making a delightful effect with
economy of means. Commissoned by Paul Hindmarsh, the work is ideal for
a church or similar building, where its resonances will be enhanced by a
spacious acoustic. It is also a finely judged example of writing for tenor, as
distinct from soprano.

The composer also suggests that three live tenors may be used for an
alternative version. In the light of today's sport-influenced vogue for tenors
in triplicate, this seems an excellent idea. Vocal timbres will have to be very
well matched of course. There is a decidedly ecclesiastical feel to the piece,
especially at the beginning and end. Now that Gregorian chant has suddenly
become popular, this is yet another reason why the piece should prove
highly successful with performer(s) and audiences.

Since the work was written, major technological advances have meant
that reel-to-reel tape is now rarely used. It is therefore appropriate for
modern digital and DAT equipment to be substituted for the machines
envisaged here, saving time and space. The live voice is recorded and played
back immediately at intervals of 1″ and 8″, creating a mosaic of overlapping
sounds. Typically, the composer's technical instructions and diagram in the
front of the score are clear and practical, showing the placing of speakers,
tape machines, and microphones. A technician will of course be needed to
operate and control this equipment. Volume has to be monitored throughout, so that the singer's sound matches that of the recorded versions. A
person with the relevant experience will easily be able to adapt the arrange-
ment to the particular venue.

The tenor soloist must be aware that every single sound he utters will be
re-examined twice more; extraneous noises have therefore to be avoided
assiduously. Quite apart from musical inaccuracies and vocal mishaps, even
a surreptitious throat-clearing or fumbled page-turn may reappear with
embarrassing clarity! Veterans of more ambitious electronic music occasions give hilarious accounts of performances ruined by perpetual
reverberations of unfortunate accidents, such as the dropping of equipment!

A light youthful-sounding tenor (or tenors, in the case of the all-live
version) will be well suited to this work. Tone must be clear and tuning
impeccable. Rhythmic accuracy, including maintenance of a steady pulse
and careful observance of rests is absolutely crucial. As when singing a
round (for this is in fact a highly elaborate way of beginning one), the gaps
between phrases have great significance. Harmonies are dependent upon

clean negotiation of intervals, although the tonality is firmly based on a tonic of F and its minor modal version, and the same notes constantly recur. Pitching should not therefore cause any problems, and there are no extremes of tessitura, so a wide range of tone-colours can be achieved without strain, and the voice is not taxed by virtuoso feats. Accents and dynamics have to be observed strictly so that they are clearly discernible in each version. The effect of the layered voices swirling round and interweaving in kaleidoscopic patterns is very exciting. The opening and closing sections involve some long-drawn-out notes that require good breath control.

The text, by the composer, consists of some evocative pattering chants in semiquavers ('play another title', 'being in a time of decay', 'keep on calling', 'death-defying', etc.). These occur in their full form in the penultimate section of the five blocks of different, yet closely related, material, that make up the work. Looking back one discovers that all the components of these fragments have been deconstructed and stripped down to phonetics, to form the text for the rest of the piece. This material is manipulated most deftly and imaginatively, the multiple repeats emphasizing syllabic details.

The piece begins on a monotone middle F, with long vowel sounds oozing and merging, until they gradually close on to 'mm'. The full span of dynamics from triple *piano* to *fortissimo* is incorporated, and the *senza vibrato* marking is a salutary warning against allowing the tone to judder. This test of control and nerve is perhaps best placed thus early in the piece, while the singer is fresh. Relief comes quickly, freeing the voice for a series of graceful intervallic motifs. These carry a mixture of accents as well as grace-notes, staccato, and glissando, all of which make an arresting effect in their undulating layers. The first two involve a very sudden diminuendo from *forte* to *pianissimo* and *piano* as the voice rises (Example 1) and the composer marks the upper notes 'head voice', so that a change of quality is inbuilt. Syllables are predominantly smooth and mellifluous: 'ba-oo-ah', 'long', 'leng', 'lang', etc. Characteristic rhythmic features, including Scotch snaps give bounce to the lines, and liquid consonants, especially 'ng', can be lingered upon and savoured. (I am reminded particularly of a similar use of phonetics in 'Sing Lullaby' by Peter Wiegold—a haunting work for soprano and double bass, based on fragments of traditional, especially Scots lullabies.) Dynamics are subtle and varied, with constant 'hairpins'. Short sharp attacks break up the lines and there is a build-up of intensity and a slight *accelerando*, before a pause heralds the change of key.

Ex. 1 McGuire

The music now enters what sounds to be an F minor mode (although a three-flat key signature is given), D flats replacing D naturals as useful signposts in the thickening texture. The time changes from 'free' simple time to a 9/8, marked 'ritmico'. The vocal fragments are very brief at first, and the composer, ever-practical and considerate, says that the live singer may adjust his rests to make sure that entries fall within gaps on the tape. This avoids the more strait-jacketed aspect of working with electronics, and the tenor can exercise some control over his own performance, and avoid any blurrings of detail.

As layer upon layer accumulates, the effect is dazzlingly colourful. Flicked staccato endings to phrases are very important in keeping the patterns precise and pointed, standing out in relief amid the waves of overlapping pitches. The music becomes denser and activity almost frenzied, trills further enriching the texture. After a crescendo, with high accented staccato 'wahs' punctuating the lines, there is a sudden change. A smooth rocking plainchant starts very high and soft on 'ee' (an excellent choice for secure placing). This can be sung falsetto. It is repeated four times, but eventually surges forward, with an enormous increase in volume, right into the next section. This, in violent contrast, consists of percussive phonetics, bitingly insistent, making a fascinating collage effect ('de-ke', 'tu-ke', 'tak-tik tah'). Considerable verbal dexterity is needed for this, with quick synchronization of palate and tongue. An exhilarating *fortissimo* is reached: the tenuto accents on the top Fs are important, since they stand out in the texture. This material is repeated during a slow diminuendo to nothing, and the composer asks for the 'k's to be eliminated gradually so that the sounds become almost murmured.

Now the words themselves are heard (Example 2). This section sounds particularly brilliant when multiplied. There are some tricky cross-accents

Ex. 2 McGuire

be a-no-ther: play a-no-ther tit-le: play a-no-ther in-ci-dent-ly:

be-ing in a time of de-cay take a — tune and play to — peo-ple,

learn-ing to keep on call-ing them to come to-ge-ther;

here, and these make all the difference to the effect. Fragments whirl around in dizzying repeats. Finally, calm is regained with a return to smooth phonetics, almost entirely vowel sounds. Once again the singer must control a long note on middle F, but this time there is a virtually foolproof device that will give security and made a superb effect. Cupped hands oscillating over the mouth perform exactly the same function as the 'wah-wah' mute used by players of brass instruments. The speed of the oscillations is indicated graphically, and the singer will have no trouble in varying it accordingly. The sound must be kept bright, placed well forward, perhaps almost with a nasal tinge (helped by an 'ee' vowel). Echoes of the opening interval fragments are followed by more of the 'wa-wa' effect. The work ends with a succession of three identical arching chant-like phrases, that evoke the sound of medieval church music. Each repeat is gradually softer, and the echoing tape is then faded out carefully to end the work.

This piece will make an ideal choice for an unusual venue—especially, as already mentioned, a church, ancient building, or gallery. Because of the amplification it would be practicable for outdoor use, in field or forest, or inside a marquee. Theatrical lighting (or even complete darkness) could enhance its magical atmosphere. In a more conventional recital setting, it will help bring variety to a programme for voice and piano. Purcell or Monteverdi arias, or Italian *arie antiche*, even perhaps Britten's *Sonnets of Michelangelo* would be appropriate stylistically. Some of the other works for solo voice in this volume could also go with it. Early music and folksong (especially Scottish) are its more obvious musical companions. Three student tenors could use it to enliven a showcase programme. It would also fit well in a concert of sacred choral music, or of madrigals involving three or more singers.

A Little Snow
(1994)

Roger Marsh (born 1949)
Text by Nicanor Parra
from *Canciones Rusas* (1963–4)
Translated by Miller Williams

T III; M IV
Solo voice (any)
Duration *c*.6'

This magical little piece is sure to appeal at all levels. It has a delicate quality that is truly fascinating, even on a first read-through. Roger Marsh has written a number of vocal pieces, and, though his work shows the strong influence of Berio and his followers, the special lightness of touch is all his own. The combination of unpretentious musicality and a permanently youthful freshness is very winning. The music is presented in a clear, uncluttered way, immediately attractive to the eye.

Singers should not be daunted by the avant-garde aspect of the notation. All is clearly explained in the frontispiece, with a most helpful and detailed guide to the vocal effects, including the variants of sung and spoken tone. Any voice should feel comfortable performing it, and it is suitable for an untrained voice too, although theatrical flair and extreme poise are pre-requisites. The musical difficulties are largely concerned with the pitching of intervals, especially quarter-tones. These involve only a slight bending of the note downwards, within a natural speech inflection, and should cause few problems. They are notated in standard fashion: the quarter-flat being indicated by a backwards version of a normal flat sign, and the quarter-sharp (used only sparingly) by a symbol resembling a normal sharp with only one set of crossed lines instead of two. For the most part, the vocal demands are slight. Everything is very gentle and a great deal of the lines consist of such small segments that breath capacity will not be taxed. Tessitura is left to choice: arrowed treble clefs indicate this, and a certain rhythmic freedom is allowed within the space-time notation of glissandos, and at the frequent pauses. Otherwise the composer has indicated note-lengths and rests most meticulously, since a feeling of regular pulse is essential for the hypnotic repetitions that form a major part of the work. At the halfway point the voice part becomes rather more complicated, sprinkled staccato scales descend rapidly in parallel lines, and a welter of activity is packed into a short space. However, since all material is to be repeated over and over again, any problem figures will soon gain in familiarity, especially in the matter of pitch orientation.

The piece is a perfect example of artful simplicity. Audiences will love its quiet, quirky charm, and they will respond to the understated poignancy of the words, in which fleeting spoken references to the death of Pushkin are submerged in the continually recurring snow motifs that form the basis of the work. A clever idea, most beautifully executed.

The music is divided into six sections of disparate length, marked A to F. This is also very helpful to the performer, since, when singing unaccompanied, it can be easy to lose track of shape and structure. It is obviously essential to assimilate all the signs and instructions given in the 'glossary' before embarking on the piece. The composer, in asking that there should be no 'artificial projection' clearly means that an operatic approach would be quite unsuitable, and larger voices will need to be well contained. Young voices will be particularly at home, although it is true that a reliable technique will always be an advantage, especially with so much *pianissimo* singing, and fine control will also be noticeable in legato phrases. The composer would prefer the piece to be done from memory, with the singer lit by one low spotlight.

Section A establishes a regular pattern of alternating lines: the first exposes the basic refrain, which occurs five times, the first repeat exactly the same, and the others bearing only the subtlest changes of timbre, articulation and timing. A breathy tone is asked for, and the singer must take care in choosing the starting pitch, since all relationships and repetitions thereafter will be determined by it. The fact that every syllable is separated by a rest means that there is a danger of overbreathing. Each full phrase should be taken as one span; if not, control may be lost, and tone-quality may waver. The composer stipulates that the chosen pitch should be 'high in the range, but not so high as to be uncomfortable'. Two special features need to be noted. The composer indicates them with (i) and (ii) at the beginning of the passages affected. (i) requires a similar approach as in Schoenbergian Sprechstimme, where notes are to be slightly pitched and then inflected downwards, to make the pitch less definable. (ii) is the sign for a passage incorporating specially softened consonants, which are placed in brackets. 'T's for instance, are to be given extra sibilance. All this is fully explained by the composer in his introduction. The words should eventually become so blurred that they 'turn gradually to snowflakes'. The performer's imagination, concentration, and sensitivity to atmosphere will be crucial in attaining this delightful effect. In between each 'half-sung' refrain, after a long pause, the singer has lines of spoken text, which are to be performed impassively, but with absolute clarity. It is very important to observe the *attacca* at the ends of lines 1, 2, and 5, and go straight into the refrain again without breathing. Pauses are also highly significant. The beauty of the piece is that the performer will immediately experience the calming effect of all this intimate detail, and will be unlikely to want to disturb the spell.

Section B begins with what seems to be a repetition of the refrain, but is soon broken up into smaller fragments, the first repeated several times before the phrase is finally completed during an *accelerando*. Here the 'breathy' indication is missing so tone can be clearer. The smoother legato material now makes a first appearance. Long paused notes are preceded by a minor seventh leap from the fast articulated 'as if'. These are very gratifying to sing. The refrain is subject to further contraction, in fast-running droplets of sound, all scrupulously notated, The smoother phrases now take over, melting into *bocca chiusa* (indicated by what is now the standard sign: an upright cross) on the paused notes. These pitches, varying by semitones provide the tonal focus for the piece. Section C continues in similar fashion, with alternations of the refrain theme and the smooth paused intervals, each breaking up into smaller repeated sections, gradually becoming much faster. The singer must make sure not to get louder because of the surge of speed. Eventually notes are accented, as fragments become even smaller, and are broken up further into their phonetic components, complete with snowflake effect.

Section D resumes, momentarily, the steady (crotchet = 60) tempo of the beginning. Now the music takes off in a whirling sequence, in which splintered, staccato bursts of the refrain, mostly on phonetics, end in rapidly accelerating droplets, in two antiphonal parallel lines falling (melting) into nothing. The notation is perhaps a little ambiguous here: the lines between the notes imply a linked glissando, but they are used merely to trace the progress of the pitches of each parallel descent. The composer wishes the staccato to be maintained to the end, continuing the snowflake effect (Example 1). It may go against the grain at first to lessen the volume as the music gets faster: there is often a habit of intensifying tone simultaneously

Ex. 1 Marsh

with speed. The fast successions of phonetics (the standard phonetic alphabet is used) may need to be practised slowly. The bracketed groups mean that the sounds contained within them can be used in any order. The composer states that 'no two gestures are identical', so the pitch should be slightly different each time, avoiding any feeling of mechanical repetition. Eventually the smoother music returns, and there is an expressive use of a fleeting hummed Sprechstimme, sounding like a gentle sigh. This involves quarter-sharps which are only found in this passage and at the very end. The hummed phrases become longer and longer, in finely spun semitones, with a flicked-away staccato at the ends. The mellifluous lines are interrupted by one final shower of descending droplets.

Section E is very brief and entirely lyrical, bringing a return of the upward seventh featured in section B. Each short phrase is followed by a pause, and there is a sudden stop on 'blood', which is sung staccato, the composer adding a timely reminder not to become melodramatic!

A very long pause prepares for the last section, F, which is again very lyrical, but reintroduces spoken fragments in between the sung phrases: a lovely encapsulation of the opening, in which the smooth hummed phrases seem to comment comfortingly on the sad tale. Timing of pauses and of both kinds of vocalizing must be judged to a nicety. There is just one spoken fragment that has rhythmic notation (notes without heads, so no pitch is specified), to help with the delivery. As the last *bocca chiusa* fades away there is one final repeat of the refrain at a slighly higher pitch than before, and once again, quarter-sharps are used to inflect the final 'a-gain'.

Such an immediately endearing work is rarely found. It will make its impact in almost any setting. It would contrast particularly well with the more overtly theatrical works of Alison Bauld recommended in this and Volume 1, but would make a haunting effect in any standard recital too. There are many possibilities for enhancing the atmosphere still further: it could be sung in complete darkness, or off-stage, provided the ambience is right and the audience quiet and attentive. John Cage's works as well as the Berio *Sequenza* would help make up a varied recital programme for solo voice. It will bring out each singer's individual qualities, giving valuable experience in communicating with an audience through a subtle blend of detachment and deep absorption.

Un Colloque sentimental
(A Sentimental Conversation) (1978)

Colin Matthews (born 1946)
Texts by various poets (in French)

T III; M IV
Medium voice and piano
Duration *c*.15′

This is a lovely work by one of our most sensitive and versatile composers. It seems beautifully balanced in structure, although the composer, somewhat surprisingly, reveals, in his note at the front of the score, that the three central songs of the five were in fact written between 1971 and 1978 for 'private pleasure'. 'Le Jet d'eau' is the composer's earliest surviving piece. Eventually he had the idea of expanding them into a cycle, by enclosing them within the two unequal parts of the setting of Verlaine's celebrated poem of the title. He has, on his own admission, also taken certain liberties with the texts, making several omissions and alterations to suit his personal responses to the special world of nineteenth-century French poetry. The refrain of Baudelaire's 'Le Jet d'eau' is not set, and is printed in small type at the front of the published score. Full texts and translations of all the poems are provided: a great boon for performers and teachers, and it is perhaps a pity that not all composers and their advisers take this amount of trouble in presenting their vocal music to best advantage.

Matthews's aim was to recapture the essence of the texts within an identifiably modern musical language, yet remain faithful to their spirit, and he has succeeded admirably in this. I find it surprising that this thoroughly appealing cycle is not already in the regular repertoire. The two contrasting Baudelaire settings, written originally for a higher voice, are also available separately as a shorter concert item.

The cycle was first performed by the Australian countertenor Hartley Newnham, who has done so much to encourage composers to write for this rewarding voice-type, with its special strength and penetration in just those areas of the range (the lower half of the treble stave) where the female voice can sometimes lack focus. It could of course be sung by a mezzo or a light baritone (the highest note is A, but *ossie* are also provided). However, it represents a real find for the countertenor of genuine musicality and enterprise. Since there are now so many fine examples of this voice, and their general level of musicianship is often well above average, this should prove an ideal vehicle. There will be a subtle change of atmosphere according to what type of voice performs it, and its adaptability for this purpose indicates the composer's extreme sensibility to timbre and its varying possibilities.

It would be impossible not to be aware of the powerful shadows of the great French song composers, most especially Fauré and Ravel, but also Debussy and Duparc. Debussy's setting of the 'Colloque sentimental' is a natural point of comparison. He and Fauré have provided the singer with many memorable settings of Verlaine and Baudelaire, all capturing the rarefied atmosphere of the era of the poetry, and displaying that flair and responsiveness to the nuances of the French language that have so profoundly affected composers following after them. However, the composer's only acknowledged specific musical references are to Schoenberg's *Verklärte Nacht* and Scriabin's *Poème d'extase*, as well as an earlier work of his own.

The words are set throughout with assurance and style, obeying the expressive inflections inherent in the language. Words are mostly set straightforwardly, note for syllable, although there are a few melismas in the second song. The musical and dramatic variety within the cycle is particularly striking. The free, almost recitative-like, enigmatic dialogue of the framing title-song is in stark contrast to the richly textured Baudelaire settings with their brilliant piano passagework, although these two songs are crucially different: the first highly chromatic and the second basically tonal. The charmingly simple, almost folksong-like de Nerval setting captures another style, redolent of 'Les Six', especially Satie and Poulenc. The piano accompaniment is exciting and unfailingly idiomatic, providing opportunities for a strong pianist to demonstrate real virtuosity combined with stylistic awareness and response to the music's natural flow. The relationship between voice and piano is constantly flexible. Sometimes it follows the tradition of earlier models, with florid figures supporting radiant cantabile vocal lines, at other times the two parts alternate, and occasionally the piano acts as commentator. Marks of expression are always helpful and well judged.

1. Colloque sentimental, 1ère partie (Paul Verlaine)

In keeping with the icy landscape of the poem, the opening is marked 'very still' and the voice part 'cold'. Successions of *pianissimo* chords set and sustain the atmosphere, punctuating the singer's plain, recitative-like comments. Syllables fall easily in the voice, and there should be no difficulty in achieving the hushed quietness required. Rhythms do not have to be rigid: the composer suggests 'poco parlando'. The 'm's on 'morts' and 'molles' can be used to place the following vowels with accurate delicacy. The singer should not be afraid to risk dying away almost to a whisper at the end.

2. Le Jet d'eau (Charles Baudelaire)

Of the two Baudelaire settings, this first is the more substantial in scope. Fountains are of course often depicted musically by rippling figures in the piano, cushioning and supporting a flowing vocal line. Fauré, Duparc, and Chausson were masters of this effect, and Matthews, too, varies the rhythmic groupings to help with subtle changes of mood, aided by fluctuations of time signature. The accompaniment here has a conventional role, providing texture and atmosphere, and the singer must take the lead in shaping phrases. The voice begins softly, rising and falling comfortably. A few cross-rhythms and triplets may give ensemble problems at first, but these will soon be overcome. One notable device employed by the earlier masters is used here to great effect: the deliberate intensifying of energy immediately prior to a sudden moment of poised raptness. The crescendo through 'nonchalante' must be fully exploited (there can even be a hint of an *accelerando*), giving time only to snatch the merest breath before landing on the magical F sharp as the accompaniment adopts a richer harmonic vein. The irregular time signatures (5/8, 7/8) contribute to a swooning effect. The tessitura rises as the text provides alliterative, shimmering sounds. Words such as 'jase' and 'extase' readily invite a concentration on their sibilance. A small acciaccatura is given for the very end of the word 'extase', so that the vowel has more space to resonate, and there is just time to enunciate, lift, and reattack for the exquisitely quiet 'Où' that follows (on an enharmonic change from E flat to D sharp). A short, expressive piano solo, arising from quintuplet figures accompanying the end of verse 1, leads into the second verse. This begins in declamatory and dramatic fashion, with some tricky rhythms between voice and piano, and then quietens into Duparc-like fast-moving ripples in the treble range, while the voice sinuously floats and dips. There are some finely spun diminuendos on final notes of phrases; a lower *ossia* is provided for those who might find an E flat awkward for this. The piano plays a vital role in maintaining elasticity and momentum through constantly shifting figurations. A crucial, low-lying melisma on 'mourante' will need careful shaping to keep it within an even legato, avoiding accents. At the end of the verse, it is again the pianist who has to steer the transition, a brief solo passage, into a calmer mode (*poco più andante*) for the last stanza. The voice now moves in quintuplets in unison with the piano's *mezzo-staccato* figures which gently support. The composer gives the instruction 'flexible in rhythm' to ensure that the effect is not mechanical. From experience, I know that this means extra preparatory work, repeating the lines over and over again so that they eventually feel natural, and there is no longer a need to emphasize the notes that coincide (Example 1). Only then can one relax into a pliable, almost swinging, effect, the words falling naturally as if speaking slowly. The dynamic remains soft, but the piano part becomes more elaborate, depicting the sobbing of the fountain. Another bar which will need preliminary work is the 5/8 at this point, where singer and pianist have cross-rhythms and the voice must keep a steady quaver pulse. Again the piano surges out into a rhapsodic solo, reminiscent of a moment in the first song of Ravel's *Trois Poèmes de Mallarmé* for voice and ensemble, when the piano suddenly takes off alone in similarly lyrical vein.

Ex. 1 C.Matthews

(*flexible in rhythm*)

Ô toi, que la nuit rend si

bel - le, _____ Qu'il _____ m'est doux, pen -

-ché vers tes seins, D'é - cou - ter _____

senza cresc.

As it calms, the singer re-enters, very softly, for the final paragraph, low in the voice. The intervals must be adroitly pitched against the piano's continuous textures, which melt away to nothing. For the singer's last note, again an E flat, a lower *ossia* is again suggested for those who might experience difficulty in achieving the very quiet dynamic (triple *piano*).

3. Que dirais-tu ce soir (Charles Baudelaire)

This second Baudelaire setting is more modest in scale. The piano still plays a leading role in shaping its progress, with abundant use of repetitive figures, yet the interpretation does not immediately suggest itself along traditional lines as in the preceding song. A subtle approach is called for, involving concentrated thought and patience. The text's images are not so straightforwardly depicted, and a questioning mood can often be difficult to convey by vocal means.

As the voice begins completely alone, pitch memory has to be retained from the previous movement (the piano's postlude has ended in a *ritenuto* to a final C natural: the accompanist should make this clear for the singer and linger on it a little). The piano part soon resumes with cascading figures, mainly in fast sextuplets, but occasionally expanding to quintuplets so that the pulse never seems rigid. The vocal line is plain and undecorated (marked 'sostenuto') and in medium tessitura, avoiding extremes, and is sometimes left unaccompanied for short stretches. Exact gauging of the basic tempo will be important: it must be steady yet flowing. The sudden interruption of the piano's line creates a feeling of hesitancy, and this is especially so in a solo passage punctuated by commas at every barline. After the opening verse, a more serene and contemplative mood takes over, the voice's lines softly yet warmly accompanied by piano figures in the bass clef. These become more ethereal as they rise in pitch, and note-groups divide in rapidly shifting patterns, again halting from time to time, with an occasional pause on an isolated diminished seventh chord. The elusive visionary qualities of the text, beyond its actual meaning, call for interpreters of keen sensitivity and accurate responses to both verbal and musical sub-texts. The piano seems to draw us into a realm of heightened expectancy. For the last stanza, the accompanying patterns slow to normal semiquavers, and the voice continues its deceptively simple discourse. A radiant coda brings illumination in a rapt declaration of spiritual identity. This movement will test the performers' ability to capture its special inner intensity and to hold the audience's concentration.

4. Intermezzo: Une allée de Luxembourg (Gérard de Nerval)

The more detached and sophisticated mood of this movement, evokes comparison with the work of 'Les Six', especially Poulenc. The piano has a gently pulsating *perpetuum mobile*, this time with chords in the right hand. The basic rhythmic tread (through changes of time signature) gives a lightly jogging effect. The voice part has immediate freshness, flair, and charm and is comfortable to sing (Example 2). After the opening verse, in a basically minor but hopeful mode, there is a sudden change at *sostenuto ma agitato* and rhythms become much more complex, involving cross-rhythmed triplets, and four-against-three relationships between voice and piano. These are of course highly effective for the *agitato* required, but will undoubtedly need some extra practice before perfect ensemble is achieved. The young man is speaking from the heart, in natural speech rhythms, appropriately non-metric in their spontaneity. A dramatic point is reached, and the music stops and starts, before the pulsing motion begins again, with little skirls in the piano's left hand, as the singer's lines are fragmented, and the tempo accelerates considerably, bursting into a brisk but passionate and heady A major section (there is a key signature here). The enchanted lover cries out in spent ecstasy, only to make a remarkable recovery in the contrasting coda. The piano gives an accented quasi-atonal introduction to the singer's final throw-away comment: 'Le malheur passait—il a fui'. This is marked 'sotto voce' and should sound confiding and agreeably surprised. The piano finishes with a sardonic flourish, after which the final setting follows *attacca*. A bracing and refreshing interlude, contrasting sharply with the other movements.

Ex. 2 C.Matthews

*In old French the 's' of 'preste' is silent. The modern equivalent of the word is 'prête'.

5. Colloque sentimental, 2ème partie (Paul Verlaine)

The cycle ends with the extended resumption of the Verlaine poem of the work's title. The piano's chiming, bell-like chords on three staves, heard at the beginning, recur here in inverted form, and, at first, the icily immobile character of the opening is also continued. The two spirit characters again have to be differentiated subtly in timbre. The compass may be some help here: the first speaker has tenuto marking, while the second's somewhat dampening replies are *sotto voce*. The singer should experiment with various types of 'white' or 'veiled' tone-colours to see which works best: often very personal to the individual interpreter, and dependent on dynamics and verbal shadings. A sense of other-worldliness is needed. Some very low F sharps should not be problematic since they are virtually unaccompanied—the merest thread of sound will suffice, but an *ossia* is given just in case. The 'v' and 'n' of 'souvienne' ought to help focus the sound at pitch in advance of releasing the vowels—a simple device which invariably works in many different contexts. The low G sharp on 'Non' is marked 'toneless' so a breathily spoken effect should work well. Quite suddenly, the music warms to an outburst of emotion and sensuality, swelling to *forte* on 'bouches', and the singer must seize this opportunity to break out of the repressed mould for a short while, until the discouraging reply of 'C'est possible' ('expressionless' as marked). The main protagonist makes another attempt at injecting some feeling, in an unaccompanied phrase, but, in a subdued *lento* echo,

Ex. 3 C.Matthews

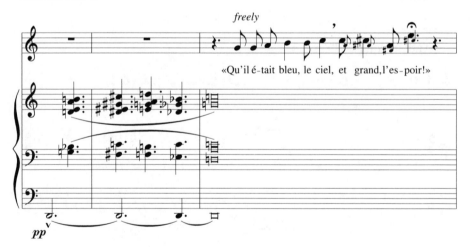

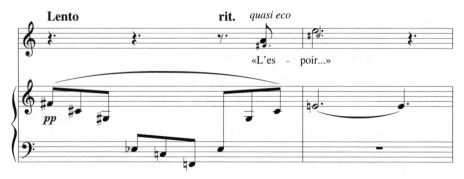

hope is extinguished (Example 3). The composer is so acutely aware of how crucial the vocal placing has to be to achieve a clear and sepulchral tone for the echo of 'L'espoir', that he has written a lower *ossia* so that it can be produced very softly, whatever the weight and natural tessitura of the singer, and there is no risk of a jarring rise in volume. The coda to the cycle is perhaps surprising. The piano provides a gentle triplet movement and the voice's final phrases of narrative (now in the third person again, as at the outset) are simple and detached over this, quickening a little as 'la nuit bénie entendit leurs paroles'. The final mood, then, is one of quiet resignation, and the piano concludes the cycle with figurations which seem to encapsulate those of the preceding movements: first, descending arpeggios, and then, a reminder of the quasi-atonal wide-ranging monody found at the end of No. 4, played *fortissimo*, suddenly cutting itself off without slowing. (The un-answered question?)

This is a richly rewarding work, full of subtlety and layers of meaning which will repay close and careful study. It is particulary important to foster that special awareness that duo partners must have for each other's roles, as the voice and piano share duties very evenly, and even take over and overlap one another's characters in a intriguing way. It is therefore most suitable for experienced performers, not so much for technical or musical difficulty, as for artistic sensibility. It would obviously sit happily in a recital of French music, especially the *mélodies* of composers already mentioned, and to juxtapose other settings of Verlaine and Baudelaire would be most appro-priate. Its ideal proportions would make it an excellent centrepiece for a standard recital. John Casken's *Ia Orana, Gauguin* (see Volume 1), which is heavily influenced by French models (and contains a direct Debussy–Baudelaire quotation!) but is otherwise quite different stylistically, would make for a fascinating comparison, but the two works should be kept in separate halves if sharing a programme. English Romantic composers, who also have much in common with French music, would also provide a large choice of companion-pieces, perhaps in the form of mixed groups of shorter songs to maintain a good balance.

The Golden Kingdom, Op. 33
(1979–83)

David Matthews (born 1943)
Texts by various writers

T III; M III
High or medium voice and piano
Duration *c*.18′

The Matthews brothers (cf. Colin Matthews *Un Colloque sentimental*) continue to produce some of the most rewarding work to come from the middle generation of British composers, yet their styles could hardly be more different. David, the elder, has a special fondness for the voice, and has written a good number of song cycles, some with orchestra. He unashamedly favours a lush romanticism, and creates a rich palette of vocal and instrumental colours set in warmly sensuous harmonic textures. This cycle of nine songs is a particularly beguiling compilation of varied settings, written over a number of years, and bound into a satisfying and nicely constructed whole. Sopranos, mezzos, tenors, or high baritones will thoroughly enjoy the blend of full-blooded expressionism and poetic delicacy. The voice is frequently given wonderfully flattering lines, the tessitura arching up and down with the natural contours of the phrases. Any note above high G sharp is given a lower alternative. The piano parts are also extremely rich in character. The influence of Britten is often apparent in harmonies and rhythmic gestures.

Over half the songs were written in 1982; the earliest, No. 6, 'Blue Butterflies' Eyed Wings' dates from 1979, and the most recent is No. 5, 'Lament of Ahania' (1983). No. 1, Shelley's 'A Bridal Song' and No. 7 'Bright Cloud' are dated 1980 and 1981 respectively. The six Kathleen Raine poems are in two blocks of three: Nos. 2–4 and 6–8, framed by the two Shelley settings that begin and end the cycle, with the more sombre Blake song placed at the centre of the work. The chosen order works very well in context, contrasting rhapsodic, contemplative, and declamatory elements. Rather unusually, the last four settings are the briefest. The last 'Fragment' is one of only three songs that bear a key signature (although the two 'Spells' are based around C major). Normal notation is employed throughout.

Though eminently and enticingly singable, the songs do require a considerable degree of vocal control and versatility of approach. Reliably intuitive musicianship will be an important asset. There are quite a few places where female singers may have to work hard to prevent words being obscured during high-lying passages. The composer is obviously aware of the sonic effects of the poetry that further enhance the meaning, and sibilant and percussive consonants need to be brought out clearly.

This immensely enjoyable vehicle gives both performers a real chance to shine. The abundant warmth of expression will come across very strongly in the act of live performance, and there is room for individual interpretative touches.

1. A Bridal Song (Shelley)

The voice begins legato 'Quietly but urgently' in unison with the piano's ripe chords. One is reminded of the start of Berg's *Two Songs*, Op. 2. Finding the opening pitch could be problematic (a discreet cue memorized off-stage is perhaps the best solution). Intervals will need the finest tuning, even though in this opening phrase each note is to be found somewhere within the piano's harmonies. The composer thoughtfully provides rests at logical places, but a few additional breaths may be necessary. A good opportunity occurs before 'kindle'. A warning 'take time' at the triplet approach to the radiant high G sharp on 'star' helps ensure a lovely effect. Vocal lines are ideally lithe and graceful, covering a wide range. The *pianissimo* high B can be floated quasi-non-vibrato, and another breath may be taken after it, if need be. An *ossia* of G natural is provided for lower voices. A passage with running piano triplets could cause intonation problems initially, since there is not much to hold on to in the accompaniment. Intensity rises dramatically, with some brilliant semiquaver arpeggio figures in the piano. These grow softer, matching the vocal line, which drops to low E on 'renew'. The vowel sound must not lose its cutting edge. Against delicate high quintuplets in the piano's right hand, the voice floats an ethereal line. The raptness required should not be allowed to hinder the precise articulation of words such as 'fairies' and 'sprites'. 'Keep' on F may be awkward for sopranos and mezzos: the vowel will have to be kept open. At a thrilling climax, the piano's strong chords, heralded by bravura flourishes, add a tremendous bounce and impetus. The voice is now given full rein. Huge leaps on 'O joy', 'O fear' are physically exhilarating. The crescendos have to match the piano's, and timing of the arrival at the top note is crucial. The voice arches down again, and the piano's shimmering figures dissolve into an impressionistic wash, while the voice murmurs one last fragment: 'come along'. This song, like others in the set, seems quite complete in itself and could be performed separately. Its mystical expressionism and sensuous harmonic language call to mind the work of Messiaen.

2. Him I praise (from Northumbrian Sequence) (Kathleen Raine)

A key signature here indicates E major (or C sharp minor), but the basic tonality is of A major with the sharpened subdominant (D sharp). One cannot help being reminded of Britten at times during this powerfully dramatic and fervent setting. It is perhaps one of the hardest of the cycle to bring off. At the beginning, each of the singer's decorative unaccompanied declamations is preceded by a ceremonial flourish on the piano. In the following section, where the piano has triplets, the singer may need extra work to consolidate pitches and rhythms, and make ornamental figures, such as the *trillo* on 'bridal', run easily within the low tessitura. There is a real danger of the piano covering words and finer details. A final recitative statement gives the singer freedom to expand, cadencing on to the pause on 'place' which leads directly into a fast *Vivo* (note the Brittenesque Scotch snap on 'darkest'). For this section the singer must be rhythmically alert, especially when swinging the duplet dotted quavers against the piano's lilting triple time. Lines become rather strenuous as they get louder, and a number of 'e' vowels have to be sung on high notes, with little time for them to 'speak'. The voice leaps to a high B (*ossia* G sharp) on 'In-to', and a strong glottal articulation should help placing. This exciting unaccompanied declamation leads into another contrasting section: a march-like *misurato*, in which the piano supports with harp-like chords in ritualistic style. The final paragraph lies very well in the voice, apart from 'mirroring seas', with its tenuto accents, placed around the female register-break. It helps to keep vowel sounds as long as possible. The singer's last phrase is most beautiful: a fleeting rest in between 'radiance' and 'shines' is one of those subtle touches that lift the interpretation. For the close, which dips on to a warm cadence in the home tonality, dynamics are very important, especially the final diminuendo. This colourful and richly varied movement could possibly be performed on its own, perhaps even in an ecclesiastical setting.

3. Spell of Creation (Kathleen Raine)

In this extremely lively and fascinating piece, basically in ternary form, chanting spell sections enclose a middle passage of dramatic declamation. The voice starts alone, *sotto voce*, in a lengthy incantation in dynamic rhythms (Example 1). This recalls, for a moment, Britten's orchestral cycle *Our Hunting Fathers*, Op.8, where the list of hounds is chanted in similar

Ex.1 D.Matthews

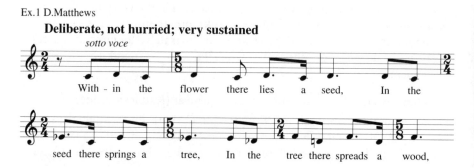

manner. The marking 'deliberate, not hurried, very sustained' indicates that, though quiet, the singing must retain intensity and a controlled pulse throughout the successions of fluctuating time signatures and irregular beats. Tone should be precise and bright, not muffled, and consonants strongly projected. This setting will fully test the singer's rhythmic accuracy and ability to breathe quickly *a tempo*. As the chanting builds and moves higher in the voice, the piano joins with syncopated chords that become fuller and richer as the voice rises to a peak of manic excitememt. Here the high writing could certainly be something of a problem. Although the line moves up and down, there is little time to rest, so the repeated Gs and later G sharps could prove tiring. It is essential to keep a feeling of lightness and flexibility, and a fairly thin clear line. Words will require a special effort if they are not to be lost. It is perhaps tempting to imitate a witch-like sound, but the characterization should not be exaggerated. A climax is reached on 'Love' (high A, or, alternatively F natural) as the *più mosso* middle section begins. Strong, accented, quasi-orchestral chords reinforce the vocal line, which is marked 'firm, declaimed'. Full breath capacity will need to be employed here, and a richer sound quality will match the luscious harmonies and provide a contrast to the chanting. The lines broaden into a dramatic cantabile, and after a searing *fortissimo* 'In the fire consumes my heart', the music gradually unwinds and returns to the faster chanting rhythms, with a slow *rallentando* as the vocal line descends and grows quieter. A ten-bar coda brings a return to strict tempo, and the voice chants the last stanza in clear rhythms over the piano's soft chords. The singer's last few words are unaccompanied. The music should stop abruptly with no suspicion of slowing. This movement is great fun to perform, and is an ideal preparation for what is to come.

4. Spell of Sleep (Kathleen Raine)

If just one song had to be picked from the cycle, this is the undoubted hit. Shining and lyrical, its beautiful vocal lines are supported throughout by regular pulsing chords in the most luminous range of the piano (Example 2). The general layout, and characteristic dipping intervals cannot help but remind one of the movement entitled 'Being Beauteous' from Britten's *Less Illuminations*. This song is a joy to sing, the raptly arching phrases perfectly shaped for vocal comfort. The opening melody shifts a third higher, entering the voice's most flattering range. After the hypnotic opening, the middle section brings more glittering figurations in the piano's right hand while the pulsing chords continue in the left. The voice soars effortlessly to a high A on 'space' (the lower octave is a far less satisfactory alternative). Words must be projected clearly; there is a danger of wallowing in the lyricism to the extent of neglecting consonants. The passage depicting images of the seabed needs particular attention, since it goes lower in the voice, and has to come through the piano's syncopated chords. There is a return to the rapt opening theme, in the higher version, for a magical final section, which

Ex. 2 D.Matthews

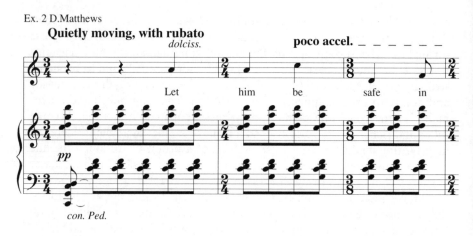

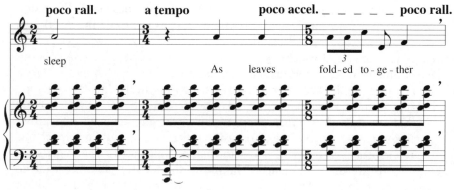

slows gradually to a peaceful conclusion. This song also exists in two alternative chamber ensemble versions.

5. Lament of Ahania (Blake)

Perhaps the most elusive of the settings for the vocal interpreter, this starts in dark, subdued mood, but becomes more passionate towards the centre. The piano's role is very strong indeed, and it dictates and shapes the progress of the whole song. A stately dirge in dotted rhythms (marked 'Grave') begins, solo, in the piano's left hand before the voice enters. It is repeated over and over again, as a passacaglia throughout the movement. The voice begins softly and broodingly. It is as well to keep vibrato to a minimum so that intervals with the piano are quite clear. If not, the result could sound turgid instead of solemn. Tessitura is quite low for the opening section, and triplets have to be plotted carefully against the piano's relent-less tread. Pitching is not easy: there are many close intervals. The piano's burgeoning textures could give a balance problem here unless the singer can command an ample tone. For the long phrase beginning 'From my soft cloud', it would be undesirable to interrupt the crescendo through 'dew'. However, 'Harvests' is not an easy word to negotiate when short of breath, and the low pitch may lack penetration. A snatched breath after the high 'fall' would be ungainly, disturbing the rhythm. Since the composer also marks a crescendo towards the end of the phrase, it is perhaps permissible to take a quick breath after 'life' if necessary. The voice rises to an exultant high A on 'joy' (F natural as an *ossia*), and eventually plunges downward for the final cadence, but its dynamic remains strong with a crescendo towards the final low D. This may be rather difficult to achieve, especially for sopranos and tenors. It is important to keep the sound clear without breathiness or obtrusive vibrato. The piano continues the passacaglia in a long solo epilogue, ending with soft slow chords and arpeggios. The next song follows *attacca*. (This setting should not therefore be performed alone.)

6. Blue Butterflies' Eyed Wings (Kathleen Raine)

This is a tiny gem (just one page, in the key of F major) and it will demonstrate the singer's ability to float delicate sinewy lines with ease in *pianissimo*. The piano has continuous semiquavers in a *perpetuum mobile* which thickens gradually. The characteristic dropping seventh in the voice's melody calls to mind that in 'Spell of Sleep'. Intervals become broader, and the voice swings higher and higher, reaching A (*ossia* F) and finally a very long paused B natural (or G) to end. It is very important to keep the tone light and flexible, placed forward with very little vibrato. A glottal start on 'I' will aid precision. Real *pianissimo* singing (as opposed to artificial covering of the voice) sometimes appears to be a forgotten art, but it is important to ensure that the voice's finer edges are still in good condition. For anyone experiencing real difficulty holding the high note, a C natural is even suggested for the final bar, for those choosing the G alternative. There is little worse than being compelled to hold a note longer than comfortable in the high range—the resultant loss of quality can be embarrassingly noticeable. The enchanting effect of the song must not be put at risk by any insecurity at the close.

7. Bright Cloud (Kathleen Raine)

Another single-page miniature, at a steady pace, but packed with incident, as in songs of similar length by Charles Ives (cf. 'Maple Leaves', 'Evening'). The pitch of the lingering last note of the preceding song has to be retained: it would not be a good idea to have a cue at this juncture. A particularly evocative verse is enhanced by soft, glowing harmonies. The piano part seems almost complete in itself, but the singer must weave soft lines, in which the natural speech rhythms often dictate the mode of delivery (as in a gentle parlando passage). The difference between 'espress.' and 'semplice' in the first line must be apparent. The most problematic passage is likely to be the high-lying section that follows (Example 3). The female singer may

Ex.3 D.Matthews

White gold and rose vi - sion of light, ___

Mean - ing ___ and beau - ty ___ im - mea - sur - ab - le.

have some difficulty in floating continuously in this vulnerable register, and too much vibrato could make words indistinct. A good deal of support will be needed to keep the sound free of throatiness and maintain legato. The lower alternative for 'vision' is the more practicable. Starting again high on 'Meaning' needs care too—there must be time to produce a hummed 'm' on the note before eliding into the vowel, which will of course have to be modified. This section will feel higher than it actually is, and the descending seventh at the end will come as a relief. The last two phrases, separated by a comma, are quite different in character: rippling arpeggios provide a misty accompaniment to the voice's smooth lines. These are marked 'pianissimo, dolciss. sostenuto', but, since they lie comparatively low, they should not be so soft as to hinder audibility, and consonants should be heightened. The song ends suddenly, with no *rallentando*.

8. Oval the Golden Moon (Kathleen Raine)

The last two brief settings have a specific connection with Aldeburgh. This one is dedicated to the late Imogen Holst (the composer's daughter, Britten's editor, and an inspirational choir trainer, conductor of the Purcell Singers, of which I had the privilege to be a member) on her seventy-fifth birthday. It is the tiniest of fragments. Falling intervals again grace the vocal line, which is meltingly soft, consisting of just six short phrases. The lower octave *ossia* for the high A could rob the song of a particularly ravishing moment. The piano part is chordal, the limpid harmonies appropriately redolent of the English Romantics. The sparse layout enables the voice to shine in purest high notes, which must not be sung non-vibrato: Imogen Holst would have disliked the starved sound sometimes found in early music singing. The *dolcissimo* marking so often used in this cycle means that the voice's expressive colours must be fully exploited. The last phrase descends to a long-held low B. This has to be controlled carefully, not allowing tone to spread, and keeping a fine thread of cleanly pitched sound. Significantly, in view of its dedication, the last song follows *attacca*.

186

9. A Fragment: To Music (Shelley)

The finale, in the key of D major, bears the dedication 'to P.P. at 70', and is a touching and apt tribute to that incomparable artist Peter Pears. The music brings together elements from the earlier songs in the cycle. The brief vocal part is surrounded on each side by spectacular piano solos, evoking memories of his matchless musical partnership with Benjamin Britten. One can clearly imagine the great tenor singing these lines with his customary commitment and compelling intensity, every care lavished on the tiniest detail. The opening piano solo is full of colour and energy, whirling arpeggios alternating with high staccato chords. A series of low chromatic chords, gradually becoming softer, leads into the middle, vocal section that seems to suggest the mannerisms of lute music. This is perhaps a reference to his other distinguished partnership with Julian Bream. The voice has catchy rhythmic patterns, in middle register, the syllables falling sweetly and naturally. The cycle ends with a long postlude on the piano: first, a moving procession of hushed chords with a lyrical melody on top, and finally, rapid rippling figures, returning to the *Allegro* of the opening, which fade away, slowing very gradually and poignantly into silence.

This rewarding assortment of songs makes an excellent and substantial programme choice for the English language group in a full standard recital. The unusual proportions are a special asset, focusing attention on the tightly concentrated miniatures towards the end. The songs could even be interspersed with others, perhaps other settings of Blake or Shelley. It is also possible to perform the longer songs on their own, especially Nos. 1 and 2. The two Kathleen Raine 'Spells' pair well together as a separate item, perhaps in reverse order. The songs of Charles Ives would provide a rich feast from which to pick suitable companion-pieces. As well as those mentioned earlier, the atmospheric 'Housatonic at Stockbridge' and 'Tom sails away' would be ideal. A cohesive programme could be built around more specific references: works by Britten (*Winter Words* or the *Donne Sonnets*) and Holst (the Humbert Wolfe songs). In view of the frequent instances of high-lying words, the tenor voice could perhaps be happiest all through the cycle, but there are some gorgeous voluptuous phrases that will suit female voices splendidly.

Our Lady's Hours
(1959)

Anthony Milner (born 1925)
Texts by various writers

T III; M III
High voice and piano
Duration *c.*12′

The choice of texts for this beautifully conceived cycle by a major, yet unaccountably neglected, composer, proclaim the deep religous faith which pervades all his works, and contributes so strongly to their conviction and integrity. Stylistically the songs are assured and vigorous, with shades of neo-classicism combined with English Romanticism. The appearance of the score is conventional, especially in its notation, with traditional key and time signatures, but the personality of the composer comes through strikingly and the music is by no means simple with its wide-ranging lines often highly decorated. Rich chromaticism and driving rhythms are a characteristic, and the piano-writing is exciting and colourful. The substantial central song is an extended *scena*, framed by two briefer songs: a simple introduction, and a flowing *Adagio* finale, which is richly textured and fervent. The result is a perfect balance, highly satisfying in construction and effect. Some of the higher-lying lines may indicate that a tenor would be perhaps the ideal voice to maintain textual clarity. An excellent technique will be needed to spin some long lines and weave the subtle phrases full of dynamic contrasts and verbal details. This music demands and deserves dedication and commitment from the singer, and it should prove a stimulating task well worth all the effort needed for a polished and unstressful performance.

1. Dawn (Sloane Manuscript, 15th century)

As suggested by the opening instruction, 'Andante con moto e ben ritmico', rhythm is extremely important to this composer, and motoric continuity is an almost constant feature even in simple forms. In keeping with its fifteenth-century text, this opening song has a vocal melody reminiscent of plainsong, subtly varied in chromatic changes but basically modal and comfortable to sing, with rhythmic flexibility provided by shifts of time signatures. Some close intervals need meticulous tuning, keeping vibrato to a minimum (Example 1). The final scoop up a minor third to high G on 'la-dye' and then pausing on the D below, makes for a flattering piece of legato singing— beware of getting too loud. This is primarily a gentle understated song, beautiful in its tender simplicity, and posing few problems for the singer.

Ex. 1 Milner

He came al so stylle To his mo-der's bowr As
dewe in A - prylle That fal - lyt on the flour.

2. Noon (Gerald Manley Hopkins)

By contrast, this much more ambitious song exercises the singer to the full, matching the scope offered by the grand proportions, colourful imagery, and heightened language of the Hopkins poem: a splendid *tour de force*. In accordance with the effortless professionalism we expect from the composer, piano flourishes before each vocal entry end on a note helpful to the singer, removing potential pitch difficulties that might have been experienced with such strong divergences from the key signature (A major) (Example 2). Marked nuances are precise, and help with enunciation. Immediately after the opening declamatory recitative there begins an *Allegro* which, the composer says, should be considered the song's main tempo. Crisp rhythms are set in action and diction is especially important: this is another case when the rests are not intended as breathing places but as punctuation. The first opportunity for a breath is after 'snow-flake' (place the 'k' exactly on the next beat). 'Fleeciest, frailest flix 'd' is something of a tongue-twister. As always with Hopkins, consonants are to be relished physically and sensously, and alliterations emphasized (lots of rolled 'r's wherever possible). Another device shows the composer's innate understanding of vocal technique: short phrases follow one another and accumulate, training the singer in readiness for the more expansive phrases which come at the ends of paragraphs.

The characteristic decorative figures in the piano's right hand at the start of the song recur in a quieter passage, the tempo flexible for a moment. A row of alliterative 'n's in succession turn to 'm's and 'l's as the music whips up intensity and rhythms go whirling on. Full use must be made of these lovely liquid consonants and their vocal mellifluousness. Breaths must be timed accurately to avoid losing momentum—the lines surge up gloriously to an exhilarating high A flat on 'Minds', preceded by a big crescendo with a quick breath immediately after it—this springboard action makes for a perfect placing, leaving no time to spoil the next note. Being compelled to plunge straight in in this way inevitably works, and is greatly encouraging to the timid. Even the breath itself becomes an expressive device as a sigh or a gasp of wonder. It must always be remembered that fast-moving

Ex. 2 Milner

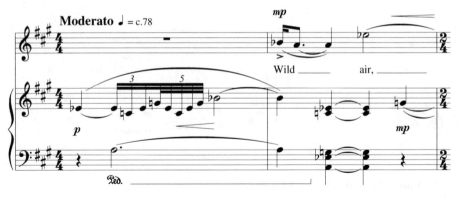

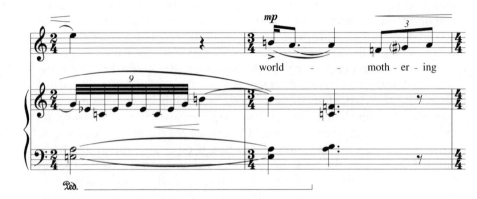

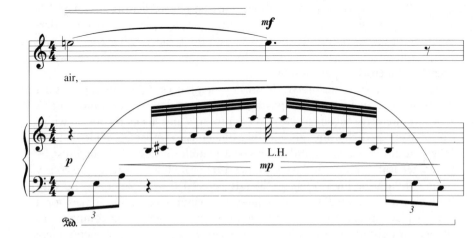

Ex. 3 Milner

This air _____ which by life's law My lung must draw and draw

Now, but to breathe its praise, Minds ___ me in ma-ny ways Of her

syllables need not seem rushed, even when they involve semiquavers on 'and', 'draw', or 'but to'. The feeling of legato must prevail (Example 3).

Some long and short triplets can swing naturally against the beat (there are plain chords in the piano at this point). Tenderness and warmth of mood return, suddenly coming to a comma in the music to prepare for the word 'Mary'—a suitably rapt moment, needing a poised and crystalline tone. Some lingering triplets make this a particularly grateful phrase to sing. A glowing radiance in the poem, heightened by much alliteration on open sounds in the text, is mirrored by glowing music, now once again in the basic *Allegro* tempo. There is an affirmative major tonality here enhanced by the word-setting. 'No way' rising to a held high G should invite a fine tone-quality. The exalted atmosphere is maintained (the long phrase beginning 'I say that we are wound with mercy' must be sung in one breath), until a darker and more introspective mood arrives, and the tessitura is accordingly lower. The words 'wild web' and 'wondrous robe' must be savoured and the notes attacked gently without accents. The softer dynamics here are important and the audience must be made to listen intently. This is a crucial passage, and a slight slackening of tempo is allowed for it to make its full impact. The voice dips a little deeper (low B natural,) but without emphasis, as more sombre tonalities occur. The style becomes more rhetorical but the dark mood prevails to the end of the paragraph, which sees a return of the piano's rhythmic whirls. After a pause the singer resumes in a more extrovert spirit, corresponding with crisp, sibilant 's's and 'sh's in the text. The sharp keys keep the music bright and cheerful and rhythms are straightforward, building to a powerful and thrilling climax. Each phrase is cumulatively higher-reaching and more expansive than the last: now the singer will be thoroughly warmed up and at fullest capacity of muscle co-ordination.

After a pause, an entirely new tempo, *Molto Moderato*, brings a magical softness, contrasting with the preceding passage's vocal exuberance. The voice spins a delicate thread and then spontaneously breaks into speech patterns, awestruck, bursting once again into a joyous major-orientated *forte*, gradually accelerating, only to wind down suddenly on to a cadence

191

for 'it does no prejudice'. A sudden, brief, spell-binding *Adagio* in *pianissimo* requires the singer to negotiate long lines with steady, intense tone and rapt concentration. The tempo quickens again for a passage of triplets. Another hushed *Adagio* phrase interrupts an exultant outburst, and a dynamic *Allegro* leads to a lovely arching arpeggio down on 'God was God of old', which must be fully emphasized, *fortissimo*, with a tenuto on every note. After the more percussive-sounding texts of the previous passage, some warmer, smoother consonants return, depicting the motherly images in mellow mid-voice. Some sibilants ('sweeter' and 'Sifted to suit our sight') should be placed well forward to keep the sounds bright and clear. The voice now moves more easily around its range, rising and falling with natural grace.

A return to the opening *Moderato* sets the atmosphere for a final section of great intensity, often subdued or deeply contemplative, but breaking out with abandon at key moments. This requires much stamina to maintain the continuous, relentless legato, underpinned by flowing semiquavers in the piano. Hard work will repay the performer—a slackening of intensity must be avoided at all costs. Phrases are very long, and breaths must be swift and barely perceptible, generating a physical response from the audience, so that they seem to be breathing with the singer. The recitative-like outbursts are dramatic, full of interpretative detail. Maintaining the mounting excitement and corresponding increase in volume may prove vocally taxing, but the singer should now be at fullest stretch. A sudden *piano* comes on the word 'isled' on a high A (no fierce glottal attack here), and the end of the song is slow and very soft, with the final note a long *pianissimo* on 'child' on C sharp—usually a safe note in most voices. The gentle marked tenuto on 'thy' is important. Timing must be exact and a tender poise achieved so that the listener is left suspended in a mood of beatific calm, ready for the last song.

3. Dusk (Hilaire Belloc)

Though much more modest in proportion than the preceding song, this one is equally impressive and full of variety within a skilfully controlled gradual build to a climax, and attainment of final serenity through three, semi-strophic verses. As usual, the music's movement is continuous and the piano figurations increase in intricacy towards the middle. A relentless tread is evident throughout. The vocal writing is conventional in the broadest sense, but it is always apt and gives the singer ample opportunity to show skill and control, starting softly in the middle of the voice, almost recalling the plainchant feeling of the opening. Pitches are used economically and each phrase begins with repeated notes, dirge-like, but with great potential for differentiation of tone-quality. The music travels somewhat dangerously through break-points in the soprano voice during the latter part of the verses, each stepping a little higher. The ends of verses descend once more with the refrain 'This is the faith that I have held and hold', which is set with moving fervour. The turbulent middle verse requires considerable dramatic force for the voice to be clearly audible over the piano's more complex textures and rhythmic march. A very loud passage, high-lying on 'And harbourless for any sail to lie' makes a searing climax and needs to be powerful and full-toned yet steady. Words do not lie quite as comfortably here as elsewhere and will need some preliminary work to avoid strain. The final verse is serene and confident. The luxuriantly long legato lines and perfectly placed consonants aid clarity. All crescendos and diminuendos are to be observed scrupulously. The final heart-rending cry, 'O my last Ally', may give tuning problems. The refrain ends the cycle simply and touchingly.

This admirable work should be given a key position in a recital. It may be interesting to compare it with the Williamson *Celebration of Divine Love* (See Volume 1), which is similarly fervent and well integrated. Song cycles of this stature are greatly needed to lift singer and audience with their firm spiritual commitment. There are interesting comparisons to be made with the works of Messiaen, too. If other English pieces are programmed with it, miniatures would be the best choice. Simple folk settings or very early music would also go well, as would Spanish music in particular (some of the piano's figurations suggest Spanish rhythms at times!). This is a tremendous vehicle for a singer of real artistry.

The Hare in the Moon
(1977)

Rhian Samuel (born 1944)
Text from a Japanese folk-tale *(Ryōkan)*
Translated by Geoffrey Bownas and Anthony
Thwaite in *The Penguin Book of Japanese Verse*

T III; M III
Soprano and piano
Duration *c*.7'

Rhian Samuel is an experienced and assured writer of vocal music, and there are several other works of hers that can be warmly recommended to readers of this book. Aided by an excellent ear and natural sense of proportion, she consistently produces vocal lines that are as pleasurable to sing as they are to look at. The beautifully neat, bold manuscript is an added attraction for the potential performer. Everything is well laid-out, with clarity and practicability as high priorities.

Subtitled 'Narrative, Threnody and Envoi', this is really a miniature cantata. The original version is scored for soprano, vibraphone, marimba, and double bass. It sits very comfortably in the soprano voice, but a flexible mezzo would also be suitable: the one very high note is so well set that it is unlikely to fail. The composer manages to incorporate spoken and Sprechstimme passages within the natural inflections of the wide-ranging phrases, and the whole piece sparkles with vitality and spontaneity. The clear-textured piano part underlines and illustrates the story, and balance between voice and piano is ideal. Despite a basically atonal idiom, the music should cause few problems for a young singer. Pitch cues in the piano should be easily detectable at key moments.

A fresh clear voice is necessary for the precise and somewhat detached delivery appropriate to the text. Oriental folk-tales have long been a source of fascination for composers: there are examples from Stravinsky to Judith Weir. Many other composers have produced Japanese haiku settings, and these have tended to encourage an especially refined mode of singing, in which small details are thrown sharply into focus in sparse, exposed lines that have a distinctively enigmatic quality. Melismas are used sparingly.

This piece skilfully bridges the gap between Eastern and Western styles and assimilates the best of both. 'Spare' parlando writing is contrasted by a rich array of neo-baroque runs and melismas, and a dazzling variety of rhythmic patterns. The narration of the tale, which constitutes over half the piece, is speeded up by passages of fast-moving, non-notated speech. The singer has a chance to characterize the creatures: fox, monkey, and hare, as well as the god in his disguise as an old man. Devices such as glissandos are used spectacularly to add to the fun. The 'Threnody' and 'Envoi' are contrasting miniature arias, the first full of virtuoso display, and the latter a tender and poetical resolution.

The soprano's opening phrase, beginning on A, is unaccompanied. It should be possible to strike a tuning-fork or touch a piano just before entering the auditorium, and to hold the note in the memory just long enough to last through the applause. It would be a great pity to spoil the atmosphere by having an obvious cue given on stage. Since it is such a short phrase, constant repetitions may even fix it in the aural (and physical) memory quite securely. After this, the piano's soft opening chord introduces a spoken passage, notated in strict rhythm with crosses for note-heads, and marked 'in a matter-of-fact way'. Subtle inflections of pitch, including a small portamento, are indicated. There is a transition from unpitched speech to pitched Sprechstimme, and it is worth taking time to acquire the ability to switch at will from one to the other. Sprechstimme (conventional Schoenbergian notation has normal notes with crosses through their stems) means that an identifiable pitch should be heard for a moment before the note is 'bent' or inflected away, as in speaking, to avoid any pure elongation of the pitch that could result in 'normal' singing. Considerable patience is needed to master these differentiations of timbre and articulation. They do of course vary according to the word or syllable, but greatly enhance the palette of available vocal colours. The line then progresses to actual singing, and the voice has a rewarding melisma, soaring up on 'bond', then falling away naturally, moving back through the various modes of delivery in reverse order, ending with a spoken word 'friendship'. This line can be useful as a study exercise for the piece in general, and the facility gained will serve for similar passages in other works. The voice part is well spaced, with plenty of chances to rest while the piano continues the story. A nimble and versatile player is needed: sensitive, delicate of touch, and quick to react to the many bold changes of mood. Each time the tale starts to race along in a fast, freely notated section, the piano's right hand has a 'box'—a series of rapid repetitions of the notes within a frame, performed *ad libitum*—while the left hand continues in strict rhythm. The singer declaims the text freely and swiftly over the top: she will need to aim for a high, piercing pitch to be audible. At the point where the god is introduced, a swirling grace-note melisma decorates the word. The voice should coast smoothly and easily over its wide range, and individual notes need not be articulated, once they have been practised slowly enough to make sure of the pitches. Once the god has assumed his disguise, there is a particularly apt use of glissando on 'Help me', marked 'whining voice', sliding down from a loud high A flat to the bottom of the range, dissolving into speech tone. There are also amusing, croaked trills on the separate syllables of 'hung-ry old'. These effects are immediate and always work perfectly. For the following piece of fast declaimed narration the composer marks the places where the voice should co-ordinate with the piano's chords: this helps to control the delivery and accentuate the alliteration in the text ('From', 'front', 'fox', 'fish'). The 'hare, hopping' is also well timed for clarity. Some separate staccato attacks lead to a swooping downward portamento on 'thing', where the 'ng' can be used to maintain smoothness.

A *meno mosso* passage is particularly rewarding, the text deftly set for maximum effect. At a faster 3/8 section the singer has groups of descending semiquavers in Sprechstimme which aptly convey the malevolence of the fox and monkey. As the hapless hare goes unwittingly to his fate, the *pianissimo* line 'Hare did as he was told' is marked 'knowingly, even ominously'—another example of the composer's instructions guiding the performer in a concise and practical way. For the sudden shocking surge up a tenth on 'then' the 'n' will prove useful for vocalizing, up to the firm, accented, glottal attack on 'In-to'. The composer, ever-sensitive to the singer's need, has marked a comma just before the exciting leap to high C on 'hurled': a perfect approach and ideal choice of pitch for syllable. Too vigorous an 'h', though, could cause trouble—the sound is more important than the exhalation, and a German 'ch' could prove most helpful here, and much more audible (Example 1).

Ex 1 Samuel

After this bout of frenetic activity and swift interplay of moods, the 'Threnody' sets an entirely different atmosphere, as the god reflects on the merits of the animals, and concludes that 'the hare was the finest'. This is a display piece containing the characteristics of a decorative baroque aria, with first triplets and then ornaments, within a poignant *Adagio*. The keyboard part takes up the baroque gestures, and leads into an *Andante*, which accelerates to a climax on a melisma on 'kind'. Intervals are crucial here as it is unaccompanied. The last section of the Threnody begins with a brilliant *arietta*, Handelian semiquaver runs repeating the words 'the finest', finally arriving on high B, and then subsiding in a 'sobbing' series of accented notes. This high-lying passage may cause some difficulty, and the singer may feel a little strangulated on the word 'finest' because of the diphthong and silent syllables 'f', 's', 't'. It is important to observe the decrescendo promptly to avoid tiring. The descent will be a considerable relief. The last lines of the 'Threnody' carry a moving description of the hare's 'promotion' to heaven, with pitches gently accented in undulating lines that flatter the voice. A long diminuendo on high G sharp is helped by the 'v' of 'ever', allowing it to be carefully poised before floating freely. Plangent two-note groups of quavers in the piano (marked 'hesitantly') form the link into the 'Envoi'. This has luxuriant and shapely vocal lines, with delicately poised melismas that are a joy to sing. Pitching may need some preliminary study, but the piano's harmonies give secure support, and conscientious preparation, line by line, should soon allow the singer to savour this most beautifully moulded concluding section, serene and rhapsodic in mood (Example 2). Even the last word ('sleeves') allows for a controlled slow fade, making the most of the vocalized 'v', so that tuning remains exact.

Ex. 2 Samuel

This 'cycle' is an ideal concert piece in length and concept. Its appeal and entertainment value are immediate. As a study piece, too, it is invaluable, enabling the singer to learn more about her own voice and its subtlest inflections, as well as utilizing a wide variety of singing techniques, from fast coloratura to raptly spun legato. Since the work is so compact and complete in itself, it could be placed almost anywhere in a recital. It could be set amid a selection of earlier music, perhaps either following or preceding a baroque or classical cantata (Handel, Mozart, Haydn). There is a wealth of material in Purcell, too, from slow-paced arias to dramatic *scene* such as 'The Blessed Virgin's Expostulation'. Framed by larger pieces, even complete Lieder cycles, *The Hare in the Moon* will stand its ground very well, and surprise and delight many a cautious audience. Other folk-tales or works of Eastern influence could be included; many composers have set Japanese lyrics (Stravinsky, Goehr). It is important, however, to avoid too many miniatures in one programme. A careful balance needs to be kept between works of varying length and level of activity, and it would be unfortunate to pre-empt this work's rich detail by placing anything too complex just before it.

Time to the Old
(1979)

William Schuman (1910–92)
Text by Archibald MacLeish

T III; M IV
Medium/high voice and piano
Duration 11′15″

This beautifully written short cycle by a distinguished US composer completely disproves any arguments that twelve-tone writing can impair lyricism and expressive freedom. One rarely finds such accurately heard use of the voice in silky-smooth lines that dip and soar and words that fall naturally. The music sits perfectly in the lyric soprano voice, but a warm-voiced tenor would find this an ideal vehicle, and flexible, light mezzos and baritones would also be at home. The vocal writing is flattering and exposing at the same time. The mood is mainly contemplative and spiritual, and tempos basically steady. Full-blooded dramatics are largely absent, and there is a spell-binding concentration on mellifluous long-breathed phrases, allowing the pitches to provide their own intrinsic colourings, unerringly precise in their aural conception. Every note seems ideally placed, and the composer is very clear about what he wants in interpretative detail. All breath marks, including optional ones, are indicated, and no more should be taken. This cycle deserves the most exquisite singing, and a fine technique will be an advantage in avoiding any unevenness in the expertly moulded progressions.

The three songs are to be performed without a break, and are sure to make a compelling effect with their intense commitment and assurance: a perfect example of writing for the voice without resort to extremes, and an important contribution to the repertoire. Much more ought to be heard of this composer's wide-ranging and exciting output, and his large-scale works involving voices are a rich resource for the adventurous programme-planner.

1. The Old Gray Couple

A series of gently glowing phrases span a large vocal range effortlessly, with all syllables helpfully smoothing the path, and crucial words pin-pointed by subtle rhythmic changes and pauses (Example 1). The natural flow of the words dictates rhythmic patterns which lie so easily that the singer can adopt an almost conversational style, with little bursts of extra energy as phrases crescendo rapidly to *forte* then back again with the utmost smoothness. The very slow tempo may prove problematic to those of limited breath

Ex.1 Schuman

They ____ have on - ly ____ to look ____ at each oth - er ____ to laugh

capacity, causing some phrases to be divided. Lines become increasingly radiant and lyrical, and a warm voice will be well suited to the closing phrases. Much poise and skill is needed for the final held E flat, *piano* with a diminuendo at the very end. This will demonstrate the singer's ability to float and control this slightly problematic note, but as always, helpful consonants provide an aid to legato ('l' to start with and 'n' to end).

2. Conway Burying Ground

Piano parts are very well integrated here, in keeping with the impression of a continuous span, rather than of three separate songs. The strumming broken chords in the first song are developed and used in a more fervent and extrovert manner in this slightly faster movement, to support the vocal line and enhance emotional impact. A ritualistic effect is achieved. The vocal line begins in mid-voice and rises in pitch and volume, reaching a climax on a high G, followed by a sudden diminuendo to *piano* for the most crucial statement 'they do not know'. This is all the more arresting for being separated clearly from the preceding paragraph, and kept *a tempo* in stark isolation, before the opening theme occurs for the third time. Each time it recurs, the lines seem to grow naturally from it with freely developing intensity, underlined by the split chords.

The last section of the song returns to the supple, wide-ranging lines characteristic of the opening setting, trailing away on a sustained 'until', with a long pause (but no marked diminuendo), which should help the singer to feel confident in keeping the note (the C above middle C) at a comfortable level, remembering to elide the final 'l' evenly and maintain tone to its very end. The word 'interval' is given subtle rhythmic treatment. The voice has to stop after the first syllable (a minim) and continue after a rest of two-thirds of a triplet. As there is a diminuendo on the first note it is probably wise to close on to the 'n' of 'in' early, perhaps even on the second crotchet count, and no breath must be taken at the rest. It is worth taking the trouble to perfect what may seem a small detail, but in music of such refinement the performer cannot afford to neglect anything, however fleeting.

3. Dozing on the Lawn

Here the piano has sustained chords, some of them broken into arpeggios as in the preceding songs. The steady tempo and calm mood of the opening are recalled, with the same luxuriant warmth of tone required to do justice to the flatteringly wide sweeps. However, an edgy precision is appropriate for the faster, more rhythmically energized phrases which intervene.

Grace-notes are used to enhance the lovely effect of the swooping downward intervals—these are a joy to sing and there is ample time to negotiate them cleanly (Example 2). The closing phrases have a rapt beauty and the singer merely has to obey the minutiae of the score's instructions. A final long-held B flat with a crescendo and diminuendo on 'lie' will be better if the 'ah' part of the vowel is used until the very end, keeping the sound bright and well forward to prevent wavering, and remembering to engage support muscles throughout.

Ex. 2 Schuman

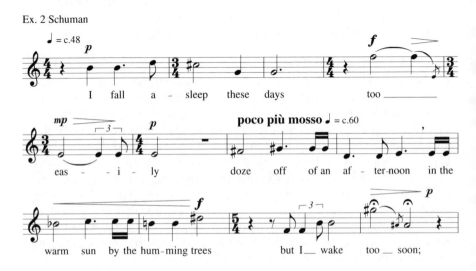

It is a tribute to the great skill and experience of the composer that the abiding impression of this work is of warmth and naturalness, and the tightly controlled compositional structure does not impose a feeling of academicism. These lovely songs are sure to sound well, especially in a lively acoustic, and, although it is the composer's wish that texts be printed in the programme, there is little danger of words being lost with such precisely judged settings.

The piece would fit happily into any traditional recital programme: its musical distinction can easily hold its place alongside major classics, especially those of the Austro-German composers. It would make a good beginning to the second half of a concert, immediately engaging the audience's concentration. A complete recital of contrasting cycles in English would be a particularly good idea. Britten's works would complement Schuman's style exceptionally well, and give the performers a chance to exhibit another side of their talents. A well-focused voice is the prime requisite, and any uncertainty in placing would be clearly discernible. It is therefore an excellent choice for training a young voice, giving time to examine the quality of each note, without being distracted by complexities of articulation.

Love Songs
(1987–90)

Malcolm Singer (born 1953)
Text by e e cummings

T III; M II
Soprano and piano
Duration 5′

Malcolm Singer is a composer whose works always give pleasure to performers and audience alike. Clearly imagined, precise, and beautifully wrought, they linger in the memory as models of unpretentious style and charm. He belongs to no particular movement but has often employed the techniques of minimalism with ingenuity and wit, to delightful and innately musical effect. The material is always meticulously organized and presented. The musical idiom is fresh, uncluttered, and accessible, yet not at all derivative.

This little trio of songs represents his small-scale occasional pieces. Each was written to celebrate a wedding of personal friends. All are apt and touching, and sweetly understated in keeping with cummings's verses, whose succintness is ideally suited to this purpose.

They are not perhaps quite as straightforward to perform as they may appear. Poised control, an even delivery, and an ability to keep a regular pulse will all be needed. As with all relatively simple vocal music, the singer is often left exposed, without spectacular vocal acrobatics to ensure due appreciation, and every note has to bear close examination. Unsteadiness or tiredness cannot easily be concealed, and there is no refuge in extreme histrionics or dramatic colourings of timbre. The unaffected manner appropriate to preform these little pieces may prove elusive at first. Young singers will sound lovely in this music. A light soprano (or even a tenor) will be happy in the middle song, but a good, well-focused middle range will be needed for the others, especially for the powerful opening—indeed a mezzo would be quite at home here. The songs do not, of course, have to be performed as a group, but can be used as the occasion demands, although the given order works well.

1. Untitled (1988)

This starts very slowly, at crotchet = 40, and is quite a big song in this context, full of drama and bold gesture. The harmony is static—a pedal F continues throughout, and a 'molto pedale' indication aids the deep supporting resonance that binds the piece. Despite this the composer works his material so expertly that there is no lack of variety. Hugely spaced piano chords, consisting of layered seconds, provide a sonorous beginning. These range up and down the octave continually, the clashing intervals occasionally resolving on to more consonant triads, providing a *perpetuum mobile* of slow oscillations. Against this the singer has to produce a firm clear line in the middle of the range, surrounded entirely by the piano's pitches. The given vocal dynamics may need to be boosted considerably to avoid balance problems. Much is made in the voice part of the minor and major third above the keynote of F. The word 'swim' on low D flat is quite difficult for a soprano: using the lips strongly for the 'w' will aid the focus, and the vowel must be as spacious as possible. After the first paragraph, the voice begins to concentrate on monotones, the volume gradually rising with the pitch. Rhythms remain well varied, and counting beats carefully will avoid possible pitfalls. Phrases often end in long notes with crescendos, so any lack of support will be exposed. The composer, obviously aware of potential problems, has given an optional breathing place just before each of these. It is generally better to be able to make a real crescendo than be inhibited by lack of power. Intensity increases cumulatively, and as the singer's repeated notes rise gradually by step until she reaches high F, *fortissimo*, stamina will be thoroughly tested. Singers will know how tiring such a seemingly straightforward ascent can be. At this point piano chords become barer, stripped of their thirds, contributing to a feeling of rigour and purpose. The singer now has some welcome relief, leaping up and down the octave in basic fanfare figures (taking care to place a tritone securely). A slow diminuendo, with the voice's notes becoming gradually more sustained, brings the song to a close, the piano's chords remaining in bare fifths to the end. A tiny coda gives the voice a somewhat cautionary final say, softly on a monotone A flat: 'Love did no more begin than Love will end'. The last word has to be held with a 'dim a niente'. The 'n' will be an important aid here to make sure of a clean fade. The song is dedicated: 'for Nina and Timothy on the occasion of their marriage'.

2. Love is more thicker than forget (1987)

Marked 'quiet and playful', this delicious miniature, inscribed 'for Gail and Phil, on the occasion of their marriage', involves a fleeting, delicate waltz. It is not at all simple, especially with regard to pitching. The music swings along continuously, commas providing quick breathing places. The construction is nicely symmetrical: two strophic verses are separated by four bars of solo piano, and introduction and coda also consist of four bars. It all makes a beautifully neat impression, and the lilting, one-in-a-bar movement of the waltz is quite irresistible. The vocal melody, though, is trickily chromatic, and there are some teasing cross-rhythms, making phrases fascinatingly varied. The piano part, in continuous crotchets, remains detached throughout. Everything must be light and seemingly effortless. The alliterations of the poem are brought out delightfully and the whole piece seems to trip along so infectiously that it is very important to polish musical details and check intervals before attempting it at full speed. Conversely, it could be useful to speak the words in rhythm at full tempo as part of the learning process. Tone should be clear and bright, high-placed, with very little vibrato. The natural fall of the syllables can dictate subtle nuances, lengthening or shortening notes very slightly to keep the waltz rhythm buoyant (Example 1).

Ex. 1 Singer

The composer stipulates a metronome mark of 92 per bar, but adds the term 'Minuet-like', giving an important hint as to style, which must remain elegant and unflustered. The fast-moving words will require excellent articulation, and the singer should make sure to release each sound swiftly and allow throat muscles to relax. A special effort will certainly be needed to preserve an even flow. As in all fast music, small notes must not be neglected or rushed. Notes before breaths will have to be shortened, and there is no time for deep inhalations. A singer with difficulty in floating head voice may have trouble achieving the precision and lightness required. If the voice is allowed to become heavy, the piece could prove surprisingly uncomfortable, despite its brevity. The very last note is a long high G sharp on 'sky' (not the kindest of words, because of its percussive consonants and awkward diphthong—it is best to sing 'Ska' and let the ending take care of itself!). This must be kept pure and thread-like

3. I carry your heart with me (1990)

This poem is another great favourite with composers: Edward Harper also sets it memorably in his orchestral cycle *Seven Poems of e e cummings*.

Here we have a characteristic example of 'systems' music. Voice and piano start together, the voice intoning middle A in steady machine-like patterns, remaining on this monotone for much of the song. The accompaniment at first proceeds in quaver chords, unpedalled but smooth. A telling feature of the early part of the movement is the constant stopping and starting, with voice and piano rests coinciding precisely. This means that ensemble has to be kept on a tight rein. There is a significant general pause between the two opening sentences, and concentration has to be held suspended through it (Example 2). The piano eventually changes to con-

Ex. 2 Singer

(a-ny-where i go you go, my dear; and what-e-ver is done by on - ly me

is your do-ing my dar - ling) i fear no fate

(for you are my fate, my sweet) i want no world.

tinuous semiquaver arpeggios before the singer's paragraph ends on a very long note, with crescendo, on 'You'. After this there is a change of character: the piano begins strong pulsing quavers on a tritone increasing the mechanical effect. Note-values condense and intensify, and triplet movement pushes the music forward. The piano's right hand is in exact rhythmic unison, while the left hand picks out the singer's pitches which now move around a little, before settling back to the repeated A. Additive rhythms need watching here; in particular, dotted quavers have to be counted scrupulously. The singer's final sentence starts low in the voice and moves around the natural speaking range, stopping on an extended low B, as the piano's patterns become sparser. After another general pause, during which it is particularly crucial to maintain tension, the song's opening makes a brief, fragmented reappearance, fading on a short pause. The piece was written for 'Polly and Theo, on the occasion of their marriage'.

As encores these charming little songs could hardly be bettered, but as a group they provide a welcome contrast to late Romanticism, for instance, or to works unencumbered by system such as the multi-faceted songs of Charles Ives. They are also ideal for informal occasions, especially wedding or anniversary parties. There is a real need for short pieces of such quality and wide appeal, and, although less-skilled singers may make a good basic effect with them, there is little doubt that a disciplined professional approach and rigorous attention to pitch and rhythmic detail will prove an advantage. The end result, however, should have a carefree spontaneity. Having attained familiarity with the 'additive rhythms', the singer can now proceed to the larger-scale cycles of Messiaen, which could form an interesting stylistic comparison.

Her Anxiety
(1991)

Mark-Anthony Turnage (born 1960)
Text by W. B. Yeats

T III; M IV
Soprano and piano
Duration 10'30"

Mark-Anthony Turnage's remarkable gifts have already been widely recognized. Despite his comparative youth, he has deservedly established a reputation as one of the most exciting composers to have emerged in recent years. His successful opera *Greek* showed his mastery of dramatic vocal writing, and intuitive grasp of the characteristics of timbre and resonance. A keen ear and natural musicality are immediately evident in this welcome cycle, and the material is manipulated with exemplary clarity and economy. The honesty and directness of the music make a powerful impact, yet the piece will not tax a young singer, nor one of limited experience. The distinctive musical language carries echoes of earlier English music, from Purcell to Vaughan Williams and Britten, but these influences are imbibed at so deep a level that all seems fresh and new.

The score is meticulously neat, with all details laid out clearly. The distribution of the four movements is particularly attractive in its symmetry: two settings for voice and piano frame short solo movements for each performer, and the proportions seem ideal. Standard notation is used, barring key signatures, and all except the solo voice movement have time signatures.

1. The Lady's First Song

It is always reassuring for the vocal performer to have the chance to launch into a bold uninhibited opening paragraph. After a piano introduction of spare, repeated, fanfare-like figures, joined to long-held chords, the soprano's sobbing, hocketed 'O's portray the Lady's agonized love-pangs. Turnage has an acute sense of the intrinsic qualities of each vocal pitch. Both E flat and B flat are excellent choices for a lingering moan, and he knows well that the middle register of the soprano voice can yield a rich variety of colours within varied dynamics. The singer will be aware of using her voice instrumentally, testing and monitoring each sound in turn in the series of stark declamations. Pitches are repeated continually, and the placing of the vocal line within the piano texture is most telling. The piano part, laid out on four staves, is so widely spaced that it surrounds the voice, which cuts cleanly through the centre. This makes a lovely bell-like effect, redolent of some of Britten's vocal writing. Rhythmic unisons between voice and piano, particularly in each note of the hockets, enhance the feeling of formal ritual, evocative of early music, wonderfully simple and direct (Example 1). Eventually a more cantabile vocal style takes over, and the accompaniment flows more smoothly for a while, before the throbbing 'O's resume, this time more continuously, yet muted and gradually fading, leaving the piano to die away with more harmonic fanfare fragments embedded amongst long-held notes.

2. Sweet Dancer

Marked 'freely', this solo movement for voice lies very comfortably indeed, and moves around the natural soprano range with great sparkle and vitality. The bright F sharp for the opening is ideally incisive, and staccatos and marked accents all work perfectly. Every detail has to be observed and subtle gradings of dynamic are crucial. Again, features of early music are clearly evident; the second phrase's paired notes aid the bouncing, dancing effect, but rests should not be used as breathing places. This line is a superb example of word-setting: the staccato 'Plot of the' springs naturally on to the high G sharp of 'Garden' in a most enjoyable way. The suppleness of the lines can be savoured without the least danger of a lapse in tonal quality, and there are virtually no hazardous syllables. Longer notes provide points of orientation and pitch memory, both physical as well as aural. The high F sharp, F natural, D sharp, and D natural are particularly useful in this respect. The sharpened notes have an important psychological role in keeping the pitching bright. For the second part of the setting there is a gentle unforced parlando on low B natural. This should fall very easily in the natural speaking range, and the speed is judged exactly right for this. The

Ex. 1 Turnage

Ex. 1 Turnage continued

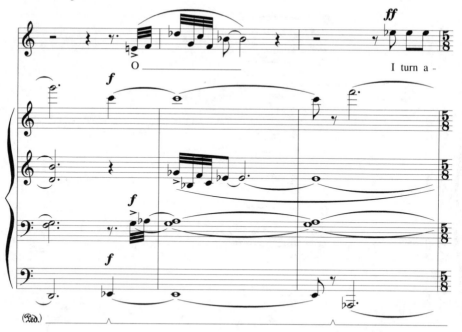

final paragraph builds and expands cumulatively, the lines dipping and darting around excitingly. Felicitous details include a swift scooping glissando up a fifth, and, as attention focuses on the repeated 'dance' and then 'Dancer', the last two phrases are glorious to sing: they contain huge intervals, with tiny low, flicked staccato springboard notes in between, and are guaranteed to come off brilliantly (Example 2).

Ex. 2 Turnage

3. The Lady's Second Song

This piano interlude is really a song without words, echoing aspects of the opening movement, and also providing a foretaste of the final setting's more elegiac mood. Dynamics are full of violent contrast, and all is written in the treble clef. Tripping, dance-like figures appear in the second half, and these then proliferate and build to a forceful climax on *fortissimo* chords. After a moment of peace, a final phrase gathers even more force, landing on a thunderous tremolando to end.

4. Her Anxiety

In this, the title-song, the harmonic language and gestures of both the English Romantics and early music are most subtly infused in the texture to beautiful effect. The soprano starts unaccompanied, and, again, there are useful pitch-pointers, in this case the long-held D and F naturals, which give a chance to focus and memorize the physical sensation of the vibrating tone. 'Spring', *fortissimo* on F, sets a somewhat familiar test in preserving tonal beauty on a potentially constricting syllable. Countless settings of Romantic poetry have given singers this uneasy task. The best course is to let go of the rolled 'r' as quickly as possible, and not to prepare the '-ng' in advance, but to leave the throat relaxed, keeping the 'i' as open as is practicable. As in all three of the vocal settings, there is constant rhythmic vitality and flexibility, and Scotch snaps are used to crisp effect. Rhythmic unisons between voice and piano are again a continuing feature. The music basically avoids counterpoint, yet the exceptional clarity and rigour of utterance never seems arid or static. There is a true nobility in the fastidious control and discipline.

The music is divided into clearly defined sections, and brief 'General Pauses' punctuate the lines. The composer is not afraid to use silence as a dramatic aid, and his sense of space and timing are unerring. Slow-moving unisons with the piano's chords on 'Prove that I lie' are most compelling and intensity builds to a peak. After a pause, the singer again has a solo line, with some baroque rhythmic elements. As the piano joins in again, the music becomes more and more impassioned, culminating in the climactic 'Love is nearer death' (Example 3). Gradually, tension relents in a chilling

Ex. 3 Turnage

series of dying echoes of 'Prove that I lie'. The tessitura descends until it falls below the stave. It should be noted that final dynamics are not all that quiet, and the composer is thoughtfully aware that a young soprano's lower range may be a little vulnerable. He therefore gives the singer the chance to keep the tone firm and well supported, averting the danger of a nervous petering-out. There seem to be two possible interpretations for the ending: it could be considered either as a murmured incantation, still and poised, and resigned, rather than turbulent, or as an exhausted last utterance, weary and despairing. However, it would be unwise to sacrifice cleanliness of tone on the last dropping minor third, since the low D flat and B flat have to be sustained and tone must be held steady. Emotions suppressed and turned inward in this way make the song almost unbearably moving. As with the first movement, the piano's top notes lie above the voice, and the texture seems translucent and uncluttered to the end.

This impressive and assuredly idiomatic work is a model of restraint, yet an audience will be riveted by it. It belongs firmly within the great tradition of

British vocal music and would sit very happily in a programme of Purcell and Walton in particular, the 'Song for the Lord Mayor's Table' making a near-ideal choice. Teachers and keen students should seize on it gratefully. Its fresh appeal conceals a formidable compositional skill, and attention to the minutest detail of vocal nuance. Even beside a spectacular vocal display piece, or florid aria, it will not be eclipsed. It should therefore take the prime position in a recital, before or after the interval. It deserves to find a lasting place in the repertory, and one eagerly awaits the composer's next vocal concert work.

First Frost, Op. 115
(1988)

James Wilson (born 1922)
Text by Kevin Nichols

T III; M II
Bass and piano
Duration *c*.18'

The work of the Dublin-based British composer James Wilson is a consistent source of pleasure. With unfaltering taste, a delicate wit, and unobtrusive technical expertise, he has evolved a flexible and confident musical language that is loosely tonal, yet with a free-ranging chromaticism. Some harmonic and rhythmic gestures are redolent of other English music, especially of Britten, yet his work has a distinctive style and exceptional emotional power. He is not afraid to portray passion, and his works leave a strong impression long after the performance. He is particularly good at sustaining atmosphere, and shows an acute response to the sensual properties of words as well as to the minutiae of their inflections. His vocal works are especially rewarding, and his choice of texts is admirable. Highly cultured and open-minded, he is able to draw on a very broad range of interests and experience, and a highly developed sense of humour is an added asset.

A substantial and most satisfying cycle for bass voice is greatly to be welcomed. Contemporary repertoire in general tends to be weighted heavily in favour of sopranos, with baritones also relatively well served. The texts are exceptional in their wide range of colours and emotions; they present a veritable cornucopia of memorable images, and the biting perceptions need no unnecessary adornment. They reflect eloquently on the relationship between Man and Nature, in particular the parallels between Death and the coming of Winter. Despite the often grim pictures, an idealism and a deep sense of inner truth and beauty prevail.

The sonic properties of the words also fall strikingly on the ear, and the singer, too, can relish the feel of them. There is abundant alliteration and onomatapoeia, and Wilson wisely does not clog the texture and risk obscuring this. Lines in general are set very sparely, and the voice is often left exposed. There are very few melismas, and the composer is obviously aware that florid writing is less effective with the heavier voices. Words are set straightforwardly, the intrinsically weighty resonances of the bass voice always taken into consideration. All nuances and inflections spring directly from the text, and the frequent switches of mood and gradations of intensity are accomplished with easy mastery. The loose recitative style which predominates allows the singer considerable room for manœuvre in shaping phrases and highlighting key words.

The piano part does not require a virtuoso, but a thoughtful, intuitive player will make much of its clear textures and intermittent word-painting, although the voice decidedly commands centre stage. Balance problems are unlikely, and there is no need to force tone even at climaxes. There are very few really loud moments, so their effect is all the more powerful. In the many unaccompanied passages, the singer can make intimate contact with the listener. Pace and dynamic are subject to the widest variation, and the general impression is of a spontaneous expressiveness.

The work is in one long span, in the form of an extended *scena*, but interest is sustained throughout. Normal notation is used, and double barlines mark the ends of sections.

After a piano introduction in sparse octaves, the voice enters gently, in flexible phrases that describe the onset of day. Rhythms are entirely natural, as if speaking in a confiding tone. The piano often seems to be a secondary, wordless voice, which provides discreet comment. At *un poco più mosso*, the accompaniment's fast repeated figures (staccato in the left hand) lead into an extrovert piano solo with shimmering tremolandos and trills. The voice's hushed musing, at first alone, brings a return to the steadier tempo, and the piano's swirling arpeggios enhance the nostalgic mood. Again, the voice is left exposed, answered only by a single line on the piano. Less comforting memories bring starker chordal support, and the singer's phrases move along in natural speech rhythms, eventually dropping low on the word 'honey'.

A new section at a faster tempo begins with a bold rhetorical piano solo, but the voice's response is low-key. The singer's terse fragments are marked 'secco', and should be enunciated in a clear, detached manner. Triplets free the lines from rigidity, and Wilson shows his penchant for throw-away lines at the ends of phrases. A delicate piano passage features dropping staccato figures that accelerate into a succession of repeated bitonal thirds. As before the voice enters alone with clipped phrases (Example 1). The music proceeds

Ex. 1 Wilson

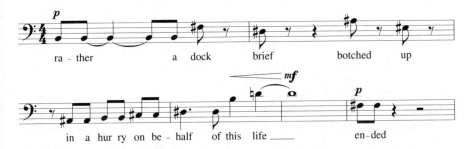

in similar vein for a lengthy stretch, alternating short piano solos with succinct vocal phrases. Gradually the voice begins to linger and swell on longer notes in the higher range. For the sentence beginning 'washed out', singing quasi-non-vibrato will help portray the bleakness of the text. The phrase 'business as usual' is repeated in resigned fashion, the voice falling to low F. A series of evocative images of birds and beasts is especially memorable: short vocal solos are answered by delicate 'brush-strokes' on the piano. The lazy triplet on 'casual seals' is a nice touch, and the lightness of the scoring throughout ensures verbal clarity. A high *pianissimo* passage beginning 'out of view' can be sung in a disembodied falsetto. The voice soon relaxes down again, the final word 'luggage' easing on to low A.

The fastest section of the work now follows. The voice's wide-ranging lines (there is a rapid descent down a tenth to low A), are underpinned by motoric dotted rhythms deep in the piano's left hand, all *una corda* and very soft. Quasi-minimalist ostinatos in running semiquavers replace them, and the tessitura gradually rises. After a pause on 'equinox' there is a complete change of character. Resonant *cantando* chords in the piano around a rapt vocal line conjure up a moment of awed radiance. The voice soars to a high E flat with a serene melisma on 'Eternal' (Example 2). The conversational

Ex. 2 Wilson

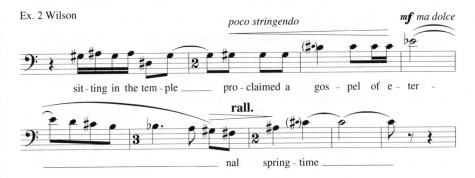

style returns, but tension builds cumulatively. The piano's material features a selection of previous motifs, such as the harp-like arpeggios, the bitonal thirds, and the low *una corda* dotted figures. The singer's phrases become more expansive but there is a sudden breaking-off at the word 'arc'.

The following section has a special charm. Fleeting piano fragments in classical style evoke memories of musical evenings of Mozart and Bach. The voice is left quite alone for a series of simple, unaffected phrases, marked 'parlando'. Bell-like held chords give occasional support, and these continue as the singer embarks on a lyrical high-lying melody, recalling the classical models. The more conversational phrase 'and ring a poignant carillon' is most vividly captured. The images are warmer and more comforting here. The voice should glow appropriately as 'the sun breaks cover'. A rather strenuous series of repeated high notes—Ds, E flats, and E naturals—bear a triumphant fanfare-like quality. By contrast the next paragraph brings a sense of doom, as winter darkness threatens the cosy images.

A more substantial piano solo, full of rippling arpeggios, initiates a change of atmosphere and a further slowing of pulse. An impressionist texture briefly depicts a sudden breeze, but lines soon thin out again. The nocturnal imagery continues at some length, with an occasional arpeggio or trill from the piano gently underlining the words. Particular details are caught to perfection ('quick as a swallow's wing', 'deadweight heart', etc.). The metre fluctuates between two and three in the bar, but eventually settles on the latter. Throughout this fluid and varied passage, it is very important to keep the sense of an underlying pulse. The singer's long 'flares' on high E flat is helped by the brief rest before it, which gives it a precise impetus. The accompaniment becomes fuller again, providing a glittering depiction of the winter landscape. The singer's most crucial moment is the rapt floating of 'netful of stars', suspended on high E. This lovely cadence ends the section.

The new tempo is faster again, and a high, sparkling piano solo heralds yet another passage of totally unaccompanied singing, plain and undecorated. For the 'November gales' there is, appropriately, more activity. Words are painted individually ('bristles', 'skeleton', 'sinew'). The thinning-out of the texture for 'aging, a loved face' is very moving, and voice and piano are spaced widely apart (Example 3). The singer's urgent questioning continues, in a mood of suppressed tension, dynamics and rhythms always finely honed to the contours of declamatory speech.

After the 'first snows fall', the final section begins. This is marked 'senza misura', and 'secco', with the voice articulating rapidly over piano arpeggios. Despite the quiet dynamic the singer should keep a penetrating edge to the sound, and breathe only where marked by the composer, taking care not to lose momentum. Curiously, there are very few written dynamics but, since the music hurtles along so relentlessly, it is to be assumed that volume can rise correspondingly with the intensity. Consonants should be exaggerated: this is the only place where the audience could miss the words. Sibilant

Ex. 3 Wilson

sounds can help considerably. A melisma on 'Go' is particularly exciting in context. The singer must snatch a quick breath after 'spent', and make a clear glottal attack on 'oxygen'. The voice's cries become more desperate, amid fears of darkness and eternal night ('the edged wind and the barbed rain wait to bundle us into the rough coat of night'—a memorable image). At the climax the singer calls passionately for 'More light'. After this rings out, softly echoing repeats gradually die away, and one last lingeringly poignant phrase climbs upwards, fading to *pianissimo*. This is quite a vocal feat to end with, and the intervals have to be managed with extreme smoothness, merging into falsetto without a break (Example 4).

Ex. 4 Wilson

light

This is a cycle of rare power, and it requires considerable stamina and artistry from the singer. It will be well placed at the end of the first half of a programme, so that its full impact can be savoured. Other pieces in the recital should be much briefer in contrast. A group of songs by Ives or Barber would be suitable, as would the Elliott Carter set mentioned in Volume 1. Early Schoenberg, Wolf, and Fauré songs would be ideal too. Because of the constant fluctuations of mood in this work, something simple, such as a Negro spiritual, could make an effective foil.

The Turkish Mouse
(1988—arr. for voice and piano 1990)

John Woolrich (born 1954)
Text adapted from a Turkish folk poem
collected by Bela Bartók

T III; M II
Soprano and piano
Duration 4'

John Woolrich is a composer who has enhanced the singer's repertory with a delightfully varied and high-quality body of vocal works, and readers of this book are urged to seek out for themselves further examples of his output. From a wealth of choice I have selected this charming miniature, which is well suited to a young soprano. It was originally written for Mary Wiegold's Song-Book, and set for voice and small ensemble. The reader is enthusiastically recommended to obtain the current list of these invaluable additions to the catalogue for voice and instruments. Several of the composers involved in that outstanding enterprise have subsequently transcribed their pieces for voice and piano, in order to increase their performance potential, and this is one such example. Short pieces are always welcome in concerts, and the discipline and economy needed to make a strong impression in a short space is a telling demonstration of compositional flair and adaptability. These Woolrich displays in abundance.

The vocal part is set in a clear and forthright manner, and the piano accompaniment shares the same characteristics of regular rhythmic patterns and short sharply accented phrases, with a good deal of staccato writing. Conveniently, since there is considerable folky dissonance (irresistibly recalling Bartókian models, both instrumental and vocal), the singer's pitches are frequently mirrored in the piano, some cunningly concealed, others in straightforward unison, so there is little risk of derailment. The singer does start alone, however, so a discreet cue will be needed. Occasionally more complex figures decorate the accompaniment, and the player will need an effortless facility and lightness of touch. A regular 4/8 pulse prevails and the basic folk-motif is subject to all kinds of subtle variation and shifts of tonality, within frequent abrupt alternations of loud and soft dynamics. Phrases sung *piano* are repeated at an emphatic *forte*, almost as if shouting to be heard: an amusing reversal of the more commonly found echo effect. The singer will need quick reactions and a clean, unforced delivery, with evenness of tone a crucial attribute. It is especially important to keep a rein on the rhythm, not allowing shorter notes to rush ahead.

The musical language reminds one forcibly of Stravinsky, especially with regard to the frequent use of grace-notes to enhance strong beats in the chugging rhythms (see *Les Noces*). These are invariably helpful vocally, the momentary 'spring mechanism' freeing the voice during potentially tiring successions of repeated notes in the vulnerable middle range, some verging on the awkward register-break area. Non-singers may be surprised to find that such writing is not nearly as simple to perform as more obviously spectacular melismatic showpieces. The insistent, mostly syllable-per-note, setting allows for very little give or take, so the singer has to acquire a good breathing discipline, taking shallow snatches of air in the offered gaps, without losing tempo. When notes are joined in pairs there are special opportunities to shape the mini-phrases, by employing the baroque practice of *notes inégales*, and shaping them deliberately in twos, as notated, instead of trying to smooth out the lines. Triplets provide still more welcome respite from the basic quaver movement.

The interpretative aspect needs some thought. In keeping with the text and parlando style, a certain faux-naïve or peasant quality may even be slightly exaggerated, especially when the volume level rises, although intonation must not suffer. Certainly, a simple, punchy directness will be in style. The voice part is non-legato throughout, although varying degrees of staccato are employed, and dynamics fluctuate quite alarmingly. There should certainly be no suspicion of an inhibited choirboy sound, and any identifiable English mannerisms should be avoided. One should beware of feyness: an easy trap to fall into in what are thought to be light-hearted items. A deadpan approach is invariably more effective; a natural innocence and spontaneity rather than an arch knowingness.

The song is full of quirky charm, always with a touch of the exotic. The working of the basic material is most ingenious, and words are set with full awareness of their natural nuances. Some trip off the tongue effortlessly, and their syllables preclude the need to notate them staccato: for instance 'chatterer of chatterers'. The most demanding passage is the very loudest: the triple *forte* on 'The mouse comes with the robbers' (immediately after a *pianissimo* version!) is followed by a string of awkward syllables, with an intervening grace-note (Example 1). The last four bars should be sung in one breath, as there is not enough time to breathe between the repetitions. The gradual diminuendo (still strictly *a tempo*) will be easier to control if air is used economically, and the throw-away ending can be placed deftly and precisely.

Ex. 1 Woolrich

'The Turkish Mouse' has a piquant, distinctive flavour that is sure to appeal to all kinds of audience, including all age groups. It would fit neatly into a programme of other folksong-based pieces, in particular the *Four Russian Songs* of Stravinsky, 'The Ugly Duckling' by Prokofiev, and any folksongs set by Bartók or Kodaly. Karel Husa's *Twelve Moravian Songs* (see Vol. 1) would also be a good choice. The pieces by Eibhlis Farrell and Donald Martino in this volume would suit a singer with the same attributes needed for this piece. From the popular recital repertoire, Mozart, Schubert, Schumann, and Poulenc would make up an attractive programme. For a subtler, and still highly appropriate complement, Chabrier's animal songs or Ravel's *Histoires naturelles* would provide a different perspective.

Postscript: After this article was completed, 'The Turkish Mouse' became available in a published version as the first in a set entitled *Three Cautionary Tales* (Faber Music). The other songs in the set are 'The North Wind' and 'Poor Mr Snail'.

Life Story
(1994)

Thomas Adès (born 1971)
Text by Tennessee Williams

T IV; M V
Soprano (or other voice) and piano (original
version for voice and ensemble, 1993)
Duration 7'

Of the younger generation of British composers, Thomas Adès has already gained a considerable reputation. His natural gifts and exceptional maturity make him an outstanding all-round musician, and his breadth of culture is an enormous asset. His vocal works so far demonstrate his fluency and his excellent ear. They may appear difficult at first: densely packed with detail in an atonal, mainstream idiom, but what may appear to be terrifying hurdles actually work in context. Rhythms seem complex but often turn out to be a refined form of written-out rubato, falling naturally with the inflections of declamatory speech.

This particular piece is a real novelty, and very entertaining. Although written originally for soprano and ensemble, it could suit any flexible voice: A is the highest note, and there are plenty of low notes to provide relaxation and avoid tiredness. Knowing of the composer's virtuosity at the keyboard, it is no surprise that, in this version, the piano part is formidable. An able pianist will welcome the challenge, and he or she will need to have quick responses, since ensemble is crucial. The singer usually leads the way, and it must all seem totally spontaneous. The text takes the form of a rambling anecdotal confession, cynical and sardonic. It is both a bitterly humorous reflection on the futility of efforts to communicate, and a protracted demonstration of self-absorption. It would be difficult to envisage it with anything other than an American accent. The histrionically gifted may even come up with a 'Deep South' version.

It is very important to read the composer's note on vocal style. He advocates the study of the late work of Billie Holliday as a model. The work is conventionally notated, the only unusual marking being 'hairpins', commonly used for crescendo–diminuendo, occurring in a wavy-lined form, to indicate degrees of intensity of vibrato. This definitely calls for a jazz technique, and the composer mentions that other gestures, such as the glissandos and the cross-rhythmed accents found throughout the piece, should be stylistically unified in similar vein. This is quite a task for the average classically trained singer, but the good breath support and wide range that most possess should prove advantageous. It is often liberating to be confronted with something that requires a different approach from the familiar repertoire.

Reading through the piece in a quasi-improvisatory way is an enlightening experience. The piano part is peppered with cunning pitch cues, embedded in the texture, cleverly guiding the singer through some of the more hectic moments. Also, unencumbered by worries about detail and, instead, aiming to give a general picture, one actually finds it difficult to be wildly inaccurate, because the notes seem to come out naturally on to many of the right pitches from the outset, and rhythms, though appearing difficult, feel suddenly manageable in context. This opens up a whole new attitude to working, and especially to the learning process. If one can shed one's fearfulness and plunge in, an approximation like this gives an idea of breath-spans and mood, and of course a most valuable insight into the piece as a whole. Details can then be honed and polished gradually until everything is secure. It is the opposite method to that of dividing a piece into small sections and chipping away at every small detail before moving on. Both methods are valid, but it is revealing to find that with a truly musical composer, brimming with natural talent, as Adès is, what may seem an indulgent extravaganza is exactly the opposite: everything is meticulously conceived, with full awareness of the practicalities. A composer-performer has a special advantage: the joy of performing pervades this piece, and it has tremendous panache and imagination. As a concert piece it is a rewarding *tour de force*.

The piano's introduction sets the atmosphere. It is marked 'vehement and exhausted', and lies low in the instrument, proceeding in fits and starts, snarling and growling in violently contrasting dynamics. The tempo is slow (crotchet = 40), but in 12/8 with so many fast notes, it will not seem so. Just before the voice enters, the piano moves higher and becomes lighter. The singer begins (after a clear cue of the opening low B at the top of the piano's held chord) in semi-casual style, in a low and very comfortable tessitura. The lines are gently conversational, incorporating longer notes for a smooth effect. That on 'or' provides the first example of the 'Billie Holliday' controlled vibrato, surrounded by glissandos, and encouraging an appropriate crooning effect. Breaths are finely judged: small rests precede each phrase, and are used for natural punctuation, so there is no need to look for other places. Singing as if speaking is always the ideal to aim for in this kind of writing, and to read the text aloud will be a good preparation. As with other American poetry, 'r's should not be rolled, and percussive consonants not overarticulated. Liquid consonants are important for keeping a legato flow. The composer is well aware of the way that syllables fall: he marks 'parlato' for a passage of more clipped sounds: 'The other party often says'. The little downward glissando on 'you' should be quite marked, its crescendo preparing the way for the rhetorical 'Tell me', where the voice opens out into an expressive, lyrical passage, and there is a chance to practise the 'vibrato hairpins' at length on an E flat and then a C. The very quick fade to triple *piano* is marked 'più disperato': a general feeling of world-weariness is always apparent in the narrative. As would be expected the composer's written instructions, abundant accents, and nuances throughout are a completely reliable guide to both performers. There are some marvellous details in the piano part, which is homogeneous and assured. Filigree rhythmic flourishes, biting accents, and subterranean rumblings all feature amid constant light and shade. The composer has an exemplary sense of balance: there is none of the muddiness that can often mar virtuoso piano accompaniments. Everything is wonderfully clear, and the frequent brief rests allow for transparent windows that keep the texture light and buoyant.

The singer's confiding asides are beautifully set (Example 1). The satirical, wheedling glissandos on 'sincerely' work perfectly. This is a very long phrase, so a breath could be taken before 'your life' so as to make sure there is plenty of room to negotiate the 'vibrato hairpins' on the F. After this, the downward glissando will provide a welcome rest.

Ex. 1 Adès

The next section continues in casual conversational mode. The lighting of a cigarette is depicted by snapping both fingers, and lines range easily up and down. Rhythms are quite off-beat but they run very naturally in the event. The phrase 'like a pair of rag dolls' etc. has triplet semiquaver groups in swung rhythms. This snaps off suddenly to make way for a loud howling *fortissimo*. The bracketed grace-note just before a swoop up a minor tenth on 'Y-ou' gives the voice an ideal springboard to release a free, open sound. The piano has long trills that complement the pulsations of the singer's vibrato, and create a distinctive bubbling texture. The extended passage of repeated 'Oh's gives the singer full rein, in expansive lyrical lines, with enjoyable glissandos and athletic leaps. The composer suggests modifying the vowel according to need: another example of his care for the performer's comfort. The piano contributes tremolandos (marked 'non agitato'), and the music gradually subsides into a series of sighs that turn into groans, and finally, after a short pause, a Sprechstimme grunt—all brilliantly effective, and delightfully easy to perform. A low, quiet parlando concludes the expressive interlude, full of inventive nuances, and ending in almost a whisper at the words 'an audible breath'.

A short piano solo, mercurial in character, leads into the continuation of the story—mundane observations thrown off with a combination of humour and resignation. As ever, seemingly complicated combinations of rhythm and accent fall into place almost immediately. The *pianissimo* at 'or one of you rises' is marked 'poco fantastico' for a particularly roguish reference, gently mocking. For the second time the voice suddenly launches into a different gear on a surge of energy. The burgeoning vibrato on the held 'their' on high G flat should be marvellously incisive. The second cadenza of repeated 'Oh's, where roles of speaker and listener are ironically reversed, is even more violent than the first (*quasi tutta forza*). Again the cries wind gradually down, but emotion is still highly charged, and subtle differences in dynamic and mood (*dolente* for instance) should be sharply observed. The final 'groan' is a little longer, and is placed more spaciously. The low parlando ending recurs, varied a little, this time fading to an 'audible sigh' (here the text is illustrated directly by the setting). For the 'quasi bisb.' (almost whispered) effect asked for, the swinging triplet figures are left unaccompanied so the breathier sound will be easily heard. The 'sigh' can certainly be exaggerated, with all the remaining breath being expelled in a rush. However, the singer must be careful not to throw the voice off-balance for the vital conclusion of the mini-drama.

The ending is masterly: the story goes on in an undertone, darkly expressive, and then suddenly peters out. After a questioning, inflected 'Then?' and a very well-timed pause, comes the dénouement. The two protagonists lapse into sleep, and disaster strikes, in a throw-away line, straight after the work's longest-held note. The combination of these constitutes the work's main technical hurdle. Not only is it quite a feat to hold the B and control it perfectly, but the last few words have to make their full impact within a very quiet dynamic, and the transitions must be slick. Timing is important, and the singer should make the most of hissed consonants- 't' and 'th' in particular (Example 2). Fortunately the voice should still feel fresh: any fatigue would tend to show at the end, so it is as well to conserve energy during the pauses in the final section.

Ex. 2 Adès

This is a most remarkable work, quite unlike a conventional song cycle. It is neither an operatic *scena* nor an elaborate show song but something in between. It would make a very strong impression in a standard recital, next to Austro-German lieder (Beethoven, Schubert, Mendelssohn, Brahms, Schumann). Other modern pieces would have to be chosen very carefully, but a selection of works setting American texts would be interesting. Actual American show songs (Gershwin, Berlin, Porter) would be ideal, and it could form a centre-piece to a cabaret evening.

Pines Songs (*c.*1984)

Daniel Asia (born 1953)
Text by Paul Pines

T IV; M VI
Soprano (or mezzo-soprano) and piano
Duration 15′

I first came across these magnificent and strongly individual songs in a version with chamber ensemble, but the richness and colour of the harmonic and textural detail is equally well suited to the medium of voice and piano. They are warmly recommended to singers and pianists of some proficiency, who are seeking something strikingly different for their repertoire. The five settings can be sung as a complete cycle or performed separately. Each is satisfying in its own right; the composer, however, states that the final number 'I walk out to the end' should not appear alone.

Daniel Asia's music is fluent and assured, happily combining many of the characteristic features and facets of American music, from mainstream to the more popular elements, in a remarkably original and powerful way. Repetitive, motoric figures are prominent, and these are expertly woven into a brilliant and kaleidoscopic mix that includes strong jazz overtones. The mordantly witty, pithily evocative poems are a special delight, too. Their extreme economy of utterance is complemented by piano parts that are highly elaborate, with lengthy solo passages that illustrate and expand the imagery. Words are set in an imaginative and very personal way, maintaining the liveliest rhythmic interest. The composer is fond of using melismas and passages of humming to extend certain words. The long luxuriant lines that frequently occur are a pleasure to sing, using the singer's full breath capacity. Everything flows easily and naturally, and the music's language, though intricate, is always fascinating and direct in its appeal.

It has to be remembered that an idiomatically American way of delivering the texts is built into the music—exaggeratedly crisp diction would ruin its special flavour. Enunciation should be as smooth as possible, ironing out percussive corners, and aiming for an easy flexibility, at times almost casual. This will only come after considerable practice, and a feeling for jazz will be an advantage in finding the appropriate style, far removed from the English school. However, some consonants are clarified in American pronunciation: 'r's are always sounded, but not rolled, even in the middle of words, and the Scottish 'wh' is properly defined. The composer's own interpretative instructions are extremely helpful in establishing mood, and he shows great care and sensitivity to phrasing and dynamics. Good breath control will be very important throughout. Musically speaking, the main problems will be rhythmic. Many syncopations and changes of metre have eventually to seem effortless, once details have been given the necessary close attention, phrase by phrase. The style may seem elusive at first, but it all falls into place quite suddenly, once words and music start to blend spontaneously, and there is time to relax into the atmosphere, and identify with the special character of the poems, without being harried by vocal or musical hurdles.

1. White Pillars

The piano's introductory solo creates a restless, distracted atmosphere, in which the pulse floats between regular and dotted quavers in short, disjointed phrases with wildly fluctuating dynamics. The opening words involve syllables that will immediately demonstrate characteristics of American diction: the 'wh' of 'white' is repeated three times, and the 'r' in 'pillars' should be fleeting but clear. Dotted rhythms should not be rigid, and the opening vocal paragraph can be sung in two phrases, the only breath being after 'floor'. Speaking the words ('somewhat ponderously' according to the composer's instruction) helps in finding the pliable rhythmic flow that establishes the style from the beginning. For 'the clock has a picture of Sir Walter Raleigh' the voice recites naturally on a monotone (marked 'acerbic') with the piano remaining still, so that the audience is immediately drawn into the poet's ironic humour and sharp observation. Unexpectedly 'on' is given a rocking melisma, with 'it' clipped off *subito piano*, with a comma indicating a glottal 'i' to separate it, rather than a breath. After a short metric passage of 4/4, the piano takes off in a dazzling solo, full of city sounds and bustling momentum, slowing down again for the voice's re-entry. Fast and slow tempos alternate, keeping concentration at a premium. The focal point of the setting is a directly personal utterance, rising in surges to a sudden *mezzo-piano* on 'I can't read' (Example 1). If the singer can manage it, the upper alternative, climbing to high C, makes a marvellous effect. It should be sung without vibrato. Breath can be taken

Ex. 1 Asia

before 'perusing': any other choice would interrupt crucial crescendos, and the high passage will be all the better for economy of air flow. Frequent crescendos and diminuendos in the course of sentences remind one of moments in Elliott Carter's vocal settings, especially 'A Mirror on Which to Dwell', where workable phrasing needs special forethought, and musical considerations should come first. The verse's closing paragraph projects the image of an old man cutting up his pancakes. Rhythms should be smooth and casual until the line rises for a loud declamation. There is an opportunity to breathe unnoticed before 'has', so that 'pancakes' can be really loud, and the diminuendo effective. After a pause there is ample time to place the last, poised entry, each syllable clearly separated. Here again there is a choice of pitches for the final held note, but in this case, the given alternative is lower. The high A is better for maintaining a straight sound. The 'w' in 'Squ-' of 'Squares' focuses the line securely, and the singer must remember to leave the ending of the word very late. The 'r' and 's' (pronounced 'z') will need to be very quick, slipping into the gap before the piano's last chord.

2. I'll never understand

A musing, contemplative feeling pervades this substantial movement, which is especially rewarding for the singer. The fine-spun phrases lie beautifully in the voice, and lines are frequently enhanced by shapely melismas. There are some very long notes indeed, putting the singer's technical control to the test. The flexible rhythms, a successful example of written-out rubato, contribute to an enjoyable sense of freedom. The singer's first pitch, C, should be picked up from the penultimate chord of the piano's introduction. The composer's note 'Very freely, wistfully' is all the indication needed. He does, however, add occasional interpretative instructions to the piano part. In the opening section the voice launches a series of graceful phrases, each heralded by a split chord. The singer is left unfettered to glide through intervals and savour every sound. Bell-like repetitions of octave triplet figures recur throughout the movement in the piano, and an extended solo passage, increasingly intense, follows the voice's opening statements. After a massive chord (the part has three staves for a moment), a very soft piping tune is heard 'emerging' (the composer's word) and this leads into the next vocal passage. This is a most attractive section, marked 'legato' to make sure that syncopations and uneven groupings run easily within the longer spans. What may seem to be complex time signatures—10/16, 14/16, 11/16—in fact have a natural swing, and are fun to work out. The composer shows a rare understanding of performance practice: the singer is kept busy negotiating these special rhythmic twists, relishing their springy quality, when suddenly a very long note occurs. The voice will be well exercised in readiness, and the 'l' of 'lines' should be placed forward, and the note kept light and clear. At the very end a semitone slide upwards helps prevent any drooping in pitch (Example 2). The uneven rhythms continue in a short

Ex. 2 Asia

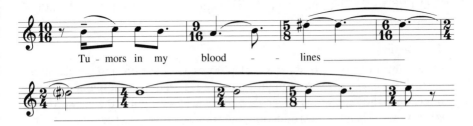

Tu - mors in my blood - - lines

piano solo, and the voice re-enters with a syncopated phrase that climbs to high G flat, dips for a moment, and then, with plenty of time to breathe, reaches a very loud climax on 'ratio'. The 'a' vowel must not be pinched: any gripping of the throat will be heard all too clearly. A final piano interlude combines the octave triplets with accelerating chords, and fades away. The voice's humming solo is a lovely touch. Freely expressive, marked 'dreaming', it contains some tricky chromatic intervals. As the dynamic rises, the lips can be opened slightly. The final line of the poem is set most memorably, with a glorious unaccompanied passage covering a huge range of volume, and ending with a portamento down a tritone, as the piano re-enters. This thrillingly abandoned moment is immediately complemented by a rapt, slow ending. The comma before 'so much as a whisper' is crucial for the sudden mood-change. The last few bars are by far the most difficult. To end perfectly on an E flat, in the register-break area demands excellent control, and breath control is also severely taxed. It is probably advisable to snatch a breath before 'as', since the important 'wh' of 'whisper' will use extra air. The floated pause at the end should be held as long as possible. The sound need only be the merest thread, now the piano's motion has ceased.

3. A Little Girl

A delicious, brief movement that perfectly encapsulates its subject-matter. The composer's unerring way with natural speech rhythms is invaluable here, and his own detailed expressive nuances and accents are a completely reliable guide. Staccato markings are especially effective, as is the glissando on 'fall down'. The lightness of touch is also evident in the piano part, and the music trips along with vivacity and charm. A brief, exuberant piano solo separates the opening descriptions from the poet's conclusion: 'she's the whole poem'. This last vocal phrase is the most difficult technically, as it scoops low in the voice, and melts into *bocca chiusa* for the last long phrase. The leap up a tenth from middle C is exciting, but closing on to 'm' on F could be problematic. As the 'm' is in brackets, it seems that the composer is aware of the danger of restricting the sound at that point. It is more practicable to keep the lips open, so the sound is more of a 'ng', until the safer lower tessitura is reached for the lovely, arching final phrase, which has to be sung with the utmost smoothness, with a gentle glissando up the final fifth to the long pause on A. This should be held until the breath is completely gone.

4. Dear Frank

Consisting only of two short vocal phrases (a question and its teasingly surreal answer), this is a piquantly memorable setting. The piano's drumming left-hand repetitions on single pitches provide a pulsating background, set up by a lengthy introduction, continuing through the singer's first phrase, and on up to the moment when the voice re-enters. As usual, voice rhythms are very natural, and the tessitura is well placed for absolute clarity. The answering vocal fragment begins in a matter-of-fact way and then suddenly swoops up to a *subito fortissimo* on 'Mexicans'. There is a characteristic drop at the end of the long-held note: this time down a tritone, with the 'n' extended on C, and the 's' (pronounced 'z') prolonged at the end. Closing on to the liquid consonant like this tends to shut off the sound. As the accompaniment (now in scintillating semiquaver figures with reiterated high octaves above) remains loud, the singer will have to work hard to keep the dynamic level high enough, by making sure that the mouth remains open for the resonance to come through. This could feel a little awkward at first, but it is important to bring off the punch-line confidently, since the start of the phrase, supported only by chords, will instantly focus interest, and dynamic contrasts should be very marked.

5. I walk out to the end

This is the most spectacular movement for the singer, full of brilliant coloratura and dramatic variety. The pianist's virtuosity too will be on show, and, as with the second setting, the poem is filled out by lengthy piano solos after each line, making it a substantial piece. Rapid rippling wave patterns in the right hand create a glittering texture above the slow tread of the bass. Mood-swings are conveyed by subtly fluctuating tempos at the outset. The voice's opening tempo sets a faster pulse than that of the preceding bar (marked 'suddenly elegiac'). The vocal lines are consistently mellifluous and rewarding, but they need a disciplined approach to make sure of nailing every detail. Their supple grace could possibly lull the singer into coasting a little too easily.

Ex. 3 Asia

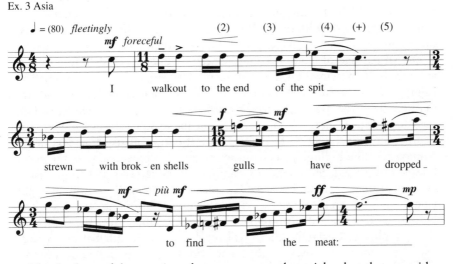

The rhythms of the opening phrase are somewhat tricky, but they provide a good preparation for what is to come (Example 3). In fact, the composer has helpfully marked out beats through the more difficult subdivisions. It is essential for the singer to acquire familiarity with the (at first) unnerving process of feeling beats in unexpected places, and adapting to constant shifts of emphasis in the patterns without being distracted. Some practice in the additive rhythms found in Messiaen, for instance, will be a distinct advantage, and it is fascinating to see how neatly it all works out. Learning to manage without the crutch of regular beat patterns is a most valuable exercise, and will eventually bring confidence. This facility will be tested throughout the movement, and note-groups have always to be articulated clearly. A breath is permissible after 'gulls' as this preserves the musical phrasing. The vowel in 'meat' will have to be modified; this is a difficult moment because of the tessitura and weight of sound required. Strong support muscles will be most needed here. For the phrase starting 'Fishermen' the tempo is a little quicker, and the rhythms even bouncier. Breathing places need careful consideration. I have found that the seemingly good opportunity of an intake after 'traps' does not work so well in practice, as it feels a trifle rushed and awkward. There is plenty of time for a good breath after 'back' (placing '-ck' on the beat), and after that it is best to follow the musical phrase, and snatch another after the run on 'wake'. There will then be enough air to last comfortably to the end of the phrase that carries the crescendo on the held D sharp, remembering to enunciate the 'd' of 'cloud' clearly. The lilting rhythms of 'dream' should be floated, preparing for the rather unexpected rise to high A flat. Here the composer has, unusually, provided two opposite alternatives for the dynamics.

Presumably, the crescendo to *forte*, his bracketed second choice, is the one intended for mezzos with heavier voices, who might find problems with the diminuendo floating to *mezzo-piano* in head voice. This is of course where a soprano will be thoroughly at home. It is rare to find a composer so acutely aware of the differences between vocal types. His solution is a most practical one, so that everyone can be heard at their best. After this there is a longish passage of piano texture, fast demisemiquavers melting into soft trills above an accented tune, and suddenly burgeoning to *fortissimo* before calming again for the vocal re-entry. Now the figures lie higher and are marked 'delicatissimo'. The singer's music here is simple and gentle, ending on a long high F sharp. A short, turbulent piano solo pauses suddenly for another slow introduction to the voice's last entry, this is again at a faster tempo, as at the beginning. The music of verse 1 is repeated, with the vocal lines subtly varied, but containing similar rhythmic tasks as before. However, breathing spans are easier. The melisma on 'smell' is just the right length and lies comfortably, as does the upward-running 'the sea'. The vowels of 'lower Broadway' are flattering vocally, and ensure the success of the last phrase. Certainly, there will need to be a breath before 'Broad-way'—the *ritenuto* allows for this. The wider American vowel of 'Broad-' will help keep the sound open and free while pausing on the high G, which is eventually left unaccompanied—a lovely opportunity for the singer. Coming out of this pause requires precision. The semiquavers are marked 'in time', and they provide a perfect springboard on to a firm-held long A. This will claim all the singer's breath capacity, and the note must be kept bright and clear with a minimum of vibrato.

This important cycle will make a splendid focus for an American programme, surrounded by such composers as Ives, Ruggles, Barber, Bernstein, Carter, Rorem, and also the best of the show songs of Porter, Kern, Rodgers, Berlin, and Gershwin. It would also contrast nicely with music of the Second Viennese School. It is the kind of piece that yields more and more rewards after close study, and it helps singers to know more about their own voices, and to relish the special qualities of American vocal delivery.

The Witches' Song*
(1990)

Alison Bauld (born 1944)
Text by Shakespeare

T IV; M IV
Soprano solo
Duration 4′

Singing unaccompanied is of course a great test of musicianship and ability to pitch accurately and maintain tuning. Without the unfair advantage of perfect pitch it is difficult to envisage the singer managing this piece without the aid of a pitch-pipe or tuning-fork, but this could be used as a theatrical prop, obviously not furtively, and would be well in keeping with the natural eccentricity of the setting and characters.

The composer gives clear and concise instructions for vocalizing this highly original and spectacular mini-drama. The singer must adopt a totally different colour for each of the three witches. Each part is written on a separate stave, and this requires a certain virtuosity in darting swiftly from one to another, but also helps accentuate the difference in the interpreter's mind. Witch I on the top line has a generally higher tessitura than the others, so a more traditional interpretation of witch-like characteristics, such as a narrow, pinched sound and a shrill, hectoring quality, will be easily practicable and splendidly penetrating. The text also invites a wheedling tone, hinting of pseudo-gentility, sickly sweet and occasionally twittery. An imaginative performer will have a field day! A lurking hysteria must be kept under control. Witch II (middle stave) is a somewhat cooler customer, sardonic and knowing. There is even a jazzy quality to some of her music, which also contains a considerable amount of Sprechstimme and speech effects. Witch III (bottom line) has a low tessitura in the main, and an open, cavernous tone, using full vibrato for dramatic effect, will make an appropriate contrast to the others.

As with all solo pieces, it is very important to establish and maintain a clear rhythmic impetus and pulse, so that the result is not amorphous. The composer requests a flexible 'ebb and flow' but momentum should not be lost, despite the lack of accompaniment to dictate the course of the music.

All three characters establish themselves in rapid succession (Example 1). Witch I's opening rhythmic staccato phrase is imitated instantly in a differ-

---

* *Banquo's Buried* and *Cry Cock-a-Doodle-Doo!* are discussed more fully under Technical III on pp. 137–142.

ent colour and register by Witch II. The verbs 'mew'd' and 'whined' give obvious word-painting opportunities at the end of the respective phrases. Witch III's first entry needs a special effort to achieve the distinctively darker, fuller timbre at a highish pitch. The slide from E sharp to D sharp then up again to E natural, in a moaning tone, is quite difficult at this vulnerable range. The sustained humming on the 'm' of 'time' is helpful. Witch I has a chanting solo in 6/8 time: a nasal quality will be appropriate to keep her in character. This is always more of a problem when tessituras overlap and there may be a danger of too much similarity between the parts. The performer can relish the gory images of the text, strictly obeying the rubato markings, and the appropriate gradation into Sprechstimme as the tension rises. Wheezy or croaking sounds can occur naturally at such moments—the great advantage of not being tied to a conventional vocal sound. The singer has to negotiate a change of tempo to *Andante*, setting the new slowly rocking rhythm without the aid of a backing accompaniment. There is an immediate cut-off for the first 'chorus': 'Double, double', etc. The composer instructs that one voice should sound as three: a special

Ex. 1 Bauld

challenge of stamina and imagination, that should make a brilliant and exciting effect. The passage is heavily accented. Witch II's next entry follows close on—so close that it is better nor to take breath before it, but to breathe well for the second phrase of the 'chorus', beginning 'Fire burn'. It will therefore come as a sudden interruption and an abrupt change of texture, but it is important to remember the more casual laid-back character of Witch II, easier to achieve in the legato phrase which follows. The 'dry squeak' on the word 'bat' is helped by a sudden climb. Use of the glottis will help here. For the *Presto—parlando*, written on a monotone low C sharp, the pitching need not be taken too literally. It is intended as a guide to the general tessitura. This rattles along at a tremendous pace, with percussive consonants making a strong contribution to whipping up the intensity, reaching a peak of excitement on 'bubble' (use a prolonged 'l' here, keeping the tongue well forward). The full 'chorus' comes again in an inverted, lower-pitched form, this time with a gradual crescendo. Again this leads directly into a solo, this one from Witch III, in 'languorous' mood. The sudden change to a quiet dynamic should be quite a shock. A hollow, crooning sound is suitable here, maintaining a sinister legato. There are some unusual pronunciations here and elsewhere, authorized by the composer, who is meticulous about correct rhymings: 'goolf' to rhyme with 'wolf'. The extended solo passage for Witch III which follows is perhaps one of the most difficult in the piece. The voice has to combine a dark colouring of timbre with a staccato, parlando delivery, in a sequence of particularly tricky syllables. According to the composer, the pitching of the Sprech-stimme need only be approximate, but the problem is one of preserving tonal evenness and the distinctive quality of this character throughout a choppily accented line. Thinking in long phrases is the answer, once words begin to flow easily. The pace changes again for a sinister cantabile, and then accelerates as images become progressively more disgusting. A violent crescendo on 'lips' leads to an explosively suppressed hiss on 'Finger of birth-strangled babe' where the composer asks for the words to be 'over-articulated'. In the next two phrases two more unorthodox pronunciations occur: 'drab' and 'slab' should have the long 'a' to rhyme with 'babe'. After these venomous outbursts, the singer begins a mocking 'nursery sing-song' (the composer's words), which suddenly rushes into a hysterical Sprech-stimme, leading directly into another 'chorus'—this one loud and furious, rising to *fortissimo*. At this point Witch II interrupts in typical style, with 'Cool it!' (Example 2). This is a key moment, and the composer's note: 'cry of the gangland' leads one to believe that this may be a passing reference to a moment in Bernstein's *West Side Story*. The mood changes totally in accordance with Witch II's suave detachment, and somewhat jazzy aura. The performer should instinctively adopt a hip manner that is likely to raise a gentle chuckle from the audience. (The pause will be needed for this.) Witch II's sweetly sinister line floats up, and is caught on a high G by Witch I, now identified as Hecate, who takes over. Their two different tone-

Ex. 2 Bauld

colours must be sharply differentiated here even to the point of exaggeration. Witch I, after holding the shrill G, collapses into cascades of demonic laughter, kookaburra style. As anyone will know who has tried it, a descending cackle is extremely easy to vocalize, especially when it follows directly on without a breath being taken. The less air remaining, the drier and more penetratingly accurate the sound. The breathing plan for this paragraph should be worked out carefully, as the laughter has to lead straight into some Sprechstimme at a 'normal' pitch range. Witch I (Hecate) continues to hold the stage with her virtuoso solo, ranging from a delirious, lilting chant to a *pianissimo* chromatic descent in Sprechstimme, which has to be casually thrown off at the end of the breath. Musical shaping and sense of timing are essential attributes here, to keep the rhythm flowing and focus clearly on changes of pace and mood. Choices of tempo are vitally important, and it is fortunate that this composer's instructions are an invaluable guide. In a master-stroke of drama, Hecate suddenly mutates into Lady Macbeth, in a series of chilling, half-whispered 'Come's, sliding down at the ends. Now we hear again Lady Macbeth's crazed lullaby from 'Banquo's Buried', the first work of the trilogy: a direct quote, which continues with the refrain 'I tell you yet again' exactly as at the end of 'Banquo', up to the muttered, repeated 'To bed'. The very last line is a whispered 'There's knocking at the gate', as fast as possible. The timing of this *coup de théâtre* is absolutely crucial, but there is little chance of the audience's attention wavering during this wonderful showpiece, which is so consistently fascinating and original.

Ideally, all three of these settings should be performed by the same artist in one evening, forming the centre-piece of a programme of music theatre. An excellent alternative is for instrumental pieces to serve as interludes: either early or new pieces. Music from Shakespeare's time would go perfectly, as would Purcell arias, or other settings of Shakespeare settings by more recent composers. A mixed recital of these would be very attractive. A Tippett cycle would be particularly interesting as a contrast (*The Heart's Assurance*, for instance) as would any more complex and florid music, but it is important not to tire the singer. The two Macbeth settings could be performed together: indeed, the order of the three pieces can be flexible in general, according to the occasion. Of course, the greater difficulty of the unaccompanied work may limit the number of performers able to incorporate all three pieces in their repertory. The pieces are also excellent material for a showcase or student concert, using different performers for each, and of course, if more ambitious staging facilities are available, so much the better. This trilogy constitutes a major addition to the genre of vocal music theatre, to which many major twentieth-century figures, such as Berio, Cage, and Kagel, have contributed.

Earth Hold Songs
(1993)

Tristram Cary (born 1925)
Text by Jennifer Rankin

T IV; M V
Soprano and piano
Duration *c*.16′

A welcome song cycle from this distinguished British composer now resident in Australia. One of the leading pioneers in the field of electronic music in this country, and also composer of many notable film scores, Cary has perhaps been less well known to us as a concert composer of acoustic music. His fine ear, wide cultural background (he is the son of the author Joyce Cary), and strong structural sense pervade all of his music, which is unfailingly well organized and presented with meticulous care and clarity. This is a rewarding virtuoso showpiece for singer and pianist. The voice part is spectacular and varied, with many chances to exhibit a fine technique and performing flair. There is liberal use of colourful melismatic writing, of word-painting, and of effects such as glissandos which flatter the voice and make the whole effort most enjoyable. It could be taxing if sight-read all at one go. Careful polishing of each movement will be the best method of approach. Each song has its own character and the musical style certainly bears more than a trace of neo-classicism in the motoric rhythms and sparkling pianistic patterns. Despite its basic atonality, the piano part provides pitch cues often subtly embedded in the running counterpoint which predominates. A high standard of musicianship and quick responses will be necessary but the result will repay the effort.

This work is substantial, always arresting, and full of energy. It perfectly exploits the special flexibility of the soprano voice, making particularly exciting use of high notes in cadenza passages. The poems too are rewarding. Jennifer Rankin's untimely death has denied her due international recognition, and her work has rare individuality and power. A gifted pianist is needed: this is very much an equal partnership.

1. I had a room

The piano part begins in characteristically rhetorical and dramatic style. After the introductory flourish, the music settles into a *più giusto* featuring pulsing repeated notes which seem to indicate the passage of time in the lonely room. The contrast of the enclosed images with those of the world outside are aptly captured. Mood and pace fluctuate continually in a restless, searching atmosphere. The singer's opening phrases have delicate melismatic figures, in rocking 6/8 metre, pausing on high G flats. A sudden fast tempo brings more fragmented lines that need to be projected strongly, before the 6/8 rhythm returns, with a wide-ranging line that is particularly comfortable to sing. There are frequent tempo-changes often with duplet divisions giving further flexibility. A spectacularly high passage, depicting the gale, has tactful *ossie* for those who could find it daunting (Example 1).

Ex. 1 Cary

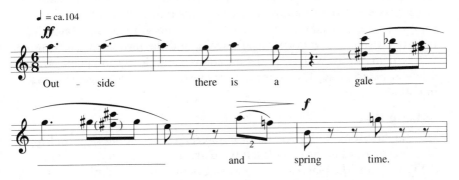

Its relentless force could give problems, but the *fortissimo* should perhaps not be interpreted too literally: the voice will be incisive enough at that range. The melisma has to be shaped within a legato, avoiding emphasis on the highest note, and not breathing until after 'spring-time'. The following slower phrase in a lower tessitura also needs to be well supported. The 'w's of 'women' and 'weeping' will help to focus the tone. The depiction of the children outside is set high in the voice. The held high C (*ossia* provided) on 'in' should not be accented; a floating quality is much safer and more appropriate in the context. Short words such as 'sash' are set very naturally and should be kept within the phrase. A sudden *accelerando* and crescendo to *fortissimo*, snapping off from an upward glissando on 'lines', is very effective, and the 'n' sound is helpful for the slide. A climactic cadenza is reached on 'sky' (marked 'ad lib.') where the singer can relish the freedom to expand on the written quadruplets and enjoy a temporary respite from the driving pulse. The final section of this movement encompasses much of the material heard before, the beat ebbing and flowing. A dramatic coup is reserved for the end: after a loud vocal melisma (again in quadruplets), the line swoops up again with glissandos and then lands on hammered accents in the middle register, depicting the threatening image of 'a great bird'. This may be quite tricky to bring off: percussive syllables should be exaggerated and timed exactly. It is essential to come out of the legato coloratura directly into the final accented line, stopping only to allow time for the piano's intervening fifth. This first song is perhaps the most demanding in stamina and musicianship.

2. Black Cockatoo

A constant beat keeps this delightful movement well under control and the singer can negotiate the springing lines clearly and accurately with as little vibrato as possible. The given loud dynamics could perhaps be modified, since the voice can attain a cutting quality in the high register that will easily come through the accompanying texture. The vocal delivery should be exactly as if singing a baroque aria: poised, supple, and rhythmic, allowing dynamics to rise and fall with the musical phrasing. There are some onomatopoeic niceties that are particularly effective ('flap-flapping', etc.) and two screeching upward glissandos are tremendous fun. Towards the end of the song the tempo steadies, but vocal lines remain grateful and rangy (the repeated 'bending', works especially well), and the movement ends somewhat enigmatically, with two brief questions, sung clearly and plainly above a slower piano pulse. The performers are instructed to end together exactly in tempo.

3. Earth Hold

Like the first song, this gives many an interpretative and musical challenge. Staccato rhythms in the piano's left hand are matched by dry, short notes in the voice part. The piano's passagework becomes more ambitious in scope, and the singer uses her full range, highlighting important words in the poem's colourful imagery. A faster tempo brings a loud 'fanfare', announcing the heron and ibis. A nice contrast is afforded by the warm sunlight, where the vocal line becomes mellower, yet rises to a climax and suddenly subsides. One of the most vocally satisying passages is an *ad libitum* solo declamation, punctuated only by spread chords—'Sea-glare, and thin houses'—which is most beautifully set, giving the soprano a chance to shine in the varied melismas and freer rhythms. Soon after comes an insistently repeated 'so, so, so' within an *accelerando*, matched by piano triplets. A rich imagery in the text inspires vibrant musical material, rising to an exciting peak on the word 'sun'. Darker, watery images are kept low in the voice, but a sudden rocking, one-in-a-bar waltz portrays the palm tress 'popping up' (another attractive repeated figure). The voice rises to a sustained high B on 'thin', where it will be a good idea to keep a steely sound as suggested by the word. After this climax the vocal lines fragment, with fleeting references to previous material, and the movement ends in reflective vein: 'mapping out my landscape'.

4. Earth Wind

This movement starts in bravura style with a wonderful virtuoso solo for the singer, highly decorative, with an exhilarating series of glissandos, illustrating the wind (Example 2). This is one of the work's high points. The piano part too is very exciting, with plenty of dashing loud trills as a recurring feature, and short sharp attacks contributing to a toccata-like percussiveness. There is certainly a feeling of wild abandon here that will be enjoyable

Ex. 2 Cary

for both performers, although ensemble will need careful attention. Long sections of strict, driving tempo are relieved by freer moments giving more space for *espressivo*. The vocal part leaps and swoops daringly in the fast tempo, and it is important not to neglect notes of smaller value. Words such as 'relentless' placed around the high register break are a little awkward to negotiate clearly. Passages of coloratura on 'wind' and 'blowing' are highly effective and should cause no problems, as they tend to occur within an *ad libitum*. The singer's final few phrases feature large intervals, sometimes dipping low, and they must be firmly centred. The last of them dies away naturally as the piano's burbling trills take over.

5. Sand

The main sections of this last setting feature a swift, lilting one-in-the-bar waltz rhythm, with suitably lithe and graceful vocal lines. The music must flow naturally, almost casually, *molto legato* with nostalgic innocence at memories of childhood. Contrast is provided by alternating passages of 2/4, which are interspersed between the waltz sections. The piano has running semiquaver counterpoint, while the voice continues to swing easily over a wide range, reaching a climax in a sequence of, sixths, in a cross-rhythmed variant of the waltz (Example 3). At a *meno mosso*, the vocal part becomes

Ex. 3 Cary

hesitant and proceeds in fits and starts, only to break into a series of full-blooded melismas, which gradually fade, ready for the waltz to resume. The nostalgia of the opening gives way to less comfortable reality. The tempo winds down, and once more, a 2/4 section interrupts, slowing down when it reaches the sequence of sixths, which, as before, are comfortable to sing, although the 'ee' vowel on 'reef' will need to be modified. A slow version of the waltz is supported by a long-held chord, and the music gradually subsides and peters out as if covered by the tide.

This cycle will provide both singer and pianist with a tremendous opportunity to develop technical and interpretative abilities. There is much scope for imagination within the predominantly metric and extremely mobile musical context. It would be a good idea to read the poems aloud, to capture their essence and picture the subtle shadings of mood. The work will make a fine centre-piece for a concert, perhaps one featuring settings of other women poets. It would be best to avoid anything else too demanding, especially involving florid passagework. Stylistically, any of the shorter Romantic or Impressionist songs (Schumann, Mendelssohn, Fauré, Debussy) would contrast extremely well.

Time Past IV
(1984)

Simon Emmerson (born 1950)
Text by Shakespeare

T IV; M III
Soprano (or mezzo-soprano) and tape
Duration 12'

A work for voice and electronics might seem to indicate a specialized and somewhat rarefied taste, but this hauntingly beautiful work is immediately accessible in its firm tonality and logical construction. It is based throughout on a single hexachord and its transposition. Mellifluous vocal lines, consisting of syllabic fragments from the well-loved text (Sonnet XXX), range widely within the chosen pitch framework, and variety is provided by decorative melismas in the form of grace-notes. A stop-watch is needed during performance to keep within the time-spans indicated. Space-time notation is used, with timings clearly marked in 5″-sections, each line of music comprising 30″. Length of notes is conveyed by proportionally varying horizontal lines radiating from the stemless note-heads. The music flows easily and naturally, and only in the more frenetically active central section is there likely to be a problem in keeping with the watch. Within this discipline, however, there is much freedom. The tape fulfils the role of conductor and accompanist combined, the only crucial difference being that it cannot wait if the singer is late! This composer is punctilious in every detail, and the score is admirably presented, all practicalities thoughtfully worked out. An assistant (with a score) will be needed to switch the tape on and off (it runs continuously) and check the balance of the two speakers (the tape accompaniment has its dynamics built-in but some adjustment of level may be necessary in different acoustics). Modern technological advances continue to make such works easier to programme. The work flows in a continuous arch, from a quiet rapt beginning, through a period of intense activity, and out again into a contemplative mood, with use of speech effects, whispering and elongated gradually mutating vowels. Meanwhile the pre-recorded tape provides textures of rippling, babbling syllabic repetitions, transformed and overlapping, creating a multi-coloured palette of vocal attacks and timbres. At key moments there are obvious cues to signal exact coincidences with the live voice. A masterpiece of ingenuity and deceptive simplicity of effect.

The stop-watch has to be switched on at exactly the same time as the tape, and the singer should not be afraid to trust the timing through the measured (10″) silence that begins the work. The tape sounds start just a hair's breadth in advance of the voice, so it is important to balance this crucial moment. The tape should be barely audible here, just enough for the singer to match pitches without seeming obvious. Once she begins, she will not be able to hear tape details for a while, until, eventually, the central section reverses the situation, the tape totally engulfing the voice for a while. Once launched into the texture, the singer should have no difficulty at all in pitching accurately within the six notes which are repeated in differing patterns throughout. Dexterity in negotiating the grace-note flourishes that decorate the main notes may take some time to acquire. As these become more compressed and the tape and voice dynamics rise, it is important not to force the tone. Commas occur at the end of large paragraphs, but the singer will need to work out more detailed phrasing within these. Breathing places have to be planned very carefully, in longish spans. Since the voice part is more or less continuous through the lengthy opening build-up, wrong decisions can have uncomfortable consequences. The vocal delivery should be gentle and smooth, without emphasis, for the first page or two, increasing in expressiveness with the rise in volume and activity. Dynamics are very important indeed, and these help the interpretation considerably. A hypnotic effect is achieved through the weaving variations of the hexachord.

The composer exploits the voice's natural suppleness, through gracefully arching intervals, and varying tessitura and pliable rhythms. Some of the lower notes may tax a light soprano, but they rarely require a strong dynamic, and the ranginess of the lines helps the voice to feel free and flexible. Grace-note groups become more intricate as the tempo increases and excitement mounts. The composer frequently places final consonants at the front of the following word or syllable, to enhance the feeling of a finely spun legato cantabile. It is best not to take breaths during a marked crescendo, and words need not be split up. Breaths after an explosive consonant work well (for example, after the words 'thought', 'remembrance', 'sought', 'waste', 'sweet', etc.). This can then dictate a suitable breathing pattern. It is worth taking the time to make a proper plan, so that strain can be avoided. It is always an advantage to organize scores before starting to sing them full voice, although of course, it may then be found that a few more breaths may need to be added when at full stretch.

Page 4 of the score is the trickiest, with a great many details to be negotiated within what will seem a contracting time-span (Example 1). The earlier passages seem deceptively spacious, but once melismas start to proliferate, seconds fly rapidly by, and the stop-watch becomes especially necessary to make sure of not being left behind. At 6′10″ the voice reaches an exciting *fortissimo* climax at the top of the range (A flat is the highest note) and this has to coincide with a sudden gap in the tape's by-now extremely dense texture. As the singer pauses for a necessary refuelling of breath and energy, the tape bursts out with a dramatic new effect: insistent repetitions of percussive consonants. They must immediately re-enter together with a low bass F. (Arrows mark these moments of exact coincidence.)

From now on, the voice part is more strenuous, involving longer-held notes, and 'stage whispers', written with crosses instead of note-heads, implying Sprechstimme. Deliberate breathiness here could prove tiring and dynamic levels difficult to achieve. A grating, dryish quality is safer than forcing out air with the voice. It is in this section that the voice should appear to be struggling to be heard above the tape, so a straining effect could be appropriate, but not at the cost of vocal comfort. The composer states that in a normal concert hall acoustic, the singer should not need amplification, but it is my opinion that a little subtle enhancement could prove advantageous here! Diphthongs are marked 's.v.' (meaning 'slow vowel'—not, as more commonly found 'senza vibrato'), so that the transition between the two sounds should be gradual, with some exaggeration of the components, using the lips for added effect. The following passages are plain and declamatory, varying sharply in mood. For the phrase 'for precious friends hid in night', a good well-supported breath is needed, in order to make the full crescendo (marked 'molto dolce e legato') and sustain a glowing top note until rescued by a new tape event (the hexachord with strong low bass F, from which spring more repeated consonants). Once

Ex. 1 Emmerson

again, timings can be deceptive, and a close eye should be kept on the watch. (A digital display, strategically placed, is probably the best option, although a watch hung around the neck on a cord can make a suitably theatrical effect.) Gradations between singing, speaking, and whispering will need some care, and the faster-moving monotone Sprechstimme passage beginning 'And weep afresh' provides a moment of relief from sustained vocalizing. From time to time the instruction 'senza vib.' appears, giving an opportunity for a plain, child-like tone in contrast to the dramatic quality of the full-voice phrases. The composer has an excellent ear, and shows acute judgement of timbre here.

At the bottom of page 6, timing is particularly crucial, and the singer's three successive held notes will need plenty of support to sustain the broad crescendo. Commas in between each note should be taken seriously, and not rushed, so that the top of the crescendo on the final E flat does not flag. A gradually dwindling bass drone on the tape stops at this point, and the voice must make a swift diminuendo and, a mere second or so later, die out at the precise moment that the low bass F re-enters on tape.

The following passage is the hardest for the soprano voice (Example 2): a series of repeated low Fs, some inflected in quarter-tones with glissandos and a juddering tremolando—just on the edge of the range, perhaps, but they do not require a refined tone-quality. In fact, a thin, reedy, chanting

Ex. 2 Emmerson

effect is most practicable. Then comes a succession of octave yodels: the low F is gently held, while the voice hockets up and down in a flicking laryngal movement—easier than might be imagined, as long as one does not push too hard). *Bocca chiusa* need not mean that the throat should be clamped. At the end of this passage, the voice floats up an arpeggio and should stop exactly with the tape. The next, unaccompanied, passage must be timed carefully so that the following series of sparser tape entries come at the correct points. As before, pitch is clearly defined and voice and tape cues provide a balanced duet, in a passage of exceptional poignancy and expressiveness. The vocal lines are tellingly simple. As the singer reaches down to a quiet low F, glissandos begin on the tape, and the singer must remain still for 30″, after which tape cues pick out chordal pitches which are then sustained and reverberate below the singer's final, most beautifully judged phrases, in a gentle cantabile in low register. The tape texture gradually dies away, and finishes just after the singer.

This work is a model of its kind, and makes an outstanding opening to either half of a recital. Because of its clear pitch framework, it is not at all difficult for an audience unused to new music. It provides variety within a recital for solo voice, as well as the traditional voice–piano programme. It goes particularly well with British music of all periods (including Shakespeare's)—indeed it would sound well in a church acoustic, perhaps as an interlude in a choral concert. It would be exciting to place it amongst other Shakespeare settings, Warlock's or Tippett's for instance. Because of its long lines, more fragmentary vocal works would make a good contrast. French music would also be appropriate in view of the 'Proustian' association of the poem's second line ('I summon up remembrance of things past').

Two Sonnets of Sir Philip Sidney (1981)

Jeremy Haladyna (born 1955)
Text by Sir Philip Sidney

T IV; M III
High voice and piano
Duration *c*.7′

Many composers of fine quality are to be found in the music departments of American universities. Jeremy Haladyna was in England for a spell during the late eighties, and has since returned to the USA where he lectures at the University of California, Santa Barbara. This powerful cycle shows his dramatic flair, sense of colour, and musical vitality. The musical idiom, though modernist and atonal, skilfully incorporates a taste of Olde England in response to the historical setting of the poems. Subtle references to the music and dance of Elizabethan times are most deftly worked into the writing, yet the general effect is not obviously English, but rather an intriguing fusion of New and Old Worlds that is strongly individual.

A singer with plenty of stamina and energy will relish these two substantial, well-contrasted songs. A tenor will probably sound best, particularly in the many high-lying passages, where a soprano's resonance could obscure some syllables. The piece blazes with passion and bold resolve. The first song is an angry, self-flagellating diatribe against personal weakness, and the destructive effect of desire, and the second brings a more contemplative mood, and, with it, acceptance of the joy of spiritual reward, and exultant affirmation of Love's eternal life-giving force.

Each song is sufficiently strong in impact to be performed separately. The composer has already envisaged this possibility, but he states in a note that the given order must be adhered to when the work is done complete. Standard notation is used for the most part, complete with time (but not key) signatures.

Sonnet IX

There is an operatic abandon to the vocal writing here, far removed from the more intimate world of the Liederabend, and piano joins in the fray with similar forcefulness. The poet's tortured struggle with self brings forth a series of defiant outbursts that ring superbly in the voice. Despite the equally strenuous accompanying gestures, these should ride the texture with little problem. It is easy to see why these marvellous words have attracted the composer. The sonic impact of successions of often violently percussive and alliterative syllables, and the striking imagery, are searingly direct and visceral. The music is marked 'quick and ominous': a significant and helpful comment. 'Ominous' could suggest a steady, brooding tempo, and it is as well to remember to keep the pace going. After a sinister introduction on the piano, the voice enters, heavily accented and wide-ranging, and the singer must resist the impulse to force the tone. Dynamics are quiet at first, but high tension is immediately apparent. It is as if the vocal line is being delivered through clenched teeth, muttering darkly and fiercely. The second phrase is almost spat out with great bitterness (Example 1). The composer is obviously aware of the effectiveness of wide leaps. Dotted phrase-marks denote the musical shapes, and can be used to determine breathing places. The piano pounds out ritualistic chords, with closely clashing intervals, as the furious complaint continues, with more alliteration on 'cradle of causeless care'. It is important not to push out the 'c' sound too hard, risking breathiness and loss of focus. Even experienced singers are apt to fall into

Ex. 1 Haladyna

Fond fan-cy's scum, and dregs _ of _ scat-ter'd thought,

this habit under duress. Timing of the transition from explosive consonant to vowel often needs to be monitored very closely. Once perfect control is achieved, every note will be secure and predictable, whatever its dynamic or articulation, and nothing will jump out of line. Throughout this passage words are set syllable by syllable with no melismas. A thrilling climax on the *fortissimo* 'wrought' is followed by a long pause.

Suddenly, a slow, quiet, more cantabile section begins, giving the singer a stunning portamento on the second syllable of 'Desire'. The huge intervals will be welcome vocally, to avoid any tiring on the long high notes. There is also a special instruction to the singer to wait until the piano's chord has cleared before gliding down. This is an important consideration, often overlooked by composers. Experienced singers do of course acquire a keen aural awareness of balance and acoustic aspects while in the act of performing: one can never stop listening while singing. The portamento recurs in similar fashion on 'long'. This is even more comfortable because of the prolonged 'ng' which can begin towards the end of the slide. Again the composer's responsiveness to the text allows for liquid consonants, especially 'l', to be used to help with legato. The paused high G on 'worthless' is also very safe if the 'w' is poised on the pitch before the vowel is released. It is in effect an 'oo' rather than a real consonant. Phrases here are long and smooth and very easy to sing. The tempo moves on a little, and the voice has a declamatory passage in faster note-patterns. These build to an angry cut-off, placed rather unusually, for special dramatic effect. The staccato 'For', belonging to the following line of verse, is joined to 'all thy smoky fire', and must stop quite suddenly for a meaningful paused rest, before the singer leads into the 'much slower' phrase, continuing the sense across the gap. The audience will be waiting in keen anticipation, and the device should bring a heightened raptness to the word 'virtue'. Syncopated accents occur throughout, and the one on '-tue' is particularly important. The music goes into free notation at the cadence, but tempo 1 soon reappears in regular 3/4, and, with it, more bold, accented outbursts, again syncopated, with every syllable stressed. Wild, high *fortissmo* As on 'Kill Desire', suddenly dropping down a seventh, stretch the singer to fullest capacity, and the piano's thunderous chords bring the movement to an end.

Sonnet X

Again the composer has provided a lucid instruction: 'Calmly, with great self-possession'. The vocal interpreter is expected to use heart and mind as well as technique to effect the change to a more inward and ultimately spiritual and affirmative view of life (and death). It will only be convincing if the singer is able to imbibe and communicate the idealism of the text. An audience is invariably able to discern and respond to serious commitment, and fidgeting is easily quelled by deep mutual concentration. The piano's introduction is surprisingly loud, but its sonorous warmth prepares the atmosphere ready for the voice's quiet entry. The singer can now enjoy some beautifully poised phrases, lying smoothly in the medium register. The piano is very quiet indeed, muffled still further by the soft pedal. The minutest inflections and variations in dynamic take on great importance, and the piano's decorative figures enrich the texture at the ends of phrases. The composer asks for 'hushed tone' for a special phrase: 'draw in thy beams'. The spiked accents used previously are replaced by bell-like tenuto marks. I would take 'hushed' to mean covered rather than breathy tone, to preserve a smooth flow. Normal tone is resumed soon after, and a rest before the accented 'humble' is a compelling touch. The voice soars freely and warmly, becoming more impassioned while declaiming the radiant affirmation of spiritual joys; phrases arch and eventually swoop down to middle C. After another brief spell of free notation, the piano's forthright chords herald the last section.

The music begins almost identically to the opening, the vocal phrases much as before, with raptness giving way to fullest rapture. At the word 'evil' there is a sudden short break, at the precise moment when the music starts to diverge from the material heard before. Resounding declamations eventually sink, focusing on middle C. The composer stipulates that the singer should close on to the 'n' of 'heav'n' early, preserving the syncopated rhythm. The passage beginning 'Then farewell, world' is deeply moving. It is marked 'lontano' and 'recitative style' as well as 'Meno mosso'—quite a lot to assimilate. Soft held chords on the piano leave the singer free to concentrate intensely, unfettered by pulse. The original tempo is resumed in a glowing *forte* (marked 'renewed') for the voice's last, ecstatic phrases. These climb very high and a full tone has to be sustained to the end, with reiterated high As making a shattering climax. The final cadence is preceded by another sudden cut-off, but an *ad libitum* allows plenty of time to breathe and to focus the paused up-beat for the final onslaught. (Example 2).

Haladyna has produced a thoroughly memorable and stirring work. Its energy never flags, and his concern for the practicalities of audibility, even at the most heated moments, is sure to be appreciated by participants and audience alike. It is very much performers' music. That rare bird, the heroic tenor, is the ideal voice for this; an English cathedral tenor would not be at all suitable. An extrovert and somewhat rugged approach is needed, and a strong dramatic presence an essential asset. Dramatic sopranos would also be thoroughly at home in the piece. As for programming, some of the 'big'

Ex. 2 Haladyna

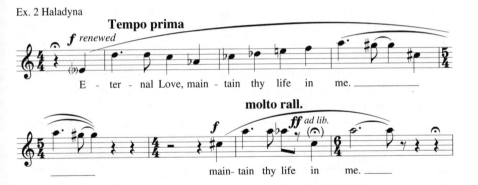

Schubert Lieder, such as 'Ganymed', would make a striking contrast, and Beethoven and Liszt would also go well. Some actual Elizabethan music, or even some of the Warlock songs that refer more overtly to Tudor models, could make an absorbing recital.

Dives and Lazarus
(1994)

Matthew King (born 1967)
Text from Luke: 16 (Tyndale Bible)

T IV; M V
High voice and piano
Duration *c.*17'

Here is a most impressive and original short cantata by a gifted and exceptionally versatile composer whose work I have known well since his student days. His Christian faith is the consistent focus of his musical vision. As a fine keyboard-player he has created a most fascinating part for the pianist, in which he acknowledges a homage to Elizabethan models such as Byrd. The vocal gestures are intended to evoke the lute songs of Dowland and his contemporaries. It is a tribute to this composer's skill that he brings off this considerable feat of technique and imagination in combining these styles in updated form, yet retaining his individuality. A particularly elegant and original type of pastiche is elevated by strong musical and artistic convictions. A fresh young voice, whether soprano or tenor, is ideal for this work, which is a major addition to the repertoire. Those who have special-ized in early music will find it particularly appealing, and extreme clarity of tone and of rhythmic articulation is needed. The delicacy of the ornamented lines, and the interplay between voice and accompaniment, are particularly striking. The composer continues to develop in assurance in writing for this medium, and this work represents another bold leap forward.

The piece is in one continuous movement and is rich in detail. The piano part is especially intricate and rewarding. Tonal centres and time signatures fluctuate continually, but there are subtle pitch cues that should keep the singer on the rails throughout, and the early music flavour is always present, however well disguised.

Harpsichord-like *una corda* opening phrases on the piano clearly establish the style with their grace-note embellishments. The voice begins to tell the parable, *poco rubato*, relatively simply at first, incorporating graceful melis-mas to decorate key words in the narrative ('purple', 'deliciously'). Dynam-ics and nuances are always carefully indicated and extremely well judged. The prolonged sibilance at the end of 'abyss' is most effective, and word-setting in general promotes clarity of enunciation. The voice must work to full capacity in long phrases, which fall naturally and flexibly. Melismas occur mainly in the middle of the range, aiding precision of pitch without strain. The harmonic relationships between voice and accompaniment have to be made clear by well-defined tone, and dissonances must also be rel-ished. There are, however, many unisons and convergences on to tonal centres, especially at cadences. Dynamics are gentle and unforced so that the story can be articulated without distractions. Tempos vary throughout this opening section, and some are very slow indeed, at moments of intense poignancy. Cross-rhythms enhance the free flow of the narrative. As the tempo moves suddenly forward after the death of Lazarus, at the words 'was carried by angels', the piano's high-lying chords and shimmering demisemiquavers decorate the voice's climb 'into Abraham's bosom', (Example 1) and the triumphant cadence is echoed, in more relaxed fashion, sinking lower in the voice and ending the paragraph on a pause.

The second stanza resumes the plain narrative style of the opening, but quickly becomes more overtly expressive, with a rapt *pianissimo* marking the moment when Dives views Abraham and Lazarus in heaven. As he calls out, the piano's brilliant left-hand scale-passages increase the dramatic tension, and the vocal part becomes more passionate, in a mood of desper-ation. The composer's instructions for shaping and colouring the phrases are meticulously thought out, and the rubato must be gauged carefully so the ebb and flow work perfectly as he dictates. This passage seems full-bloodedly Romantic, almost Expressionist as in works of the Second Vien-nese School even though the vocal part preserves the flavour of early music. Balance problems at the heightened dynamic are avoided by the low tessit-

Ex. 1 King

Ex. 2 King

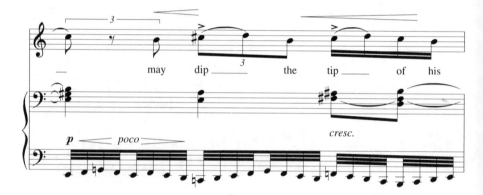

ura of the accompaniment (Example 2), yet lighter voice-types may find the low B flats in the slower section, beginning with Abraham's response, a little difficult. However, the following section, marked 'tenderly' is beautifully set. Descriptive adverbs such as this invariably help an interpreter, and can make an enormous difference to the way a performer thinks about a certain passage, colouring the words and music instantly in intuitive response. Arpeggiated, harp-like chords contribute to the seraphic effect. The tone-colour should glisten appropriately without becoming too operatic. An intimate quality is always present. The composer's characterization of the dramatis personae is carefully imagined. There should be a marked difference between the impulsively emotional utterances of Dives, and the firm, sympathetic authority of Abraham, for instance. The piano accompaniment accentuates the contrast: spare lines, with hands widely spaced, radiant, harp-like strummings, for Abraham; dense, tortured rumblings with a fast-running bass for Dives. Abraham's oration is the central dramatic focus of the work, and it continues in more elaborate style up to a pause. The piano again descends to the depths for Dives's response. Even at this level of dynamics, the cross-rhythms and phrasing still bear reference to early music, especially in the relationship of voice to keyboard, and these features must be keenly delineated as the music surges forward. Again, tension dissipates for a serene cantabile phrase from Abraham, accompanied by a two-part fugue. Passages in quotes have to be differentiated clearly from those outside: always a tricky interpretative problem, requiring intense concentration and focus on the text's subtlest implications. The performer's artistry is called upon to portray each character within the narrative. Satie's *Socrate* is an example of a work that gives the singer this specific task throughout its considerable length and always makes an extremely moving effect despite the uniformity of material and infrequent dynamic variation. It represents perhaps the highest form of artistic sensibility. A spiritual message cannot be delivered by forcing or exaggerating. Control is always present in this more intimate type of drama—a totally different approach from that of the operatic platform, where roles are allocated to widely differing voices and persons. Since heaven is the setting for a major part of this piece, a sense of ethereal detachment is appropriate.

The exchanges between Dives and Abraham continue to be marked by contrasting musical material. Dives's final impassioned *fortissimo* outburst eventually falters into weaker repetitions (Example 3), and Abraham's reply is supported by thin, broadly spaced chords, which now float above the vocal line. At the words 'though one rose from death again', the piano's right hand states a theme based on a rising scale, with tenuto accents. It is important for the singer to allow this to come through clearly, because this material is to be worked and developed into a three-part contrapuntal texture, beneath the final vocal paragraph. The voice, too, eventually takes it up in the form of a gentle, gliding melisma on the word 'rose', before the cadence in B flat, which seems almost Purcellian. The piano then has a solo coda, underlining the final message of eternal life, and triumph in death, with a direct quote of 'See the conquering hero comes' from Handel's *Judas Maccabaeus* (a tune perhaps even more widely known in the revivalist hymn 'Thine be the Glory, risen conquering Son | Endless is the victory Thou o'er

Ex. 3 King

Death has won'). This also is worked into a contrapuntal pattern, with more overt references to early music in style and ornament, finally coming to rest on an unresolved cadence.

This original and deeply felt work gives a fresh slant to the traditional cantata on a biblical theme. It would be interesting to compare it with the Britten *Canticles*, in particular 'Abraham and Isaac'. Another intriguing parallel, especially since it features the discourse of souls entering heaven, is Messiaen's little-known mini-cantata *La Mort du Nombre* for soprano, tenor, violin, and piano.

Dives and Lazarus is of course eminently suitable for a church recital, surrounded by examples of early music, especially Purcell. Keyboard solos could also be interspersed, and it would go well as part of a mixed programme of chamber music, featuring other instruments. If there is to be another modern vocal work in the programme, perhaps a virtuoso unaccompanied piece (see Knussen or Lefanu in this volume) would be suitable as a contrast. The rarefied atmosphere it evokes must not be spoiled by inappropriately melodramatic juxtapositions. A very wide range of moods are covered within the work's modest scope, and it needs to be lived with for a period of time so that its special spirit can be thoroughly absorbed by both performers. Despite its immediate attractions—it falls very easily on the ear and is full of wit and ingenuity—there is nothing superficial here. It constitutes an auspicious addition to the repertoire of sacred music, and is to be warmly recommended to talented performers seeking a fine example of work from the younger generation of British composers.

Three Poems of Irina Ratushinskaya (1991)

John McLeod (born 1934)
Text by Irina Ratushinskaya
Translated into English by David McDuff

T IV; M V
Soprano and piano
Duration 7'45"

The searing emotional power of the work of the young Russian poet Irina Ratushinskaya and her defiant optimism in the face of horrific experiences in a Soviet labour camp, have moved and inspired artists everywhere. Since her poems became known here, several composers have responded to their vivid and visceral immediacy: Brian Elias, for instance, has produced a fine orchestral song cycle.

The striking and characterful music of the Scottish composer John McLeod is perfectly suited to these vibrant texts. Full of drama, contrast, and rhythmic drive, the three settings make a most satisfying and well-proportioned cycle, with the fiercely dynamic middle song the most ambitious in scope. The piano part requires a player of exceptional flair and strength, quick to respond to and lead the varying tempos and moods. Abrupt and dramatic changes of tempo are a feature of the composer's work, and metronome markings should be observed closely. Balance between voice and piano is crucial: there is quite a lot of loud music, and although relatively short, the piece will test the stamina of both performers. A warm and expressive soprano voice, well centred and penetrating over a wide range, yet able to float *pianissimo*, will show the music to best advantage. Considerable stage presence is required to carry conviction, in closest identification and empathy with the poetry. A fairly high standard of musicianship too is needed: pitching is not at all easy in the highly chromatic idiom, and intervals have to be tuned scrupulously. Rhythms have a flexible spontaneity, often obeying speech patterns, but they will need detailed work at the learning stage. The bravura sweep of the lines communicates energy and intensity which hardly ever lets up. The singer's skill in articulating syllables high in the voice will be an important asset. Not all phrases are ideally comfortable at first, but after several repetitions the work begins to settle into the voice. Too hectoring a style should be avoided: there is often more time for semiquavers than one imagines, and percussive consonants must not be allowed to restrict the tone in high-lying passages. Swift reactions in letting go of the muscles used to produce them will free the voice's natural resonance even *in extremis*, but this, too, only comes after long practice. Rehearsals should be well spaced to avoid fatigue from overenthusiastic projection before ensemble is secure. The performers are equal partners, and must remain closely in touch: it may be difficult for the singer to hear the piano in very active passages when she is singing strongly in a high register. The pianist's rhythmic groupings have to be clearly defined: textural clarity is most important, and pedalling should be carefully adjusted to suit the acoustics.

1. Where are you, my prince?

The audience's attention is instantly held by the beautifully judged opening setting, ideally paced so that the atmosphere can be savoured. After a loud piano flourish, the singer enters quietly, poised on high F, and her questioning first phrase pushes the music along a little. Pitches fall easily in the voice at first, establishing a poignantly direct utterance, before a sudden anguished cry leaps up to top C flat on 'My eyes' (Example 1). Since no accent is marked, the large interval can be spanned legato, as long as it does not impair clarity. The downward plunge to 'fire' is tricky. The quick notes must have identifiable pitches, and the brief rest is unsuitable as a breathing place. 'Fire' will be firmer in tone if the percussive attack is not forced. The singer's questions and asides to herself, in short, pithy phrases, are contrasted by the violent outburst describing winter's harshness, which forms the centre of the movement. The sweeping lines cover a tremendous range, and the music's intensity heightens the impact of the text's haunting imagery. 'Drives' on *fortissimo* high B is particularly effective. A breath snatched after the second 'round' could prove awkward, and it is best to wait until after 'circle', when a quick intake may help the descending phrase, and enable the 'p's in 'point of despair' to be heard clearly. There is a difficult transition, from a triplet figure on E flat up a tritone to A natural on 'grille', for the tempo-change to *Adagio*. The 'i' vowel must not be constricted, and the palate and tongue have to be relaxed very quickly after the consonants: a prolonged rolled 'r' should help, and there should be no attempt to enunciate the final 'l' too far back in the throat. The preceding

Ex. 1 McLeod

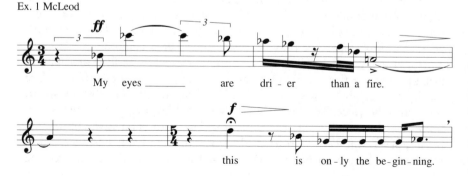

note on 'the' should be as legato as possible, taking time to poise the diminuendo. The song ends softly, with simple, touching fragments of wistful contemplation, and a final hushed murmur of 'I'll dream of you tonight' (marked 'pianissimo espressivo').

2. I will travel through the land

The raging momentum of this movement means that it actually takes less time than the opening setting despite its substantial content. The basic *Allegro feroce* is now and again interrupted by a short *Adagio* passage before the music surges forward again with tremendous force. The pace and energy required will put both performers severely to the test. Text audibility could be a real problem, and consonants will need to be exaggerated. Percussive and sibilant sounds must be given special attention, so that despite the animated and sharply accented delivery, they do not bounce out of control and blur rhythms. The very first note of any loud phrase should never be pushed too hard. The frequent presence of short rests in mid-phrase could encourage hectic breathing resulting in gustiness. The tessitura of some words may affect clarity and penetration; for example, 'human suff'ring' set very low in the middle of a virtuoso wide-ranging phrase. The 'u' sound is not one that invites a cutting edge, and the 'h' could make for a bumpy or delayed start—there is very little room for correcting imprecision at speed. The singer should aim for a lean accurate tone, and keep vibrato to a minimum. There is room to expand a little in the slower phrases, whose timing is of utmost importance. The composer repeats some key words in the poem to enhance the drama. Double-dotted descending hockets on the reiterated 'walk' lie very well vocally, and the accent also aids articulation. Similarly, the repeated 'everything's nearer the end, again in sharply defined rhythms, help control some subtle tempo adjustments, and the gradual winding-down of dynamic level.

A *più mosso* in 2/4 a third of the way through the piece, provides a hypnotic contrast to the reckless outbursts that surround it. The poet muses on the subtle and mystical transference of physical similarities between wives and husbands. The pianist has oscillating triplet quavers in the bass clef, and the soprano transparent and uncluttered lines that gradually build to a climax on 'last vein', ending in a spine-chilling fade on 'skins'. There is opportunity for some imaginative tone-colouring here, and the pitches are practicable for this, especially the B natural at the end, over the piano's *molto ritenuto*. The renewal of the *Allegro feroce* brings yet more uninhibited declarations of defiance. Dynamics and rhythms again must be given fullest attention. When the whirling pace is resumed after another beautifully placed *Adagio* phrase, there are further tests of slick enunciation ('That most ancient of words'). The very short, clipped 'light' at the end of the sentence must linger just long enough to reveal a clear pitch centre. The last *Adagio* section is the longest, incorporating the repeats of 'everything', then unfolding into a free passage, marked 'quasi recit—whispering'. A slightly breathy quality, mysterious and intense, works very well for the predominantly low part of the phrase, and consonants can be heightened, but it will be much safer to preserve quality on the higher 'from me' by keeping tone pure. The pause would otherwise be difficult to manage. For the final *Allegro feroce*, the repeated 'How' and 'What' make an exciting effect, but may carry the risk of wasting air on the first, separated sound. Ideally, the singer should aim to encompass the whole paragraph within two spans, refuelling only after 'last'. This will make the melismas on 'breathe' and 'live' more even. As the voice breaks off the piano launches into an even faster coda of manic power; *con tutta forza*.

3. No, I'm not afraid

This last setting, of the poem which bears the title of the volume, conveys most stirringly the vast range of emotion exposed with such painful directness by the poet. The piano begins alone with a funeral march, which is violently interrupted by the singer. Despite the force of the interjection, the vocal part is marked 'with dignity' to guard against any lapse into hysteria. This is, perhaps, the key to the interpretation of the whole work. Such powerfully dramatic material does not need overemphasis, and a disciplined, almost austere approach can be infinitely more moving than a more overt depiction of harrowing moments. The sudden *piano* after the opening declaration is excellently placed vocally, allowing the singer to keep words clear, making good use of the sibilant sounds ('prison nights', 'survive' 'sadness', 'escape'). A deftly judged piece of onomatopoeia introduces the cockerel (Example 2). The singer can take full advantage of the scooping

Ex. 2 McLeod

The cock-er-el will weep free-dom for me   And here knee deep in mire

line and characterful rhythm to give a close imitation of a cock-crow. Colourful images proliferate, and the rhythmic *Maestoso* tempo returns with the heart-rending cry: 'How am I to carry to an alien planet, what are almost tears?'

The cycle ends with a shattering admission of fear, contradicting the opening statement's defiance. The timing of phrases is vitally important. A comma separates the quiet 'It isn't true', from the soaring glissando up a minor ninth on 'I am afraid', starting very fast and slowing to allow for clear enunciation at a very high pitch. This may be hard to accomplish at first, although the repetition of the words takes away some of the burden of achieving total clarity. The singer must not rush this passage and risk sounding strangled. Her final phrase is deeply moving: 'But make it look as though you haven't noticed' is intoned, *parlando senza vibrato*, on low D. This should not be hurried, and should have a disembodied quality. Intense emotion is now internalized, and concentration is held to the very last, ending quietly without a *rallentando*.

John McLeod has given singer and pianist a memorably dramatic vehicle with which to develop powers of communication and sharpen responses to one another. The experienced singer will relish the opportunities to display her range of colour and dynamics over such a broad range. It would obviously be appropriate to place the piece in a recital of Russian music. Some Tchaikovsky or Rachmaninov songs could frame it. Prokofiev and Shostakovich world also provide a rich source of complementary material. By contrast, some French music would be a good choice, particularly in view of the composer's fondness for the work of Messiaen. (*Poèmes pour Mi* makes an excellent companion piece.) A church setting, as long as it is not too resonant, is as suitable as a concert ambience. A degree of quiet formality will focus audience concentration all the better.

Cycle for Declamation (1954) (Solo voice)

Priaulx Rainier (1903–86) Text by John Donne

T IV; M III Tenor (or other voices) (unaccompanied) Duration *c*.8′

This is quite simply one of the outstanding solo-voice works of the century. Written for and dedicated to that consummate artist, the late Peter Pears, it was an ideal vehicle for his unrivalled intensity and compelling presence. Such timeless and inspiring texts (from Donne's *Devotions*) demand, and receive, music of the highest calibre. Rainier, a much-loved figure, originally from South Africa, but long resident in Britain, was justly revered by connoisseurs and those lucky enough to be her students, but, like others of her generation, did not really attain the wider international recognition she deserved. The uniformly high quality of her work stands as a testimony to true values, at a time when these are needed more than ever. She has produced a work of startling power and memorability. It is particularly exciting in a church resonance, of course, but as a concert piece it is guaranteed to hold the attention. It demonstrates the singer's control and artistry through a rigorously disciplined approach. There are no flashy displays here—just a series of ringing phrases, not all of which fall easily in the voice, but which are infinitely rewarding after long practice. It is perhaps better suited to the tenor range than the soprano. Some parts are uncomfortably high, making it difficult to keep words clear at the higher octave, especially in the first setting, and the second movement exploits a particularly vulnerable transitional register. The composer, ever-practical, states that other voices, including soprano, may transpose the whole piece to suit their range. This does, however, alter the colour of the phrases, and the high, gleaming pitches originally chosen do seem to be ideally appropriate, even if they may require extra work. Excellent breath control (as exemplified by Pears) is a prime requirement, as is clean intonation. The musical idiom combines some neo-classical features with strong references to modal folksong roots.

1. Wee cannot bid the fruits

A thorough preliminary warming-up will be essential before the voice is ready to launch into the first phrase. This features a loud, sustained succession of high Gs on a range of differing syllables, involving some awkward groups of consonants. It pays to be analytical about the word components and seize every natural opportunity for legato. Since there are also heavy accents, there is a real danger of forcing or constricting the sound. Here in particular, a reverberant church acoustic will help to smooth the edges (Example 1). To be specific, the problem syllables in descending order of difficulty are: 'sticke' (the short 'e' vowel is framed by two lots of silent aspirate–percussive consonants, and the accent may encourage pushing), 'bid', 'De-' 'leaves', and the initial 'Wee', where, at least, there is a chance to establish the line on the 'oo' of 'W' before releasing the 'ee'. The following 'c' of 'cannot' must not bounce the sound out of position. The singer must listen to the resonance, and be satisfied that quality is uniform,

Ex. 1 Rainier

avoiding gripping the diphthong ending of 'May'—the first breath-point—where the sound should be left hanging in space. The trick is to restart in exactly the same position (the 'n' of 'nor' is helpful). It is important not to rush semiquaver groups, but to ensure that each note has a discernible pitch centre, free of the surrounding consonants. Special care is needed for the end of the phrase, which lingers a very long time on '-ber'. The whole phrase, if practised assiduously, will prove a valuable lesson in intensified legato singing that will serve well for other repertoire, in particular the songs of Schubert, which often feature words set in a way that can mitigate against immaculate delivery by all but the most experienced artists. After the crucial opening phrase there is a sudden slight increase of speed, in contrast to the spaciously ringing first line. There is no need to breathe after 'give'. This extrovert and portentous declamation is as if a sermon were being delivered from a high pulpit. The few melismas ring out like bells. At the paragraph commencing 'Reward', a more inward feeling prevails, with softer dynamics accordingly. It is important to mark the difference between tenuto accents and the sharper kind indicated by small arrows. Rhythms and dynamics are less predictable here and must be carefully observed. At the lower-lying section beginning 'Feare' a darker, fuller tone is appropriate, and, as before, the double-dotted rhythm is to be brought out clearly. If the singer lives the words, a sense of conviction carries the piece triumphantly. Intonation will need care at 'friendship', and there is a tied triplet over the barline which gives a feeling of rubato for a moment, otherwise a strong pulse should be evident. There is time to colour 'natural affection' in a glowing and tender *piano*. The crescendo at the end should be exaggerated to prepare for the strenuous closing decalamations, which are relentlessly high-lying, as at the opening. Words are, however, a little easier to negotiate, with the exception of the hammered out 'that knows not their season' where the semiquavers must remain steady. The long note on high A on 'lose' is helped by preparing the 'l' and then singing through the '-se' (pronounced 'z') and on to the vocalized 'the', landing safely on the forcefully accented 'fruits' with a rolled 'r'. This final word snaps off quite suddenly, and a resonant acoustic will enhance the effect, which almost seems to invite an echo. On a personal note: I have tried transposing this movement down a whole tone, but in the end decided that the higher version's ringing quality was worth the extra effort.

2. In the Wombe of the Earth

Of the three movements this is probably the most difficult vocally, as it requires enormous control. There may even be serious intonation problems since there is a great deal of floating around E and F natural, which could expose any insecurity, especially in the female voice. Transposition will help considerably of course, but it is perhaps a pity to alter the pitch relationship of the three pieces to one another. This movement has a modal D minor tonality. The tempo-marking (minim = 58) is reassuring if checked with a metronome. It is easy to inflict self-punishment by lingering unnecessarily in slow tempos. As before, much breath support is needed, and, in general, the expectation of a male chest capacity is a challenge to the female interpreter. Vowels are especially crucial, and need to be examined in detail. There are very few percussive attacks here, and accents are mostly of the softer, tenuto kind. The singer has to find exactly the right quality from the beginning: soft and sinewy, with a clear centre that can be manipulated instrumentally, making sure that the pitch does not droop. He or she will become acutely aware of the need to maintain the brighter, nasal resonances, helped by the 'ee' vowels, but at the same time, the tone must not be pinched or reedy. The written dynamics are tricky, especially the diminuendos at the ends of phrases. As with the first movement, the beginning and end of the song provide the most testing moments. After wafting between D and E for long stretches, it will be a relief to reach an 'official' resting-place, with three whole minims worth of silence. (These must still be counted out.) Firmness in the middle register is needed for the central section, where accents are particularly telling. Phrase-marks divide the music into long spans, and snatched breaths in tempo must not interrupt the flow. It is important to avoid bumpy restarts. Intensity builds, and notes need to be sung to their fullest length. The line soars up rapturously, and the high Gs are a welcome release, mellifluously set in phrases that weave graceful patterns. The minor third in the middle of 'transported' will seem a large leap in this context, and there will have to be a portamento through it to sustain the rapt legato. Another chance to rest occurs before the final, most demanding phrases. The fragment 'our dust' must be accurate in rhythm, thinking through the following rest. The melisma on 'blown' gives a chance to prepare for the greatly extended final line, and to focus perfectly the repeated oscillations of half- and whole-tones that make up the work's most difficult passage. Exceptional control of breathing will ensure that the final held D does not waver or fade too soon. The placing of the first few notes of the phrase will determine the fate of the whole. The last possible breathing place is after the fragmented 'with', and the composer has put a helpful diminuendo just after this, to prevent the singer from using up the new intake of air too soon. The placing of the 'w' of 'wind' will have a far-reaching effect. It is best to vocalize a 'w' on the pitch and ensure a continuous line; any unnecessary gaps will waste precious air. Having reached the high F safely (another wide-seeming minor third) this very long line must be floated and not held with the throat. Soft palate and jaw muscles should be relaxed, and an open head resonance felt, with no sensation of pushing individual notes. The lilt of the 2/2 rhythm should still be noticeable, and awareness of the continuing pulse will help the singer psychologically. It is very important not to diminuendo too soon on the final note, but instead to let the tone fade naturally as breath expires. This means keeping the support muscles of chest, diaphragm, and abdomen taut and fully energized to the very last moment, so that the tone has a thread-like clarity of pitch and does not flatten or become clouded.

3. Nunc, lento sonitu

This last and longest movement contains some of the most stirring words in our entire literary history, familiar to almost everyone, and assured of tremendous impact wherever they are heard. It is probably the easiest of the three to perform, since it moves around the range constantly, the tempo varies and there are many chances for the singer to dictate pacing and take a rest in between strenuous passages. The sonorous, deep bell-peals of the opening provide a recurring motif that is wonderfully effective. They also afford vocal relief after the preceding movements' more stressful demands. At the start, the final consonant of 'Nunc' should be placed exactly on the second beat, establishing a steady pulse. Dynamics are exceptionally well varied in this movement, and they make an indispensable contribution to the dramatic effect. Singers sometimes lack the daring to exhibit their full dynamic range. In the interests of preserving a warm tone, a *mezzo-forte* is too often the quietest level of sound on offer. The demands of singing over an orchestra, especially in an operatic context, can lead to habit-forming overprojection. There are special rewards to be gained from the more intimate and subtle nuances possible in the recital hall. As before, lengths of rests are equally important as note-values. Trumpet-like fanfare figures occur throughout, excitingly immediate in their effect. Choice of breathing places needs forethought, especially in the third and fourth lines, where there are many rests, but the continuity of sense is vital. The reiterated 't's provide a clue as to structure: it is very important not to interrupt the crescendo on 'Sunne' but to go through to 'but', placing the 't' on the following half-beat. This then provides an ideal breathing place, with a natural springboard effect, propelling the voice onward to the final 't' of 'Comet'. Another breath can be taken here, again making sure of the rhythmic placing of the 't'. Awareness of the text's alliteration is an added enhancement. The tension remains high for the thrilling outburst of 'Who lends not his ear'—a sustained 'trumpet blast' for which the composer herself has provided a breathing mark. A syncopated rhythm here should be well delineated. Now the reason for the breath mark becomes clear: the singer must continue the phrase after the onomatopoeic 'rings', arching down to the soft bell-chime that follows (Example 2). Another gleaming rhythmic fanfare passage is followed by a sudden diminuendo to a floated, sustained D, requiring the same technical approach as the end of the previous movement. Again, the 'w' sound is helpful vocally. This time there is a pause, at the singer's discretion. The timing of the restart, the repeat of the opening's deep bell refrain, and its soft echoing answer, is of great importance. There is no need to hurry. This is the very heart of the work. After the first statement of 'No man is an Island', and the pause that

Ex. 2 Rainier

Who casts not up his *Eye* to the *Sunne* ___ when it

ri - - ses? but who takes off his *Eye* from a

Com - et when that breakes out? Who ___ bends not his *eare* ___ to

an - y *bell,* which up-on an - y oc - ca - sion rings?

naturally follows, there is a sudden quickening, as the text races on to another peak on a high G on 'were'. There must be no interruption after 'maine', and breath should be taken after 'Continent' (another carefully placed 't'). Again the composer, realizing possible ambiguities, has written breathing marks in this important paragraph. Of these, the more difficult is the one after the dotted quaver of 'were', since a quick snatch is all that is possible. It is important not to lose hold of support muscles, or let rhythm slacken. This last phrase may seem a long haul, but the sustained liquid consonants on 'thine owne were' will aid focus. The vowel of 'were' should be left to resonate freely, not clipped off with an enunciated 'r'. The ending of the piece is truly memorable and impressive. The tempo reverts to the steady pulse of the outset, and the text's second most familiar passage is now declaimed with ringing clarity. The crescendo up to 'in-volved' is especially moving in its intensity. The English text is regularly interrupted by the gentle Latin echo motif of 'Morieris'. The choice of tessitura for 'for whom the Bell tolls' is ideally bright in resonance. It is important not to break the line after 'tolls': the pulse (a funeral dirge) dictates that it continues on to 'it', and from here until the end of the work, the beat must be constant. The last, prolonged, hushed 'Morieris' can be even quieter than marked, tenuto accents keeping the tension going to the very last.

It is difficult to imagine a situation where this important work would not be a happy programme choice. As already mentioned, its spiritual content fits it for church performances, including organ recitals, but its message is equally appropriate for non-believers. Its uncluttered lines and immediate musical language will pose no problems for even the most conventionally minded music club audience. It provides a perfect complement for any of the major vocal classics, especially the weightier cycles of Schubert, Brahms, and Schumann. A solo-voice work of this quality always gives a welcome change of emphasis in a programme for voice and keyboard. It would also be equally useful in a chamber music recital. Because of its deep emotional force, it is as well to allow time for recovery afterwards. It is perhaps best at the start of a recital, or just after the interval, when the audience is at its most receptive and concentrated. Despite its technical demands, it deserves to become part of standard repertory.

Songs from the Exotic (1987)

Judith Weir (born 1954)
Text from traditional folk material from Serbia (in English translation), Spain, and Scotland (No. 3 in Spanish)

T IV; M III
Medium voice and piano
Duration *c.*10'

Judith Weir continues to delight us with the freshness of her ideas and her firm grasp of practicalities. She has discovered how to write accessible music that is not at all facile or superficial: a rare feat. Her musicianship is completely at one with her literary imagination and her sense of fun—also, her innate good taste. These gifts enable her to steer close to the areas of pastiche and parody without losing her individuality, or offending purists. Since the highly original, much-admired solo opera *King Harald's Saga* (1979) she has written many more vocal works, including three full-scale operas, and her instinct for vocal writing is even more assured. Particularly noticeable is her sensitivity to the voice's capacity for long-breathed phrases, and also to the varied nuances of articulation. Her music is as attractive to perform as it is to listen to. It also looks good on the page: an aspect often neglected. Her instructions are concise and invaluable. She has the ability to express herself clearly and is unfailingly tactful and helpful when working with performers. It is hardly surprising that her attributes are now more widely recognized.

She is attracted by folk music of many countries, including that of her native Scotland. Curiously, and endearingly, a Scottish flavour is always faintly discernible in her music, even when the subject-matter emanates from quite another culture—proof, perhaps, of the deeper influences that bind all folk art. She has a winning way with words, often reworking source-material in her own original way, yet demonstrating an instinct for the natural inflections of other languages, and an awareness of the quaintly humorous undertones that often lurk beneath the most sombre themes. An interest in the folk tradition of Serbia, represented here by the first two movements, also inspired her chamber work *Serbian Cabaret* for 'Speaking Piano Quartet'. It is of course extremely unfortunate that current events have given this area painfully uncomfortable overtones, but a genuine folk tradition should be immune from nationalism's more destructive aspects. As for the Spanish setting, this shows the flair demonstrated more extensively in her *Spanish Liederbooklet*—a cycle to be warmly recommended to high sopranos.

The vocal parts of this present work may appear relatively undemanding, as they are mostly in simple note-values, in a medium register. However, as any trained singer knows, the hardest test of all can be to keep an even flow when there are no spectacular runs or melismas to free and display the voice, perhaps even concealing deficiencies in control and purity. As with the Berio *Folksongs* there are moments when a raw, quasi-non-vibrato exaggerated chest voice could be highly appropriate, but unless this sound is produced properly, with full support, it is dangerously unreliable, especially with regard to intonation, and can ultimately be monotonous. If a rough tone is deliberately used for colouristic effect, it should also be possible to demonstrate normal lyricism as a contrast. Throughout the piece, the voice–piano idiom is effortlessly mastered and the lively keyboard parts are enjoyable to play. A boundless vitality is evident from start to finish, and material is ideally balanced and varied, yet retaining a cohesiveness of style.

1. Sevdalino, My Little One (A Serbian folksong)

The opening immediately grips the attention. Brightly oscillating chords in the piano, *molto legato* and *una corda*, create a constant high-lying texture cushioning and supporting the voice, and dictating the many exhilarating harmonic shifts. The composer is fond of using the piano in this colourful, almost orchestral way. Here the sound resembles that of a concertina, enhancing the ethnic effect. In the middle of this continuous pulsation, the voice has to draw clean legato lines, placed clearly and precisely. Breathing places should be kept to a minimum so that the vocal sound too is instrumental with a cutting edge to it, and vibrato well controlled (Example 1). The music's forthright impression is reinforced by the number of cadences: the composer is not afraid of closing phrases in a pointed and concise manner, entirely in keeping with the words' directness. Dynamics at the

Ex. 1 Weir

cadences, however, are sometimes unexpected: for instance there is a series of sudden decrescendos on final notes. The movement is marked 'semplice', and its simplicity will need to be of the artful kind: flow should seem effortless within the constantly changing rhythmic patterns. The singer should always keep the tone luminous, and guard against the pitch sinking. At this level, it is often wiser to think high to stay in tune and chime with the piano's resonance. Close intervals need to be checked scrupulously, especially at crucial harmony changes.

2. In the Lovely Village of Nevesinje (from a Serbian epic)

This provides a considerable contrast, and is more obviously histrionic and dramatically varied than the previous movement. The mixture of direct and reported speech is characteristic of Weir's choice of vocal settings, and there are strong reminders of *The Consolations of Scholarship*, (despite its oriental background) as well as of *Serbian Cabaret* in the declamatory style. The accompanying piano figures here are tremendously varied, sometimes becoming extremely elaborate. However, the keyboard role is always that of partner rather than of competing soloist, the relationship being directly comparable to that found in the great German Lieder repertoire, for which the composer acknowledges a special fondness. The piano's opening chord progressions are marked 'level and distant'. Weir always chooses words carefully to guide the performers, frequently crystallizing a mood succinctly in this way. The movement begins *misterioso*, and the voice's entry is 'detached and sinister'. The singer has a low, chanted recitative that sets the scene, underlined by the piano's interspersed chord sequences. The threatening mood is conveyed by a gradual crescendo. Pronunciation guidance is given for the Serbian proper names in the text. At 'suddenly furious', the accuser speaks. Tessitura here is well chosen, and the singer's chest register should pierce through the piano's deep rumbling demisemiquavers ('like a rolling wave'), with the triplet figures projecting clearly. The voice becomes more impassioned, and there is an (unconscious?) reference to no. 5 ('Répétion Planétaire') of Messiaen's *Harawi* in the wild, primitive call of 'Ahi!' (pitches are also similar). Rhythms will need care here, especially in a passage of vocal hocketing. An abrupt change of texture begins *mezzo-piano*, 'with suppressed fury'. The piano's nervous syncopated chordal patterns build tension as the voice dictates 'three choices' with menacing clarity. Against some florid piano demisemiquavers, the singer must make sure to time syllables well, taking full advantage of any sibilant or percussive opportunities. The angry diatribe, first issuing a challenge to fight, and then a calculated insult, ends 'with suppressed violence', as the piano part dissolves into a light staccato that suddenly peters out. Tension should be felt through the ensuing silence. The coda, marked 'epic', is full of hidden meaning, understated, but weighty in implication (and delivery—marked 'massive'). Despite the brevity and deceptive simplicity of this passage, it requires a considerable effort of interpretative concentration to bring it off. The singer has to convey a commanding presence in just a few words, ending with a flourish.

3. The Romance of Count Arnaldos (A Spanish song, 15th–16th century anon.)

For this early, anonymous Spanish verse, the composer provides an English translation directly over the corresponding words in the text. This device ensures that the meaning is assimilated from the first, and becomes integral to the interpretation, even during the early learning process.

The composer immediately captures the appropriate Spanish flavour, (even recalling the *Canciones populares españolas* of Falla) with the aid of light ghostly staccato chords in the piano, hands alternating. These continue throughout in irregular quaver groupings, dance-like, but not too hectic (the tempo is marked 'easy and relaxed'). The text relates the legend of Count Arnaldos, his sighting of a mysterious sailor, and their ensuing dialogue: enigmatic, tantalizing, and inconclusive. The composer seems to have a taste for texts which leave things unsaid, so that the music can contribute an extra dimension. The continually shifting emphasis of the rhythms will entail a good deal of preparatory work to avoid faltering, and some pitches are not easy, although piano chords are a help (Example 2). The singer has

Ex. 2 Weir

to convey clearly the conversation that follows the opening description with its evocative images. Tessitura dips into the lower reaches, but tone should remain light and clear, so that details can come through without strain. Phrases are often fragmentary, and the singer should take care not to rush or force them. It is best to have a breathing plan worked out well in advance, limiting main breaths to the start of each section. The singer's only chance of an easy legato comes on an elongated final syllable, at the end of the first and last stanzas, alternating Ds and E flats, first at the lower octave, and then up at the end. This is a charming song, but one that will need particular polish to make it seem effortless.

4. The Song of a Girl Ravished Away by the Fairies in South Uist (A Scottish-Gaelic folksong)

This traditional folksong is set in a most arresting manner. The accompaniment at first merely enhances and amplifies important notes in the vocal melody, as if strumming a stringed folk instrument. As the folk-tune is repeated, undergoing various transformations, the accompaniment touches in yet more unisons with the voice part, pointing rhythms with very brief single notes (Example 3). The singer should make sure that intonation is exact, and that tone-quality matches the style. There should be very little vibrato. Despite the 'prompt' touches, pitching is not as easy as might be expected. The resonances set up by the striking harmonies can be very

Ex. 3 Weir

deceptive and a steely accuracy will be needed to centre the notes firmly. In the central section, swirling demisemiquavers in the accompaniment recall moments of the second song of the cycle, and the voice encompasses a wider range of pitch and expression. Dynamics are to be strictly observed, especially the diminuendos. For the last verse the piano has high, bright, chiming chords, which ring on through the vocal lines. The piece ends abruptly, a tempo, without a hint of a *rallentando*.

This is a thoroughly entertaining concert item which requires a disciplined approach by singer and pianist. As with Lieder, folksong calls on a vast array of subtleties and controlled inflections that may not be obvious to the unschooled listener. The desired end result is that naturalness which is in fact the result of a great deal of thought, acquired skill, and commitment. There is no doubt at all that an audience will enjoy this piece, and it can easily be placed in a standard Lieder recital, or next to some straight folksongs. Other vocal works from Spain or Scotland would make an appropriate, thematic programme. The cycle will also be suitable for a baritone, or a countertenor, and, as the tessitura is not demanding, sopranos and tenors with a reliable lower range would be quite comfortable. A lighter voice will have the requisite flexibility for the faster moving passages, but each singer will be able to create an individual interpretation. Freedom to interpret intuitively within clear given guidelines is the wish of most performers, and Weir is well able to satisfy this. Her music is deservedly popular with professional and amateur performers alike.

Carte du tendre
(1993)

Caroline Wilkins (born 1953)
Text by Charles Baudelaire (in French)

T IV; M III
Soprano and prepared piano
Duration *c*.10′

The remarkably evocative and highly original work of the British composer Caroline Wilkins has already won her an international reputation. Currently resident in Germany, she is at home in both acoustic and electro-acoustic music, at the cutting edge of modernism, and her work, beautifully heard, experiments with sonority and articulation in a most arresting way. A substantial period of residence in Australia has also broadened her perspective.

Her music is luminous and clear in texture, each individual resonance clearly plotted. She manipulates her material expertly, and is not afraid to let the music stand still: repeated notes are a constant feature in both voice and piano. Decorative figures are delicately worked into the spare lines, which have an oriental fastidiousness and economy. This music is far removed from the world of Second Viennese School Expressionism, apart from certain harmonic and intervallic relationships.

The composer explains the reason for the title: 'Carte du tendre' was the ancient code of courtly love. The three familiar Baudelaire poems with their basic sonnet form gave her the idea of codifying the text, using selected fragments—now a fleeting phrase, now a word or repeated syllable. Admirably, the complete poems, and the fragments used by the composer, are printed out in full at the front of the score. The details for the preparing of the piano are also explained fully and clearly. The general effect produced is intended to suggest the quality and intonation of a nineteenth-century barrel-organ, as would have been heard in the time of the poet. Unusually, the actual quality of sound resulting from each 'inside piano' treatment is described: the small implements placed between upper strings produce a 'metallic ring'; strips of plasticine, lined by paper, a 'thin, silvery tone'; and plucking the strings by hand, a 'metallic reverberation'. Each has been tried and tested thoroughly. The composer's vocal instructions further exemplify her refined sensitivity to aural ambience, and the subtlest acoustic resonances: she use triangular note-heads for whispered effects; those to be half-spoken have crosses through the stems. Standard symbols indicate the gradual opening and closing of the mouth on long vowels: an open 'o' for open, and a 'closed' dot for closed, with arrows between. The only sign that could be ambiguous is that consisting of slurred groups of staccato repeated notes where note-heads are smaller than normal, indicating a 'barely audible echo'. The discrepancy in size is not too obvious and might possibly be overlooked. However, it is found only once near the end of the cycle.

High A flats feature repeatedly, and later an A; otherwise the vocal range is undemanding, and the sparse layout gives ample time for rest. Entries are frequently spaced far apart, the piano echoing, amplifying, and developing the singer's often very simple material. There are several passages of notated speech (with their crossed note-heads suggesting shape rather than exact pitches). The piano part has relatively few chords or sustained harmonic moments. Pointillistic repeated notes, wide-spaced intervals, and scurrying groups of demisemiquavers feature throughout in varying combinations. Voice and piano are equal partners; this is not a soloistic vehicle, but, thanks to the extreme sensitivity and strong personality of the composer, the effect will be memorable. The voice will need to be in fresh condition, since any problems with singing softly could be cruelly exposed, but a singer with a well-placed head register should find it very comfortable and flattering.

1. Harmonie du soir

After the piano's quiet magical beginning (marked 'molto sostenuto e rubato'), long voiced 'v's are used tellingly in the singer's opening fragment. Ideally the reiterated 'i's on high A flat should be attacked cleanly on the glottis so that they are precise and predictable. The climb up to them is very smooth and easy, preparing the way. Single acciaccaturas in the piano add to the oriental impression. The voice's entries consist of fleeting words and syllables. The spirit of the poem is captured in a haunting, almost secretive way, wisps of sound acting as brush strokes. The piano has the major role, using the utmost economy of pitch and gesture. Some off-beat accents in a repeated-note figure in the second vocal entry are rather unexpected (Example 1). Apart from these delicate figures, the voice has some lovely glowing

Ex. 1 Wilkins

(va) ___   qu'en ___   cen ___   soir _

notes, beautifully placed for natural resonance. Every sound can be savoured and it is very important not to allow the dynamic level to rise. Good *pianissimo* singing is of course a very clear indication of technical accomplishment, and any labouring could be painfully obvious. Later the voice has spoken syllables (crosses for note-heads—marked 'hesitant, reflective') and the atmosphere is even more rarefied. There are subtle glissandos to inflect the pitch, and fingernail pizzicatos for the pianist give a tingling intensity. A soft floating B flat, fading from triple *piano* to almost nothing is marked 'non vibrato'—quite a tall order. The voice's hushed syllables (rather surprisingly marked 'with darker colour') become more sibilant: 'Le soleil s'est . . . son sang . . . se . . . se', leading to repeated dropping sevenths, gently rocking, each separated by a comma. At the end, the fade on '-soir' is very exposed and needs the finest line possible. The soprano should have no problems at all with pitching: there is ample time to pick up cues from the piano, and the constant repetition helps to focus the physical memory of each note in the voice.

2. Recueillement

The voice begins alone, whispering on 'Sois sage': a little subtle amplification might even be appropriate. After so much breathiness it can be difficult to find a clear tone immediately, but the 'm' of 'ma' is a help. After another pitched note of pearly clarity, there is more speech, meticulously plotted with accents and gentle staccato. The piano then has successions of stark, long-held intervals. After so much stillness comes a sharp contrast, with fast arpeggiated piano figures, marked 'senza espressivo, very articulated, meccanico'. The voice has some longer notes, based on the components of 'remords', and, eventually, the whole word. The level of intensity continues to rise, and *mezzo-forte* will certainly seem very loud in this context. The singer must follow the piano's uneven rhythmic patterns very closely while sustaining her notes. Vocal crescendos end in mid-air and break off abruptly. Just as suddenly, calm and quietness return and the voice is left unaccompanied for a stretch: first a few scattered sung pitches and soft spoken sounds, the latter, rather significantly, carrying both staccato and glissando markings, and then a considerable slowing of pace at the word 'loin', which has a long diminuendo on E natural—another test of vocal security. As so often, the French double vowel is helpful in keeping the sound forward, the 'w' sound bringing the lips into play. The whispering returns, with heavy use of sibilance. The voice has a radiant high A flat, and a succession of delicate repetitions of 'en', on D natural. These prepare for a hypnotically pure series of tenuto F naturals (*lontano e molto sostenuto*), and the voice again dissolves into softly intoned speech at the end, while the pianist has to negotiate some tricky harmonics inside the instrument.

3. La Mort des amants

Marked 'Agitato' and 'flottant, leggiero', this final movement is much more declamatory and overtly dramatic than the others. There are no long phrases: the vocal part consists of disjointed fragments, featuring many repeated notes as usual. Tremendous care must be taken to observe all the finer details of nuance and dynamic. The indication 'flottant' occurs often during the movement, and should act as a discouragement to heaviness. All is to be kept pliant and delicate. Vocal entries are again very sparse, and the piano is used percussively. A sung trill is answered by an even longer one on the piano. Over the piano's bright ringing *fortissimo* the singer has repeated 'é's on a staccato quintuplet preceding a sustained high G. The last section is full of contrast. *Lontano* repeated B flats on 'sang-lot' are particularly appropriate to the word (sob) (Example 2). It is here that the very soft echo effect occurs, and the composer repeats her earlier notation instructions in the score, to save the performers looking back. After a piano trill, the voice re-enters with a sudden burst of power on 'Viendra ranimer', the triumphant high A ringing out, before the line drops down by way of grace-notes. This is the work's longest and most complete vocal phrase, and makes a

Ex. 2 Wilkins

wonderful effect. The voice is then left entirely alone to finish the work on a highly concentrated long B where all the singer's powers of control will be put to the test. It is here that the gradual opening and closing of the mouth is featured: the 'm' of 'flammes' helps to maintain true intonation to the very last, exposed diminuendo, and the final gasped '(m)ortes' should empty the lungs' last reserve of air.

The piece depends a great deal upon the finesse and sensibility of the performers, and, in particular, on the steady nerves, solid technique, and powers of concentration of the singer. The atmosphere has to be absolutely right, and a darkened auditorium is essential, with perhaps some theatrical lighting. The acoustic must not be too dry. *Carte du tendre* will make a wonderful contrast to a more conventional recital work. Certainly, French music will go admirably with it, and Debussy's *Cinq Poèmes de Baudelaire* are virtually ideal. Other Baudelaire settings by Fauré and others can also be considered. The work by Colin Mattews featured in this volume could precede it, or, even more appropriately, the John Casken work *Ia Orana, Gauguin* in Volume 1, which has certain syllabic repetitions and pianistic figurations in common with it, albeit within a totally different musical context. One other more avant-garde work could be included; perhaps something involving tape, or just for solo voice. It should also be remembered that Caroline Wilkins is recognised as an Australian composer in that country, and her work is therefore suitable for a programme of Antipodean music.

Abendlied
(1989)

John Buckley (born 1951)
Text by Brentano and Eichendorff (in German)

T V; M V
Soprano and piano
Duration *c*.12'

John Buckley is one of the most gifted and assured of the middle generation of Irish composers, and is deservedly enjoying an increasing international reputation. His music is richly cosmopolitan, showing the influence of major Continental masters such as Messiaen.

This cycle makes a fine recital item, but none the less calls on considerable reserves of stamina from both singer and pianist. The vocal tessitura is consistently high, there are constant demands on breath capacity, and the ability to sustain long notes in the upper register is exhibited to the full. However, word-setting is thoughtfully worked out, so that syllables are not lost amid the frequent melismas.

The piano-writing requires a player of great proficiency. It is a particularly satisfying assignment for a fine artist who can display soloistic panache, as well as intuitive accompanying skills. Separate rehearsal at the preliminary stage is practicable, since there are many stretches of piano solo, which give the singer a welcome rest in between potentially exhausting passagework. The voice part will also benefit from a good deal of advance technical work, strengthening support muscles to cope with the high placing of most phrases. The effect is brilliantly resonant, and very beautiful.

Two well-known poems, Brentano's 'Hör', es klagt die Flöte', and Eichendorff's 'Mondnacht' (so memorably set by Schumann in his *Liederkreis*, Op. 39) are juxtaposed, and complement each other perfectly in their subtly contrasting musical treatment. The first half of the piece (the Brentano setting) is full of dramatic tension, and the second poem is, in general, set more simply and gently. Long melismas on the final words of phrases are a common feature of both settings, those in the first poem rather more elaborate.

As often happens, the very slow tempo (crotchet = 42) stipulated in the score has been adapted to the realities of performance. It can certainly move on a little without disturbing the luxuriant effect of the glistening long lines. Enharmonic relationships within coloratura will need constant checking to avoid mistakes. It would be all too easy to give an approximate account, glossing over details. Pitching is helped greatly by cues on the piano just before each vocal entry. The singer's dynamics are often light, and a high soprano's gift for poised floating will be fully exploited. A good technique is therefore needed, but singers should not be deterred by initial problems while learning the score. The gradual development of increased muscular strength will soon pay off, and mastery of the expansive phrases will prove physically satisfying. In the second portion of the work, the singer should be at full stretch, easing herself through the long-breathed spans of 'Mond-nacht', where entries are closer together, and each phrase in turn uses full capacity. As with Messiaen's *Harawi*, the voice is warmed and loosened as the piece progresses.

The notation is admirably clear, apart from a few anomalies with acci-dentals within bars. Many widely accepted modern conventions are em-ployed, such as the graphic representation of *accelerandi* and *rallentandi* within melismas. As many will know, this involves 'hairpins' to show the gradual increase and decrease of note-values and their corresponding amounts of ligatures.

A prolonged piano solo begins the work, setting the nocturnal scene most evocatively. Arpeggios, grace-notes, and repeated notes create a shimmering texture. The voice enters on a rapt high F sharp on 'Hör'—the 'h' very helpful for clearing any unwanted 'frogs'. Gentle, meandering melismas begin almost immediately, and the technique of letting go of the throat, allowing the tone to float suspended, is instantly called into play. The practicability of the work is determined by this factor. Failure to achieve a high-enough placing could cause discomfort, and every phrase has to be held securely, never allowing support to slacken. Filigree details, including syncopations, can be traced in within a legato flow that must seem free and spontaneous, never rigidly metronomic. The composer always allows the singer time for a good breath at the start of the long phrases, and there are very few ensemble problems. The pianist must pay close attention to the singer's needs, and never rush her at these poised moments.

The first elaborately elongated melisma occurs on 'rauschen'. The written-out *accelerando–rallentando* has to be negotiated with dash and bravura, avoiding any feeling of metric rhythm. It may take a while to acquire this freedom, especially since accidentals need watching assiduously (Example 1). If necessary, a quick breath can be taken before the verb. The high-lying 'Golden' should be unproblematic, and the paragraph ends safely and comfortably, as the piano takes over for a substantial solo. The soprano has to catch the end of the piano's semiquaver groups at the *poco più mosso*, but the tempo steadies again as she enters on 'Stille'. Here the voice part is simple, and the piano supplies the decoration. A loud, reiterated bird-call is now introduced on the piano. It quickens excitingly, heralding the voice's re-entry in exalted mood. It is certainly unusual to find the word 'schweigt' (is silent) sung *fortissimo*. However, the ringing, declamatory style provides a chance to shed inhibitions. There is another rapid melisma on 'laute' which has fast repetitions of a three-note figure. The singer must

Ex. 1 Buckley

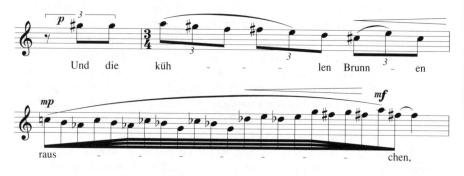

Und   die   küh   –   –   –   len   Brunn   –   en

raus   –   –   –   –   –   –   –   chen,

be alert here: the piano's 3/16 solo bar goes by in a flash, and the soft vocal re-entry comes sooner than expected. Happily, the rolled 'r' on 'rauscht' allows a little time, as does the piano's broken chord. It may be advisable to breathe after 'Erde', depending on the tempo, although the composer marks an official breath-point in the centre of the prolonged melisma on the 'äu' vowel sound. Grace-notes adorn an already intricate line, and these should be speedy, helping to emphasize the main notes of the melody. As the voice lingers on a high note, the piano begins another solo, again featuring the bird motif, this time starting *pianissimo* and building to full throttle.

After much vocal display, the following section has somewhat plainer lines, including a rewarding, wide-ranging sweep on 'alte Zeiten'. 'Trauer' is, however, given a very long melisma, with a rest for a breath just before the cadence. (The syllabic distribution is a little misleading: '-er' should not occur until the final, held D flat.) A piano cadenza announces the voice's most dramatic outburst (Example 2). This phrase needs considerable vocal virtuosity—the accelerating semiquavers must convey powerful momentum, culminating in the exciting swirl of notes on 'Wetterleuchtend' (sheet-lightning): appropriately brilliant and incisive. However, the singer must brake with alacrity, changing mood and colour ready for the calm, dipping cadence on to low E on 'Brust'. This will feel very low indeed in context, and

Ex. 2 Buckley

Und es   schwei – fen   lei   –   –   se   Schauer _____

Wett - er - leuch   –   tend ____   durch die   Brust _____

must be kept firm and steady. (*Mezzo-piano* should not be interpreted too softly at this level.) This marks the end of the first setting, and the transition to the Eichendorff poem is effected by another piano solo, which ends with the bird-call re-echoing, gradually resolving on to a repeated note.

The singer has ample time to gather her resources for a poised *pianissimo* entry. Long notes at the ends of phrases must not waver, and the hushed atmosphere is beautifully caught. Throughout 'Mondnacht' there is a subtle ebb and flow between the performers. At the end of each phrase, the piano's passagework pulls the tempo back (*poco rall.*), and it is up to the singer to re-establish strict tempo for the next line of the text, after a lingering up-beat. *Pianissimo* is to be maintained throughout, apart from what is pos-sibly the work's most hazardous phrase: the athletically ranging 'Nacht' ending on a sustained high B flat (Example 3). This is not nearly as difficult

Ex. 3 Buckley

So stern-klar war die Nacht

as it would seem—the composer tactfully provides a warmer dynamic (*piano*, rising to *mezzo-piano*) and the wide intervals help to free the voice. A short breath could even be snatched after 'sternklar', to make things even safer. As long as notes are joined in a perfectly even legato, even verging on glissando for the final climb of a major seventh, all will be surprisingly effortless. As 'the soul spreads its wings', the voice's final phrases feature still more of these long-drawn-out spans of elaborate, often syncopated figures, in increasingly relaxed vein. If a breath is taken before 'spannte', it will be easier to incorporate all the details and emphasize the word-painting. Before the voice can relax completely, however, the penultimate phrase has to be accomplished. An ornate melisma on 'Lande' rises to F sharp and then descends a semitone. This is a little awkward to focus, but a *poco accel.* and a rising dynamic level (to *mezzo-piano*) help considerably. Only then can the singer intone the last comfortable, medium-range cadence, with clear simplicity. A lengthy and atmospheric piano solo ends this impressive work, and the birdsong is heard again to delightful effect.

A high-lying youthful soprano voice is ideal for this piece, but a good degree of technical security is essential. It would make a splendid exercise in head-voice singing, and, like Messiaen, Buckley employs the singer's full lung capacity. Audiences will be held spellbound, both by the physical and mental concentration involved, and the bell-like resonances and character-istic glittering textures of the idiomatic piano-writing. It would be a lovely idea to place it alongside other settings of the same texts, especially the Schumann. The fact that it is quite far removed in style from the German Lieder repertoire, would make for an admirable contrast. Classics of the Second Viennese School (Schoenberg, Berg, Webern—even Schreker or Zemlinsky) could make up an attractive twentieth-century recital. Dallapiccola's *Quattro Liriche di Antonio Machado* would suit a similar high, flexible voice. After an interval, some French music, such as Satie or Poulenc, could contribute a lighter mood. It is a most welcome addition to the concert repertoire, and the hard work it necessitates is duly rewarded by its ready appeal and durability.

She is Asleep
(1943)

John Cage (1912–92)
Text: phonetics only

T V; M III
Voice (any) and prepared piano
(alternative version for 4 Tom-Tom players)
Duration *c*.6′

A hauntingly memorable and original work from this great and influential figure, who has been a source of inspiration for so many composers and performers in all branches of the arts. It has a hypnotic quality that focuses the audience's attention from the outset. There is no doubt that the singer/vocalist needs to be experienced and confident, with excellent powers of concentration and strong nerves. This is exactly the kind of music that can reveal hidden weaknesses in the middle of those voices that sound most impressive when singing strongly at the extremes of their range.

The piano is prepared by placing thin pieces of rubber around the first and third strings of the keys indicated in the score, near the bridge—a typically simple effect that works beautifully, creating a fascinating muted resonance. The keyboard part is in fact limited to a very few pitches, all of them at the bottom of the instrument (notated 16va): notably a perfect fifth from G to D, and then the perfect fourth from the C a seventh above to the F above it. The patterns made from these pitches are as varied as can be, first appearing as a complete chord, and then split into repeated figures in fluctuating rhythms. The voice part, too, is built from a small number of notes. The major triad on middle C plus the supertonic D and the submediant A predominate throughout, with very occasional excursions down to low G, A, and B for much more sustained singing. These lower pitches help to rest the voice. The work is described as a 'Duet' and both participants are very much equal partners.

As often with such works, the simplicity of approach that is needed to execute it requires the highest degree of skill and control, and the composer's instruction to use no vocal vibrato is easier read than obeyed. The exhaustion that can come from holding support muscles tautly for long stretches, can result in exactly the kind of wobbliness that is least welcome, and the medium range of the piece is not necessarily the easiest to manipulate and maintain a pure thread of sound. The composer asks for vibrato on specific long notes, marked with a tremolando sign, similar to that used for the 'dental tremolo' pioneered by Berio for seminal vocal works of a later period. (This turned out to be more of a jaw wobble, the fast oscillation producing the desired effect.) Here it is rather more difficult to predict what Cage actually likes best: he was always disarmingly non-committal when questioned closely by performers, often repeating 'do whatever you feel comfortable with'. However, his acute ear and refined sensibilities were daunting models, and each piece, however slight in scale, has a rarefied quality that cannot be taken lightly.

Choice of vowel-sound has been left to the singer, but a small list of suggestions are given. I have found it practicable in general to sing short accented attacks on 'wah' (by far the most rewarding and reliable of the list for short vowels), using a mixture of Oh and Ah, sometimes eliding them, for the majority of pitches, and reserving the 'U' (oo) for the vibrato–tremolo notes. A muted pigeon-like 'coo', rapidly repeating the note, as used in Cage's 'A Flower', seems to work better than the jaw tremolo. It is difficult to believe that Cage really means, by his instruction to exaggerate vibrato at these points, that one should adopt an unfocused over-rich basic sound: operatic vibrato would not have been to his taste, and the gentle bird-like noises would seem more in keeping with his spirit and meditative inclinations. Placing the lips forward in a rounded shape helps to control the ululation. There is even a possibility that a gentle rolled 'r' with the tongue fluttering just inside the lips, would make an even more pleasing effect, also giving the singer a chance to relax the tongue muscles.

The piece begins with the voice exposed alone in a long *pianissimo* solo, starting on middle C. A glissando from D to a very short C at the end of the first phrase, must be as slow and gradual as possible. For the accented G, 'wah' is a good choice to make it really clear, and impel the voice forward for the very long E that follows, which has to change to a vibrato halfway through before dropping on to a staccato C. (This should be very short.) Obviously, breath control is of prime importance. The next two lines for the unaccompanied voice feature repeated short accented staccato attacks punctuated by rests which must be counted out carefully. A low D has to be held steadily until the piano entry, which will come as a relief, and a welcome support during a series of more prolonged notes which follow. The work's most demanding breath-span involves D with a glissando up to held E and then eventually down again. It is comforting to remind oneself that the pulse is crotchet = 104, and there should be no undue lingering. It is useful to acquire an ability to imagine a clear but invisible (and inaudible) beat moving the music along steadily. When suspended on long pitches it is possible to lose track of progress.

As the voice part becomes suddenly more active, the burden of vocal control is lessened, to be replaced by the problems of adhering to strict rhythms, taking breath in time, and maintaining perfect ensemble with the keyboard player. The piano part becomes a great deal more elaborate, with uneven rythmic groupings, syncopation, and even groups of grace-notes. The 4/4 must still be discernible, and the singer has to negotiate a succession of tremolandos, separated by very short single notes. Another very long phrase starts on a prolonged low A, sliding up to B and ending in an extended tremolo, slipping back down to A at the very end. Through all of this, the piano part must be followed closely so that the end can be well co-ordinated (Example 1). The voice is allowed a short rest afterwards, before

Ex. 1 Cage

a rhythmic dialogue proceeds, each part with fanfare-like figures, the voice's with vibrato. Again the singer must focus on a series of long Es, some with glissandos, and one in particular with a crescendo–diminuendo. Dynamics are crucial. In this basically quiet and delicate music, the difference between *piano* and *pianissimo* seems highly significant, and the occasional *mezzo-*

forte has great impact. The singer begins a long section in which E and D alternate in patterns of, first, repeated triplet figures, and then groups of semiquavers with syncopated accents. A clear thin tone like a muted trumpet will help articulate the detail, amidst which dynamics and shadings play an important part. In this passage, the voice is left almost unaccompanied, the piano touching in occasional single notes or bare fifths. The next section is an extended keyboard solo, in which the voice takes the accompanying role, providing a few gentle low notes. These gradually fragment and contract, and a more dramatic interplay features very long held notes in the voice, and occasional accented figures, with more frenetic drumming patterns answering on the piano. A momentary *accelerando* dissolves into steady quavers and at the return to strict tempo the voice must prepare for an ending just as exposed as at the beginning of the work. First, though, the keyboard has a cadenza-like passage of complex rhythms, during one of the voice's longest held notes. As the accompaniment thins out, the voice alternates between plain held notes and their tremolando versions, with the brief staccato figures in between as before. Lone piano chords provide the cut-off for each long note, preserving the pulse to the very end without slowing. As previously, it is essential to count the rests accurately.

To be able to sing this piece successfully is a sure test of technical expertise and stamina, as well as of musicianship. Intonation must always be secure, so that constantly repeated pitches are consistent. A large voice is certainly not required, and could even prove a handicap. The composer's own stated preference for the works of Erik Satie should be borne in mind when choosing companion works for a programme. His other works, such as the very similar 'A Flower' or the justly admired 'Wonderful Widow of Eighteen Springs' also come to mind, but they should not be performed consecutively, but interspersed with contrasting material. The words of James Joyce were also important to the composer, and some more Joyce settings to go with the 'Widow' would be most appropriate. A dramatic solo work, full of colourful images, such as Alison Bauld's 'The Witches' Song' or the Rainier featured in this book, and, in particular, the Aston 'Crazy Jane' settings would be excellent. It is possible to imagine this piece in a rather different context than that of a conventional recital—as an interlude in a poetry evening for instance. It is a most attractive piece for an audience, even if the performers themselves cannot afford the luxury of relaxing and enjoying its special atmosphere.

Nachtlied
(1984)

Jonathan Harvey (born 1939)
Text by Goethe and Rudolf Steiner (in German)

T V; M VI
Soprano, piano, and tape
Duration *c*.23'

This intense and committed cycle by one of our most sensitive and versatile composers is an important addition to the electro-acoustic music repertoire, and adds an interesting dimension to a straight recital. It uses both the words and the music of Schubert's setting of Goethe's 'Wanderers Nachtlied' ('Über allen Gipfeln ist Ruh''), as its base material, retaining the original key of B flat. Excerpts from this (both vocal and keyboard parts) plus sung and spoken fragments from the Steiner texts were recorded in advance by the original commissioner and performer (myself). These have been elaborately transformed, treated, and realized at the electronic studios of City and Sussex Universities. The finished tape, for use in concert performance, is available on hire from the publishers. Recent advances in technology mean that a DAT copy may now be the best option, more practical and portable. Otherwise, the original version is on reel-to-reel tape: a good quality recorder is needed. There must also be two matching speakers, amplifier, and a technician available for setting and adjusting balance. During the work's course the tape has to be switched on and off at intervals, so an assistant armed with an extra copy of the score (and someone able to follow the manuscript!) is also essential. This may seem to involve rather a lot of trouble but the work is well worth the effort. The atmosphere of the piece is darkly dramatic and powerful, and the singer is given a chance to display virtuosity as well as a pure, simple line at the outset. A highly resourceful pianist with quick reactions is needed. With a tape, there is no give and take: cues have to be identified instantly, and if co-ordination is not achieved the tape goes on relentlessly, leaving performers embarrassed! I have always found it exhilarating and challenging to work in this way, and 'live' and electronic sounds can make an intriguing blend in the right context. Since acoustics tend to change in between a rehearsal in an empty auditorium and a well-attended concert, a last-minute sound check is always advisable. Despite all these necessary extra preparations and accessories, an audience usually responds warmly to the stimulating experience of being drawn into a magic world of electronic sounds, which can greatly enhance the expressive effect of a performance.

It has to be said that the appearance of the score, reproduced from the composer's manuscript, is a little daunting at first glance. There is not always enough space between staves, and both performers, and any score-following assistant, will need to resort to heavy markings, ideally with coloured highlighters for the text, delineating each part in order to avoid confusion, especially between piano and tape cues. The amount of staves per page varies considerably throughout the work, and speed of progress through the music can therefore be deceptive in relation to its visual impression. There is no doubt that a substantial rehearsal schedule will be needed. There is no room for hesitation or spontaneous rubato in the passages where the tape is running. Of course it is reassuring to know that the tape will always be the same, but there are many places where exact coincidence is necessary, and mistakes will be noticeable.

As is often the case, taped sounds take some getting used to. It is wise to listen to the tape part on its own several times to identify any crucial, quieter cues that have to be picked out from the texture. It also helps to add some extra private timings in tacet passages: a stop-watch is useful for this.

Once practicalities have been sorted out, however, the piece is enjoyable to perform. One aspect that will need special attention nearer the time of the concert is that of the cues for stopping and starting the tape. Leader tapes mark the beginning and end of each cue, but some of these follow on quite closely. There are two places where, if the tape is allowed to run on, its next event will drown and disrupt an important solo passage. These unfortunately occur at moments where the performers themselves are too busily occupied to be able to signal to the tape operator. He or she therefore needs to be briefed very thoroughly. Ideally, a printed sheet of instructions should be provided. As long as there is adequate rehearsal time in the venue, all should be clarified by an extra run-through. Since, quite frequently, the composer, or a similar expert in this specialized field, is present, one can occasionally be lulled into a false sense of security. It is as well to take a realistic view of the situation from the standpoint of a non-specialist, and prepare accordingly.

A discreet use of a pitch-pipe or tuning-fork (preferably backstage at the last moment before entering) will be necessary at the very beginning of the piece: a slow hypnotic vocal solo. This is a highly decorated variation of Schubert's melody, featuring the complete Goethe text. The opening is marked 'pale, eerie, "lonely" with a deathly calm'. Tone has to be very clear and pure, with grace-note groups delicately turned, and close observation of the given dynamics and nuances. The text is set comfortably, and breathing is exceptionally well gauged. A tiny echo phrase at the end of one particularly effective line drops naturally into a thread-like tone when breath is virtually spent, and yet can be clearly heard even at the softest dynamic (Example 1). Uneven groupings, including quintuplets, and successions of dotted quavers, contribute to a feeling of rhythmic freedom. The soprano voice is well suited

Ex. 1 Harvey

Die   Vög - lein   schwei   -   -   ge - n,

schwei - - gen   im   Wal - - de.

to this sort of filigree writing, and the audience's attention is immediately held by the rapt, exposed lines, spun with grace and springy lightness. Towards the end of the verse, there is a slight quickening of tempo at 'Warte nur', heightening the suspense, before a long-drawn-out *rallentando* at the close. After a short pause, the voice begins again, with the same material, this time followed in a musing, almost semi-conscious, fashion by the piano, which echoes and decorates key pitches. It is obviously important for the singer to keep her tuning scrupulous, so that there is no embarrassing discrepancy at the piano's entry. At the end of the second phrase, which is decorated a little more, both performers enter a free section. After restarting in B flat, each goes their separate way. The piano has a fascinating series of extended flourishes, involving rapidly repeated note-patterns, chords, and grace-notes. This continues over a lengthy stretch, and is written out in the normal way. The soprano, however, has one of those games with which modern music specialists will be familiar. She is given seven fragments, all variants of the Schubert–Goethe. Some of these involve special effects, such as wide trills, including one with a glissando at the same time—not at all difficult. There are also some notes designated for breathy sound, the most awkward of which is certainly the one marked 'in-drawn' on 'schweigen'. To be asked to gasp in more breath than one needs can be uncomfortable, and it should only be attempted with care, and not allowed to disturb vocal poise. Happily, pauses are provided in between each fragment. The fragments are to be sung in sequence as written, and then repeated in random order, gradually extending the intervening pauses, until the piano has reached the end of the section. The danger of losing one's place is very real, and I would advocate some kind of agreed signal between the performers, to warn the singer of the impending cut-off. One of the fragments does, in fact, invite the voice to improvise on the piano's material at that point, which gives her a chance to catch up on proceedings. Repeated rehearsals will, of course help the singer to gain familiarity and arrive at a consistent time-span, and to grow accustomed to certain distinctive moments heard in the generally impressionistic texture.

It is at this point that the tape enters. The sounds are very slow indeed and so low-pitched as to be somewhat hard to hear, especially while singing. This passage is perhaps the most difficult of all for the singer, mainly because of the need to control the breath and listen acutely at the same time. Phrases are extremely long, and the sonorously chiming bass-line of the tape (still quoting from Schubert—as is the vocal part) may be covered. Some higher vocal sounds on the tape give vital cues, and timing is crucial. The bass chimes are often not easy to recognize, and the live piano interpolates more elaborate textures in similar vein to the previous section. It is extremely important to have the volume level high enough, to aid perfect ensemble. A cadence is reached with a long-held middle F on 'Du'. The tape runs continuously through a short gap. Then comes the most rigorously rhythmic section where the pianist has the considerable responsibility of co-ordinating exactly with a lengthy sequence of measured running quavers (with some off-putting changes of colour and tessitura on the tape). It is important not to hurry, but to adhere rigidly to a steady pulse. The soprano joins in, first, declaiming snatches of the Steiner text (in tandem with a taped voice) and then in a long cantilena, rapt and flowing, and eventually extremely florid with some exciting coloratura, when lines are repeated. This passagework should be polished in privacy, so that it runs easily. In the context of a run-through with the tape going, there will be little time for lingering or for accommodating any hesitancy while concentrating on minute vocal details. The singer also has to keep a constant pulse, and not be distracted by some swirling interruptions from the piano. Again the spacing of the notation (conventional, including accidentals, but no barlines in this section) is not entirely helpful. Melismas are given extra room, and it is wise to mark the whole passage out in quavers. Some rhythms are quite tricky, especially those with notes tied across beats—a feature that is to recur frequently throughout the work. Particular care is needed when changing to a new line: it is here that a beat is all too easily dropped. A particularly dazzling piece of *fioritura* embellishes the repeat of 'Aus dem Reich der Daseins hüllen' (Example 2). The soprano part is thrilling and full of wide soaring leaps. As voice and piano go into an *accelerando*, and the voice suddenly dies away, the tape cue ends, and must be switched off immediately, wound through the short leader tape, and switched on again. Within the few seconds' gap, the piano just has time for a succession of octaves, continuing the *accelerando*, and ending in rapid grace-note figures.

The tape sound re-enters (Cue 2) with a harpsichord-like effect, featuring grace-note groups, and, as the piano's long trills subside, there follows a long tape solo: a welcome rest for the live performers after the work's most demanding section (especially as far as concentration is concerned). Towards the end of the tape interlude, fragmented, echoing voices are heard on the tape, for 11″ before the soprano enters the central portion of the work, in which she shoulders the responsibility of keeping with the tape in a series of 'choral' passages. The piano keeps a low profile here, and it is up to the

Ex. 2 Harvey

Aus __ dem Reich der Da-seins-hül — len   Aus dem __ Reich __

_____ der __ Da _____ seins __ hül _____

len _____

singer to count carefully, and, at the same time, listen to the taped vocal trio, to which she adds a fourth (top) layer. These four *a cappella* sections are in two sets of two, separated in the middle by another substantial tape solo. The tempos of each are varied, and the flow of the music can be deceptive at the first attempt. It is unwise to wait for the other voices in order to co-ordinate, as this can cause lateness. The best course is to establish the pulse and press on in a positive manner. Only during rests can one have the luxury of checking up on the answering voices. Dynamics on the tape vary a great deal, and some voices sound more prominent than others. It pays to famil-iarize oneself with every small detail of the tape cue that precedes these voice sections. The first necessitates a particularly speedy reaction after counting the eleven seconds. It is a good idea to count a little fast and then get ready to poise the high B flat on 'In', after just one note (a D sharp) has sounded. The soprano's opening bars involve extreme changes of tessitura, which are not as difficult as they might appear. Stretching the voice while listening seems to encourage a lighter touch, avoiding strain: thus the very low notes (G sharp—but an upper *ossia* is provided) are not forced. Pitch relationships at the end of this passage will need care, as the tape voices are only a semitone away. The short tape interlude here is relatively easy to follow. Its last 'event', pulsating chords with B flat at the top, lasts about 5″, and the voice on the tape follows close on at the same pitch. This is very faint, and again the singer's reaction has to be razor-sharp, yet it should be noted that this tempo is a little steadier and will feel markedly so in context. For this section, the pungent rhythms must be well defined and there is a catchy lilt to the music. The long tape solo gives some respite for the singer, but the pianist has to negotiate some tricky moments of co-ordination with a series of running figures, and a fleeting reference to the earlier 'Schubert' material. At the end, fragmented layers of voices on the tape give way to a deeper, burbling texture. This lasts about 6″, and again, the singer must become swiftly orientated to the strict, brisker tempo of the next 'choral' section. The first bar may be a bit shaky at first, but as confidence grows, and rhythmic discipline improves through practice, it all falls into place relatively easily. A silence in the middle can be unnerving, but is also a good place to ensure a perfectly accurate restart. As before, it is important to tune intervals accurately with the taped 'trio'. The next brief tape segment features fragmented voices overlapping with 'perforated chords' (described thus in the score and easily identifiable). The utmost concentration is needed here, since the layered voices, singing 'li' at the end of the tape interlude do tend to melt imperceptibly into the vocal solos of the 'trio', and the opening cue is incredibly quiet, and only detectable by a sudden change of acoustic. It is much fainter than the surrounding vocal texture which continues through this section. The tape will have to be listened to several times to be sure of identifying this entry. After that, the section proceeds as before, and is 'plain sailing' vocally. The wide-ranging vocal fragments are very rewarding to sing, and can be floated with no fear of inaudibility.

Now comes the second instance where the tape comes to an end, and must be switched off and on again very rapidly. Again the short interval is covered by a piano solo. The tape part from now on is more freely notated and the performers are no longer bound to it. However, soprano and piano must still maintain good ensemble through some syncopated passages. A climactic high C for the soprano heralds release from the metrically controlled music. Long chords on the tape form a basic framework within which the piano weaves an intricate and prolonged solo. This features the trills, repeated notes, and running passagework heard earlier. Some 'Musique concrète' effects on the tape ('wind' noise and more metallic 'perforations') occur just before the tape falls silent momentarily (but is kept running), and eventually ends after another burst of 'choral chords'. The voice re-enters, very low at first, in two declamatory bars of strict 4/4. At the end of this the next cue has to be given very clearly to the tape operator (preferably by the soprano herself who can then remain in vocal control). There follows a substantial section of free music, in which voice and piano negotiate many grace-notes punctuated by cadences, while keeping a close eye on one another. The soprano takes the lead in this section, apart from one brief moment where a held non-vibrato note, echoed on the tape, has to be coordinated exactly. The free-ranging lines continue, many of them elaborating traditional Romantic decorations, especially a characteristic Schubertian turn. A tremendously energetic and exciting *accelerando* leads to the last spectacular vocal coloratura passage, as the tape again disappears. It is imperative for it to be switched off here—there is a very real danger of the last tape event running on and spoiling the ending. The pianist supports with measured octaves, recalling fleetingly the earlier, 'chiming' passage

(Example 3) until the soprano takes off on her own, gauging a careful diminuendo.

The final paragraph is very poignant. The phrase 'Tritt mein Ich' is repeated in unhurried style, well spaced, the piano in close attendance. Suddenly the soprano becomes almost skittish in some unvoiced phonetics on 'T' and 'rr' (ability to roll an 'r' is indispensable here). The tape's final

Ex. 3 Harvey

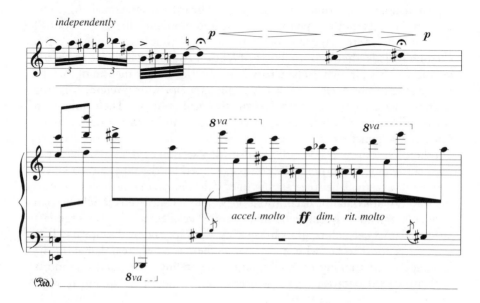

entry adds still more rolled trills and gurgles. The singer must be quick to catch the end of these—as they stop dead she has to put in an 'i-T'. After a brief wait she speaks the text, ending in a slide upwards on the 'ss' of 'bewusst'. Micro-timing is needed here, as the tape voice supplies the 't' to end the word, and then live and taped voice must coincide for the work's final 'mein Ich', the soprano prolonging the 'ch' into silence.

This substantial and satisfying work is most unusually structured. It seems to become more ethereal as it progresses. The music represents a spiritual journey, and acquires cumulative radiance as it reaches its climax. There is an impression of casting off earthly burdens and attaining a carefree lightness at the end. The variety of vocal material provides a challenge to the singer, but it all lies extraordinarily well, despite extremes of range. To precede it with the original Schubert song on which it is based makes a lovely effect in a recital. In fact, it could be a good idea for a whole group of Schubert's Goethe settings, ending with the 'Wanderers Nachtlied', to lead directly into the Harvey. This would of course necessitate setting up the tape and other equipment early so there can be a smooth transition.

Harvey's strong commitment to religious and philosophical issues link him with other contrasting figures, most notably Messiaen. The *Chants de terre et de ciel* would go very well in the opposite half of the programme. Since tape equipment is available it would be a good idea to have a work for tape alone, or perhaps the pianist could give a solo with or without tape. John Tavener's *Three Surrealist Songs*, also with tape, would contrast by their brevity, and other epigrammatic songs would also provide a balance. With a work that demands a good deal of special concentration, it is best not to load the programme with obvious blockbusters, and carefully selected German Lieder (especially Schubert, Beethoven, and Wolf) are probably the best options.

A singer with an unflappable temperament and good musicianship will be in her element, and it is essential that the pianist chosen is someone able to be an equal partner and contribute a strong, soloistic personality.

Four Late Poems and an Epigram
of Rainer Maria Rilke
(1988)

Oliver Knussen (born 1952)
Text by Rainer Maria Rilke
Translation in English by Stephen Mitchell

T V; M VI
Unaccompanied soprano
Duration *c*.9′

A new vocal work of compelling quality is always welcome, and this piece was certainly worth the wait over a relatively long period of gestation. The composer's personal style and command of his medium are instantly recognizable. An idiom with strong elements of post-Viennese serialism provides the voice with graceful leaping lines, exhilarating and full of colour. A short refrain (the epigram: 'Rose, oh pure contradiction') stated at the beginning, is repeated exactly between Nos. 1 and 2, and appears in inverted form between 2 and 3. The dynamic range throughout is extraordinarily varied, and the many markings, including those indicating stresses and subtle shadings, demonstrate the composer's aural refinement and awareness of syllabic detail, creating a memorable effect. Though fragmentary in appearance, the music flows in long paragraphs, and the singer will need to be well exercised and 'sung in' to maintain a smooth tone-quality. There are a number of places where intensity of declamation could result in hardening of tone and loss of natural resonance. Some words are set rather high and there are sections which could be a little uncomfortable at first, especially at moments of high tension in Nos. 3 and 4. The final song 'Gong' is wonderfully effective on its own, with its repeated onomatapoeic use of the title-word, and its dizzying shifts of mood, rising to a shattering climax before the gong chimes fade into silence.

Pitching is always something of a test when singing unaccompanied, and chromatic relationships will need care, but the music is so precisely and logically structured, that, as with all the most naturally gifted composers, it falls into place much more easily that might at first be imagined. Pitch centres stay in the memory from an early stage of preparation. Audiences will respond warmly to this piece, held by its unfolding drama. Timing is all-important without the discipline of an accompanying partner to regulate the pulse. A resonant acoustic enhances the piece greatly, allowing the singer space to relish the resonance between phrases, thereby learning to judge exactly when to move on and when to hold back. It is a thoroughly poignant

and absorbing work, full of passionate energy. It requires a singer possessing control and imagination in equal measure, and will show a fine technique to advantage.

Epigram

The work begins quietly with the statement of the motto which punctuates
major sections. A slightly ambiguous marking, 'on the breath' for the
opening note, actually means (on the authority of the composer) 'slightly
breathy'. Certainly a rapt, intense feeling of suppressed awe and excitement
is needed, and the quick decrescendo–crescendo on the note helps. A rolled
'r' will aid the entry. It is worth spending some time over this small detail,
especially as it is to recur. The timing of the '-se' (pronounced 'z') of 'rose'
is also important. Pulse and dynamics fluctuate constantly throughout this
brief paragraph, and there are many accents and changes of emphasis to
negotiate (Example 1). The E flat of '-ny' is potentially the most difficult

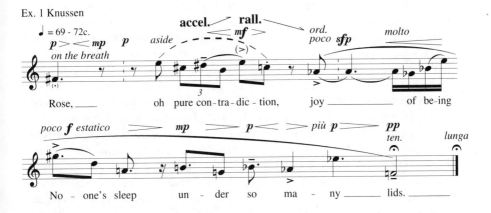

Ex. 1 Knussen

note: it should be kept open and floated freely, taking care to join it to the
following, much lower pitch, for which a long-drawn-out 'l' on 'lids' will
help considerably. It is also worth remembering that there is a final chance
to end the last *pianissimo* note smoothly by singing through the 's' (voiced
'z') keeping pitch focused to the very end. A suitably long pause capitalizes
on the effect of this delicate opening statement. A calm unflurried deport-
ment is exceptionally important when singing solo, to make the most of the
direct contact with the audience.

1. Idol

The composer tactfully provides a slightly higher alternative for the opening
B, since lighter voices may find the lower pitch awkward. However, that
particular low note is to be exercised fully in the course of the piece, so it is
as well to become accustomed to placing it firmly, not allowing the percussive 'g' to throw the note off-balance. It is healthy to be able to relax the

voice downwards into a normal speaking range. The springboard device of using lower notes to loosen the voice ready for a leap upwards is well exploited. Some of the passagework in this movement will need to be practised slowly, because of the many varied dynamics and articulations required. Glissandos cover some of the wider leaps and these are always flattering vocally. The snapped-off accent on 'cats' is set with perfect precision. In most cases, the composer's detailed indications merely confirm the appropriate nuances that come out naturally when the text is declaimed *espressivo*. The words 'sweet-grown nectar of vision' and, later, 'palate's crypt' will need to be enunciated with care (the former also lies in a vulnerable part of the voice), and the 'vi' of 'vision' may have to be modified to give space for an open resonance. Awareness of the varied tone-colours inherent in the text's images is essential, and the composer's expressive suggestions, in Italian, are very helpful. His marked phrasing must be carefully observed, and pauses well judged to maintain tension and momentum. This movement contains the first 'gong-beats' on the low B, that are to be a distinctive feature of the cycle. The 'ng' should be prolonged with as much resonance as possible. The final paragraph provides the work's most exposed moments, and requires considerable support to sustain breath. As singers will know, really soft singing requires the strongest muscular control. The *pianissimo ma chiaro* on the word 'What' on low G sharp (a D is provided as an *ossia*) is crucial. Even experienced singers can fail to find a firm tone when starting so low in the voice, but it is often a question of habit. If the approach can be exactly as if about to speak, it all becomes much simpler. An optional breath is marked very early in the phrase. As the composer is obviously aware, there would be a natural hiatus after 'casts' because of the percussive consonants. Some rocking triplets within a very soft melisma must be kept very smooth, and breathing places well organized. Again the composer is the best guide, and his staccato and accented markings should be scrupulously adhered to. For the melismas on 'spell' and 'cunning' the liquid consonants are elongated and used as vowels, and the sudden lessening of volume is achieved quite easily. For the word 'escape', since the 'p' cannot be elongated, a similar effect is made by using a *bocca chiusa* which has to be joined smoothly to the 'p'. A good accent on 'sca' helps to impel the singer into a well-focused sound before the sudden diminuendo. Another optional breath comes before the last phrase, but it is better not to interrupt the flow of a somewhat awkwardly placed section. The jaw needs to be kept relaxed and 'e' vowels must not be allowed to tighten. Decorative melismas should seem almost casual (but always accurate) and the music flows with spontaneous momentum right up to the final paused 'pow'r'. This requires courage, since it has to left floating freely on a single vowel. It would be unwise to attempt the actual triphthong at this height. The 'ng' at the end of the preceding word can be prolonged, easing the throat for a moment and keeping the tone going while planning the leap up a diminished fifth. This passage will need practice before it runs easily.

Replica

There now follows after a brief pause, an exact repeat of the opening epigram. As before, there is plenty of time to hold the final note and pause before going on. As with Schoenberg, (cf. 'Pierrot Lunaire') pauses are carefully graded and meticulously worked into the scheme of the work's span.

2. Gravity

Tempo relationships from movement to movement are another crucial factor in shaping this work. This movement should move along briskly. It starts non-vibrato in mid-voice, which should produce a distinctive unearthly sound. As before, flexible rhythmic patterns range over the stave, with glissandos and staccato markings occurring at appropriate moments. The swift, high-lying 'winning yourself back' will need speed of muscular co-ordination to avoid restricting the tone. It is important not to hold on to the 'w' or 's' but to relax facial muscles instantly. The same two pitches (B natural and G) are used for the repeat of the non-vibrato 'center'. This appears suddenly out of a passage of normal singing. A long pause then allows for the contrast to make its full effect. A spectacular wide-ranging phrase, with some helpful grace-notes, is particularly rewarding to perform, although pitching will need care. It must not be rushed (Example 2). The

Ex. 2 Knussen

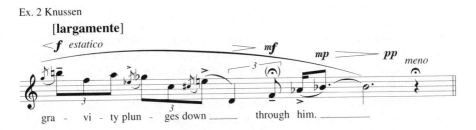

tempo slows again, and another challenging passage ends the movement. Once again, correct breathing is the key. Starting with mellifluously arching intervals the voice has to move directly into a series of high notes, marked 'senza vibrato, legatissimo'. It is a considerable relief to arrive at the subsequent resumption of ordinary voice, on a helpfully accented short trill on 'cloud'. The singer has then to scoop up to delicate *pianissimo* on 'rain', and descend to a low resonance for 'heavy'. It must all seem effortlessly graceful.

Double

The opening motto now occurs in inverted form, each phrase turned upside-down, but with the same proliferation of changing dynamics, some slightly adapted. This means that the final held 'lids' comes on a D sharp, which is not so easily floated. It will help to keep the 'l' well forward, touching the teeth with the tongue.

295

3. Imaginary Life

This movement provides a colourful and highly dramatic narrative, angry and nostalgic by turn, full of sudden outbursts. Consonants must be projected strongly and rhythms well articulated, but without forcing the tone. This is a very direct catalogue of personal experience, the changes of mood often abrupt and shocking. The long rolled 'r' on 'terror' works marvellously well. Two extremely taxing melismas on 'school' and 'slavery' will repay detailed work. Cross-rhythmed accents in the course of them add to the challenge (Example 3). Despite the spiked accents and *sforzandi*, a basic

Ex. 3 Knussen

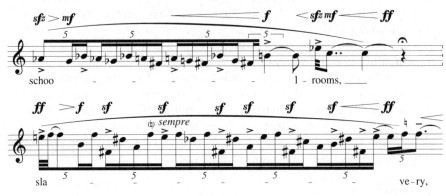

thread of sound must bind the phrases together. An anguished 'yowling' rather than a grinding effect will convey the tedium of school, but the later 'slavery' can work up to a froth of anger, never actually losing control of the detail. In this 'furious' section the singer should literally hurl herself through the phrases, right up to the downward lunge on 'deep loss'. There is then time to gauge the change of emphasis for 'Defiance', and the emotive reflections on stereotypes that follow, in list form, each with a clearly differentiated mode of delivery. This movement is particularly rewarding for the interpreter. For the fanfare-like interval on 'victor' the composer writes 'like a trumpet', so vibrato should not be allowed to hinder the clarity of attack. The upper-note crescendo then stops, resonating in the air. A similarly exciting blast occurs at the end of the next phrase, on the high B flat on 'blow'—again trumpet timbre should be borne in mind. After this tremendous surge of energy, there is a complete change of atmosphere, for the *meno mosso* which ends the movement in an agonizingly poignant way. Plaintive, gentle fragments are punctuated by brief, murmured, echoes, hummed *bocca chiusa*. Most of these lie rather unkindly around the register-break area, and could be vulnerable to sudden cutting-off if not placed perfectly within a seamless legato. It can be inhibiting to think of these hummed passages too softly. The *bocca chiusa* restricts the sound considerably in any case so it is as well not to be too daring with the *pianissimo*. It is extremely important not to lose track of the text during the musing hums. The flow of the text must maintain its hypnotic intensity, making the shock ending all the more effective. The singer must not breathe before 'God leapt out' despite the rest and crescendo. The notes will come out much more clearly and emphatically without the extra air, and this applies especially to the accented 'God'. For the last line there is also a sudden change to a livelier tempo. It should give the audience quite a jolt after the lulling intimacy of quiet nostalgia. The last movement follows *attacca* before tension can slacken.

4. Gong

The singer must plunge straight down on to the deep 'gong' resonance, with a sense of continuity from the preceding, emotion-packed movement. A ritual, declamatory style is instantly established, with space for the music to breathe, and for the audience to reflect on each highly charged statement. The cycle is ideally constructed so that the drama is cumulative, and strokes become broader and bolder, after the more fragile and decorative opening stanzas.

As before, timing of pauses is of prime importance. Each thought needs time to sink in before moving onward. The opening lines have a simple austerity, with a moment of exultant freedom on 'into the open' as the voice suddenly soars up. The composer envisages a slight *accelerando* at this point, after which the thrilling high B can be left to ring out. The vocal articulation is quasi-instrumental, with flourishes still evoking ceremonial brass instruments. A clean delivery and scrupulous tuning of intervals in almost steely precision will suit the louder moments. 'Gong-strokes' divide each section. It is enjoyable vocally to make the most of the long paused *morendo*—it is relatively easy to negotiate a finely spun diminuendo at this level on the 'ng' sound. The *intimo* passage beginning 'sum of all silence' is particularly haunting, and here the lower part of the voice should produce a natural unforced colour and clarity on the repeated 'self'. The phrase which follows needs detailed study to incorporate its many inflections and nuances. The very short 'in' must not be thrown away, but given just enough space for a pure 'pitch kernel' to be heard. Each phrase ends on a poised note which allows the singer to relish the acoustic effect. From now until the end, crucial details abound, and exact observation of even the most fleeting nuance is of great importance. The work's final page again exploits the most rewarding area of the voice for 'You whom one never forgets'. It is sometimes difficult to monitor tone in relentlessly loud high passages, since the upper harmonics resonate in the head. Tone will need to be rounded out on 'invisible lips' as 'i' vowels could sound too thin at the high pitch, especially with a sudden *pianissimo*. The alliterative 'l's should be light and placed well forward, using the tip of the tongue, and the 'v' should also be pitched, helping a smoother flow. There is a final passionate climax, rising to a peak and then leaping down a tenth on 'ev'rything'. At the close, three more 'Gong's on low B ring out, dying away gradually, in an ending that is truly magical in effect. The last note must be held as long as possible, perhaps gradually closing the lips (they can be opened slightly on 'ng' to give a change of colour). There is a feeling of vast space and distance, and this will be enhanced by a lively acoustic, especially a church.

This fastidiously written work is a major addition to the repertoire. It certainly requires a high degree of musicianship and ample time must be allotted for preparation, as it may not 'sit' in the voice immediately. Certain high-lying sections on 'e' vowels, and very subtle fades and surges will take time to fall naturally. However, the rewards gained from intensive work on this piece will be enormous. Its stature will impress all who hear it, and the performer too will learn a great deal. For the interpreter, technical and musical details are bound together so closely that it is impossible to see them separately. The formal structure seems ideally balanced. The piece can happily stand alongside the most substantial established classics for voice and piano, particularly those from the Romantic Austro-German repertoire: the major cycles of Schubert for instance. Schumann and Mendelssohn would also be good choices. The composer's own fondness for Ravel could also be borne in mind, and Russian music could make an effective contrast. It can make a fine start to a programme as long as the artist is confident. Equally suitable for the mature artist as for the gifted student, the work provides rich study material, particularly in rhythmic flexibility and timing.

But Stars Remaining
(1970)

Nicola Lefanu (born 1947)
Text by C. Day Lewis

TV; M VI
Female voice (solo)
Duration *c*.8′

This early work by Nicola Lefanu already shows her flair and professionalism, qualities that continue to characterize her work, now that she has become deservedly established as a leading figure in the British contemporary scene. It remains a great favourite in my own repertoire, with its freshness and immediacy. Doubtless, her mother, the late Elizabeth Maconchy, provided an ideal role model during her compositional development, and like her she shows a special awareness of the needs of the performer. Her music is eminently practical and meticulously worked out, the notation always clear, with exceptionally careful attention to interpretative nuances.

The composer envisages the piece sung as from a high rock, the voice flung across a spacious valley. Thinking of this adds an exhilarating outdoor feeling to the piece. The splendid imagery of C. Day Lewis's poem, with its vivid depictions of birds (kestrel and dove) as symbols of spiritual release, is set most appropriately, and there are a good many innovative vocal devices and gestures. The composer has gone to a great deal of trouble to annotate each detail clearly. Conventional notation is mostly used, although there are a few passages of free rhythm, when note-stems are absent. Quarter-tones are used to inflect the text most subtly, and these are written in what has come to be the accepted manner: a sharp with only one cross-bar for a quarter-sharp, and a reversed flat sign for a quarter-flat.

Many subtle shadings of whispered and spoken tone are employed, some eliding off the ends of phrases. Making the transitions from one shading to another may necessitate some preparatory work to make everything run smoothly and naturally. It was a great advantage to have had the opportunity of working closely with the composer in advance of the première. Some nuances may even elude adequate symbolic representation, and need verbal explanation. Such refinements do require patience at the preliminary stage, but the singer will gain enormously thereby in technical control and analytical awareness of the capabilities of her instrument.

Significantly, the wonders of creation: sun, moon, sky, and stars, and, especially dawn, figure often in texts chosen by Lefanu (and also in those set by Maconchy). An instinctive affinity with natural things is developed with craft and experience. The verse is always used most imaginatively, with repeated words and echo effects providing a fascinating mosaic of vocal fragments interspersed with longer lyrical phrases.

Pacing of the work is very important. Main tempo-changes are clearly marked, but there is much use of rubato within subsections. The music often seems to be in a state of flux. Spontaneity will dictate the general flow, but breathing has to be organized in advance. Some gestures only convince at a particular speed, and the singer must take care to iron out any bumps, concentrating firmly on the text's images pictured in the mind's eye. Lefanu uses bursts of coloratura and glissandos with great expertise, judging range and speed for vocal practicability and comfort. Frequent repeated syllables add impetus, and the generally fragmentary nature of the piece makes it most suitable for a resonant acoustic. A musicianly and technically accomplished singer should be very happy with this spectacular showpiece. Discreet use of a pitch-pipe at the end of sections is permissible if needed.

The work falls into three main sections. A prolonged, basically extrovert 'exposition' describing the kestrel, is followed by a brief, contrastingly slow and contemplative interlude. The tempo suddenly becomes much brisker for the arrival of 'dawn's dove', at the start of an extended final section. However, tempo and dynamic changes come so thick and fast throughout that transitions between sections are gradual, with frequent harking back to previous material, The 'dove' paragraph is surrounded by passages of slow murmuring, and there are many other subsections, some ending with a coloratura flourish up to a held high note. As soon as the word 'stars' occurs, a lyrical peak is reached, with a gorgeous arching phrase that includes a high B flat. The work's opening phrases are repeated at the end, and glowing echoes of 'but stars' reverberate into space. The general effect is exuberant and mercurial yet satisfyingly cohesive.

The opening is marked 'ringing tone', and the soprano has to find a suitably bright quality instantly. The following echo can be non-vibrato for maximum contrast. The demisemiquavers help impel the tone forward. The voice has to drop naturally into speech at the ends of phrases here. It may take a while for this to feel natural, but once attained, the facility will be used again and again, and it is of great importance in capturing the essence of the piece (and of others in the genre). For the echo on 'elate' the '-te' has to be pitched, however. The music swings along spontaneously and dynamics are scattered in dazzling variety. The singer will begin to acquire a natural sense of timing, dropping each note into space with aplomb. After the first written pause, the forward impulse of the music is stemmed, until it picks up again for the 'kestrel'. The disjointed staccato triplets on 'e' have a dancing quality. As in all unaccompanied works, rhythms need discipline, and any identifiably metric moments should be seized upon. Quick reactions are needed to respond to the constant fluctuations of pulse. Quite often the music surges quickly to a climactic display phrase within the framework of a larger section. The exultant leap up a minor ninth on 'joy' is particularly rewarding. It is followed by an exciting snatch of coloratura, peaking on a held high A. The fast septuplet figure will need slow practice to make intervals accurate; at speed, it will be impossible to check this properly, so the notes must be worked into the voice until they run automatically. The gentle staccatos on the syllables of 'hover' fall easily in middle range, but the repeated 'wind' will require careful spacing. The first '-nd' is marked as an unpitched grace-note, and the second is within a smooth *pianissimo*. These details are important.

The opening tempo returns, complete with muffled echoes, even more arresting when sung non-vibrato in this higher range. The word 'furiously', which occurs as the tempo picks up again, is brilliantly set. The singer can attack with vigour, first enjoying the melisma, and then incorporating one of the work's most original effects: a high unpitched yelp. Here a cross is substituted for the note-head, and the singer should aim as high as feels natural, before swooping down to normal singing in low register. This is not nearly as hazardous as may be feared (Example 1). There is no need to force out the top note: a gentle yodelling motion in the throat does the trick, and the instantaneous loosening of muscles provides a useful exercise for future vocal freedom. Balance and poise must be undisturbed, since the music calms very rapidly to a gently spoken (but pitched) 'rest'. The vowel can trail away into breathiness to avoid any sung tone at this comfortably low register. The word 'chaired' is given space-time notation to keep the rhythm flexible, and a paused 'wind' on low E flat is marked 'breathy'. This is followed closely by a high G flat to be sung 'clearly'. This is probably the work's most challenging moment. There is an element of risk if too much breath is used. It can help to linger on the 'w' of the 'clear' note, so as to focus the tone securely once more, in case placing has been thrown momentarily off-balance. 'Breathy' requirements, though effective dramatically, ought to be used sparingly, as here, otherwise there is a danger of jarring the voice. Happily, the singer is immediately given a chance to relax and enjoy a sweeping upward phrase on 'Shouting', the '-ting' cried out rather than sung. This means stifling the tone very quickly before it can bloom. Now comes the culminating section of complex and varied coloratura: this is rewardingly wide-ranging. Staccato and legato fragments are punctuated by commas in a spectacular display of vocal agility, which surges forward excitingly, finally leaping to a glorious long high A sharp. Momentum must be maintained until this peak is reached.

There is a long pause before the middle, slower section begins. This is marked 'dolce tone, intense', a helpful guide to a sensitive interpreter. A suitably glowing quality on 'joy' should be relatively easy to achieve, and warm resonance and tonal beauty are priorities here. Fragments of previous material, 'hoverer', 'wind', 'furiously', and 'rest' recur in a kind of codetta summing up the work so far. Now follows the prolonged section of soft, low-pitched speech, beginning with the repeated word 'rest'. Free notation is used here, and the subtly shaded nuances of dynamic are very important. Breathing could be problematic: it is surprising how quickly air runs out when speech drops to a part-whisper. The whole passage is marked 'gentle, without stress', but the singer must support all phrases with full muscular strength to prevent seepage. There is often a tendency to suspend physical effort in quiet low passages; this leads to feathery and unpredictable quality, and the audience will perceive the reduction of energy. Pauses between phrases should not be hurried—the singer can easily compel attention by an

Ex. 1 Lefanu

301

intensely concentrated approach. The passage may prove a little tiring at first, so comfortable gaps should be left between entries. The visual effect of space-time notation could mean that rests are overlooked. Inflected quarter-tones have to be manœuvred with skill, especially on 'loving', where 'normal' singing is to be resumed directly out of speech (Example 2). The top

Ex. 2 Lefanu

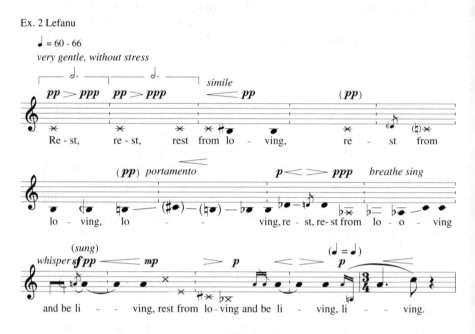

two staves of this page probably offer the most testing series of refinements in the piece. Sung notes have to be very clear, with minimum vibrato, to make sure that each gradation from speech to song can be evident. It is wise to take a good breath after the B quarter-flat before the long, sliding portamento, and the two notes before the comma can be shortened a little in contrast. After the repeated 'rest' another full breath will be necessary to support another awkward transition from breathy to sung tone. There is no helpful impelling consonant here, and it is hard to avoid unevenness at the start of the low A flat. It is useful to remember that, for a sound that is entirely breath, as here, a gentle, sustained version of the German '-ch' makes the right effect without much air being expelled. The whispered grace-notes 'and be' should come out naturally, springing easily on to the sung A natural. 'Rest from loving' can be spoken in plain, slightly clipped fashion, with the quarter-tones slightly 'bending' the notes, so that it all seems casual and unforced. After this, some rhythmic impetus returns; repeated notes and decorations add to the engaging effect, especially the bouncing reiterations on 'fallen'. This intimate and fascinating section ends with a throw-away, gently murmured 'fallen'.

A sparkling new tempo brings 'dawn's dove'. Bright high notes afford relief from the muted intensity of the previous lines. A flicked 'yodel' down a wide interval on 'Fire' is enjoyably simple to negotiate. There must be no hesitation; the loose movement of the larynx frees the voice ready for a firm attack on the low A, leaping up a ninth immediately after. A charming, delicate interlude softly repeats the word 'dove', and spacing of the notes is crucial. The soft, murmured speech returns a second time for a prolonged sequence of subtle 'brush-strokes', again notated freely. Glissandos and quarter-tones are again featured, in variations of inflected speech. The singer has to emerge from a deep whisper to a ringing middle A natural, and the voice can then soar rapturously in some rapid coloratura. This cuts off suddenly, as the mood changes from irrepressible joy to a calm serenity, bringing a steadier tempo. 'Naught', though notated conventionally, is marked 'almost speech': this works very well at the given pitch. The echoed 'morning' is very well judged, and the singer must not overlook the spoken inflection on the final syllable. The word 'stars' on high G, dominates the last section of the work, and the singer should take the opportunity to acquire physical memory of what is often a favourite note with sopranos. Beautiful lyrical phrases culminate in the arching melisma with the work's highest note (B flat). Fleeting references to earlier material appear during a slow unwinding of tension. 'Sink lower' rather unexpectedly occurs on an upward quarter-tone curve, and 'as dark womb recedes' dips deep into chest register for the last time. This serves to relax the voice in readiness for the return to the opening theme. Just before this there are a few more details to be worked on: the composer adds the words 'almost whisper' and 'almost sung' on 'creation' and 'will step' respectively, so that the minute tonal gradations will be smooth. Again, a practicable breathing pattern has to be planned: ideally, there should be no intake after the last 'fade'. It would be a pity to spoil the up-beat springboard on 'step', by interrupting the exciting swing directly into the return of the opening refrain on 'Now'. As the repetitions of 'but stars' reverberate into the distance, the singer has time to place each high G comfortably without rushing, and a chance to exploit the acoustic resonance, adapting to the venue.

This attractive showpiece goes very well in a traditional recital programme. It certainly requires a high degree of musicianship, and a conscientious approach, but the vocal writing is idiomatic and rewarding. Quarter-tones and speech-effects will require extra work but will surely prove beneficial in developing technical and interpretative skills, and cultivating awareness of vocal possibilities. This work would also enhance a recital of mainly twentieth-century classics, perhaps interspersed with brief, more recent pieces (including others in this volume). A solo work always excites an audience, and the acoustic can be used to advantage here. A church or even an outdoor venue will be particularly suitable. It would also fit nicely into a chamber music concert—in view of the feeling of distance, Schubert's 'Der Hirt auf dem Felsen' would be a perfect companion piece in a recital with clarinet and piano.

Three Sonnets to Orpheus
(1993)

David Ward (born 1942)
Text by Rainer Maria Rilke (in German)

T V; M V
Mezzo-soprano and piano
Duration *c*.10′

A welcome new cycle from this composer, who is now resident in Shetland, and continues to write steadily. Frequently influenced by High German Romanticism, he has produced several carefully crafted vocal chamber works, including some for music theatre. A small output of high quality pieces reveals a strong and individual voice, rigorous in finely honed detail, and uncompromisingly committed to his own high standards, irrespective of popularity. He does admit, however, to adapting his vocal style to suit the language, and his settings of English texts, which clearly reflect his heritage and present environment, are palpably different from these Rilke songs. Here he shows a close identification with the Austro-German tradition, and in particular, with the Second Viennese School, especially Berg, and there are also shades of Hindemith. The musical idiom features leaping lines, heavy chromaticism and, notably, a full-blown Expressionist piano part which demands considerable virtuosity—indeed the textures often seem to invite orchestral treatment. Though brief, this cycle packs quite a punch, and requires stamina and concentration from both performers. The singer (a dramatic mezzo is the ideal voice for this) will need to sustain an even tone through a very wide compass. A strong presence and sense of style, and some experience will be a distinct advantage: these are not beginners' pieces. The marriage between words and music is extremely successful, sometimes even invoking Wolf: this, despite the fact that the composer admits that he does not actually speak German. The analogy is that of the sailor who does not swim: he is imbued with the spirit, rather than the surface facility.

This challenging and memorable mini-cycle makes a strong impact, and is worth the effort of mastering its tougher moments. The score is neatly presented, and words are printed in full, with an English translation, at the front. Clear references are provided, so that the chosen excerpts from the Rilke Sonnets can be identified in their original context. Since Rilke is notoriously difficult to translate, the colour and rarefied atmosphere have to be gleaned, almost by osmosis from a succession of at times bewildering images, but the exultant celebration of the forces of Nature and Art is highly potent.

1. A Tree Ascending

The voice starts very low, launching immediately into a wide-spanning line, supported by a demanding accompaniment with a decorative left-hand part (Example 1). In between similar soaring, Expressionist bursts there are

Ex.1 Ward

sudden moments of stillness, leaving the voice almost alone, intoning softly and simply, in a low register. Staccato and *pianissimo* can be achieved naturally and still remain audible. The *sotto voce* unaccompanied fragment of 'Tiere aus Stille' involves an octave leap up from low G sharp, but this should cause no problems if touched lightly at the start. Sibilant sounds can be emphasized to enhance the hushed effect. The dynamic subtlety recalls that of Webern, and continual rubato keeps the pulse fluid. Just over halfway through the song, there is a change to 6/8, but the beat remains the same. The last paragraph of flowing lines, with full-blooded accompaniment, especially in the bass, unfolds gently into music of quite a different character. Voice and piano have light, flexible figures, quasi-*scherzando* in style, especially in the piano's staccato groups. All is delicate and precise, until a sudden slower tempo brings a darker interlude, with the voice intoning in a low tessitura, over pedalled arpeggios. A final, burgeoning, Expressionist paragraph brings the movement to an exciting close, with the piano's texture at its richest and most virtuosic in contrast to the singer's sustained line.

2. Dance the Orange

The composer's instruction 'Suggesting a waltz' is significant. The parody of Viennese schmaltz is clear, despite the lack of obvious repetitive waltz figures. A lilt has to be maintained, and rhythm must never sag. In keeping with the mercurial nature of the text, the music is fragmentary, and the many rests should not interrupt the sense. Breathing should be economical, and the singer's agility will certainly be fully tested. The phrase marked 'breathily' could perhaps stray towards Sprechstimme. There is almost a feeling of a *danse macabre* in this substantial setting, especially when the singer is left alone in syllabic emphasis and marked staccato for 'tanzt'. A clean delivery is very important, as well as a quick adaptability to the rapid shifts of colour that follow. Familiarity in the language will help with the cabaret style, sometimes reminiscent of Weill or Eisler (even Hindemith) that seems appropriate here. A sudden quadruplet against running bass triplets must not seem contrived. This is marked 'hollowly' and should be projected strongly against the piano's crescendo. Balance will need careful attention at such moments, and timing throughout requires considerable skill and panache. To sing 'sweetly' on 'Süss-sein' should give no trouble, and the sounds of the syllables should be savoured. A rapturous phrase: 'sie hat sich köstlich zu euch bekehrt' is doubled by piano octaves, enriching the sound in stark contrast to the sparser layout of the opening section, and of the frequent parlando fragments. The penultimate section relaxes into a steady 4/4, with some very tricky triplet subdivisions in voice and piano. The vocal lines are, however, marked 'almost sleazy' so a good deal of licence can be allowed to produce a suitably slurred effect. Keeping track of beats will be no easy task, but the decadent atmosphere can be indulged without inhibition (Example 2).

Ex. 2 Ward

For the final paragraph, the opening 'waltz' is resumed at a heady, almost intoxicating *fortissimo*. This could possibly lead to forcing if the singer is not careful. The best solution is to keep the sound clear and cutting, shaping phrases boldly, and emphasizing strong down-beats and any percussive consonants. This should create an impression of forceful projection while saving energy for the tops of phrases. Triplets within the 3/4 (again the voice is doubled by piano octaves for these) must not be allowed to obscure the basic waltz feeling. This last section will need some work before it runs easily.

3. '...I Exist'

The last setting, the shortest, is by no means simple to bring off. Again it requires a deep identification with the Expressionist world, this time in more reflective vein, the dynamics generally at a gentler level, the tempo a slow crotchet = 42. Tessitura is extremely wide-ranging, and phrases luxuriantly long at times. The voice begins with a rapt *pianissimo* on low A, unaccompanied. (The piano's one introductory note gives the pitch.) Undulating phrases build gradually, with rhythms moving flexibly in combinations of triplets and slow semiquaver groups, obeying the drawn-out speech patterns. The coda brings a sudden onset of power—rather unexpected in view of the text, which does not seem to invite a violent outburst! The piano's tolling chords crescendo to *forte* and the singer's last few phrases ring out in declamatory fashion, cadencing triumphantly in 'D major' (but without the third in the triad) with a thrilling unaccompanied octave leap, from high A down, on 'Ich bin'.

This is a work capable of making a very strong impression in concert, but a great deal of responsibility rests with the skill and unflappable musical command of the two performers. A substantial period of preparation should be allowed for the music to feel entirely secure. Ward's deeply felt response to the texts manifests itself in a thoroughly extrovert way, unflinchingly passionate and heedless of any possible accusations of excess. One is reminded of the work of Alan Bush in the unwavering conviction, and fearless expression of unbridled feeling and high tension, not sparing the decibels. I feel that the repertoire is enlivened by such music, and audiences will find it very exciting. Rhythmic control needs to be kept through the complex subdivisons, so that the effect does not become undisciplined.

This piece will make a strong antidote to French music in a programme. The singer can exhibit her versatility by putting it alongside some Debussy, for instance, even Poulenc, which could form a bridge to the cabaret element. A more obvious choice would be to place it in a classic Viennese evening, with Strauss, Mahler, Schreker, or of course Schoenberg, Berg, and Webern. The audience needs to be a fairly sophisticated one, well attuned to late Romantic, early twentieth-century influences.

Awa Herea (Braided Rivers) (1993)

Gillian Whitehead (born 1941)
Text by the composer
First two sections translated into Maori by Keri Kaa

T V; M VI
Soprano and piano
Duration *c*.18′

A truly outstanding piece by one of the most consistently rewarding representatives of New Zealand's art and culture. Gillian Whitehead has long been admired for her poetic vision, natural musicality, and craftmanship. Resident in Britain for many years, she now divides her time between Australia and New Zealand. Her output includes several operas and many other vocal chamber works, and all these show her exceptional lyrical and dramatic gifts. A real performers' composer, she has often collaborated with New Zealand poets, most particularly Fleur Adcock. A personal and deeply felt response to the nature and folklore of her native land, always present in her music, shows particularly strongly in this superb cycle, for which she has written her own text. Intimate spiritual contact with her heritage (she is one-quarter Maori) manifests itself in both a special sensitivity to the sights and sounds of nature—birds, beasts, plants, landscapes and climate, and their signficance in Maori culture—and a fierce resistance to the commercial interests that threaten to destroy them.

The work is divided into seven movements, some overlapping into the next, exceptionally well integrated into a balanced whole. After an unaccompanied wordless Vocalise, based on birdsong, and a Karakia (Maori incantation), the title-song (split into two parts) frames a central sequence of four poems in English, each of them recalling specific sights and impressions of New Zealand's South Island. The title-song's theme of plaiting (braiding), is applied to human life as well as to the natural world. The basic message is that a single thread is vulnerable and finite, but that threads woven together form stronger and more lasting bonds.

The soprano writing is most satisfying, veering between chanted ritualistic monody and sweeping lyricism. The Maori texts should cause no difficulties: translations are provided, and pronunciation is mostly phonetic, with vowels a little shorter than in Italian, and diphthongs smooth, yet with their components delineated. The only unexpected feature is that 'wh' is always pronounced 'f'. The piano provides the most delicate support in simple repeated notes, and later launches into more virtuosic solo passages, yet balance is unlikely to be a problem. There is no doubt that the singer's standard of musicianship will need to be reasonably high, especially with regard to pitching, but the composer is always immensely practical, and potential performers should not be daunted by the task. The musical language is basically simple and uncluttered, and rhythms are flexible and relatively undemanding. The mellifuous vocal part includes a few phrases that are to be spoken, some free, some in notated rhythms. This is a most beautiful and hauntingly memorable work, and a major addition to the repertoire. Sadly, Tracey Chadwell, its dedicatee and commissioner, died early in 1996 aged 36. The piece is a fitting memorial to her distinctive artistry and generosity, and will continue to bring pleasure to others.

1. Vocalise

This is an ideal way to start the cycle. Unaccompanied singing always focuses the audience's concentration and creates a special atmosphere of intimacy and direct communication. Birdsong effects feature constantly, depicted in delightful chirrupings and grace-notes. These are interspersed with long-held notes on gradually changing vowels. Some of the bird imitations are extremely close, such as the whispered 'ch-k-ch-k-ch-k'. For this, vowels are put underneath to indicate the mouth shape required to subtly alter the sound. Then there is a 'Tssss' which also has a glissando. All these effects work brilliantly and are fun to perform. A pitch-pipe may need to be on hand, especially for the opening note: a long mid-range G flat. The timing of rests and pauses is very important, and any flaws in technique are liable to be exposed at times. Tone-quality should be steady, with very little vibrato, but never nasal. Intervals always seem logical, and the voice learns very quickly to feel secure on the written pitches. The aspect of physical memory is central to the learning process. A passage of metred triplets will sound even more bird-like if the 'k's are made very resonant in 'Kua hoki mai', etc. (the only words in the Vocalise—they presage the start of the following 'Karakia'). For a sequence of fast repeated semiquaver triplets the composer asks for a slight throbbing pulse on each note. Her interpretative suggestions are succinct but imaginative: 'laid back', 'bell-like', and so on. The soprano must be able to float in *pianissimo*—the last line of this movement is the most testing in this respect. It rises to a long B flat, but a lower option is provided. A radiant high G at the end of the singer's last phrase begins the next setting, to be joined by the piano on middle C. This must be a perfect fifth in all senses! This delightful solo calls to mind other memorable uses of birdsong by composers such as Messiaen and George Crumb.

2. Karakia

The title is the Maori word for 'prayer' or 'incantation'. The piano's solo reiterates middle C in pulsating patterns, providing a pitch pedal throughout the movement, gently supporting the voice and keeping it on key. After the singer enters, the piano's rhythms are no longer notated, but are left to the player's fancy, although the composer stipulates that there should be no octave transpositions. She also suggests an occasional (inside piano) pizzicato according to taste. The vocal phrases, by contrast, are smooth and undulating, in a mainly low to medium tessitura, moving in quavers in close intervals. Significantly, the singer's lines are marked 'mezza voce' (actually 'm.v.' in the manuscript—not everyone would know what this means). There are two different ways of approaching this: either with hushed intensity, as if bottling suppressed energy, or more pale, feathery, and distant, perhaps covering or hollowing the tone to give a muffled effect. Whichever is chosen, consonants must remain very clearly projected. The grouping of notes and syllables is irregular and the lines can roam freely and supply (Example 1). This is all very comfortable to sing, but a few decisions

Ex. 1 Whitehead

about phrasing have to be made. A quick breath can be snatched before the high G on 'ta-', and, ideally, no more until the end of the word. A similar opportunity is offered in the middle of the last phrase after 'koutou'. Tuning of the close chromatic intervals will need careful attention. It may help to make mental enharmonic changes, converting D flat to C sharp for instance. The open Maori vowels help to achieve an even, chanting tone, and a ritual style that is distinct from Western song tradition. Vibrato should be kept to a minimum. Halfway through the 'Karakia' the piano's pedal-note changes to the G above. The voice ends on a sustained middle C, making another perfect fifth, overlapping into the next movement.

3. Awa Herea

The title-song consists of eight evocative fragments of text, translated into Maori. Alternate fragments are variants of the opening incantation: 'Braided rivers, braided vines, braided voices'. The lines in between continue the theme of weaving and plaiting. This movement covers fragments 1–5 only. The repetitive, chanting vocal style of 'Karakia' with its close intervals, is found again here, but the piano's role is much more prominent, and is strictly notated, and the dynamic level is more varied. After the reflective opening with brief, drifting phrases, the piano begins a sprightly solo in octaves, two octaves apart. The voice starts by speaking in written-out, unpitched rhythms, which must not be too rigid. The syncopated, layered piano part is loud at this point, so the vocal sound should be pitched well up for audibility. The 'r' in 'herea' should be rolled gently. Thereafter the texture becomes very sparse. The voice's sung incantations are low-pitched, with trills and ornaments, supported by occasional piano octaves. Rests and punctuation dictate a practical breathing pattern. A solo piano interlude, mostly in two gently flowing parts, builds to a repeat of the voice's opening declamations. After a pause, the fourth fragment is sung almost unaccompanied. A rapt purity is needed, and the composer suggests a dynamic of *mezzo-piano*. The piano then resumes its solo, alternating between cool meandering and dynamic repeated chords, which eventually lead to a spectacular cadenza passage. The singer finishes by speaking, in natural rhythm, almost casually, the final refrain fragment, in between the piano's loud, clashing chords. The vocal dynamic will have to remain up, but it must not be overdramatized.

4. The Berries

After a long pause, the group of English song-settings now begins. This one is fairly substantial. It describes the crimson berries on the forest floor, whilst 'a front rolls in from the sea'. Here the voice part is more wide ranging and virtuosic than in the two previous movements, and broader intervals are featured. These may take a while to become really accurate. Crucial phrases are lightly scored, the piano having sustained chords which contain some useful pitch cues, for example those for 'canopy' and 'crimson'. However others are rather less helpful, and the singer will have to work hard to be really confident of staying in the centre of notes. For the lovely rising line (to high B natural) on 'glow', an *ossia* is also suggested, for which the piano will also have to be adapted accordingly. It will be more comfortable to take a quick breath before the word and to keep tone light and placed well forward. There is a sudden change of character halfway through the song as the weather turns. The piano has rippling sextuplets, septuplets, and finally demisemiquavers, depicting the waves. The voice enters with a particularly high-stepping line, in which the words may prove a little constricting at first. The piano continues the exciting build-up, breaking into raging arpeggio sextuplets, over which the singer projects a strongly rhythmic line. This reaches a climax on 'thrashes'—an especially taxing piece of coloratura which contains some awkward pitch intervals. An *ossia* is also given for this, but this would lessen the impact considerably (Example 2). After a comma, there is a sudden drop to *mezzo-piano*, and the singer has some beautiful lyrical lines to end the movement, supported by chords on the piano, its syncopated rhythms gradually subsiding on to low harmonies. The next song follows without a break.

Ex. 2 Whitehead

The ca-no-py thra – – – – –   shes

* ossia

thra – – – – –   shes

5. Lake Ianthe

The poem describes a peaceful lake, with trees reflected in the water. But, close by, trees are being cut down, and the sounds of axe and saw are heard. The piano plays a dominant role here, its loud, driving rhythms depicting the arrival of the machines of destruction, starting with a vigorous opening solo. The singer has only three extended entries, in luxuriant, arching lines. Breaths can be taken after each of the long tied notes in the first vocal entry, but a smooth legato must be maintained. The piano bursts in with another dramatic solo, building further momentum, its surging semiquavers re-placed by hammered whole-tone clashes in 7/8 time just before the voice re-enters. Here the tone can be more incisive, and non-legato, and breathing has to be worked out carefully. The piano's dynamic may need to be toned down in order not to drown the singer. The best places for taking breath are after 'images' and 'axe', keeping the quavers absolutely steady. It may help to mark the irregular quaver groupings with signs indicating twos or threes. Then for the long 'whine' it will certainly be appropriate to indulge in some word-painting, using a 'keening' quality, sliding from note to note, with a bright steely centre to each. The irregular rhythms may take some time to acquire the effortless precision needed. The ending is calm again, the singer repeating the opening phrase, expanded slightly for the last few notes, To finish, she chants a Maori proverb (in the original), on middle C, over a held chord: 'The descendants of Tane (God of Forests) are laid low.' Although not marked in the score, this should be very loud and suddenly dramatic, in a fierce, almost raucous, non-vibrato.

6. Scale and Perspective

The composer's text muses upon the different lifespans of nature's crea-tions, from its vaster wonders to the smallest forms of life (glacier to microbe), listing on the way animals, birds, and insects, often by their Maori names (translated at the front of the score). This movement has a basically steady tempo, the voice ranging in fairly simple flowing lines over a piano part consisting mainly of stark bass octaves. A central passage of chanting (the 'list') on the C above middle C will need very careful counting—the rhythms are quite tricky (Example 3). The style can be quasi-parlando here, with some fleeting moments of word-painting for the sounds and impressions of birds and insects. There is another subtle piece of onomatapoeia on 'overlapping'—again, it is important to keep track of the pulse. The last section is lyrical again, but some intervals may be difficult to pitch accurately at first, as they involve enharmonic changes and close chromaticism, and the lines are quite exposed. The very long held B natural must be absolutely clean in pitch. The whole phrase could prove taxing in one span: a breath after 'microbe' will make it more comfortable. The very last, unaccompanied, line requires the purest tuning, but the notes lie extremely well for verbal clarity and vocal ease.

Ex.3 Whitehead

7. The Sandfly

This is an amusing miniature, lasting only a matter of seconds, the text consisting of just one sentence, split into two tiny fragments. The New Zealand sandfly, though minute, has a lethal bite that can linger in the bloodstream for years, far outlasting its own lifespan. (I can testify to this!) The ironic humour of the situation is nicely caught here. The voice has brisk parlando rhythms in between the piano's stabbing ('stinging') chords and brief running passages. Poise and careful synchronization with the piano are all that are required.

8. Awa Herea (conclusion)

The cycle now reaches the second half of the enveloping title-song and the return of the theme that overlays (binds) the whole piece: (the fabric of life is strengthened by many threads). Here, voice and piano are kept separate. The singer has ordinary declaimed speech to begin with, and then launches into an incantation, similar to the first part of 'Awa Herea', but with the lines moving around a wider range, the phrases stretching into lyrical shapes at the ends. The voice has a chance to shine, free from restrictions of ensemble or the need to balance with the piano. After a piano interlude there is more 'natural speech', and, towards the end, the 'Karakia' (prayer chant) is briefly recalled at a slightly higher pitch. Trills and decorative features again occur, marked 'mezza voce' as before. Finally, the piano begins a repetitive pulse on middle C, over which the soprano floats her last graceful lines, beautifully quiet and understated, this time fitting with the piano's hypnotic throbbing. The music phrases itself very naturally—short breaths after each dotted note help to clarify shapes and enhance the exquisitely poised cadence. The composer has added a pause between the singer's two last phrases, after 'Kou-tou', to allow plenty of time for a poised re-entry, while the piano continues the pulse.

This work will deservedly win many admirers for its sheer beauty of sound and its deep spiritual strength and memorability. The contrasts of light and shade, and activity and stillness are woven into a perfectly balanced structure, full of character and flair, and constantly fascinating. It is a gift for a recitalist. A lovely programme could be made up of works containing references to birdsong. A superb twentieth-century classics recital could comprise George Crumb's 'Apparition', this work, and then after an interval, Messiaen's *Harawi* (in which bird-calls and ritual chanting are basic features). Music from the Antipodes often refers to non-Western cultures, and other composers, such as Australians Peter Sculthorpe and Ross Edwards, show the influences of their geographical placing. Works by Japanese composers such as Toru Takemitsu would also go well with Whitehead's haunting piece. Nicola Lefanu's lovely solo piece 'But Stars Remaining' (in this volume) is also all about birds. From the classic repertoire, Mozart, Schubert, even Beethoven could precede this cycle, and either French music (but not 'Les Six') or English Romantics could follow it, but a juxtaposition with anything urbane or satirical could spoil the atmosphere. This must be one of the very best song cycles of recent years, and is worth every bit of the time taken to master it.

Supplementary List

DAVID BEDFORD (b. 1937): *O now the drenched land wakes* (1966). Baritone and piano duet; Text: Kenneth Patchen; Duration: *c.6'*. T II; M II.

This is one of a group of Patchen settings which include the soprano piece 'Come in Here, Child' (see Vol. 1). It is not as difficult as the free notation might indicate. Vocal lines are fragmentary and the effect is extremely atmospheric. The pianists play inside piano as well as on the keyboard, and, during a short interlude, the singer also contributes by plucking strings, and hitting them with a 'cluster stick' (available from the composer). Original and fascinating. (Available from Universal Edition/Schott, 48 Great Marlborough Street, London W1V 2BN.)

DAVID CARHART (b. 1937): *Tanka* (1979). Soprano and piano; Text: Japanese verse translated into English; Duration: *c.8'*. T IV; M V.

A typically mellifluous and well-crafted work from this pianist-composer. The five aphoristic verse fragments (very similar to the more well-known haiku form) are interspersed by piano interludes of equal delicacy and fantasy. The third, central, setting is the most substantial, and sections become shorter towards the end. This is suitable for a flexible soprano with a wide range, able to enjoy the Webernian curves and leaps, which lie very well in the voice. (Available from the composer at 20 Standish Road, London W6 9AL.)

REBECCA CLARKE (1886–1979): *Song Album* (1995): Shy One (Yeats); The Cloths of Heaven (Yeats); Infant Joy (Blake); Down by the Salley Gardens (Yeats); The Seal Man (Masefield); June Twilight (Masefield); A Dream (Yeats); Eight O'Clock (Housman); Greeting (Ella Young). Medium/high voice and piano; Durations: *c.2'* each. T II; M II.

A selection of individual songs, not a cycle, written in the twenties by this important British composer (and distinguished viola-player) who settled in New York. This handsome new publication is most welcome. A revelation: a wonderfully varied and compelling collection certain to win many admirers for this neglected figure. (Available from Boosey & Hawkes Music Publishers Ltd, 295 Regent Street, London WIR 8JH.)

LEON COATES (b. 1937): *North-West Passage* (1990). (3 poems from a *Child's Garden of Verses*: Good Night; Shadow March; In Port.) Soprano or treble and piano; Text: Robert Louis Stevenson; Duration: *c.6'* T II; M II.

A delightful and beautifully produced short album from a composer especially sympathetic to the medium of voice and piano. He frequently gives recitals with his wife the soprano Heather Coates, to whom the piece is dedicated. A straightforward yet fresh and appealing musical idiom. The cycle can be performed complete or individual songs selected. Suitable for a bright, high-lying youthful voice. It would go well with the Stevenson settings of Williamson and Robinson also recommended. (Available from the Hardie Press, 17 Harrison Gardens, Edinburgh EH11 1SE.)

MARTIN DALBY (b. 1942): *A Muse of Love* (1968). Five Elizabethan Love Lyrics: What Thing is Love? (George Peele); When to her Lute Corinna Sings (Thomas Campion); O Gentle Love (George Peele); Cupid and Campaspe (John Lyly); Take O Take Those Lips Away (Shakespeare). Medium/high voice and piano; Duration: *c*.8'. T III; M III.

A lovely cycle, with plenty of coloratura writing, and a very clever pastiche of Elizabethan style in both vocal and keyboard parts. Excellent for a recital including early music. The piece is perfectly proportioned and has ideal clarity of texture. It ought to be very popular. A clean vocal delivery is necessary. Not suitable for heavier voices. (Out of print but copies available from Boosey & Hawkes Archive, 295 Regent Street, London WIR 8JH.)

PETER DICKINSON (b. 1934): *Stevie's Tunes* (1985). (An anthology of nine songs: Heber; To the Tune of the Coventry Carol, O Happy Dogs of England; In Canaan's Happy Land; The Heavenly City; . . . And the Clouds Return After the Rain; The Devil-My-Wife; Le Singe qui Swing; Unser Vater.) Mezzo-soprano and piano; Text: Stevie Smith; Duration: 13'. T I; M II.

A gift of a party piece and hugely enjoyable for all. One of a number of pieces written for the artistry of the composer's sister Meriel, and for his own considerable pianism and wide stylistic sympathies. The tunes all come from well-known hymns or popular songs, as either specified or implied by the poet herself in her own inimitable sing-song readings of her verse. Ideal for a late-night recital or cabaret. The score is a model of clarity and helpful information. (Available from Novello & Co. Ltd, c/o Music Sales Group, 8/9 Frith Street, London W1V 5TZ.)

ERIKA FOX (b. 1936): *Frühling ist Wiedergekommen* (1988). Soprano or mezzo-soprano and piano; Text: Rainer Maria Rilke; Duration: *c*.5'. T V; M VI.

There is plenty of energy and virtuosity in this brief, but powerfully emotional, piece. An accomplished singer with a very high standard of musicianship will find it a satisfying vehicle. The vocal part covers a large range and there are some difficult rhythms. The 'advanced' style continues the Second Viennese School tradition. The piano part is also demanding, and ensemble will need considerable attention. See also 'Singender Steige' for soprano and flute (*c*.2') also to words by Rilke. (Available from the British Music Information Centre or from the composer at 78 Peterborough Road, London SW6 3EB.)

ERIC HUDES (b. 1920): *Romancero a la Muerte de Federico Garcia Lorca* (1970). Soprano and piano; Text: Leopoldo Urrutia, in translation by Sylvia Townsend Warner; Duration: *c*.8'. T II; M IV.

A lyrical 'elegy' in the form of a free-ranging narrative, which shows the composer's meticulous attention to vocal detail. The soprano part has many wide intervals and glissandos, and there is also some Sprechstimme. There is an alternative version for soprano, flute, clarinet, viola, and guitar. A steady, clear vocal quality is required. It would be interesting to perform this alongside Satie's 'La Mort de Socrate' (the last movement of *Socrate*). (See also the following work.)

(Available from Anglian Edition, Parsonage Street, The Old White Horse, Halstead. Essex CO9 2JZ.)

MIKLÒS KOCSAR (b. 1933): *Lamenti* (1968). (Cycle of 3 songs.) Soprano and piano; Text: Federico Garcia Lorca (in Spanish); Duration: *c*.10'. T V; M VI.

Arguably one of the most impressive song cycles of the last half of the century, able to stand alongside those of Dallapiccola (his *Quattro Liriche di Antonio Machado* would be an ideal companion piece) and Webern. It is also stylistically close to Boulez and George Crumb. Colouristic vocal and pianistic effects are used with mastery, and it makes an immediate dramatic impact, showing off the performers' talents to greatest advantage. There are three starkly contrasted settings: 'Clamor', 'Malagueña', and 'Lamentaciòn de la Muerte'. Notation is clear and without barlines. Some speech effects in the last song. (Available from Editio Musica Budapest Vörösmarty tér 1, PO Box 322, Budapest, Hungary.)

ANDREW LOVETT (b. 1962). *Ophelia* (1990). Mezzo and piano; Text: George Heym (in German); Duration: 11'. T V; M V.

A striking and dramatic cycle by a gifted young composer which requires a strong and characterful interpreter. The piano part also demands a soloistic approach. Vocal technique must include a wide range of dynamics and colours—there are some long floating *pianissimi*. The musical idiom is influenced by both Stravinskian and post-Viennese models, but sounds fresh and full of variety. It would go very well with the David Ward work in this volume. Clear standard notation. (Available from the composer at 27 Lyonsdown Avenue, New Barnet, Herts. EN5 1DU.)

BUXTON ORR (Scotland) (b. 1924), *Ten Types of Hospital Visitor* (1986, revised 1991). Medium/high voice and piano (original version for voice and double bass); Text: Charles Causley; Duration: *c*.15'. T IV; M IV.

An important work from this imaginative and rewarding composer, set to a marvellous text. It gives a substantial opportunity for vocal characterization and virtuosity. Each 'visitor' is portrayed in a dazzling parade of contrasting cameos within a basically neo-classic idiom. The humour is often bitingly accurate, and not always comfortable, and mood and tempo switch abruptly throughout, ending on a sober, fateful note. Stamina, diction, and rhythmic reliability will be thoroughly tested. It would be appropriate to have the poems read aloud before the performance, since there are so many nuances of wit and perception to savour. (Available from the composer at Church House Barn, Llanwarne, Hereford HR2 8JE.)

MICHAEL ROBINSON (b. 1933), *A Child's Vision of Night* (1964). (Seven Songs: The Lamplighter (R. L. Stevenson); Nocturne (Osbert Sitwell); Shadow March (R. L. Stevenson); Silver (Walter de la Mare); Falling Asleep (Siegfried Sassoon); The Hag (Robert Herrick); The Bellman (Robert Herrick).) Medium voice and piano; Duration: *c*.12'. T II; M III.

A real gem of a song cycle by a distinguished scholar whose music deserves to be much more widely recognized. Beautifully written settings of some very well-known poems are gathered into a balanced and cohesive whole. The style is a fluent and distinctive fusion of traditional and mainstream contemporary idioms, with perhaps a hint of an American flavour. The composer's aural acuteness is particularly impressive; he is not afraid of simple, uncluttered lines in the middle of the voice, and the texts are never in danger of being obscured. The vocal writing seems ideally idiomatic and the piano parts are also rewardingly varied. The de la Mare settings of Elaine Hugh-Jones in Volume 1, and the Stevenson songs of both Malcolm Williamson and Leon Coates mentioned in this book, make interesting points of comparison. (Available from Northridge Music, Northridge House, Usk Road, Shirenewton, Chepstow, Gwent NP6 6RZ.)

ROBERT SAXTON (b. 1953), *Brise Marine* (1976). Soprano, piano, and tape; Text: Stéphane Mallarmé (in French); Duration: 4'. T IV; M IV.

An early work by this outstanding composer, and so far his only piece for voice and piano. The pliable vocal lines fit the text beautifully and will suit a high-placed, pure soprano voice, able to place intervals cleanly and cope with flexible rhythms in 'written-out rubato'. The tape merely involves the singer pre-record-ing, on cassette, the short passage of wordless vocalizing which is to be found on a second stave below the live voice at the start of the final section. This is to be switched on at the given point in the score, so that the live soprano can sing in duet with herself: a nostalgic and dream-like effect appropriate to the valedictory quality of this haunting little piece. Alternatively, if there are no suitable technical facilities, another singer (perhaps off-stage) could perform as an *alter ego*. (Available from Chester Music, c/o Music Sales Group, 8/9 Frith Street, London WlV 5TZ.)

NICOLAS SLONIMSKY (1894–1995). *Five Advertising Songs* (1925). (1. Make this a day of Pepsodent!; 2. And then her doctor told her. . . .; 3. Snowy-white; 4. No more shiny nose!; 5. Children cry for castoria!) Any voice (No. 5 involves falsetto for male voices); Original text from published advertisements; Duration: *c*.10'. T I; M III.

Slonimsky was justly revered as conductor, composer, academic, and author of in particular the *Lexicon of Musical Invective*. This is a hilarious party piece and quite irresistible, full of wicked parody and invention. The last song ends with some high shrieking after a passage of fast speech. It would go perfectly with other 'newspaper cuttings' by Eisler and Mossolov. (Available from Cambria Publish-ing, Lomita, Cal. 90717, USA.)

RANDALL WOOLF (b. 1959), *Shreffler Songs* (1988). Medium/low voice and piano; Text: John Schreffler; Duration *c*.5'. T II; M I.

An appealing and memorable miniature cycle of four songs, which lie very comfortably, and, apart from one sudden burst of coloratura in No. I, have fairly simple vocal lines. The idiom leans strongly towards minimalism and should prove accessible to a wide audience. Texts are poignantly evocative, and the settings are clear-textured and uncluttered. The manner of vocal delivery should be straightforward and unaffected, without heavy vibrato. Louder dynamics tend to happen quite suddenly in marked contrast. The composer's written interpret-ative markings are admirably clear, and should be obeyed. The piano part is also most attractive and varied. (Available from Davidge Publishing, 990 Glen Hill Rd. Shoreview, Minnesota, Mn. 55126, USA.)

Of composers who have written a considerably body of vocal music, but whose works have not been featured in the main text, I would like to recommend especially: GEOFFREY BUSH (Novello), NED ROREM, DOMINICK ARGENTO, and ROBIN HOLLOWAY (Boosey & Hawkes), BETTY ROE and MADELEINE DRING (Thames), TREVOR HOLD (Ramsey and Thames Publishing), and MICHAEL FIN-NISSY and ROBERT SHERLAW JOHNSON (Oxford University Press—these last two for the more advanced professional singer). Also, the self-published BRIAN DENNIS (30 Runnemede Road, Egham, Surrey TW20 9BL), JOHN HEARNE ('Longship', Smidskot, Fawells, Keith Hall, Inverurie AB51 0LN) (both singers), MICHAEL PARSONS (148 Fellows Road, London NW3 3JH), RICK POTTER (Flat 3. Solsgirth House, Langmuir Road, Kirkintilloch, Glasgow G66 3XN), and TIMOTHY SALTER (USK Edition, 26 Caterham Road, London SE13 5AR) and, one whose works are particularly suitable for educational use at beginners' level, the Scottish composer LAURA SHUR (75 Hodford Road, London NW11 8NH).

Acknowledgements and Publishers' Addresses

Thomas Adès: *Life Story*. © 1993 Faber Music Ltd., 3 Queen Square, London WC1N 3AU, by whose kind permission the examples are reproduced.

Avril Anderson: *Her days shall pass*. Avril Anderson, by whose kind permission the examples are reproduced, 28 Cavendish Avenue, London N3 3QN.

George Antheil: *Five Songs*. © 1934 Boosey & Hawkes Inc. Boosey & Hawkes Music Publishers Ltd., 295 Regent Street, London W1R 8JH, by whose kind permission the examples are reproduced.

Violet Archer: *Epigrams*. Examples reproduced by kind permission of the composer. Score available from the Canadian Information Centre.

Daniel Asia: *Pines Songs*. Theodore Presser Co., Presser Place, Bryn Mawr, PA 19010, USA, by whose kind permission the examples are reproduced.

Peter Aston: *Five Songs of Crazy Jane*. Novello & Co. Ltd., by whose kind permission the examples are reproduced, c/o Music Sales Group, 8/9 Frith Street, London W1V 5TZ. Text (extracts) reproduced from *The Collected Poems of W.B. Yeats* by permission of A.P. Watt Ltd on behalf of Michael Yeats.

Tzni Avni: *Beside the Depths of a River*. Examples reproduced by kind permission of the composer. Score available from the Israel Music Institute. © Israel Music Institute. Reproduced by kind permission of Alfred A. Kalmus Ltd., 38 Eldon Way, Paddock Wood, Kent TN12 6BE.

Alison Bauld: *Banquo's buried; Cry cock-a-doodle-doo!; The Witches' Song*. Novello & Co. Ltd. (see under Peter Aston) by whose kind permission the examples are reproduced.

Richard Rodney Bennett: *Dream Songs*. Novello & Co. Ltd. (see under Peter Aston) by whose kind permission the examples are reproduced. Text (extracts) reproduced by permission of the Society of Authors on behalf of the Literary Trustees of Walter de la Mare.

John Buckley: *Abendlied*. Examples reproduced by kind permission of the composer. Score available from Contemporary Music Centre, Dublin.

Glenn Buhr: *Lacrimosa*. Score available from Glenn Buhr, by whose kind permission the examples are reproduced, c/o Hart/Murdoch Artists Management, 204A St George Street, Toronto, Ontario M5R 2N6, Canada; perusal score available from Calgary office of the Canadian Music Centre.

John Cage: *She is asleep*. © 1960 Henmar Press Inc., New York. Edition Peters No. 6747. Peters Edition Ltd., 10–12 Baches Street, London N1 6DN. Reproduced on behalf of the Publishers by kind permission.

ACKNOWLEDGEMENTS & PUBLISHERS' ADDRESSES

Tristram Cary: *Earth Hold Songs*. Tristram Cary, by whose kind permission the examples are reproduced, 'The Southern Dot Factory', 30 Fowlers Road, Glen Osmond, SA 5064, Australia.

Lyell Cresswell: *Three Songs*. Examples reproduced by kind permission of the composer. Score available from the Scottish Music Information Centre.

Simon Emmerson: *Time Past IV*. Simon Emmerson, by whose kind permission the examples are reproduced, 15 Holligrave Road, Bromley, Kent BR1 3PJ.

Eibhlis Farrell: *Five Songs for Children*. Examples reproduced by kind permission of the composer. Score available from the Contemporary Music Centre, Dublin.

Irving Fine, *Childhood Fables for Grownups*. © 1955, 1958 Boosey & Hawkes Inc. Boosey & Hawkes (see under George Antheil), by whose kind permission the examples are reproduced.

Christopher Fox: *Anna Blossom Time*. Christopher Fox, by whose kind permission the examples are reproduced, Fox Edition, 3 Old Moor Lane, York YO2 2QE.

Julian Grant: *Despondent Nonsenses*. Julian Grant, by whose kind permission the examples are reproduced, 7 Thackeray House, Herbrand Street, London WC1N 1HN; also British Music Information Centre.

Edward Gregson: *Five Songs of Innocence and Experience*. Edward Gregson, by whose kind permission the examples are reproduced, c/o Royal Northern College of Music, 124 Oxford Road, Manchester M13 9RD.

Piers Hellawell: *Fatal Harmony*. Maecenas Music, 5 Bushey Close, Old Barn Lane, Kenley, Surrey CR8 5AU, by whose kind permission the example is reproduced.

Jeremy Haladyna: *Two Sonnets of Sir Philip Sidney*. Jeremy Haladyna, by whose kind permission the examples are reproduced, c/o College of Creative Studies, University of California, Santa Barbara, California 93106-6070, USA.

Jonathan Harvey: *Nachtlied*. © 1984 Faber Music Ltd. (see under Thomas Adès), by whose kind permission the examples are reproduced.

Christopher Hobbs: *Drei Lieder aus 'Der Struwwelpeter'*. Christopher Hobbs, by whose kind permission the examples are reproduced, 202 Green Lane Road, Leicester LE5 4PA.

Derek Holman: *The Centred Passion*. Examples reproduced by kind permission of the composer. Score available from the Canadian Information Centre.

Elaine Hugh-Jones: *A Cornford Cycle*. Elaine Hugh-Jones, by whose kind permission the examples are reproduced, 95 Church Road, Malvern Link WR14 1NQ.

Betsy Jolas: *Mon ami*. Heugel & Co., 56–62 Galerie Montpensier, Paris, by whose kind permission the example is reproduced, c/o United Music Publishers Ltd., 42 Rivington Street, London EC2A 3BN.

Matthew King: *Dives and Lazarus*. Matthew King, by whose kind permission the examples are reproduced, Brook Garden Cottage, Troytown Lane, Brook, Ashford, Kent TN25 5PQ.

Oliver Knussen: *Four Late Poems and an Epigram*. © 1988 Faber Music Ltd. (see under Thomas Adès), by whose kind permission the examples are reproduced.

ACKNOWLEDGEMENTS & PUBLISHERS' ADDRESSES

Bjørn Kruse: *Altra risposta*. Examples reproduced by kind permission of the composer. Score available from the Norwegian Information Centre.

Libby Larsen: *Songs from Letters*. Oxford University Press, New York, by whose kind permission the examples are reproduced, and c/o Oxford University Press (New Music Promotion), 70 Baker Street, London W1M 1DJ.

Nicola Lefanu: *But Stars Remaining*. Novello & Co. Ltd. (see under Peter Aston) by whose kind permission the examples are reproduced. Text (extracts) reproduced from C. Day Lewis *Collected Poems 1954* by permission of the agency Peters, Fraser, & Dmlop, on behalf of the Estate of C. Day Lewis.

John McCabe: *Requiem Sequence*. Novello & Co. Ltd. (see under Peter Aston) by whose kind permission the examples are reproduced.

Edward McGuire: *Prelude 8*. Examples reproduced by kind permission of the composer. Score available from the Scottish Music Information Centre.

John McLeod: *Three Poems of Irina Ratushinskaya*. John McLeod, Griffin Music, 9 Redford Crescent, Colinton, Edinburgh EH3 0BS, by whose kind permission the music examples are reproduced.

Roger Marsh: *A Little Snow*. Maecenas Music (see under Piers Hellawell), by whose kind permission the example is reproduced.

Donald Martino: *From 'The Bad Child's Book of Beasts*. Donald Martino, Dantalian Inc., 11 Pembroke Street, Newton, Mass. 0128, USA, by whose kind permission the examples are reproduced.

Colin Matthews: *Un colloque sentimental*. © 1978 Faber Music Ltd. (see under Thomas Adès), by whose kind permission the examples are reproduced.

David Matthews: *The Golden Kingdom*. © 1992 Faber Music Ltd. (see under Thomas Adès), by whose kind permission the examples are reproduced.

Anthony Milner: *Our Lady's Hours*. Novello & Co. Ltd. (see under Peter Aston) by whose kind permission the examples are reproduced.

Dominic Muldowney: *Songs from 'The Good Person of Sichuan'*. © 1990 Faber Music Ltd. (see under Thomas Adès), by whose kind permission the examples are reproduced.

Per Nørgård: *Six Songs*. Wilhelm Hansen, Bornholmsgade 1, DK-126 Copenhagen, Denmark, by whose kind permission the examples are reproduced, c/o Chester Music Ltd. (see under Anthony Payne).

Martin O'Leary: *Three Japanese Lyrics*. Example reproduced by kind permission of the composer. Score available from the Contemporary Music Centre, Dublin.

Anthony Payne: *Adlestrop*. Chester Music Ltd., by whose kind permission the example is reproduced, c/o Music Sales Group (as Novello; see under Peter Aston).

Priaulx Rainier: *Cycle for Declamation*. © Schott & Co. Ltd. (London), 48 Great Marlborough Street, London W1V 2BN, by whose kind permission the examples are reproduced.

Rhian Samuel: *The Hare in the Moon*. Rhian Samuel, by whose kind permission the examples are reproduced, 47 York Terrace East, London NW1 4PT.

William Schuman: *Time to the Old*. © Merion Music, Inc. Reproduced by kind permission of Alfred A. Kalmus Ltd. (see under Tzni Avni).

Ruth Crawford Seeger: *Five Songs*. Peters Edition Ltd. (see under John Cage), by whose kind permission the examples are reproduced.

Malcolm Singer: *Love Songs*. Malcolm Singer, by whose kind permission the examples are reproduced, 29 Goldsmith Avenue, London W3 6HR.

Howard Skempton: *The Maldive Shark*. Howard Skempton, by whose kind permission the example is reproduced, Flat 11, 11 Warwick Place, Leamington Spa, Warwickshire CV32 5BS.

Russell Smith: *Six Blake Songs*. Examples reproduced by kind permission of the composer. Available in facsimile edition from Werner Becker Verlag, Giselherstrasse 10, D-80804, Munich, Germany.

Bernard Stevens: *The Palatine Coast*. © 1953 Alfred Lengnick & Co. Ltd., by whose kind permission the examples are reproduced, distributed by Elkin (William) Music Services, Station Road, Industrial Estate, Salhouse, Norwich NR13 6NY.

Mark Anthony Turnage: *Her Anxiety*. © Schott & Co. Ltd. (London) (see under Priaulx Rainier) by whose kind permission the examples are reproduced.

David Ward: *Three Sonnets to Orpheus*. Examples reproduced by kind permission of the composer. Score available from Vanderbeek & Imrie Ltd., 15 Marvig, Lochs., Isle of Lewis, Scotland PA86 9QP or for perusal from the Scottish Music Information Centre.

Judith Weir: *Songs from the Exotic*. Chester Music Ltd., by whose kind permission the examples are reproduced, c/o Music Sales Group (as Novello; see under Peter Aston).

Martin Wesley-Smith: *Ten Songs*. Examples reproduced by kind permission of the composer. Score available from the Australian Music Information Centre.

Gillian Whitehead: *Awa Herea*. Examples reproduced by kind permission of the composer. Score available from either the Australian Music Information Centre (Sounds Australian) or the New Zealand Music Centre (SOUNZ).

Caroline Wilkins: *Carte du tendre*. Hug & Co. Musikverlag, Limmatquai 28–30, CH-8022, Zurich, Switzerland, by whose kind permission the examples are reproduced.

Malcolm Williamson: *From A Child's Garden*. © 1968 Josef Weinberger Ltd., 12–14 Mortimer Street, London W1N 7RD, by whose kind permission the examples are reproduced.

James Wilson: *First Frost*. Examples reproduced by kind permission of the composer. Score available from the Contemporary Music Centre, Dublin.

John Woolrich: 'The Turkish Mouse', now available as the first of a set of *Three Cautionary Tales*, © 1989 Faber Music Ltd. (see under Thomas Adès), by whose kind permission the example is reproduced.

If the reader has difficulty contacting publishers or composers, the national music information centres may be able to help:

American Music Center: Suite 1001, 30 W. 76th Street, New York, NY 10010-12011.

ACKNOWLEDGEMENTS & PUBLISHERS' ADDRESSES

Australian Music Centre (Sounds Australian): The Argyle Centre, Playfair Street (PO Box N690 Grosvenor Place), The Rocks, Sydney NSW 2000, Australia.

British Music Information Centre: 10 Stratford Place, London W1N 9AE.

Canadian Music Centre: National Office, Chalmers House, 20 St Joseph Street, Toronto, Ontario M4Y 1J9.

Israel Music Institute: PO Box 11253, Tel-Aviv, Israel.

(Ireland) The Contemporary Music Centre, 95 Lower Baggot Street, Dublin 2.

New Zealand Music Centre (SOUNZ New Zealand): PO Box 10042, Level 3, 15 Brandon Street, Wellington, New Zealand PO Box 10042.

Norwegian Music Information Centre: Tollbugt 28, 0157, Oslo, Norway.

Scottish Music Information Centre: 1 Bowmont Gardens, Glasgow G12 9LR.

See also:

Contemporary Music-Making for Amateurs (COMA): 13 Wellington Way, Bow, London E3 4NE.

Appendix
A Note on Practising

Examining this selection of works closely has led me to crystallize a few thoughts on the learning process. Certain practicalities cannot be ignored: overpractising is a real danger and all hard work may go unnoticed if the voice is tired by the time the performance comes around. Anyone who adjudicates will be familiar with the situation where larger voices that impress during the earlier stages of a competition can begin to sound a little frayed by the closing rounds, while lighter ones may gradually blossom and shine, reaching their peak at the finals. A flexible approach should be cultivated, and practising methods adapted to suit the needs of each individual piece. Boredom can be allayed by converting each practice session into a puzzle-solving exercise. Working in short bursts divided by periods of rest is better than ploughing through doggedly, determined to get to the end whatever the cost in fatigue. Problem moments can be isolated for intensive work, and there is no need for continual run-throughs, in which stumbling often occurs at the same places. Singers should be gentle with themselves in private practice and learn their own pacing. Analytical bar-by-bar scrutiny without vocalizing can save a lot of time. Phrasing, notation, and text can be sorted out, and beats marked in: all this will ensure the proper use of formal rehearsal time without unnecessary hold-ups. Speaking the text aloud, cultivating awareness of percussive or legato elements in the syllables, as well as of the overall meaning, is also valuable. A work often seeps into consciousness during the gap between rehearsals. A grasp of the piece as a whole comes from an unforced familiarity. The 'pioneer' of new music may lack confidence initially. Being called upon to evolve an interpretation with no previous models to follow can be unnerving. It is certainly useful to hear another performer's version, particularly at an early stage, but parroting another's efforts, and using recordings as a short-cut way of learning should not be encouraged. I usually decline to provide tapes for this purpose, believing very strongly that everyone should have the freedom and courage to work out their own interpretation. (Unfortunately, publishers who readily supply 'promotional' tapes can unwittingly contribute to the 'quick-fix' approach.)

Apart from preliminary work on the score and text, there are at least three working methods from which to choose:

1. For less difficult music that can be read virtually at sight, the conventional way of learning through continual repetition is useful for deciding phrasing and breathing places, and discovering potential problems of stamina. The interpretation grows gradually in tandem with vocal and verbal security.

APPENDIX: A NOTE ON PRACTISING

2. More complicated or lengthy pieces require a rigorous sifting process. Problem corners, words, and phrases have to be identified and worked upon intensively, starting under tempo and building up gradually until everything feels safe and runs smoothly without faltering. Difficult intervals may need patience until the voice learns them: physical memory as well as musical memory is an attribute worth cultivating. Dynamics are perhaps the last refinements to be filled in. There is little point in attempting to run the whole work until small obstacles have been ironed out. A personalized programme of vocal exercises can be built from specific fragments that give problems and, eventually, the work can be divided into small sections, of one or two pages at a time, so that each can be practised separately. Eventually of course, Method 1, above can be applied, when the work is ready to be sung complete.

3. Some especially complex works may respond best to what I call the 'swimming-pool' method. One dives in and gradually works outwards, achieving a basic sketch of the work, and filling in details along the way. This is particularly effective in theatrical works, where gestures and nuances become closely entwined with the music as both are learned together. Priority is given to general character and concept, glossing over finer points which can be worked in later. This method can result in an almost improvisatory freedom which is rather exhilarating.

Changing from one way of working to another alleviates any possibility of mechanical routine. There must always be time for complete relaxation, and for monitoring one's own vocal development. It is easy to forget that the voice is constantly learning new tricks and gaining in technical control, and that difficult passages may not always feel the same, once their hurdles are overcome.

Composer Index